Building Linux and OpenBSD Firewalls

Wes Sonnenreich
Tom Yates

Wiley Computer Publishing

John Wiley & Sons, Inc.

NEW YORK · CHICHESTER · WEINHEIM · BRISBANE · SINGAPORE · TORONTO

Electronic Products, Associate Editor: Mike Sosa
Text Design & Composition: Benchmark Productions, Inc.

Designations used by companies to distinguish their products are often claimed as trademarks. In all instances where John Wiley & Sons, Inc., is aware of a claim, the product names appear in initial capital or ALL CAPITAL LETTERS. Readers, however, should contact the appropriate companies for more complete information regarding trademarks and registration.

This book is printed on acid-free paper. ∞

Published by John Wiley & Sons, Inc.

Published simultaneously in Canada.

This publication is designed to provide accurate and authoritative information in regard to the subject matter covered. It is sold with the understanding that the publisher is not engaged in professional services. If professional advice or other expert assistance is required, the services of a competent professional person should be sought.

Library of Congress Cataloging-in-Publication Data:

Sonnenreich, Wes, 1974–
    Building Linux and OpenBSD firewalls / Wes Sonnenreich, Tom Yates.
      p. cm
    ISBN 0-471-35366-3 (pbk. : alk. paper)
    1. Computer security. 2. Linux. 3. Operating systems (Computers)
    I. Yates, Tom, 1967– . II. Title.
    QA76.9.A25S66 1999
    005.8--dc21   99-35419
                                                                CIP

Printed in the United States of America.

10 9 8 7 6 5 4 3 2

Wes would like to dedicate this book to the memory of his grandfather Anthony Simeone and his late uncle Joseph Sonnenreich, both of whom would have read this book cover to cover.

Tom would like to dedicate this book to his wife, Caroline Brossi Yates, who has read this book cover to cover and would have been a co-author had not modesty prevented her.

CONTENTS

Part II

Part III

ACKNOWLEDGMENTS

Thanks are due to all the people the world over who have given their time and expertise to create Linux and OpenBSD, particularly Theo deRaadt and the OpenBSD team; Linus Torvalds and the Linux hackers; and Richard Stallman and the volunteers of the Free Software Foundation.

We'd like to explicitly thank the following people for the following contributions, all of which were invaluable to the production of this book:

Theo deRaadt, for extensive feedback on the OpenBSD portions of this text.

Dave Pascoe, Network Guru, for teaching Tom about real networks and encouraging him to be a network guru himself. Dave bears no responsibility for any errors in this book, but he sanity-checked some of it.

Erik Fitchner and Brendan Conoboy, the authors of the IPFilter how to document, for their comments and corrections on the IPFilter section of the text.

Warren Toomey, Unix Historian, for help in ensuring the veracity of our "brief history of Unix."

The British educational system, for providing Tom with the tools and opportunities that were needed. Special thanks to Carol Perry.

Jason Albanese, founder of JP Consulting, for reviewing and testing the Linux portions of the book.

Sean Ingles, system administrator for //pharmatrak, for reviewing and testing the OpenBSD portions of the book.

Our editors, Cary Sullivan and Christina Berry, for their patience while we wrote this book, and their enthusiasm to get it on the shelves in time for the usual Easter dense-technical-book buying spree.

We'd also like to acknowledge a few of the people who poured the foundation upon which the authors stand today:

Larry Isaacson, for all of his work with the MIT Brass Ensemble. Were it not for him, the authors never would have had the opportunity to build a life-long friendship based initially on rude trumpet player jokes and the superior volume of our mutually cherished instrument-of-mass-delirium: the trombone.

Frances Sonnenreich: with unending dedication and devotion she continues to flawlessly perform the strenuous and oft-thankless job of being Wes's mother.

Ruth Yates, for her love, encouragement, help and guidance, since the days when Tom was too short to reach a keyboard.

We would not value our education so had our parents not sacrificed so much to give it to us.

Thank you for buying the sequel to the greatest tragedy of all time: Hamlet. You might not recognize it as such, and we apologize for any confusion this may cause. Due to logistical issues, we simply couldn't house and clean up after the infinite supply of monkeys and typewriters required to properly complete such a project. So we had to settle for only two primates (albeit hairy ones) sitting in front of computer keyboards. It's actually quite a testament to the laws of probability. After three months of banging on the keyboards randomly we had forty thousand pages of usable text. Once we edited out all of the unnecessary characters, we were left with this very book. True, some sentences were difficdfgult twsen edit dowan. But for the most part a bit of creative writing allowed us to retain sense and continuity. Five apples were lost, horatio.

After reviewing the final product we feel that as a sequel to Hamlet it's a resounding success. We're still not sure why our publishers insist on marketing it as a book about firewalls—a trite modern-day concern compared to the evocative and timeless drama that we have crafted. But you have seen through the ruse and have bought our masterpiece anyway. We guarantee that it will not disappoint.

What This Book Is Really About

Okay, back to reality. This is a cookbook for building firewalls using Red Hat Linux 6.0 and OpenBSD 2.5. It contains step-by-step instructions on exactly how to build a very useful and powerful firewall from scratch. This book assumes you are starting with nothing more than the processed tree flesh you're holding in your hands. It will then walk you through some basic security theory, the process of selecting between Linux and OpenBSD, getting the right hardware for your system, installing the operating system, configuring the firewall, and detecting and dealing with security breaches.

We're going to go out on a limb and guess that you want to connect a local network—even if it's just one machine—to the Internet. You've decided that a firewall would be an excellent way to help you get from your network out to the world without inviting the whole world back in for a visit. Good for you.

But why would anyone want to build their own firewall? What we all want is a box with two holes and a button: Into one hole we plug the Internet and into the other hole we plug our local network. Then we push the button on the box labelled "Be A Firewall," and everything just kind of happens, right?

Wrong.

A lot of people out there will be happy to sell you a box with two holes and a button, to be sure. When you try and set it up, though, you find the box wants to be told all about your network, what sort of services you want going in and out, and answers to all manner of other questions. To answer these, you find you have to understand much more than you'd bargained for about what your network does. When you plug the firewall in and push the button, however, you still don't know what's going on inside, and you only have the manufacturer's word that things are secure. These days, let's face it, not all computer makers are completely honest about the shortcomings in their own products.

So what can you do? Well, you can take responsibility for your own network and its security. If you take time to understand your network, you can build a firewall from publicly available, free software. This software has been created by highly knowledgable enthusiasts and scrutinised, line by line, by the whole world. If anyone finds a hole in this stuff, it's not going to get sat on by some heavy-handed corporate marketing department while the world's crackers pass your network's secrets around behind your back. Holes are made public within hours, and very often fixed within the same day. We're not joking, here—never in world history has there been a software development engine as fast or powerful as the free software movement.

Take their effort and expertise, apply it to your own network, and be secure in knowledge.

What This Book Isn't About

We did not want to create yet another text on firewall theory. We want this to be a practical book that gives you all the information you need to create a working firewall. Nonetheless, the astute reader will note that there are a number of Chapters (1,2,3, and 11) which cover more theory than practical implementation. This is because a solid understanding of security is as valuable as, if not more than, the firewall itself. That's a really important point, so will state it again here, and numerous times throughout the rest of the book:

A firewall is only secure once you understand what it's securing, how the security works, and what's not being secured.

The chapters on theory are there to help you understand the fundamental security issues of network security, and then specifically of Internet security. We have taken every effort to make these chapters as readable as possible. Our goal was to provide just enough technical information so that you could fully understand the issues and implications. This book is not meant to be a replacement for more authoritative texts on network, security and firewall theory. The curious reader will want to learn more about many of the topics we skim over. O'Reilly has an excellent series of such books that are easily recognizable by two distinguishing features on the cover: 1) titles that are comprised of seemingly random combinations of 3 and 4 letters to form words that supposedly have some meaning, like sed, awk, perl, dns, nis, nfs, and so forth, 2) woodcuttings of bizarre animals that have no immediately obvious meaningful relationship to the title (assuming the title has any meaning to you in the first place).

With any luck, the story of your firewall will not resemble the story of Hamlet, or it's modern day spin-off, Rosencrantz and Guildenstern are Dead. Instead, we hope it's more like an episode of the 80's Saturday morning cartoon series "GI Joe." The bad guys are always repelled or defeated at the end, and we all learn that "knowing is half the battle."

Why Linux and OpenBSD?

This question is very similar to the Mac vs. Microsoft Windows debate. Macs are easy to use because they limit the amount of control the average user has over their system. Windows is more difficult to use, but give the end user greater flexibility. Novice users tend to prefer Macs, while more experienced users like the flexibility of Windows. Both are capable of performing the same tasks equally well (which may not be all that "well" when compared to either Linux or OpenBSD, but that's a totally separate flame war).

Likewise, both Linux and OpenBSD will make excellent firewalls. They are both open software, although the licensing is different. Linux is easier to work with and better supported in the community and by the distributors. OpenBSD was built with security in mind and has a number of powerful security features not found in Red Hat Linux (Red Hat can't include strong encryption due to US export restrictions; OpenBSD comes from Canada so everything's fair game, eh?). Linux and OpenBSD have many commonalities, but also use two totally different systems for packet filtering.

If you've picked up this book with a preconceived notion as to which OS you're going to use, we'd like to ask you to put that notion aside until you've finished reading Chapter 4 "Choosing an OS: Linux versus OpenBSD." We don't expect most readers to have heard of OpenBSD. We do expect that after reading Chapter 4, all of our readers will have a better appreciation of the relative strengths and weaknesses of Linux and OpenBSD, and will be better placed to make a decision on which one suits them best. They both exemplify the power of the Open Source movement. That both OpenBSD and Linux exist and are thriving (along with numerous other open source operating systems such as FreeBSD, NetBSD, the Hurd, for example) is a testament to this power.

Regardless of the choice you make, your willingness to trust the security of your network to an open source initiative is what counts. Both the Linux community *and* the OpenBSD community understand that it's not about which open source system is better. It's really about choosing open source as a viable alternative in the first place.

Why Red Hat?

We chose the Red Hat distribution because it is the most popular distribution of Linux. This means that they are well understood and heavily supported by the user community. Red Hat also comes with real commercial-grade installation support. If you're having trouble, you can make a phone call to a live person that will help you out. There are some technical advantages to the Red Hat system, including a good installer and powerful tools for configuring the system, such as the Red Hat Package Management system (RPMS). We were able to save space for firewall issues and not waste it on OS installation by using the Red Hat Linux Installation Guide as our example.

However, we should stress that the tools used to build the firewall come with any Linux distribution that includes a 2.2.x kernel (which nearly all modern distributions do). Ninety percent of the Linux-specific parts of this book apply equally well to other distributions.

How This Book Is Organized

This book can be read in a number of ways. We first suggest skimming the entire book through, including the installation and configuration sections for each operating system. Then read the chapters that were most interesting. When you're ready to install your firewall, turn to the step-by-step instructions for the operating system of your choice.

The book is structured in three major sections.

Part I

Part I is networking theory, as clear and simple as we could make it. Don't know your IP from your UDP? Always thought that TCP was an antiseptic, or that the ICMP was guys in funny clothes upholding the law in Canada? Chapters 1 through 3 will take you through networking until you feel confident enough to face the rest of the book—and the rest of the Internet—with equanimity.

Chapter 1, "The ABC's of Network Security," is a broad overview of security issues in any networked environment. First we look at why security doesn't come naturally with the Internet. Then we step back and ask why we want security in the first place—what is it that we're trying to protect? The job of the firewall is to protect your network from outside hackers, but what happens if the hacker is on the inside? We wrap up Chapter 1 by looking at internal security and its implications on the design of your firewall.

In Chapter 2, "Fundamental Internet Security Issues," we look at how the Internet works, how core protocols work and the vulnerabilities inherent within these protocols. Specifically, we look at the TCP/IP suite of protocols. We also deal with some general techniques for attacking machines over the Internet, including buffer overflows.

Following our discussion of the underlying Internet protocols, Chapter 3, "How Secure Should Your Network Be?," contains a detailed look at all of the major services and protocols built on top of TCP/IP. These include the services and protocols that enable email, the Web, chat, and file sharing. We'll tell you how they work, how they're vulnerable, and what you can do to make them more secure. This chapter also describes issues pertinent to the configuration of your physical network and managing your users.

Part II

Part II gets down to nuts and bolts. Chapter 4, "Choosing an OS: Linux versus OpenBSD," discusses the history, the development, and the consequent pros and cons of the two operating systems we deal with, OpenBSD and Linux. Hopefully, this will help you make your choice.

Chapter 5, "Getting the Right Hardware," assumes you've made your OS decision and are now ready to acquire the equipment you'll need. Many readers may have picked up this book thinking, "I've got an old 486 that will make a great firewall." You're right. It will make a great firewall, but it might not be very easy to get all of the necessary hardware working with the operating system. If at all possible, you're better off acquiring a system that fits our recommendations.

Then you've got to install the OS, and at this point the linear flow of the book stops (to resume in Chapter 10). Chapters 6 and 7 are for Linux users, Chapters 8 and 9 are for OpenBSD users.

Chapter 6, "Installing Linux," and Chapter 8, "Installing OpenBSD," deal with installing the operating system. They are not installation manuals. Instead, they're meant to be read alongside the installation manuals and other supporting documents. The purpose of these chapters is to guide you through the installation knowing that the ultimate goal is a firewall system. When a choice is presented to you, we'll help you make the right choices for a firewall. After the system is installed, we'll also discuss a few further configurations you'll need to make before you can start working on the firewalling rules.

Chapter 7, "Configuring the Firewall under Linux," and Chapter 9, "Configuring the Firewall under OpenBSD," deal with writing firewalling rules for Linux and OpenBSD. Both operating systems use different packet filtering packages. Linux uses IPChains while OpenBSD uses IPFilter. These chapters explain the syntax of the packet filtering rules and explain how the filters work.

At this point, you've got a running machine and you know how to write packet filter rules. Chapter 10, "Tuning Your Firewall," revisits the protocols described in Chapter 3 and takes you through the finer points of configuring your firewall to handle them as you wish. Extensive examples are given for both Linux and OpenBSD. By the time you leave this chapter, you'll have a working firewall.

Part III

Part III explains how your work is not yet done. You need to think about what happens when things go wrong. How do you know things are going wrong? What do you do once you know? Chapter 11, "Intrusion Detection and Response," deals with figuring out when someone's been in your system (intrusion detection) and what you do about it when it happens (response).

Chapter 12, "Loose Notes," is a catchall chapter for things we allude to in every other chapter but don't deal with explicitly. This includes references to other sources, scripts, and more theory. We also include a brief tutorial on the standard Unix editor, vi.

I Don't Like Reading

If you want to set up a working firewall without reading anything extraneous, you could get away with skipping Chapters 1, 2, and 3. Skip Chapter 4, go with Linux as an operating system and read Chapter 5. This will help you pick out some hardware and put it together. Then read Chapter 6 to learn how to install the operating system, and Chapter 7 to learn the basics of firewall configuration. Finally, Chapter 10 will show you how to configure your firewall, in detail. It will also direct you to the sample firewalls on the book's companion Web site, and you can pick the one that best suits you and use that as a starting point.

That should get you up and running. However, come back later and read the rest of the book. Really, we mean it. It all applies to you.

Who Should Read This Book

The answer is anyone who's got one or more computer connected to a larger public network such as the Internet. Even if you just have one computer at home, you might want to build a firewall to protect yourself against attacks from the outside while you're logged in. This is especially true if your computer is Windows or Macintosh based. Nothing is more frustrating that losing an hour's worth of work because some teenager ran WinNuke (a program that crashes Windows machines) on a bunch of random IP addresses, one of which happened to be yours.

Home networks and small companies on a budget will benefit from this book the most. You can get commercial grade firewall protection from a very small investment in hardware. The process of learning about security will also be of great benefit to you as the network administrator for this small or medium network.

We don't expect too many large companies to be reading this book—they're more likely to go straight for a commercial firewalling solution thanks to traditional FUD (fear, uncertainty, and doubt) techniques used to make managers wary of open source solutions. That's a shame, because the firewall you'll build in this book is every bit as powerful as any commercial firewalling solution. Sure, the marketing hype makes it sound like the commercial packages are better, but the reality is the knowledge gained from going through the process of building the firewall adds more to the security of your network than all of the "advanced" firewalling features on the most expensive commercial firewalls.

That said, we still discuss certain issues from the perspective of the large company network, because we expect that many of the small and medium networks administrators that are reading this book today will be managing a much larger, more complex network within a year's time. Therefore it's useful to understand how your decisions will affect you as your company grows.

We expect that the average reader of this book will be of at least intermediate computer skill. This means that you've opened up a computer before, you've installed software and hardware, and you're comfortable configuring aspects of the computer. Knowledge of Unix is not assumed—we provide explicit instructions for all tasks. Nonetheless, learning a little bit about how to work within a Unix environment will be necessary to adequately maintain your firewall. You'll pick up a lot from this book, and we'll point you at plenty of other great educational resources.

Won't This Book Be Out-Of-Date Soon?

We are fully aware that by the time most of our readers get this book, Red Hat will have gone through a number of additional releases, and OpenBSD will have gone through at least one or two more revisions. This is not a problem—this book was specifically designed to be just as relevant two years from now as it is today.

There are two ways to deal with future revisions. The first is to simply ignore them—initially. Just get your hands on a Red Hat 6 CD, or burn an OpenBSD 2.5 CD from the OpenBSD Web site, and the book will be 100 percent accurate. Once you've finished installing and configuring the firewall with Red Hat 6 or OpenBSD 2.5, you can then upgrade to the most recent version. This will often be an easier process since both operating systems come with installers that also can upgrade old systems while maintaining all configuration data. Furthermore, after going through the process a few times with the Red Hat 6/OpenBSD 2.5, you'll be comfortable enough to handle a later version on your own.

The other alternative is to get the latest release and look at our Web site (www.wiley.com/compbooks/sonnenreich). We'll be placing information on the Web site with each release that highlights the major points of departure from the text. We've already done quite a bit of forward looking, and here's what we've found:

Installing a firewall in Red Hat 6.1 is not going to be radically different from 6.0. There may be a few minor changes, but nothing a page of errata on the companion web site won't fix. A year or so after 6.1, its expected that Red Hat will change from the 2.2.x kernels to the 2.4.x kernels. The 2.4.x kernels replace ipchains-based firewalling with netfilter/iptables-based firewalls. Luckily, the iptables syntax is very similar to the ipchains syntax, and there's a backwards compatibility option for people who wish to continue using ipchains which the developers expect to remain supported until late 2003.

The installer in OpenBSD 2.6 will be almost identical to 2.5, with a few minor enhancements. Once again, these will be mentioned on the companion web site. OpenBSD will most likely stick with IPFilter as its firewalling tool for some time to come.

What's on the Web Site?

Lots of naked and totally exposed text files. Everything you need to fulfill your fantasies of tightly secured networks and hairy sysadmins. Tools for spanking script kiddies. Penguins.

Okay, that might be a bit much—the penguins bit, that is—but the Web site will have some rather useful information on it. As we mentioned above, the Web site will be used to help keep the book up-to-date as future OS releases flood the market. Furthermore, we've placed numerous scripts and utilities on the site. There are three firewall scripts for each operating system: One low-security script, and two higher security scripts (with and without a DMZ). There are also other scripts to help in installing and removing various firewall components.

A Brief Word on Nomenclature

We are well aware that Linux has become the phenomenon it is today for several reasons. One of them is that Richard Stallman and the other GNU project members at the Free Software Foundation had all the tools and utilities a Unix system could need sitting ready for Linus Torvalds to drop his shiny new kernel into, back in 1991. Since then both the Linux kernel and the GNU software have gone from strength to strength. We fully believe that neither would be what it is today without the other. We have used the term "Linux" to refer to what should properly be called "GNU/Linux systems" throughout this book for the sake of brevity, *and for no other reason.*

Summary

With all that said, roll up your sleeves and get ready to learn about stuff you never thought you'd understand. By the time you're done with the next few chapters, you'll be a bona-fide networking geek. You'll have an entire arsenal of networking terms and security vulnerabilities at your command. Watch your boss quiver with fear when you tell him or her that the computer is susceptible to "cache poisoning." Use their panicked reaction to gregariously increase your budget and your importance—". . . the only way to prevent cache poisoning is to undergo a comprehensive security audit and infrastructure upgrade. You can call in expensive consultants, or I can do it—but I'll need a budget increase and some additional staff. . ." You get the picture. Enjoy the power trip and read on. . .

CHAPTER 1

The ABCs of Network Security

This chapter offers a broad overview of security issues in any networked environment. First we look at why security doesn't come naturally with the Internet. Then we step back and ask why we want security in the first place and what it is that we're trying to protect. The purpose of a firewall is to protect your network from outside hackers, but what happens if the hacker is on the inside? With that in mind we'll wrap up this chapter by looking at internal security and its implications for the design of your firewall.

Why Is Security an Issue?

This isn't as daft a question as it first appears. Inasmuch as it was designed at all, the Internet was designed so that moving information around would be as easy as possible, mostly in a university environment. Security was not so much a lesser concern as a positive hindrance.

You doubt us? Consider the ubiquitous http protocol, in many ways the heart of the modern Web. It was originally designed not for online shopping, but for publishing and distributing research papers with greater speed and flexibility than printed media. The idea was to get information to as many people as possible, as quickly as possible. Preventing people from reading your papers, acquiring your credit card number, and altering your payroll information just weren't the major considerations. If it had been any other way, the Internet would probably be a much more secure place, but you probably wouldn't have heard of it.

TIP

The Internet doesn't do security for you. Its openness is its strength.

The design criteria of the quiet past are inadequate for the stormy modern Internet. Most machines and networks connected to the Internet are still inappropriately secured. Why is this? Since you've read the previous two paragraphs carefully, you get no extra points for correctly deducing that it's because security is still often not a major design consideration. During design, security gets sacrificed to other requirements like usability, cool graphics, and other kinds of chrome.

> **Chrome:** Showy features added to attract users but contributing little or nothing to the power of a system. "The 3D icons in Motif are just chrome, but they certainly are *pretty* chrome!" Distinguished from *bells and whistles* by the fact that the latter are usually added to gratify developers' own desires for featurefulness. Often used as a term of contempt.
>
> —*Jargon File 4.0.0*

Invariably, moments before deployment, everyone decides that the new system ought to be secure as well. Mass pandemonium ensues, iron Band-Aids are slapped on the ailing project, and marketing touts the airtight security of the new system. It's only a matter of time before somebody falls through that kind of security. In case you haven't guessed, we think this is a bad idea.

TIP

Security is not an afterthought. If you try to deploy a system, then add security afterwards, the system will be either unusable, insecure, or both. Security must be designed from the beginning.

Including security from the beginning means understanding what security is. Understanding the nature of security means understanding the threats against which you wish to secure, the assets you wish to secure against those threats, and the technology available for so doing.

TIP

Work out what you've got, who wants it, how they can get it, and how you can stop them. That's appropriate security.

Security can be overdone. You don't have to lock yourself up in an iron box to have appropriate security. Consider car alarms and other forms of car security. They can't render a car unstealable. Nothing can do that. What they can do is make your car harder to steal than the next equally attractive car. When you buy car security, you're not setting out to stop all car theft. You're setting out to stop the theft of your car. That's an important difference. However, if you choose to live without car security, then sooner or later your car will be stolen. If you choose to connect to the Internet without network security, then sooner or later the crackers will find you. If you're really unlucky, both things will happen on the same day.

What Are You Protecting?

Formally, security is the prevention of unauthorized access to your data, to your computers, and to your reputation. These groups are interrelated, meaning that harm to one often harms another in passing. As you read each section, think about what assets you have that fall into these categories and how they might be abused.

Data

The term *data* refers to more than one *datum*, which is a unit of information. You have more data than you think. Your data include *inter alia*:

- Documents and databases stored on your systems
- Passwords and other tokens transmitted across your network
- Electronic mail stored in queues or in mailboxes
- System files that direct the behavior of your systems
- Logs that the systems produce in the normal course of operations

What happens if crackers or other bad guys access these data? One or more of three things: (1) people read (and disseminate) the data; (2) people change the data; (3) people delete the data. All of these will cause you headaches. If someone gets into your corporate payroll system and discovers the salary of every employee in the company, the loss of privacy will cause headaches. If this information gets posted on an internal bulletin board system—or worse, on a USEnet newsgroup—it'll cause migraines. If payroll information gets altered, and people are paid too much or too little, addiction to painkillers may become your second most serious problem. Finally, if all payroll records are erased and the payment of salaries halted, pain killers may become inadequate and you'll need a suicide hotline.

Even machines containing only public data need security: When the *New York Times* Web site was cracked in September 1998, everyone had a laugh at their expense. You can do without that kind of publicity.

One of the worst aspects of unauthorized access to data is that it can be so hard to detect. If someone copies your payroll records and doesn't make them public, you may never know. If someone changes a single bit in the middle of the binary of your latest software package, the one you were about to ship, you may not hear anything until a horde of irate customers camps outside your front gate. Even if you can tell that a machine's been compromised, you may well have no idea of the extent of the damage.

TIP

If a machine is found to have been penetrated, you need to treat it as having been fundamentally compromised, even if nothing appears to have been changed.

The data, the OS, and any other machine that trusts the compromised machine, are all now suspect. You will need to go over them with a fine-toothed comb before you can trust them again. This can take a monstrously long time. Reinstalling from scratch may well be quicker. In many ways, it is easier to recover from the cracker who brute-force erases your entire hard disc than it is to recover from the machine which shows a couple of privileged logins from off-site. Later in this book, we will cover tools designed to deal with the difficulty of intrusion detection, and we will also cover what to do if you believe you have been penetrated—namely, incident response.

Computers

You know what your computers are: They're the actual machines with the hard discs, right? Well, yes, but they also include the network that connects them to each other and the Internet connection that connects that network to the outside world, your backup tapes (you are keeping backups, aren't you?), and in brief, just about anything that's hooked up to one of your computers that isn't breathing.

If a cracker comes in and uses your computers but doesn't touch your data, has any harm been done? Well, for companies in the business of selling those resources, such as Internet service providers, computer resources being used by bad guys can't be sold to paying customers. If your company's product is not the services of its computers, it almost certainly uses the computers in the process of selling; if the computers slow down or even crash, the sales process stops. If your Internet connection is completely full of people downloading pirate software that some cracker made available on your corporate file server, email from legitimate customers may not reach you.

A whole class of attacks, *denial of service attacks,* is designed not to access your computers but to prevent the authorized users of the computers from being able to use them. They can be depressingly sophisticated, such as network attacks that rely on known weaknesses in your network code. They can be depressingly simple, such as rapidly and repetitively downloading a short file from your FTP server, to flood your log files and shut the server down. As operating systems become increasingly secure against intrusive attacks, denial of service attacks are becoming more and more common. They are in many ways harder to defend against than more intrusive attacks because they overuse, or abuse, services you genuinely wish to offer, instead of accessing services not intended for use. Fortunately, there are defenses against some of these attacks.

Reputation

This is in many ways the trickiest of all casualties of unauthorized access. You can lose the confidence of your customers, your staff, your coworkers, your service providers, and the rest of the world in general. Being successfully attacked is not necessarily embarrassing. Failing to notice the intrusion, ignoring it, or handling it badly, is. If someone penetrates your network, he or she can not only damage your internal data, but your reputation as well. Attacks on other sites can be launched from your site, which will not endear you to other administrators or law-enforcement personnel; the intruder can send email or post to newsgroups in a manner that looks very authentic. If an intruder sends mail to all your customers from your mail server, insulting them and including a couple of dirty pictures, people will remember that for a long time.

Earlier, we said that you can overdo security. Why would we say such a thing? Why not just lock everything down tight and eat the keys? Because security is a trade-off with convenience. The least secure operating system in the world can be secured by turning the machine off and locking it in a sealed room (don't forget to post armed guards). This machine is now pretty much invulnerable to any form of subversion. On the other hand, it's not going to do anything useful anytime soon. Every step you take back from security to help usability—the guards need holidays, someone wants to go in the room to clean the windows, "Could I just turn it on for two minutes to get some data off it?," "I only hooked it up to the modem to check my mail."—opens the machine up to subversion. To get the trade-off between usability and security right is to have an appropriately secure system.

TIP   Appropriate security strikes the right balance between "secure enough to be safe" and "insecure enough to be usable."

Internal Security

Threats come from both inside and outside of your company. Frequently, the combination of both is what creates a real security breach.

The average user is not actively concerned about security. Security becomes a concern when it creates inconvenience for the users, or when there's a security breach that directly and negatively impacts the users. Because of this, a system administrator can't assume that users will ever think about how their actions affect the security of the network. In fact, the average user will probably lean toward insecurity, since it's more convenient.

What prevents this leaning is your security policy. In its simplest form, this is a list of things users should do and things they must not do. This list should be written down and easy to find. A good security policy will keep security breaches to a minimum.

Preventing problems is always a thankless job: The better you do your job, the less anyone knows about it. Users will undoubtedly complain about the inconveniences of your security policy, saying "but nothing has ever happened, so why are you worried?." The proper response is to repress the desire to smack them silly and explain that the reason nothing has happened is because of the very security policy they're trying to subvert. If they pull rank, or try to go over your head for approval, make sure you have a very clear paper trail of your strong opposition to the issue. When the wall comes down, you don't want to be under it. A good security policy also helps keep itself intact—it's easier to enforce something that clearly, in black and white, applies to everyone.

This book is primarily about firewalls, so once we leave Chapter 1, we will not be concerned with internal security. But protection against threats from inside is very often overlooked. Internal security shouldn't be overlooked, and this part of the book is where we don't overlook it. If you choose to ignore it, you have only half a security policy. While discussing internal security, we will give concrete recommendations when possible. However, not all organizations are identical, and we have tried to break down recommendations into "home office," "small business," and "larger installations." Practices that everyone should follow comprise the first set. The second set is practices that apply to a network of 10 to 20 computers. The third set is not so much our advice to enormous corporations as they are practices you should progress to as time and resources allow, ideas to get you thinking about how security can be a real design criterion for you. Wherever possible, these practices should be followed as a matter of policy. And don't just follow them, write them down and tell people where to find the piece of paper.

Physical Security

Securing the important machines makes it much harder for someone to gain physical access to them. It's nearly impossible to prevent a machine from being subverted if someone can get to it physically. At MIT, network security and authentication are handled by a software system called *kerberos* that makes it extremely hard to lie about who or where you are on the network. The kerberos system, however, is only as secure as the machine which approves all the other requests for authentication. This ticket-granting server, as it is known, lives in a locked steel cage inside a room with a hefty lock on the door. Very few keys to the padlock on that cage exist. All the network services that might be used to compromise the machine have been turned off, to be sure, but MIT has put as much effort into the physical security of the machine as they have into its network security.

Home offices should consider moving crucial machines out of public view. At the very least, make it difficult for someone to accidentally type on one. If any of your crucial services are running on desktop machines, try to migrate them off as soon as possible. Start to distinguish between servers and desktops, and secure the servers.

Small businesses should consider moving all of the servers, along with the Internet connection, into a single room with no people in it. This makes providing other services that computers like (for example, uninterruptible power and air conditioning) easier as well. Then, put a good lock on the server room door and don't hand out keys.

Larger installations should review their policy for access to the servers. A two-tier architecture may be appropriate: Group the servers into ones that people need access to sometimes, and ones that people never need to access. The server that writes backup tapes certainly needs to be in a sheltered place accessible by the person who changes the tapes. The primary database server and the firewall are like MIT's ticket-granting server; they should be well away from everyone else's eyes.

Physical security shouldn't stop at servers. Have you ever told your email package to store your password so you don't have to type it each time you want to check your email? You're not the only one. People store their passwords on their computer. As a result, as far as your computers are concerned, possession of someone's desktop machine amounts to possession of their identity. A good password-protected screensaver that cuts in after a machine has been idle for a few minutes can stop opportunistic walk-up cracking. It would be better if people could be prevented from storing their passwords on their computers, but this can prove extremely difficult to do. Never doing it yourself is a good start. In any case, desktop security shouldn't be neglected (see the upcoming section, *Host-Based Security*).

Network Security

Securing the network hardware is particularly important if you have *shared* rather than *switched* Ethernet. To explain this will take a moment; the explanation only applies if you are using what's known as *twisted-pair* Ethernet. You can tell that by looking at your network cable. If it terminates in something like a fat phone plug, you most likely have twisted pair. If it's anything else, you don't, so you can skip the next few paragraphs and secure your network hardware *right now*.

In traditional shared Ethernet, every packet sent to every machine is seen by every other machine on the same subnet (strictly speaking, in the same collision domain, but let's not complicate matters). This means that passwords sent from your desktop to your servers can, in principle, be read by any machine on your subnet. In fact, there exist hardware and software systems known as *sniffers*, designed to exploit this very fact. They nose around all network traffic and capture the interesting-looking bits. Worse, and contrary to common belief, there is no generally valid way to spot a sniffing device (even programs like AntiSniff can't detect all sniffers). With switched Ethernet, on the other hand, switches learn which machines are attached to which ports on the switch, and don't send traffic to machines that don't need to know it. You can see how this will help—the password you are sending to the server is seen by only yourself and the server.

Maybe an analogy will help clarify this. Suppose you need to tell a secret to Fred, who lives somewhere down the other end of the office. Perhaps you need to tell him where you keep the spare key to your front door hidden. But you don't remember which cubicle he works in. Now, you could stand on your chair, howl "Fred!" at the top of your voice, and then shout out the location of the key. Your coworkers will know that the message is for Fred, not for them; therefore they'll ignore it, right? Well, yes, they should, but I hope you haven't anything valuable in your front hallway. That's how shared Ethernet works, though. Now suppose you decide against shouting, you get down off your chair, and you ask a trusted coworker to go and tell Fred where the key is. The coworker knows where Fred sits, and he walks down to Fred's cubicle and quietly tells him the message. Only you, Fred, and the trusted coworker know the message. That's how switched Ethernet works, with the switch playing the part of the trusted coworker (also starring Fred as "the server").

Telling which kind of Ethernet you have can be tricky. Go look at your network concentrators, the boxes into which all your network cables are plugged. If they are labeled as switches, they probably are. Most other things indicate a shared network. Whether you're shared or switched, making sure people can't plug things willy-nilly into your network is a good internal security measure.

Passing on from the network, desktop modems are considered a very insecure idea indeed. Individual users generally don't have the ability to securely use a modem. Dial-in and dial-out should both be handled centrally if at all possible.

For dial-in, there are a variety of devices that can receive calls and authenticate properly (often using one of the remote authentication protocols described in the section titled *Password Security*). Centralizing dial-in will also give you the option of ensuring that dial-in users land in some secured part of your network, one that won't let them behave as if they were inside your building.

For dial-out, there are network-based modems that can be accessed like any other IP-based network device. Furthermore, they can be carefully configured to only allow certain classes of outgoing call, and can be made to log all such calls. Yes, these are more expensive than just slapping a 56k modem on someone's office PC. However, while it can be hard to resist the siren song of someone who just wants to pop a modem on their serial port to dial this or that bulletin board, try to do so. It is always better to offer these services in a structured, well-designed, audited way.

Some network services are just implicitly insecure. Email, for example, is plain text, which can be read by any administrative user on any machine it passes through on its way across the Internet. Make sure your users understand what things are implicitly insecure, and the implications of this. Make sure your users know what isn't confidential. This applies even more so if you are deliberately being insecure. For example, you may find it necessary to monitor keystrokes, email messages, and/or telephone calls. Unless you'd like your company to be at the center of a huge privacy scandal, you'll need to have a clear policy in place that explains what you may be monitoring. You should also state how the data will be used, who can access it, and how it will be protected from unauthorized access.

So, to summarize:

Home offices should make sure that visitors don't plug laptops and other devices into their network. If you use modems for dial-out, make sure the modems won't pick up the phone if someone dials in. If you use modems for dial-in, make sure there's decent authentication on the line. Don't assume that an unlisted number adds any degree of security. There are hundreds of free programs that will test every number in an exchange for a modem. They're called *war dialers*, and they're very effective.

Small businesses should consider replacing hubs with switches.

Larger installations should already be using switches. If there are any modems left in the building, hunt them down with spears and kill them like the dinosaurs they are (throw them in a box with some AOL floppies and send them to your competitors). All of your dial-in and dial-out should be centralized.

Password Security

Passwords are a classic weak point in security. Since most organizations assign usernames on a systematic basis, the password becomes the final line of defense. Let's be clear about this: If a cracker can work out your username, the only unknown he or she needs to convince the system of his or her authorization is your password. Once the cracker has that, the cracker is you. The age-old problem with picking passwords is that if passwords are too simple they are subject to easy discovery; if they are too difficult, they will be regularly forgotten or (worse) written down. You can usually set passwords to expire after a set time, then the user has to change it. Opinion is divided on the merits of this, but we recommend against it for a variety of reasons. Our preference is to ask users to take a little time and choose a single, easy-to-remember but hard-to-guess password, and then make sure the central username/password database gets consulted for everything. Most software systems want to include their own dinky little username/password database, instead of consulting the central one, but if you push the vendor, they'll often own up to how to make the software consult the central database. If they claim their product won't do it at any price, don't buy it. Each new password your users have to remember makes the choice of a bad one more likely.

Home offices should start using passwords. Yes, administering these does take time, but you will have to start someday. Today is a good day.

Small businesses should ensure that password security is in their written security policy. This will ensure that employees know they have a duty of confidentiality regarding their passwords, as with other access devices such as keys, and ensure that they are clear about what constitutes a bad password.

Larger installations should start running proactive password checkers to ensure that passwords are good at the point of setting, as well as regularly running a password cracking utility. "Crack" is a good utility for Unix passwords; "l0phtcrack" is good for NT passwords. References for both these packages can be found in Chapter 12. The first time you run a password cracker, you should expect to crack around 40 percent of your passwords. If you can crack your passwords, someone else can too. Do it before they do.

Make sure that people are not fooled into parting with passwords. No user should need to disclose passwords, particularly not by telephone or email. Tell your users that they should not be disclosing passwords, even to people who claim to be authorized. It's very easy for a cracker to get a password by calling up some poor peon in the systems group, pretending to be the VP of sales, and shouting at them until the peon changes the VP's password. Make sure those staff who are authorized to change passwords have a clear policy about how people should request changes. Tell them that it's okay to tell anyone to go through the proper channels if they're trying to sidestep those channels. Be prepared to take the heat when the CEO is infuriated because some systems group peon refused to let him read his own email. We mean it.

What's a Good Password?

Sorry, can't tell you. We can tell you, though, some characteristics of a bad password. Bad passwords include:

- Any word or words in any language that can be represented in the roman alphabet
- Any word or words varied by changing letters into numbers, or prefixing and/or suffixing numbers
- Anything that's all digits
- Any variation of the username; if your username is sbn914, then 419nbs is a lousy password
- Any variation of your full name or any portion thereof
- Anything based on publically accessible information about you—particularly items such as your birthday

Avoid these and you'll be doing better than 95 percent of people. That's pretty good.

Administrative Security

As Juvenal once said, *quis custodiet ipsos custodes,* or *Who is to guard the guards themselves?* Someone has to have absolute power over the machines. However, this power is often spread much wider than need be. There is a tendency to hand out administrative (a.k.a. *root*) access at the drop of a hat to people who, for example, only need to change tapes. Given half a chance, the machines can look after their own security quite well, but not if every user is handed the magic password that gives complete access to the whole machine.

The lady who labels the backup tapes only needs to run the tape-labeling program as root. How to let her label the tapes without giving her the root password? Under Unix, there exist utilities like *sudo,* which can be used to restrict root access to only certain commands for certain people (more information about sudo can be found in Chapter 12). The man who updates the list of employees needs privileged access to the employee file, but only that file. Does he need the root password? File access can often be better handled by making new groups and adding people to them as needed. When handing out privilege to enable a task, spend a little time to establish the minimum amount of privilege needed to accomplish the task, and hand out only that much.

For home offices, think about who has root access on the important machines. If you do everything yourself with root access, stop doing that.

For small businesses, review who has the root password and why. Could you perhaps get by with three less people knowing it as long as it were written down in a sealed envelope somewhere? Could you institute alternative procedures for doing things that would let you get it back from anyone?

For larger installations, something like sudo is a must. This is partly because of better security, partly because it reduces the chance of mistakes being fatal, and partly because it keeps an audit trail of who issued what command with what arguments. Logging is an important part of administrative security. Don't overlook it. Larger installations should also start to take back administrative control from senior management. This last can be like drawing teeth, but it's necessary—no one who doesn't actually need to exert absolute authority over the machines should possess the ability to do it.

Host-Based Security

Some might contend that host-based security doesn't belong under internal security. We disagree. Neither your belief in everyone's basic goodness and trustworthiness, nor having the world's soundest firewall at the entrance to your network should stop you from plugging host-based security holes as and when you can. By *host-based security* we mean security holes that are discovered in particular operating systems or software packages. For NT and Windows, this generally means keeping up with the latest hotfixes and service packs. For Unix-based operating systems, this means keeping up with vendor-released OS patches and package-specific patches from individual suppliers. Some very competent organizations exist whose sole purpose is to make information about recently discovered holes and their fixes available as fast as practical. Keep an eye on them. Avail yourself of their free services (more information about them is available in Chapter 12).

For home offices, keep up with your patches. Check out the resources we specify in Chapter 12. Check your OS vendor's Web site. Avail yourself of any security mailing lists they, or others, provide. Talk to other admins.

For small businesses, think about the trust relationship between your machines. Do they all trust each other equally for reading and writing to data? Do they trust each other for remote access? Having identified your servers and protected them physically, now is the time to make sure there's no easy path in via the network, except where needed.

For larger installations, don't accept software upgrades or patches from Web sites without some kind of digital signature or other confirming authority.

In case you thought that last suggestion was overkill, we offer the following story from the Jargon File.

> There is a classic story of a tiger team penetrating a secure military computer that illustrates the danger inherent in binary patches (or, indeed, any patches that you can't—or don't—inspect and examine before installing). They couldn't find any trap doors or any way to penetrate security of IBM's OS, so they made a site visit to an IBM office (remember, these were official military types who were purportedly on official business), swiped some IBM stationery, and created a fake patch. The patch was actually the trapdoor they needed. The patch was distributed at about the right time for an IBM patch, had official stationery and all accompanying documentation, and was dutifully installed. The installation manager very shortly thereafter learned something about proper procedures.

—Jargon File 4.0.0

A word on virus scanners. Unix-based systems, by their design, tend not to suffer from viruses. PC systems, by their design do tend to suffer from viruses. Viruses can make your life as an administrator very unpleasant. They can introduce nasty security holes, both by design and by accident.

For home offices, there is no substitute for good virus-scanning software on the desktops.

Small businesses should be thinking about how people bring viruses in, and why, and introduce alternative practices wherever possible. Make sure that your virus scanner's signature files—the files that tell the scanner how to recognize common viruses—are kept up-to-date.

Larger installations who think there's a real problem might wish to use hardware and/or software to control access to the removable media. These usually include the floppy drive, and possibly the CD-ROM and/or tape drives on a machine.

There is also a class of viruses called *macro viruses* which spread in the context of a software package instead of an OS; Word and Excel viruses are classic examples. These are particularly susceptible to transmission by network, and in particular by email. It is currently fashionable to try and screen these viruses out at the firewall with some automated package that examines incoming mail and rips macro viruses out. Such a procedure is doomed to be partially successful at best, because there are so many different ways to include a potentially infectious document inside an email. If you believe you have a real problem with these, it may be worth investigating the technology.

For particularly crucial hosts, packages such as *tripwire* (see Chapter 12) are worth a look. These monitor specific files on your system to see if there have been any changes in them since the package was last run. It can't tell you if a file is safe or unsafe, but if you've spent time making sure that your system configuration files are sound, it can automate the process of checking that they haven't been changed, either maliciously or thoughtlessly. If you find this idea attractive, note that just checking datestamps on a file is not sufficient to see if it has been changed; forging datestamps requires relatively little effort. Packages like tripwire use sophisticated checksums that make it extremely difficult (read: impossible in your lifetime) to alter a file and not trip the alarms.

In General

True security requires smart administration. This means spending time, effort, and intelligence on it. Be clear on your security procedures, and on what day-to-day things are supposed to be happening on your computer systems. How can you know if someone's performing unauthorized tasks if you don't know what is supposed to happen on your network when it's running normally?

However, there's no point putting more effort into network security than you do into other forms of security. We know of a company that was worried that the source code of the company's software product was being disclosed to competitors. They installed software to scan every outgoing email for codewords that suggested that source code might be included in the message. While wrapped up in their paranoia, they neglected to notice that they tape drives and tapes had been provided in profusion to employees. There were no procedures to check why a tape might be being written, or to keep logs of who took tapes. For all anyone knows, the entire code base left the building every night in someone's briefcase. If you credit your employees with sufficient immorality to steal from you, then credit them with enough sense to do it the easiest way. There is no point securing your internal network to a vastly higher standard than you secure anything else internal.

In the end, your internal users work with you, not against you, and if you make their jobs harder than need be, you're shooting yourself in the foot. If management is treating them so badly that they are driven to theft, that is a social, not technical problem. You cannot solve social problems with technical solutions; if you let your security policy become a vehicle for social fixes, it will achieve neither those fixes nor security.

Threats from Outside

Although historically over half of IS security breaches have come from inside companies, this statistic changed recently. We confidently predict that this trend will increase. People on the inside have historically represented the greatest threat, not because your employees are abnormally bad, or even averagely bad, but because there weren't many crackers out there in the big bad world. The really good ones had other things to do. These days, any fool can be a hacker—nip off to www.cracking.is.fun and pick up your zip file full of exploits, give the IP address of the target, and click *start*. Nowadays, it's no longer a question of *whether*, it's a question of *when*. The good side of this is that, by and large, keeping a tight ship against the most common exploits will keep you reasonably safe. If someone with sufficient skill gets sufficiently mad at you, they will get in, but such people are rare, and (we hope!) unlikely to have a grudge against you.

Good internal security helps external security. If a bad guy walking into the building can't put a sniffer on the network, or grab passwords off people's screens or fool users into parting with them, his only way into your network as an authorized user is to fool the machines, and that means subverting the firewall. You have now simplified your problem.

By now, you will naturally be thinking about putting a firewall between your network and the Internet to keep the bad guys from getting inside your network. A firewall is a very, very good thing to have between you and the rest of the world, but it's no panacea. What a firewall can do for you is distinguish between your authorized users and the rest of the world. If done properly, it can go a long way toward keeping the rest of the world out of your network, except in the precisely defined way that you want them inside it. What it can't do is solve everything in a single go. A firewall is no substitute for a good internal security policy, nor for good host-based security. However, it will be the single strongest element of your attempt to keep the bad guys out.

Summary

In Chapter 2, we talk about the fundamentals of network security. You'll learn how the Internet works and why the design of the Internet in inherently insecure. Finally, you'll learn how to protect yourself against these insecurities. In Chapter 3, we start to list, in detail, what your firewall should do. However, we will rapidly discover a trade-off between security and convenience—for each task you wish to prevent coming in from outside, there are tasks that users will no longer be able to do easily from inside. If you start thinking now about what you absolutely don't want people to be able to do from outside, and what you absolutely do want people to be able to do from inside, it will be easier to match them up as we go on.

2

Fundamental Internet Security Issues

A surprisingly large number of people would be hard pressed to explain the difference between the Internet and the Web. In fact, many people aren't aware that there is a difference. Even email, the killer app of the decade, is now a Web browser function for many Internet users. Fundamental cluelessness is not just limited to the Internet novitiates; many savvy Internet users don't understand why Microsoft Word insists on capitalizing the *I* in Internet. Even we thought it was yet another attempt by Microsoft to dominate our minds by subtly altering our concept of the English language, but upon further inspection we learned that the founding fathers of the Net specified the capitalization in their early documents.

In order to protect yourself on the Internet, you need to have a fairly solid understanding of what the Internet is at a fundamental level. Once you have this understanding, you'll be able to evaluate the security risks associated with the various needs of your users. You'll also be able to detect problems and figure out solutions before the problems become too catastrophic.

This chapter will teach you about the fundamentals of an internet. We'll look at how data are transferred between computers, and how computers find each other on a large-scale network. We'll also look at how machines can work with more than one networked program at a time. For each of these topics, we'll explain the various security risks, how hackers tend to exploit these security

The Why of the I

There is a generic concept of Internet which refers to any set of networks built upon the protocols we will describe in this chapter. There could be many such networks. There happens to be one particular Internet that everybody uses. This network, surprisingly enough, goes by the name of the *Internet*. It originally was called *ARPAnet* (Advanced Research and Projects Agency, or ARPA, is the research department of the Pentagon), then at points was called the DARPA Internet (*D* for Department of Defense). Eventually, as more and more of the public sector connected to the network, the DARPA was dropped and the "network of networks" became officially known as the Internet.

There also exists a concept of an *extended* Internet, which includes the various networks that internally do not run on TCP/IP but are connected through a gateway. The term for this larger network is not really standardized, mostly because the majority of the population is not aware of the distinction. Thus, many people simply refer to the whole shebang as the Internet. Others use terms such as the Matrix, the Extended Internet, etc. The Matrix was a popular one among the founders of the Internet (it originates from the classic William Gibson novel, Neuromancer), but now the term is trademarked and belongs to Hollywood. It probably won't be long before the founders of the Internet are slapped with a trademark violation lawsuit.

holes, and what you can do about them. When you're finished with this chapter, you'll be ready to think about security on your own network.

How the Internet Works: The Quick Explanation

Connecting to the Internet means different things for different users. Some users have dedicated lines running into their computer. They are always connected to the Internet. Others use modems to dial into Internet service providers. There are many ways of establishing an Internet connection, and it would be very difficult for an application to figure out which type of connection is being used. Even if the application could interface with the connection directly, it might interfere with data being sent and received by other programs on the computer.

Instead of trying to interface with the Internet connection directly, networked applications "talk" to the operating system and ask it to either send data to, or retrieve data from, the Internet. The operating system knows exactly how your specific machine is connected to the Internet. The interface to the operating system is called a *network driver*.

The Network Driver

The network driver abstracts away the details of how the operating system is dealing with the programs that need to access the network. Each program can "pretend" that it lives in its own world and can simply ask for or send information from or to the network as though it were the only program running on the machine. If multiple programs want data from the network at the same time, the network driver will mediate among the programs, hopefully ensuring that each program gets the data it needs as quickly as possible.

The Internet Protocol

There are many types of network drivers, and different drivers are used to connect to different types of networks. Each type of network has its own special rules for how data is to be passed around. These communication rules are known as *protocols*. The Internet Protocol (IP) by definition is the standard for Internet communications and specifies how data is to be transferred from machine to machine. By using a standard protocol, one machine doesn't have to know what type of computer is on the other end of a transaction. The computer (via the network driver) handles converting the data into a form that it can use.

How Data Moves on the Internet

When data is transmitted across the Internet, it is broken up into small chunks called *packets*. Each packet is sent out separately from the transmitting computer. All that the packet knows is the address it's supposed to get to. It has no idea how to get there. The method it uses is very similar to the way mail gets from your local mailbox to its intended addressee.

Consider a packet to be equivalent to a letter you're sending out to your cousin in a small mining town in Alaska. You "send" the letter by dropping it off in the mailbox at the end of your street. Of course, the letter doesn't get magically transported to your cousin. A postal worker comes by and empties the mailbox at about 5:45 P.M. He has no idea how to get your letter to Alaska, but he does know how to get it to the local post office. He takes it there and drops it in a bin with the rest of the mail.

Later that day, the postal workers sort the mail and see that there's a letter bound for Alaska. They don't know how to get it to Alaska, but they do know how to get it to a central dispatch office, which may have a better idea of what to do with it. They put the letter in a hopper that is bound for a central dispatch office. A truck comes by, picks up the hopper, and takes it away.

This process of getting the letter to various central dispatch offices continues until one of the larger offices actually knows how to get the letter to Alaska.

A worker at that office puts it in a hopper that gets loaded onto a plane bound for Anchorage.

The plane lands in Anchorage, and the postal workers there look at the letter. They know where the small mining town is, but they don't have any trucks that go directly there. So, the letter travels to a larger, nearby town. The postal worker in the larger town is going to visit a friend in the mining town later that week, so he takes the letter with him and delivers it to your cousin when he arrives.

What was the point of that long and complex story? It actually illustrates quite a few points. The first major point is that if you replace the postal workers with computers known as *routers* and the trucks and planes with Internet wires, you have a pretty good idea of how data get from point A to point B on the Internet. A router is essentially a digital postal worker. Just as a postal worker passes mail to a post office closer to the address on the envelope, a router is a computer that is dedicated to passing information on to other computers nearer the intended destination. The first few routers may not know how to get the data to its intended location, but they can pass it on to other routers that may have a better idea. Eventually, a router somewhere along the line "knows" how to get the data to the right recipient.

How do the first few routers guess where to send the information? Each computer on the Internet has a unique address in the form of a four-part number known as an *IP address*. This address is very much like a telephone number, in which the first part is the country code, the second is the area code, the third is the exchange, and the fourth is the phone itself. The routers look at the IP address, which is a combination of four numbers, each of which can be in the range of 0 to 255. For an explanation of IP addresses, please see the sidebar titled, *What's in an IP Address?*

The first router looks at the first of the four numbers in the destination IP address. If it knows how to get information to a router with the same first four numbers, it sends the packet along in the proper direction. If it doesn't know where the network is, it will send the packet to another router that may have a better chance at locating the destination in question.

If the packet is being sent in the right direction, each router it gets to should know how to get the packet to a machine that's closer to one on the actual destination network. This process occurs until the packet is at a machine that's on the network itself.

If at any point along this chain a router knows that it is directly connected to a computer within the destination network or possibly even the destination computer itself, it will send the packet straight there, bypassing all of the homing in work. Going back to our original letter-to-Alaska example, imagine if your hometown was near the central dispatch station that knows how to send mail to Alaska. Your letter would get there much faster because it would bypass many of unnecessary steps to other dispatching offices.

What's in an IP Address?

An IP address looks like this:

18.62.2.61

The IP address is composed of four 8-bit numbers (0–255 in value), which are called *octets,* separated by dots. Using this system, there are 4 trillion possible IP addresses. It would obviously take a very powerful computer to store the route to all of those addresses. Therefore, a method of grouping these addresses into blocks was devised.

There are three basic groupings, which are known as Class A, B, and C networks. The first IP address number (18 in our example) happens to specify a particular Class A network. Only 128 Class A networks are possible, specified by a first number between 0 and 127. Over half of these groupings are reserved for special purposes. The rest are only available to governments and very large organizations. The reason for this is that a Class A address holder has control over all of the addresses that are formed from combinations of the remaining three octets. Each Class A network contains 16.7 million individual addresses. *Very* few organizations control entire Class A networks. Massachusetts Institute of Technology (MIT) is one of them, and our example points to a specific machine on MIT's campus (gsd.mit.edu, home of the Global School District). Any IP address that starts with 18 will therefore point to a machine that is part of MIT's network.

Class B networks have a first octet number between 128 and 191. Unlike Class A networks, a Class B network is determined by fixing the second octet at a particular number. The holder of a Class B network can assign all of the addresses that result from combinations of the last two octets, for a total of 65,000 or so possible addresses. A total of around 16,000 Class B networks are available, and most of these have been assigned already.

Class C networks are the most limited type of network. The first octet can be within the range of 192–223. The second and third octets are fixed. The Class C administrator thus has only 254 possible IP addresses available to assign. Over 2 million Class C networks are available.

This method of breaking down the possible IP address numbers means that a core router would only need to know how to get information to about 2 million networks, instead of 4 trillion addresses. Most routers don't even have a complete routing table (the full 2-million-plus addresses) but instead know how to get information to a backbone router (a router that has a much more complete table). From there, that router will have a better idea of how to get the packet to its destination. A quick note on domain names: Because long numbers are difficult for humans to deal with, a system was created for matching names to the numbers. Special computers called *Domain Name Servers (*DNS*)* are designated to translate these names into the proper addresses. When you type an address into your Web browser, such as www.yahoo.com, a domain name server in your network translates this entry to Yahoo's IP address (204.71.200.69). We'll talk more about this service in the next chapter.

Now we've got enough background to address the real issue. Remember how we said that data gets broken up into little chunks, and these little chunks are called packets? The route from one computer to another is only as good as its weakest link. If the postal worker in Alaska forgot to deliver the letter when he got to the small mining town, your cousin's letter would be lost. If the worker postponed his visit for a month, the letter would be very late. Similarly, in the network world, if a router is not functioning properly or if there is a very large amount of data coming through at any particular moment, data could very easily get delayed or lost. Packets are often intentionally dropped when the load on a router is high. Additionally, one packet doesn't necessarily have to take the same route as the next one. If the second packet takes a much faster route, it will arrive before the first one.

Now that you understand the basic principles of routing, it's time to start looking at the various programs that create these packets in the first place.

Who Are the Protocols in Your Neighborhood?

Most networked applications can be viewed of in terms of the "client/server" model of computing. The *server* is a program that is waiting for a client to connect. It must always be running, since it doesn't know when the client will want to communicate. The *client*, on the other hand, can be run at any time.

The term server is often used loosely, and can refer to a single program running on a machine, or an entire machine that is running one or more server applications. To help avoid confusion, a more specific term for the individual server application is frequently used: *service*. Thus, a server machine provides one or more services to its clients.

A *protocol* is the language that the service uses to communicate with its clients. There are a number of international organizations that work together to standardize important protocols. Without standards, every networked application would have its own proprietary protocol, client, and server application. Imagine what the Internet would look like if Netscape Web browsers could only communicate with Netscape Web servers. The reason why Netscape browsers can talk to Apache Web servers is HTTP—the HyperText Transport Protocol. All Web browsers and servers use the same language to communicate, ensuring that any HTTP compliant browser will be able to connect with any HTTP compliant server.

Open-standards protocols have helped the Internet evolve rapidly. A programmer doesn't have to worry about creating both the client and the server software if a standard protocol is used. This ultimately gives the end user the greatest flexibility. Because of this, many networked applications communicate via one of the standard protocols. Nonetheless, new protocols do appear, and a few proprietary protocols do become popular. This, of course, only makes your job harder.

Your firewall will sit between the client programs on your user's machines and the network services they want to access. The only way anybody will be able to use these services is if you explicitly provide access through your firewall. If you're a control freak, you are probably foaming at the mouth with excitement. Everyone else can groan at this point, because it means understanding and evaluating many things you probably never wanted to think about.

Most protocols are built on top of one or two other base protocols. This structure allows the protocol developer to abstract away the details of transmitting data across the network and instead focus on controlling the data flow. The Transmission Control Protocol (TCP) and the User Datagram Protocol (UDP) are used to handle the network data transmission. These two protocols are in turn built on top of IP, the Internet Protocol. We've already visited IP briefly. IP is the foundation for almost every Internet communication (with the exception of ARP/RARP, discussed later in this chapter).

Let's take a look at each of these core protocols in more detail.

The Foundation: IP

Data that are sent over IP are sent as a series of fragments, called *packets*. A large chunk of data is broken up into many packets. The key to IP is its simplicity. IP provides a mechanism for delivering packets across a network. What it DOESN'T do is ensure that the packets get there, or that they arrive in any particular order. If a router doesn't know how to get an IP packet to its destination, it simply throws it away and sends back an error message.

When you can't guarantee a packet will get to its destination the framework is called *unreliable*. If there's no information that could help you relate one packet to the next, the system is called *connectionless* or *stateless*.

Very few applications deal with IP directly. It is usually handled in the kernel (core) of an operating system. Instead applications use TCP and UDP, which provide a higher level interface to IP. There is a class of applications that deals with IP directly—these are the various packet monitoring tools that we'll be looking at in Chapter 11, "Intrusion Detection and Response."

Every packet sent across the network resembles a Russian doll (see Figure 2.1). Each *shell* is a header and possibly a trailer. The header is information that is placed at the beginning of a data chunk. The trailer likewise refers to information that appears after the data chunk. Inside the shell are the data, which are often other smaller Russian dolls.

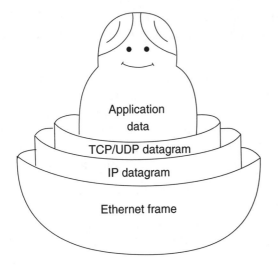

Figure 2.1 Ethernet packets depicted as a badly drawn Russian doll.

The combination of header, data, and trailer is called a *datagram* (the term "Russian doll" was never officially adopted by government officials, possibly because most of the initial technology was developed by DARPA during the Cold War, but most likely due to the fact that I just made up the term). The process of placing one datagram within another is called *encapsulation*.

The outermost datagram is called the *Ethernet frame*. It contains a header and a trailer. In between is the IP datagram. The IP datagram contains a header and another datagram, which is usually either a TCP or UDP datagram. TCP and UDP datagrams may contain raw data or may have other protocols encapsulated within.

The process of unwrapping the layers in a packet is called *demultiplexing*. The Ethernet hardware demultiplexes the Ethernet frame and passes the encapsulated IP datagram to the IP service. The IP service then demultiplexes its datagram and passes the resulting information to the appropriate service—usually the TCP or UDP service.

IP Vulnerabilities

Before going into the various IP-based attacks, we need to introduce a critical concept called *spoofing*. It is very easy to create a packet that has a fictitious source IP address. When another machine receives this packet, it may believe that the packet originated from the fictitious sender. This process is called spoofing the target machine. Attackers use spoofing for a number of reasons.

One of the most common is to gain anonymity. By spoofing packets, the attack appears to be coming from somebody else's machine. Attackers also use spoofing when they want to assume the identity of a machine that has privileged access to certain resources. In order for spoofing to work, a number of other factors often need to be at play; we'll approach these in greater detail throughout the chapter.

There are numerous attacks that can be mounted with a simple IP packet. We will touch on a few specific attacks that have caused considerable havoc over the past few years. By examining how these attacks work, you'll better understand the basis for new exploits when they appear.

TIP

Understanding how an exploit works helps you more thoroughly evaluate the threat and enables you to implement effective safeguards.

Ping of Death

The simplest IP-based attack is probably the infamous *Ping of Death* (PoD). This attack is effected with a single packet with a length that exceeds the maximum length for an IP packet, as stated within the protocol specification. Creating such a packet is exceedingly simple. In fact, Win95 provides a program that can do this in one line from a DOS prompt (specifically, ping –l 65510 the.target.ip.addr). Unix systems provide a similar command, although many recent versions don't allow the generation of such pathological packets.

How does the Ping of Death work? It has to do with the way IP packets are broken up (fragmented) into small pieces that fit within an Ethernet frame. When an IP packet is larger than the maximum size for an Ethernet frame (minus the header/trailer), it gets split up and sent as multiple frames. The receiving computer extracts the fragments and assembles them back into a complete IP packet.

Normally, the IP header contains the length of the entire IP packet. When an IP packet is fragmented, the header contains the fragment's length instead. None of the fragmented packets contains the length of the complete packet. Thus, when packets are fragmented the length of the fully assembled packet can only be determined after all the fragments are received.

The IP specification sets a maximum size for an IP packet. The Ping of Death is effective because some packet handling routines assume that packets larger than this maximum size would never occur. The packet reassembly code only sets aside enough memory for the maximum IP packet length. When the over-sized packet is reassembled, the extra data in the packet overflows into other memory areas. The result is that it throws the operating system into an unstable state. The operating system desperately clamors for stability, and invariably ends up in the most stable state of all—dead. This is a typical type of buffer overflow attack. We describe the process of buffer overflows in greater detail at the end of this chapter.

NOTE The ping program made this type of attack so easy that it became the weapon of choice, and ultimately the namesake of the attack method. Although most PoD type attacks are performed with "ping," the attack could be accomplished with other tools or custom programs. Protecting yourself solely against "ping" requests will not adequately address this vulnerability.

The best way to prevent the Ping of Death is to patch your operating system to a version that is not susceptible. The kernel will no longer attempt to reassemble packets that exceed the maximum length. It is very difficult to catch this attack at the firewall level because the individual fragments look perfectly normal. It's only when all of the fragments are assembled into a complete IP packet that the problem occurs.

NOTE The only way to effectively block this attack at the firewall level would be to assemble every fragmented IP packet at the firewall and check to see if it's too long before passing the fragments on to the destination machine. This can be time- and CPU-consuming, and could create problems for real-time communication or bandwidth intensive services. Nonetheless, most firewalls have an option for doing this.

Teardrop

Along similar lines to the PoD is the *Teardrop* attack. Here, the fragments of a large IP packet overlap, instead of properly lining up end-to-end. In Figure 2.2, packet one has an offset of 0 and a length of 10. Packet two has an offset of 5. This means it starts midway through packet one. This creates a 5 byte overlap. The kernel attempts to eliminate the overlap, but if an overlapping fragment is smaller than the size of the overlap (as shown in Figure 2.3) the kernel finds itself in a state that it isn't prepared to handle. This is lovingly referred to as a *kernel panic*. Kernel panics are frequently accompanied by unhappy death-like manifestations from the unfortunate recipient machine.

These problems aren't necessarily due to the nature of the IP protocol—they're simply common holes in many implementations of the protocol. The next hole is actually created by a feature of the IP protocol.

NORMAL IP FRAGMENT OVERLAP RESOLUTION

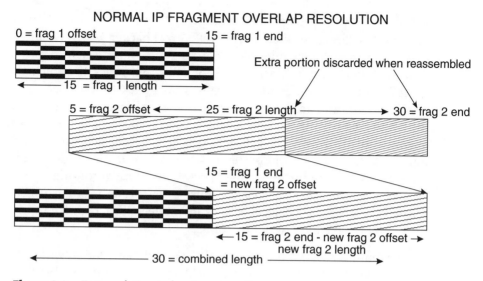

Figure 2.2   Two packets overlapping normally.

TEARDROP IP FRAGMENT OVERLAP RESOLUTION

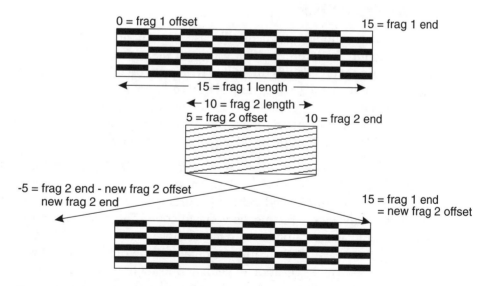

Fragment 2 doesn't have enough data to cover the overlap region.

When the new end of fragment 2 is calculated by subtracting the new offset from the end location of fragment 2, a negative number is achieved. When the kernel allocates memory for copying fragment 2 into the reassembled IP packet, it gets a negative amount of memory to allocate. The kernel interprets negative numbers as a ridiculously large number and promptly runs out of memory.

Figure 2.3   A teardrop overlap.

Strict and Loose Source Routing

The best hackers cover their traces well. A real hacker will never directly send a packet from their machine to a target machine—it's too easy to trace. Instead, they will work through a network of other machines to which they have gained unauthorized access. This causes the attack to trace back to someone else's machine and account. An extra layer of confusion can be added by taking advantage of a few options within the IP protocol that are implemented on a number of systems. One such option allows the packet to specify the path it must take to its destination. This is known as *source routing*. There are two types of source routing: *loose* and *strict*. Loose source routing allows you to specify machines that the packet must pass through, but it can also pass through a number of other machines in-between. Strict source routing forces the packet to take the prescribed route.

Source routing allows a hacker to craft attacks that are not traceable, or appear to be originating from one of your machines. Source routing also allows hackers to impersonate trusted machines. Luckily, source routing is not used by any major services. Therefore, we can have our firewall filter out any source-routed packets that appear on our network.

The Control Freak: TCP

The IP is a very simple system. Its only task is to standardize the way information moves around the Internet. What it doesn't do is ensure that the data leaving point A arrive at point B. It's difficult to write networked applications if you can't assume that the packets you send will be received in the order you sent them. It's even tougher if you don't know whether all of the packets made it there in the first place! Therefore, most applications do not use IP directly. The *Transmission Control Protocol (TCP)* was created to make the life of developers easier.

TCP is a system that provides a mechanism for sending a reliable stream of data over an unreliable network. It accomplishes this goal by keeping track of whether data are duplicated, sent out of order, or lost. If it notices a problem, it corrects the mistake. This means you can count on packets arriving in order and without gaps or duplicates. In fact, TCP lets you avoid dealing with packets altogether. Give TCP a chunk of data and the other end will receive that chunk of data. The application developer doesn't have to deal with breaking it apart into smaller chunks. This allows an application to stream data across a TCP connection without worrying about how the data are transported across the network.

When TCP is layered on top of the Internet Protocol, the resulting system is known as *TCP/IP*. This system provides programmers with a level of abstraction that lets them avoid having to deal with the issues involved in verifying the data that is received from the Internet.

TCP Ports

TCP also handles another major issue: What happens when multiple servers are running at one IP address? Many programs use the TCP protocol to provide reliable connections. On one machine, it would not be unusual to be running a Web server, a mail server, and an X Windows server, all using the TCP protocol to accept connections from other computers (called *clients*). How would a machine know which service a client wants to connect to when it establishes a TCP connection with that machine?

The IP header contains the address of the destination machine, but there's no information in the packet that points to a particular application. Since many services may be associated with a given IP address, this is clearly not enough information.

The solution is called the *TCP port number*. The TCP port provides an address for each piece of server software running on the machine. When a server starts on a machine, it must tell the machine what TCP port number it wants to use. Then, whenever a client wants to connect to a particular server, it connects to the machine that the server is on and asks for a connection to that specific port number.

Each server application is bound to a particular port number when it opens up a TCP connection. There can be only one application bound to a particular port number on a given IP address at any one time (or else a Frenchman with a bad Scottish accent appears and slices the extra application's head off with a big sword). The client application places this port number in the TCP header of each outbound packet. TCP automatically delivers the packets to the proper server application based on the port number. Most common protocols have standard port numbers to which servers are usually bound.

The client application also opens up a TCP connection (TCP connections are also called *sockets*) on the client machine. The port number and IP address of the client are also included in the header of each TCP packet sent by or to that client. The port number used by the client is rarely standardized, since the server can obtain it by looking at the TCP header. There are a few important cases where these ports are standardized, which we'll describe shortly.

There are two ways for a client to know which port its respective server is on. If the server is designed to receive connections from a specific client software package, the port will probably be hard coded into the client. This usually occurs with small or proprietary client/server packages. If the server is supporting a standard service—a Web server, an FTP server, or a Telnet server—there are standardized port numbers for each of these services. For instance, Telnet servers are usually run on port 23; IRC servers are usually run on port 6667. Web servers are usually run on port 80.

NOTE Have you ever noticed that some URLs have numbers next to the host name, but others don't? The numbers tell the browser that the Web server is running on a port other than 80. For URLs without numbers, the 80 is implied. For instance, Web browsers consider the URL www.news.com equivalent to www.news.com:80 because port 80 is the default Web port.

This port number system allows you to run several servers on the same machine—even servers of the same type. For instance, MIT's Student Information Processing Board (SIPB) runs two Web servers on www.mit.edu on ports 80 and 8001, which can be accessed at www.mit.edu and www.mit.edu:8001 respectively. If you look closely at these URLs, you will see that these return the same pages, but they don't necessarily have to.

The reason that these two Web servers return the same Web pages has a lot to do with how servers earn their own standard port numbers. Back when the Web was a neat little novelty that virtually nobody knew about, Web servers didn't have a standard TCP port to call home. SIPB decided to set up a Web server on port 8001 of one of their machines. They called the machine www.mit.edu (which sort of ticked off MIT's administration later on when the Web became popular and the name www.mit.edu was already taken). By the time the Web had become popular and had a standard port, thousands of MIT students, faculty, and labs had already written Web pages on www.mit.edu and registered the URLs on places like Yahoo! using the port 8001 URL. This eventually led to much confusion among people who didn't understand the concept of typing ":8001" in a URL. To rectify this issue, SIPB added a redundant Web server on port 80 that mirrors the old server at 8001.

SIPB's non-standard choice of port number was not due to some oversight or error. Port numbers under 1024 are generally reserved for established protocols; at the time that the www.mit.edu server first went online, the Web was far from established. The way in which these ports are reserved on Unix/Linux systems is that a user must have privileged access to a machine in order to activate a server that sits on (binds to) a port below 1024. This is a security measure to prevent a random, nonadministrative user of the machine from running a Trojan mail server, Web server, or Telnet server, to name a few possibilities (such a server could intercept data traveling to the reserved mail, Web, or Telnet ports). Windows does not enforce this restriction. The person who initially set up the SIPB Web server may not have had privileged access to the machine, thus forcing the use of port 8001.

Why are we getting this technical in regards to TCP and IP? Because the firewall sees the IP packet before it gets demultiplexed. Each layer of encapsulation provides a header that can be used for filtering the packet. In some cases we'll need to filter based on just the IP header. In other cases we can use information in the TCP header to filter, such as the port number. For example, one of the easiest ways to firewall is to block access to all ports except those that are used by your critical applications. Naturally, there are limitations to this method, otherwise this chapter would be a lot smaller.

TCP Vulnerabilities

The LAND attack is one of the simplest TCP attacks: A TCP packet is created where the source and destination IP address and port are set to the same values. The address must be the address of the target machine and the port must have an active service running. The LAND attack has the remarkable effect of rebooting or otherwise killing numerous machines!

NOTE

Setting the source IP address to the target machine's address requires pretending that your machine *is* the target machine for the purposes of constructing the packet. This is accomplished by "spoofing" the target machine. As we mentioned earlier in the chapter, a spoofed packet appears to be coming from some location other than its true origin.

The reason for the LAND attack's effectiveness is rooted in the reliable nature of TCP. In order to make connections reliable, TCP performs two critical tasks. The first is *session initialization*. A process known as a three-way handshake exchanges initialization data between the client and the server. This establishes a reference point for all future communications, known as the *sequence number*. The sequence number helps TCP reorder packets and determine if packets have been lost. The other critical task involves sending acknowledgments with each packet received. If the acknowledgment isn't received within a certain amount of time, the packet is retransmitted.

The LAND attack takes advantage of the way in which acknowledgment occurs during the initial connection establishment. The key to the attack is that the server side and the client side each has its own initial sequence numbers. For example, the server's sequence might be 1, 2, 3, 4... while the client's sequence is 1000,1001,1002, etc. For every transmission, the receiving end sends an acknowledgment that contains the next sequence number expected from the transmitting application.

The attack starts with the attacker sending a random sequence number as the first handshake. The target computer says, okay, here's my own random sequence number. I'll acknowledge your number by incrementing it and sending it back to you. This is the second handshake. If this were a normal situation, the attacker's machine would be listening for the number and would send back a third handshake by incrementing the target's sequence number and sending it back as an acknowledgment. Now both machines know each other's sequence numbers and can properly track packets. Figure 2.4 illustrates a typical three-way handshake process.

The trick to the attack is that the target machine actually sends this packet to itself (remember, the source and destination IP addresses are the same, so it thinks the sender is itself). The problem is that the target is waiting for *its own sequence number* as an acknowledgment. Instead, it gets *the acknowledgment it*

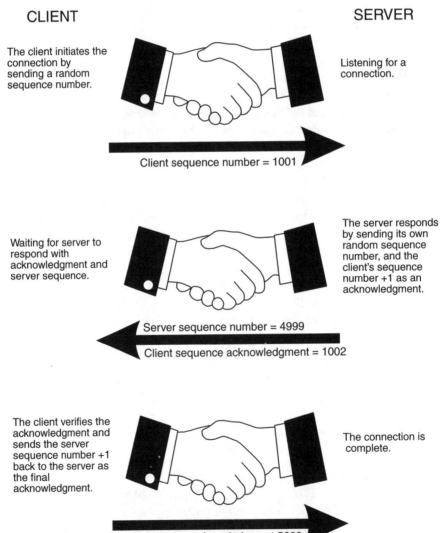

NORMAL THREE-WAY TCP HANDSHAKE

CLIENT   SERVER

The client initiates the connection by sending a random sequence number.

Listening for a connection.

Client sequence number = 1001

Waiting for server to respond with acknowledgment and server sequence.

The server responds by sending its own random sequence number, and the client's sequence number +1 as an acknowledgment.

Server sequence number = 4999

Client sequence acknowledgment = 1002

The client verifies the acknowledgment and sends the server sequence number +1 back to the server as the final acknowledgment.

The connection is complete.

Server sequence acknowledgment 5000

Figure 2.4   TCP's three-way handshake.

just sent out, with the attacker's sequence number. Because this sequence number is so wildly different from the one it's expecting, TCP knows that it can't possibly be an out-of-sequence packet. Thus, it sends the same sequence number out again. This is interpreted by TCP to mean "that's not what I expected, try again." This creates an infinite loop—it keeps sending itself the wrong acknowledgment, hoping to see the right sequence number in return. All that it ever sees is the acknowledgment it just sent out. Figure 2.5 should help you visualize this process better.

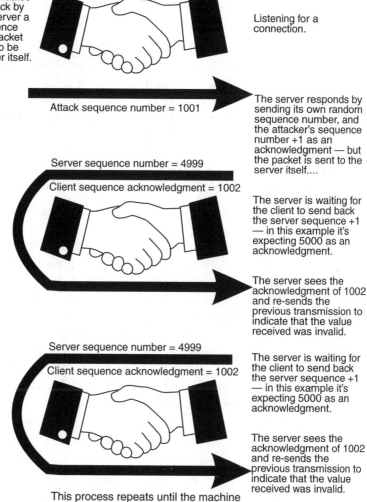

LAND ATTACK TCP HANDSHAKE

ATTACKER

SERVER

The attacker initiates the LAND attack by sending the server a random sequence number in a packet that appears to be from the server itself.

Listening for a connection.

Attack sequence number = 1001

The server responds by sending its own random sequence number, and the attacker's sequence number +1 as an acknowledgment — but the packet is sent to the server itself....

Server sequence number = 4999

Client sequence acknowledgment = 1002

The server is waiting for the client to send back the server sequence +1 — in this example it's expecting 5000 as an acknowledgment.

The server sees the acknowledgment of 1002 and re-sends the previous transmission to indicate that the value received was invalid.

Server sequence number = 4999

Client sequence acknowledgment = 1002

The server is waiting for the client to send back the server sequence +1 — in this example it's expecting 5000 as an acknowledgment.

The server sees the acknowledgment of 1002 and re-sends the previous transmission to indicate that the value received was invalid.

This process repeats until the machine spontaneously combusts.

Figure 2.5 The evil handshake of death.

Why does this kill a machine? TCP is a high-priority kernel-level process. This means that it takes priority over all nonkernel applications. It basically interrupts all normal system operation so that it can claim kernel resources to processes incoming data. The infinite loop rapidly consumes all of the system's resources and on most systems causes a painful death. On some systems, TCP will eventually time-out, but few popular operating systems are stable enough to survive when kernel resources are maxed out for an extended period of time.

There's something else to watch out for—a variant of Teardrop that is combined with the LAND attack, hitting your system with a double whammy. Teardrop and LAND attacks can be fixed by downloading a patch for your operating system. Both OpenBSD and Linux have been patched. Most versions of Windows also have LAND patches. The companion Web site contains links to major security patches for each platform.

OK, that one was easy. Now let's get into some really serious TCP issues. We just described the process by which TCP connections are initialized. We also talked a bit about how TCP sends acknowledgments after each successfully transmitted packet. What you might have noticed was missing was an *authentication mechanism*. That's because there is none. TCP assumes that the data are acceptable as long as it receives properly formed packets with acceptable sequence numbers. Once the connection has been established, there's no way for a server to determine whether the data are coming from the client machine or from a machine pretending to be the client machine.

Imagine the following situation: A client program is communicating with a server via TCP. An attacker uses the ARP technique (described later in this chapter) to intercept and redirect the flow of data from the client and the server to the attacker's machine. The attacker doesn't want to be noticed, so all of the client's commands are passed through to the server and the server's responses are passed back to the client. To the client and the server, it appears as if they're communicating directly with one another. Because it's watching the sequence numbers, it can place its own spoofed packets into the TCP stream as needed. This allows the attacker to access the server with all of the privileges of the spoofed client. The attacker can also watch for any output related to the attack and NOT pass it on to the client. Thus, the attack becomes transparent. In such a situation, the attacker doesn't even need to figure out a password to get access to the machine. The attacker simply waits until the user has logged in and then hijacks the session stream. Figure 2.6 shows how an attacker hijacks a TCP session.

The trick here is being able to position a machine in the middle of the data stream. As we will show later in the chapter, this is not very difficult. There are security holes throughout many TCP/IP implementations which enable such

NORMAL TCP COMMUNICATIONS

CLIENT   SERVER

HIJACKED TCP COMMUNICATIONS

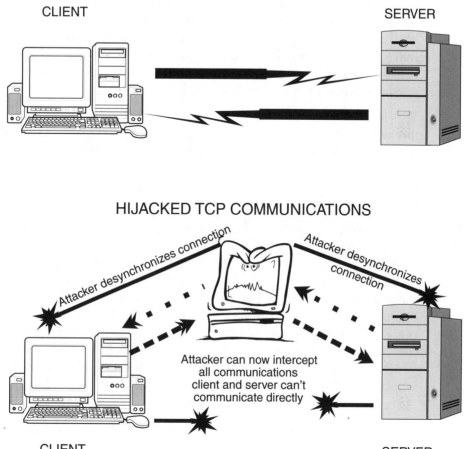

CLIENT   SERVER

Figure 2.6   Hijacking a TCP session.

an attack. There are also holes within TCP itself that allow this type of masquerading. Even if obtaining the pass-through position isn't possible for the hacker, there are many equally potent variations on the theme.

One technique that can be used to hijack a TCP session is called *desynchronization*. To explain, we need to go back to our triple handshake model:

Handshake 1. The client sends the server a synchronization packet and its sequence number, Client_Seq. The client waits for an acknowledgment.

Handshake 2. The server sends back an acknowledgment (Client_Seq + 1) and its own sequence number, Server_Seq. The client is in the *connection established* state, but the server is waiting for an acknowledgment from the client.

Right after the second handshake, the attacker jumps out of the shadows and fires a reset packet at the server, impersonating the client. The server sees this packet and assumes something has gone wrong in the handshake process. The server ends its current connection and listens for a new one. While this was happening, the client sent out a real acknowledgment to the second handshake, but by the time the acknowledgment gets to the server, the attacker has already closed the original connection. The server sees the client's acknowledgment, but ignores it because it's no longer relevant.

The client is oblivious to this entire exchange. Since it is not expecting any further acknowledgment from the server, it has no idea that anything has gone wrong and remains in the established state. The client thinks the server is still active, but it isn't. The server thinks the client has closed its connection, but it hasn't. Both the server and the client have misconceptions about the state of the connection. This is called a *desynchronized state*.

Desynchronization can also be accomplished by feeding both the client and the server a lot of null TCP packets. Null packets are those that will be accepted by the client or server but will not have any noticeable effect. The result is that the internal sequence numbers on each end will advance without the other side realizing it. For example, if the server's number was 5, a bunch of null TCP data could raise it to 5000. The client would still think the server's sequence was 5; the server would therefore view subsequent packets sent by the client as out of sequence. There is a TCP setting, known as the "window," which determines the maximum difference between the internal sequence number and the number given in a received packet. By exceeding the window, the connection will become desynchronized.

Once a desynchronized state has been achieved, the attacker is ready to open a can of whoop-ass on the TCP connection. Here are the steps that the attacker takes:

Handshake 1. The attacker restarts the server connection by sending out a synchronization packet on behalf of the client, using its own sequence number: Attack_Seq.

Handshake 2. The server responds with an acknowledgement to the client (Attack_Seq + 1) and its own new sequence number: New_Server_Seq.

Handshake 3. This time the attacker responds with an acknowledgement (Server_Seq + 1), still impersonating the client: (Attack_Seq + 2).

Now when the client sends data to the server, the server ignores it because the sequence number (*Client_Seq*) is wrong. The attacker sees it and does what he or she wants, usually recreating the packet with the new sequence number (*Attack_Seq*) and sending it out to the server. When the server responds, the client ignores the response for the same reason (it's expecting *Server_Seq* and sees *New_Server_Seq* instead), and once again the attacker manipulates the data before reformulating the packet and sending them back to the client (with *New_Server_Seq*).

What we just said is mostly true, but we glossed over a very important detail. Neither the client nor the server ignores the data with the incorrect sequence numbers. Instead, an acknowledgment is sent back with the bad sequence number. This is interpreted as "bad sequence number, try again." For example, when the client tries to send data to the server, an acknowledgment from the server is generated, saying it was expecting *Ax*, and includes its sequence number *New_Server_Seq*. The client receives the ACKs and freaks out, because it's expecting a sequence number of *Server_Seq*, not *New_Server_Seq*. So the client sends an ACK back to the server with sequence *Client_Seq*. The server gets this and mirror's the client's reaction, because it was expecting *Attack_Seq* instead of *Client_Seq*.

Is this starting to sound familiar? The result is a storm of ACKs very similar to those generated by the LAND attack. The difference is that these acknowledgments don't loop forever inside the kernel—they're sent back and forth across the network. This can flood the network and eat up a lot of bandwidth. Luckily, the attacker can end the storm by forging the acknowledgments that each side is expecting. A smart attacker will run programs that do this automatically, minimizing the storm to a few ACKs.

These attacks assume that it's possible to sniff the packets on the network in order to determine the sequence numbers. There are other approaches that work even if it's impossible to sniff network traffic. For example, the attacker can forge packets from a trusted machine and establish a connection *without ever seeing any of the replies from the server.* This can be done if the attacker can guess the server's sequence number. Many implementations of TCP use a predictable method of generating sequence numbers, so this isn't as hard as it sounds. Once a one-way connection has been established, the attacker can potentially execute commands that create a more flexible hole. Really good attackers may even be able to accomplish all of their goals through such a connection.

Unfortunately, there's not too much that can be done against this sort of attack. One solution is via hardware: buy switches instead of hubs (you'll hear this many times over the next few pages). Switches make it very difficult to sniff a network. This will prevent hackers from directly obtaining sequence numbers.

Another option is to encrypt your TCP communications via a system such as ssh (Secure SHell). Ssh encrypts all communications between client and server at the application level, and by using public-key encryption allows you to ensure that the same two machines are connecting each time. By preventing data from traveling over the network in clear-text format, you make the hacker's job much harder. Unless the hacker can crack your encryption key, they won't be able to forge or read any of the data within the intercepted packets. They also won't be able to establish connections without the encrypted authentication. We'll talk more about ssh and its many applications in the next chapter.

Newer implementations of TCP may use harder-to-predict methods of generating sequence numbers. You should make sure your machines are all running the latest versions of every TCP/IP service, to the extent that it's practical to update and administer these machines.

One general point: You should not be basing trust relationships between machines on IP addresses or hardware addresses. Trust relationships should be based on encrypted password exchange or some other complex system. IP-based trust is too easy to compromise.

The Free Spirit: UDP

There is a price that you pay for using TCP. The process of verifying that the packets are complete and in order creates a considerable overhead. A lot of extra data is generated and transmitted to control the flow. Additionally, TCP has to wait until it is sure that it has the right data before passing it to the application. If there's a significant amount of packet loss or network congestion, TCP connections suffer dramatically.

Some applications don't really care if the data arrive out of order or are missing. The performance gain from not using TCP can sometimes outweigh the drawbacks of lost or scrambled data. The classic example is streaming audio/video. A missed packet can be skipped without creating much of a problem for the user. Out of order packets also have minimal effect. Enter the *User Datagram Protocol* (UDP) packet.

UDP is a stateless, unreliable transport mechanism. It basically adds a port number to an IP packet. It also contains a length and a checksum value for packet level data integrity checking. It contains the minimum information necessary to get a packet from one application to another.

Streaming video and audio servers use UDP to send the data stream to the client. By not using TCP, less data need to be sent, which results in better playback performance.

Often the client will implement its own data integrity checking when UDP is used. With some creative programming the client can compensate for the garbled data.

Of course, there's nothing stopping an application from using both TCP and UDP. In fact, most streaming video/audio packages use TCP for the control commands and statistic information sent between client and server. TCP makes sense because this information is not critical to playback performance but needs to arrive intact.

Although both TCP and UDP use port numbers to identify individual services, their port scheme is separate. This means that a TCP client and a UDP client can both connect to the same port number at the IP address. The IP layer will properly route TCP packets to TCP and UDP packets to UDP.

UDP Vulnerabilities

One typical attack carried out with UDP is the Teardrop attack. UDP is used to create the offset fragments used in a Teardrop attack. This was explained in the IP attacks section. Another type of attack is a Denial of Service attack called *fraggle*. In order to understand fraggle, you'll need to refer to the sidebar about unicasting, broadcasting, and multicasting.

Unicasting, Broadcasting, and Multicasting

When one computer sends data directly to another computer, it is called *unicasting*. If a computer sends data to all of the computers on a subnet at once, it's called *broadcasting*. Every subnet has two reserved addresses: a *network* address and a *broadcast* address. Each computer on the subnet listens to its own IP address(es) and the broadcast address.

There's a third option for sending data called *multicasting*. There are situations where a message needs to be delivered to some of the computers on a network, but not all of them. Multicasting is similar to broadcasting, except only hosts that wish to receive the multicast tune in to the specified multicast address. Hosts can listen to multiple multicast addresses, and can send to a multicast address even if they're not listening. If the message is long or frequent, multicasting can reduce the network traffic by only sending the message once.

To effectively fraggle a machine, you need to broadcast a UDP packet spoofed from the target machine. The packet should be broadcast on a number of highly saturated networks (where most of the IP addresses in a subnet have computers on them). The key is to select an interesting UDP port. If the port is unreachable, the result will be a flood of "ICMP port unreachable" messages. One interesting port is the echo port, which simply sends (echos) the packet back to the target machine. If the spoofed port is also the echo port, one could potentially set up a loop where the target machine is constantly trying to echo a huge number of machines. This will quickly flood out the target machine (probably faster than it would flood any of the broadcasted machines). Figure 2.7 shows how a fraggle could rock your network. There are other UDP ports that can wreak equivalent havoc. We'll address a few later in Chapter 3, "How Secure Should Your Network Be?."

The Fraggle Attack

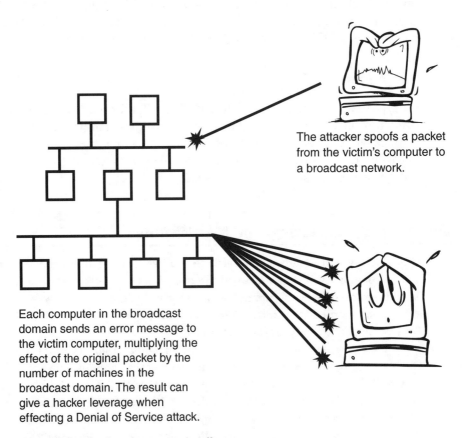

The attacker spoofs a packet from the victim's computer to a broadcast network.

Each computer in the broadcast domain sends an error message to the victim computer, multiplying the effect of the original packet by the number of machines in the broadcast domain. The result can give a hacker leverage when effecting a Denial of Service attack.

Figure 2.7 The fraggle process in effect.

For the most part, blocking UDP fraggle attacks is tough unless you plan on denying all UDP services. Any exposed UDP port is susceptible to the fraggle attack. Closing ports that aren't in use helps. Blocking ICMP unreachable requests at the firewall could also help prevent floods. The most effective thing you can do is ensure that your network isn't used for a fraggle attack. Since the principle here is very similar to a number of the ICMP attacks, you should refer to the ICMP section for more information on securing your network.

The Translator: ARP/RARP

Until now we've ignored the fact that every IP packet is really encapsulated in an Ethernet packet, or frame. The Ethernet hardware doesn't know anything about IP and doesn't understand IP addresses. Ethernet has its own addressing scheme based on unique hardware (MAC) addresses. The Ethernet header contains the source and destination hardware address. Ethernet frames are sent from the source interface through Ethernet cabling to the destination hardware interface. The destination interface is almost always on the local network—routing is done by the IP layer, not the Ethernet layer.

NOTE

Although it's by far the most common physical network technology, Ethernet is not the only network that IP packets can be sent across. Likewise, other protocols could send data across an Ethernet network. One could say that Ethernet deals with the hardware while IP deals with the software.

The problem is that IP doesn't know anything about the hardware address of the destination interface. It only knows the IP address assigned to that interface (one hardware interface can have multiple IP addresses, but multiple interfaces on the same Internet cannot share an IP address). The mechanism that translates an IP address into a hardware address is called the *Address Resolution Protocol*, or ARP.

When IP needs to convert a destination IP address into an interface address, it sends out an ARP request. This request is broadcast to every machine on the local network (see sidebar on unicasting, broadcasting, and multicasting). When a computer that has the destination address sees this request, it sends back an acknowledgment (it doesn't need to broadcast this since it can read the hardware and IP address of the sending machine from the ARP packet), giving its hardware address in the reply. The originator of the request sees the reply and extracts the hardware address. It then stores this address for quick future reference. Now the IP layer can construct the full Ethernet frame with the proper source and destination MAC addresses.

The trick with ARP is that it is *not* encapsulated within an IP packet. ARP has its own packet format. The Ethernet layer sends ARP requests and replies directly to the ARP service, without going through IP. This means that ARP is always running, awaiting possible requests or replies. This is important, because the very nature of ARP creates some security risks, which we'll talk about momentarily.

The sidekick to ARP is the *Reverse Address Resolution Protocol* (RARP). Some networks have machines that are diskless terminals and therefore do not contain any means of storing their IP addresses. These machines read all of their boot information from the network. But in order to form packets to send out, they need to know their IP address. RARP allows a diskless machine to ask RARP servers for an IP address.

RARP servers have a list of IP addresses mapped to hardware addresses. When a machine sends out a RARP request, it doesn't need to include its IP address—it only needs its hardware address. The RARP server looks up the address in the mapping table and sends a reply with the requesting machine's IP address.

RARP also uses a different packet format, one that is very similar to ARP. Unlike ARP, RARP is not a necessary service. RARP is not a very effective way for diskless machines to learn their IP address. BOOTP and DCHP provide better mechanisms for the task. Unless some strange circumstance requires it, we would recommend disabling RARP, if possible.

ARP/RARP Vulnerabilities

The largest problem with ARP is that it is *stateless*, which means that the process that listens for replies is unaware of the process that sends requests. This means that if an ARP reply comes to your machine, there's no way to tell if you ever sent an ARP request.

Imagine a situation in which your machine receives a false ARP reply that maps the hardware address of another machine on the network to the IP address of the router. This updates the ARP cache on your machine with the new incorrect mapping. This technique is known as *cache poisoning*. Suddenly, all packets destined for the router get sent to this other machine. If the other machine is compromised and is set up to analyze the packets and then forward them to the real router, you may never know the difference.

The router isn't the only machine worth impersonating. A smart hacker might choose to impersonate a file server or a database server. With some knowledgeable customization, the hacker could intercept database files or queries. A more complex approach might involve two deceptions—the database user's machine would think that the hacker's machine was the database. Likewise, the database would think the hacker's machine was the user's machine. If you think about it, you'll realize that there is a lot of power in this type of attack.

The ARP cache does expire after a short period of time, but a simple piece of software can constantly send the ARP reply, thus ensuring that the cache entry stays valid. Some implementations of ARP also attempt to update their cache by sending out ARP requests to each entry in the cache. This creates a minor problem for the attacker, since the machine with the real IP address will respond with its proper hardware address. Once again, the stateless nature of the ARP system comes to the hacker's rescue. Sending responses to the requests *before* the requests are sent will actually prevent the requests from being sent in the first place. This technique is shown in Figure 2.8. Thus, an attacker can successfully have one machine impersonating another with relatively little effort. There are programs available on the Internet that can make this process even easier.

ARP CACHE POISONING

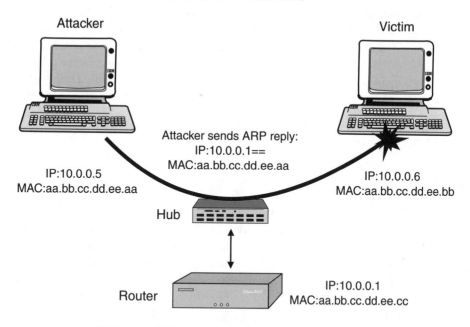

Victim now thinks attacker's machine is the router.

Figure 2.8 ARP cache poisoning.

Impersonation is one use for ARP, Denial of Service is another. Cache poisoning can make a machine very difficult to reach. A Web server that doesn't know where the router is won't be serving many pages. A little effort could easily warp the ARP caches on the entire LAN, rendering the entire LAN worthless for quite a while. ARP gives a creative hacker a wonderful palette of vibrant colors with which to redecorate your network.

We assume that the majority of our readers are terrified of ARP attacks by now. A significant percentage of you have just unplugged every network cable in your home/office. Before the pandemonium goes any further, let's talk about the limitations of this attack and what you can do to prevent ARP attacks.

ARP attacks can only be used to impersonate machines within the local network. This means that a hacker must already have access to a machine that is within your network. The machine that's being poisoned could possibly be outside the LAN though. Furthermore, ARP requests are almost never sent through routers; therefore the impersonated machine must be connected to the compromised machine via a simple hub or a token-ring network. Don't breathe yet—most networks do have simple hubs all over the place. A good hacker will probably be able to get into at least one machine on your network.

Your best defense against ARP redirection attacks is through hardware and intrusion detection software. Buy switches instead of hubs. Yes, they're more expensive, but they offer many benefits that more than justify the cost. Many switches can be configured to associate specific hardware addresses with specific ports on the switch. The switch prevents other hardware addresses from registering their presence on these restricted ports. Traffic that is intended for these new, naughty hardware addresses will simply not be sent to those ports.

Intrusion detection software can be configured to recognize ARP attacks on a LAN. We'll discuss this further in Chapter 11.

The Gimp: IGMP

We talked briefly about multicasting in a sidebar a few pages back. Multicasting is easy if all of the machines on a LAN are connected to one hub. The moment a router is involved it gets a little more complicated. There's no point for a router to forward multicast packets across its interfaces if nobody is listening on the other end. A system is needed so that routers can figure out whether anyone on a subnet is listening to a particular multicast. Enter the *Internet Group Management Protocol* (IGMP).

IGMP is an IP level protocol, meaning that each message is encapsulated within an IP datagram. IGMP messages are very simple—they're all only 8 bytes long and there is no header. There are two types of messages: a query, which is sent by multicast routers, and a report, which is sent by hosts in response to a query. Because IGMP messages are sent out via IP, there's no guarantee that they make it to their destination. Messages are repeated at random intervals to increase the likelihood of the packet making it to all the necessary machines.

Multicast communications are sent to groups of listening programs. Groups are designated by Class D IP addresses. Each address within the Class D space is a group number. A program can join multiple groups on the same hardware interface, as well as the same group on multiple interfaces. Unlike the port concept, multiple programs can join the same IGMP group on a given interface.

A host joins a multicast group by sending an IGMP report to the router. This tells the router that it should start forwarding multicast packets for that group to the host's subnet. Routers will send out queries at regular intervals during a multicast. When a multicast router sends a query, at least one multicast host on a subnet needs to respond for the router to forward multicast packets to that subnet. It doesn't matter if more hosts respond—in fact, many systems are designed to not respond if another host on the multicast network has already responded to the query. This helps cut down on bandwidth usage. If no responses are received after a while from a subnet, the router can stop forwarding multicast packets to that subnet.

IGMP Vulnerabilities

There has been relatively little talk on the net about IGMP exploits. This doesn't mean that IGMP exploits are not possible or don't exist. Multicasting does not get used nearly as much as other methods of communication; therefore, less attention has been paid to multicasting security.

IGMP does not have any type of security built in, meaning that anyone could technically listen in to any multicast available on their network. All aspects of multicast security are left to the application level. The only way to make a multicast session eavesdrop-proof is to encrypt the data stream. There are numerous projects underway to help make IP multicasting secure.

There are other potential problems that Multicasting can create—for example, it's another doorway for DoS attacks. One can create a DoS condition by using spoofed IGMP packets to subscribe entire subnets to many heavy-volume multicast sessions. Another potential security issue involves multicast clients. There are a number of popular multicast applications (CUSeeMe) in which the client application may be susceptible to a buffer overflow condition. A hacker could exploit vulnerabilities during a multicast session to gain control of a large number of client machines within a very short period of time. There also could be buffer overflow potential within the IGMP implementation on certain platforms.

The moral of this story is: If you don't need IGMP, don't use it. Disable it at the router level, and if possible on the client level also. If you do need it, look into the issues around secure multicasting.

Speedy Delivery: Your Friendly Network Routing Service

At this point, we have an Ethernet packet that's sitting on the edge of the interface card, all dressed up and ready to go. It knows where it came from, and it knows where it's going, but because the destination isn't on the local network it doesn't know how to get there. This section describes the protocols that allow different machines on the Internet to find each other and send data to one another.

The Internet is a collection of networks, linked together with devices called *routers*. There are a few large networks run by communications carriers which have wires that run all over the world. This is called the *backbone*. Smaller networks run by ISPs and other major network providers connect to the backbone at various points. These smaller networks have their own infrastructure and hierarchy of smaller and smaller networks. At every connection point between networks, there's a router.

Routers can be viewed as junctions on the, dare we say, information super-highway. Each router connects to one or more networks. The more important routers connect to many networks. These are the routers found at ISPs and on the backbone itself.

Each router usually only knows about the routers nearby. When a router receives a packet, it needs to send it off somewhere. The router figures out where the packet should go based on a few critical pieces of information:

- If the destination is a machine directly on the router's network, it will send the packet directly to the destination machine.

- If the destination is elsewhere, the router will check its routing table. This table maps IP address ranges to hardware interfaces on the router. If a router is connected to multiple networks, this table helps the router figure out which network is most likely to contain the destination machine. Entries in a routing table can be specific,—e.g., a host is directly connected to a specific interface—or more general, based on network numbers and network masks. For example, an entry might say to map all packets destined for the network 10.69.0.0 with mask 255.255.255.0 to interface #3. This means all IP address from 10.69.0.1 to 10.69.0.254 can be located off of interface #3. There's always a default route, which is the interface packets should go to if they're not covered by the routing table.

The key to routing is the routing table. For major routers connected to many networks, this table can get very complex. To make matters worse, there are many redundancies built into the infrastructure of the Internet. This means that if a core router goes down, a packet will be able to reach its destination via an alternate route.

There are two types of routing: *static* and *dynamic*. Static tables are changed very rarely—only when error messages force the table to update. Dynamic routing involves constantly seeking out neighboring routers. Both methods are used heavily throughout the Internet.

Static Routing: ICMP

Small networks and individual machines need a simple mechanism for routing. Lets say a host is connected to a hub that has two routers. How does the host decide which router gets the packet? Same situation if a host has multiple interfaces. The answer is that a host machine has its own static routing table.

A static routing table can be initialized by hand, or it can be initialized through router discovery. Most tables are initialized by hand with one or two entries—a default entry usually points to the host's router. Router discovery is used for systems that boot without a disk or are connected to more complex networks. Routers which service simple networks (one or a few routers total) also may have simple static routing tables.

Even though the tables are simple, there still may be some incorrect routes within the table. Maybe a host is not reachable, or maybe a router goes down. In these situations, error messages are sent which advise of a change or inaccuracy within a routing table. These messages are part of the *Internet Control Message Protocol* (ICMP).

ICMP allows machines on a network to notify other machines that errors have occurred. It also can be used to find more optimal routes to a host if a better route is known. The most common ICMP messages are echo requests/replies, destination unreachable errors, and redirect errors. The redirect errors are used to update routing tables with more optimal routes. According to the Host Requirement RFC (a standard that specifies the protocols which a host must implement to function properly on an Internet), ICMP redirect messages must be received on all hosts and are only optional for routers.

ICMP Vulnerabilities

Few protocols scream abuse me like ICMP. One of its key features is the ability for redirect errors to help routers build more accurate tables. Unfortunately, the redirect error can carry inaccurate information just as easily. A maliciously created ICMP redirect could cause a host or router to start redirecting traffic to an arbitrarily chosen machine, possibly one that's not even on the local network. At the best it will just mess things up. At the worst it could be one aspect of a security breach. Unlike the ARP redirect attack described above, routing table entries don't expire, so an unnoticed attack could leave a security hole indefinitely.

The only real solution to ICMP redirect attacks is to filter them out with your firewall. This will protect you from outside redirect-based attacks. Unfortunately, it does nothing to improve your internal security. Imagine a disgruntled employee wants to intercept all traffic coming from the CEO to Human Resources. The employee sets her machine up as a router. A quick redirect packet to the CEO's machine sends all default traffic to the employee's machine. Now every packet that goes out from the CEO's machine passes through the employee's machine. With some basic packet sniffing, the employee can see quite a lot of information. With more advanced techniques, the employee could hijack and manipulate the CEO's communications.

The best defense against internal security breaches is to buy some extra equipment. Put particularly sensitive equipment behind smart switches or additional firewalls. Determine which machines need to talk to one another and create filtering and routing rules that only allow those connections. Finally, intrusion detection (as discussed in Chapter 11) will at least notify you when the thing you didn't think about becomes the hacker's exploit du jour.

Of course, you hear very little griping about ICMP redirect attacks. That's because they require a little bit more knowledge than the average exploit and usually are a component of a more elaborate breach done by professionals. The ICMP attacks that really give ICMP a bad rap are the Denial of Service type attack and the Ping of Death attack. We mentioned the PoD attack before as an IP attack. While it truly is an IP level attack, the messenger used to deliver the attack is often the Ping program, which is an interface to the ICMP echo request/reply system. There is nothing about PoD that is unique to ICMP echo request/reply.

DoS attacks involve flooding a machine's IP stack with too many packets, thus preventing the machine from processing normal traffic. ICMP echo requests are a popular vehicle for crafting this attack. A packet is created which appears to originate from the target machine. It is an ICMP echo request. This packet is sent to the broadcast address of a very large subnet. The result is that every machine on the subnet replies to the echo request, sending an echo reply to the target machine. Repeatedly sending these spoofed echo requests out to many subnets multiple times will flood the target machine. The first of these attacks was known as the smurf attack. A short while later the UDP-based "fraggle" variant described earlier was created.

The annoying aspect of the DoS attack is that the ICMP echo request is a useful feature that allows a machine to determine if another machine is "alive" (actively reachable). It also allows the machine to determine the condition of the route between the two machines. A number of programs depend on this data to optimize their connections across the network. It is a low-level process that is often handled within the kernel of the operating system. This makes it difficult to turn off, unless you have direct access to configuring the kernel. The timestamp and address mask ICMP request/reply systems are also kernel-level, and could also be used for this type of exploit.

To prevent a spoofed DoS attack, you have few options. The first is to filter out all ICMP echo request/reply packets at the firewall level. This is often not a satisfactory solution, since it effectively disables any services that rely on ICMP echo request/reply. Additionally, you will still experience some effects of the attack because your upstream provider still ends up routing all the traffic. You may want to consider placing high-profile machines on somebody else's network. If your Web server is likely to be the target of such attacks (maybe you're running a Bill Gates fan site or something), you may want to consider colocating your server with a major ISP. They will have the bandwidth to sustain an attack, and will also have the capacity to hunt down and crush the perpetrator. Often, perpetrators of DoS type attacks are *not* savvy hackers.

At the very least, you have a moral obligation to ensure that your network doesn't contribute to a DoS attack. The easy way to do this is to add a filter that blocks all incoming broadcast traffic to your network. Another filter can prevent outbound traffic that hasn't originated from a machine within your network (thus catching the spoofed packet). If you are the benefactor of another administrator's moral laxity, you may consider yourself righteously sanctified in converting the heathen by revealing the one true path.

Dynamic Routing: RIP and OSPF

People don't pick IP addresses out of thin air. The Internet Assigned Numbers Authority allocates them to ISPs and other large network providers. These network providers in turn allocate blocks of addresses to smaller networks. As networks come and go and move about, these numbers get reassigned. The numbers are not tied to any geographic locality and can move around as needed. Some networks dynamically assign IP addresses as needed. Because of this, routes to IP addresses or network addresses can change on a moment to moment basis. In these scenarios ICMP redirects or router discoveries aren't enough.

The *Routing Information Protocol* (RIP) is the most popular, though not necessarily the best, solution to complex routing needs. It provides a mechanism for routers to inform each other of the networks to which they connect. RIP communications are sent as UDP packets, the standard RIP port is 520.

RIP is a relatively simple service: upon initialization it sends request packets out every available interface, effectively asking every directly connected router for a complete routing table. Each router running RIP responds by sending its routing tables. RIP processes the response and builds its own routing tables accordingly. From that point forward, RIP broadcasts its routing table to its neighbors at regular intervals. When something changes, RIP also sends out a specific update detailing the change.

As simple as RIP is, it has a number of problems that make it less than optimal for modern networks. One replacement for RIP is *Open Shortest Path First* (OSPF), which fixes the problems with RIP and anticipates some future issues as well. OSPF utilizes IP directly, and therefore must be supported by the IP handler in the kernel of the operating system. Most new OS releases support OSPF.

RIP Vulnerabilities

RIP suffers the same problems as ICMP—by its nature it is set up to receive route changing information. Default installations of RIP allow intruders to send commands which can redirect traffic to critical network resources. In small local network environments, one is better off using static routing. In more complex environments, a newer protocol such as OSPF will offer more security. Routers should be extremely suspicious of any route changing information, and should use all available resources to verify the necessity and veracity of the change request.

Buffer, the IP Slayer

We're going to take a short diversion to discuss a very important topic. Many hackers never need to use *any* of these techniques to gain access to their target machines. The most popular method for hackers to gain access to resources is by way of the *buffer overflow* technique. Buffer overflows are the result of poor programming practices, and are available in a surprisingly large number of popular applications (most Windows-based applications have at least one such error, and often many). When a buffer overflow is exploited, a hacker can execute arbitrary programs on the compromised machine. This is a complete and total security breach, since the programs can be run at the highest priority and access levels.

This technique owes its effectiveness to the popularity of the C programming language. In C, memory needs to be carefully allocated and managed. When a programmer wants to store data in memory, the proper amount of memory needs to be allocated. If the size of the data being stored increases, it's the programmer's responsibility to make sure that the allocated memory also increases. If the data being stored require more space than has been allocated, a buffer overflow condition occurs. Figure 2.9 depicts this life-draining process in graphic detail.

Memory management can be a very difficult task in a complex application. If an application is not carefully planned out from the onset, management of memory can become even more daunting. To make matters worse, a number of standard programming functions do not allocate memory properly. Novice or lazy programmers use these functions instead of using a memory-safe alternative. This is where the fun begins. Any program that allocates fixed memory space for data

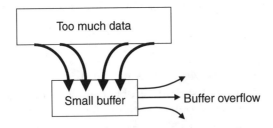

Figure 2.9 Overflow in the buff.

which may be outside of the program's control (such as user input) is probably going to allow buffer overflows. You would be shocked at how many programmers repeatedly make this elementary mistake.

So now you know that buffer overflows are caused by a program trying to store too much data in a chunk of memory that's too small. What we haven't explained is why this enables a programmer to execute arbitrary code.

The secret lies within the way that memory is used by the computer. When a program is running, there are three types of information it needs to access. The first is the program instructions themselves. It also needs access to data that the program will manipulate. Some of this data is fixed or *static* and will not change while the program is running. Other data is *dynamic* and may change while the program is running.

The third type of information pertains to *functions*, or subroutines. Programmers use functions to simplify writing their programs. If a task is done many times within a program, it helps to write the instructions for the task once and then just point to those instructions every time the task needs to be run. The task becomes known as a *function*. Whenever the program wants to use the function, it *calls* the function.

A program is a series of instructions. Many of these instructions will be calls to functions. When the program runs, it processes the instructions in order. When a program calls a function, it pauses processing its own instructions and processes the function's instructions. Once it's done with the function's instructions, the program continues with its own instructions. In order for this to happen, the program needs to keep track of where it was before it called the function. This piece of data is called the *Instruction Pointer* and contains the memory address of the program's next instruction.

The portion of memory that stores the dynamic data for the function, as well as the Instruction Pointer, is called the *stack*. Figure 2.10 shows a simplified view of a stack being flooded.

The Stack Overflow

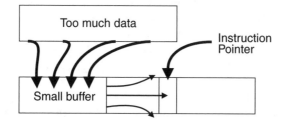

Figure 2.10   A simple stack overflow.

When a programmer allocates memory for the dynamic data and then stores too much data in the region, the data can overwrite the memory containing the Instruction Pointer. Now, when the program finishes the function and looks at the Instruction Pointer to find the memory address of the next instruction, it sees the wrong value.

The adept hacker will fill the buffer with his or her own code, and then over-flow the buffer in such a way that the Instruction Pointer gets overwritten with a value that points right back to the start of the hacker's code in the buffer. The result? The next instruction executed by the computer is the hacker's code. The size of the allocated buffer limits the amount of code a hacker can execute, but this doesn't really cause many problems. Hackers can create very malicious code within an incredibly small space, often on the order of a few bytes. In the case where the buffer is too small, there may be other buffers between the buffer in question and the Instruction Pointer. These can be used to add to the space available for the hacker's code.

Programmers are finally starting to use coding standards and helper libraries that minimize the occurrence of buffer overflows. Nonetheless, these problems do occur, and the likelihood of occurrence increases with the complexity of the application. Programs such as Microsoft's Internet Explorer are so complex that they become riddled with buffer overflow bugs.

More detailed explanations of buffer overflows are available on the Internet. One good paper was written by Mudge of the l0pht, another more detailed arti-cle was written by aleph1 of the Underground. We suggest you check them out.

Mudge's paper can be found at www.l0pht.com/advisories/bufitos.pdf

A tutorial by Mudge can be found at www.insecure.org/stf/mudge_buffer_ overflow_tutorial.html

Aleph1's paper can be found at www.insecure.org/stf/smashstack.txt

Summary

We've just looked at the core Internet protocols in thorough detail. Hopefully you now have a decent understanding of the way data move about the Inter-net. Maybe you've even started thinking about attacks you'd like your firewall to protect against. That's great, because the next chapter is going to make you really think about the ultimate role of a firewall in your network.

In the next chapter, we're going to look at many of the common Internet appli-cations your users may need to access. The ultimate goal will be to create a pol-icy for providing Internet access to the members of your organization and providing the outside world with access to your network.

How Secure Should Your Network Be?

D o not skip this chapter. Even if you think you know everything we have to say, humor us and read it anyway. Why? Because by the end of this chapter we'll have forced you to think about security in a very practical way. We'll sit you down at the keyboards of your users, then at the keyboard of a hacker. When you finally sit back down at your own keyboard you'll have a raging headache, a moustache, and you will have changed your name to Eric (see www.tuxedo.org/~esr/ecsl/).

In this chapter we'll address two aspects of network security in detail. The first will be the physical network; we'll look at the security issues of various network layouts. Then we'll deal with the various network services your users will need to access.

Contrary to marketing hype, there is no magic bullet for security. When firewalls first hit the scene, firewall vendors proclaimed that having a firewall made your network secure. Virtual Private Network and Intrusion Detection System vendors have also been spewing forth similar magic-bullet hype. Middle management loves the idea of a magic bullet—they just pay once and can assume their network is secure. Even if they're smart enough to know better, they're eventually won over by the snake charmer's hype.

The truth is that all of these technologies are good for improving the security of a network, but nothing can make a network totally secure. Furthermore, if you don't understand what you're securing, why you're bothering to secure it, and how it's secured, then your security system won't work. Anyone who tells you that they can simplify this process without reducing the security of the end product is lying.

Nonetheless, this chapter *does* simplify many of the issues, but purely out of necessity. Any of the topics discussed herein can be expanded into an entire book—some already are. If we go into too much detail on a few of the topics, the information becomes dated and useless. The result is that this chapter won't solve your security problems, *but it will alert you to the fact that you have far more of them than you originally thought.*

Reading this chapter should leave you with more questions than answers. That's because our goal here is not to answer questions, but instead to point out things that you'll need to think about and possibly research further. The astute reader will notice that this chapter covers a lot of ground. The bored reader will notice that they have many pages to skim over. Well, that's what you get when the chapter's title is a rhetorical question.

The Physical Network

The physical end product of working through this book will be a machine configured as a firewall. In order for the firewall to be of use, it must be strategically situated on your network. There are many ways of constructing a network, but for the sake of a saving a few trees per book, we will deal with the networks that result from two of the most common firewall locations. To do this, we will have to introduce two concepts: the DMZ and IP Masquerading.

The DMZ

The De-Militarized Zone, or DMZ, is an expression that originates from the Korean War. There, it meant a strip of land forcibly kept clear of enemy soldiers. The idea was to accomplish this without risking your own soldier's lives, thus mines were scattered throughout the DMZ like grated Romano on a plate of fettuccine. The term has been assimilated into networking, without the cheese. Network geeks use it to mean: "a portion of your network, which, although under your control, is outside your heaviest security." Compared to the rest of your network, machines you place in the DMZ are less protected, or flat-out unprotected, from the wrath of the Internet.

Once a machine has entered the DMZ, it should not be brought back inside the network again. Assume that it has been compromised in some way. Bringing it into the network is like calling up Troy and asking if they could send over a few more of those neat wooden horses.

Use of a DMZ

If you decide to build one, what do you do with it? Machines placed in the DMZ usually offer services to the general public. Such offerings often include Web services, domain name services (DNS), mail relaying, and FTP services (all these buzzwords will be explained next). Proxy servers can also go in the DMZ. If you decide to allow your users Web access only via a proxy server, you can put the proxy in the firewall, and set your firewall rules to permit outgoing HTTP access only to the proxy server.

As long as you've attended to the following points, your DMZ should be okay:

If you put a machine in the DMZ, it must be for a good reason. Sometimes, companies will set up a few workstations with full Internet access within the DMZ. Employees can use these machines for games and other insecure activities. This is a good reason if the internal machines have no Internet access, or extremely limited access. If your policy is to let employees have moderate access from their desktops, then creating workstations like this sends the wrong message. Think about it: The only reason why they would use a DMZ machine is if they were doing something inappropriate for the workplace.

It should be an isolated island, not a stepping stone. It must not be directly connected to the internal network. Furthermore, it shouldn't contain information that could help hackers compromise other parts of the network. This includes user names, passwords, network hardware configuration information, and so forth.

It must not contain anything you can't bear to lose. Any important files placed on the DMZ should be read-only copies of originals located within the network. Files created in the DMZ should not be able to migrate into the network unless an administrator has examined them. If you're running a news server and would like to archive news, make sure the DMZ has its own archival system. What sort of things shouldn't you do? Example: If you're running an FTP server in the DMZ, don't let users put confidential information on there so they can get it from home later.

It must be as secure a host as you can make it. Just because you're assuming it's insecure doesn't guarantee that it is. Don't make it any easier for a hacker than absolutely necessary. A hacker may not be able to compromise your internal network from your DMZ, but they may decide to use it to compromise somebody else's network. Give serious thought to *not* running Windows on your DMZ machines; it's inherently insecure and many types of intrusions *can't* be detected on Windows. Linux or OpenBSD can provide most, if not all, of the needed functionality along with a more secure environment.

IP Masquerading

While nearly all IP addresses specify a machine on the Internet, some have been set aside by the Internet Assigned Numbers Authority (IANA) as "reserved for specific purposes." For example, the address range starting with numbers from "224." through "255." is dedicated to various uses including multicast communications. Every address starting with "127." is reserved as the *loopback network*; 127.0.0.1 is specially reserved as the loopback address for the local host. The loopback device provides a machine with a convenient way to communicate with itself. The client program thinks it's sending data out to a regular IP address. A server running on the same machine sees the data as if they were coming from a machine on the network. Most importantly to us, three ranges of addresses have been deliberately held back for internal network use: 10.abc.def.ghi, 172.jkl.abc.def, and 192.168.abc.def (where abc, def, and ghi are numbers between 0 and 255, and jkl is between 16 and 31).

Addresses in all of the reserved ranges are *unrouted*. This means that the Internet as a whole doesn't have any idea how to deliver packets sent to these addresses. In consequence, these addresses are available for you to assign to your machines with impunity. Most people use either the first (10.abc.def.ghi) or the last (192.168.abc.def) group (we don't know what they've got against the middle one).

The immediate implication of using private address space is that machines on the Internet will not be able to send information to your private machines. For example, if a computer on your internal network asks for a Web page from the Internet, the target Web server will not be able to send the Web page back to your internal computer. This may leave you wondering why anyone in their right mind would elect to use private addresses on their network.

What appears to be a major problem with private addresses is actually a desirable feature for some people. In many cases, you may not want machines on your network to have any communications with the Internet. By assigning these machines unrouted IP addresses, they are impossible to reach directly from the Internet. If the rest of your network is configured properly, this strategy can significantly increase the security of critical internal machines.

Another major advantage to private address space is the wealth of freely available private IP addresses, versus the rapidly diminishing pool of routed IP addresses. Your ISP has a limited number of IP addresses to assign to all of their customers. Each extra address they give you lowers the potential number of customers they can have (once they run out of IP addresses, it's expensive and increasingly more difficult to get another block). By using private addressing, you can have millions of networked computers without any problems (due to running out of address space, that is. With millions of networked computers, you're likely to have *many* other types of problems).

Of course, the miracle of modern technology let's us have our cake while eating somebody else's. It *is* actually possible for machines on the Internet to communicate with machines within private address space. The amazing solution is called *IP masquerading* or *network address translation* (NAT). This technology allows many machines using private addresses to hide behind one or more real IP addresses.

In order to use NAT or masquerading, you need a machine that is configured as a *masquerading router* (a fairly straightforward process for Linux and OpenBSD, described in Chapters 7, "Firewall Rules under Linux: IPChains" and Chapter 9, "Firewall Rules under OpenBSD: IPFilter," respectively). The masquerading router works by intercepting the outward bound packets from the private network. It rewrites the packet header so that the packet appears to be originating from the masquerading router (which has a real IP address). We will call this process *rebadging* the packets. It then sends the rebadged packets out to the Internet. The Internet thinks they came from the masquerading router, so responses are sent back to that machine. The masquerading router then works out which private machines the responses are really intended for, rebadges those responses with the appropriate private addresses, and sends them into your privately numbered network. The packets then happily reach the intended recipient.

The moral of this story is: If you have 20 machines, and your ISP will only give you a block of eight addresses, or four, or even only one, IP masquerading is going to be your friend. If you are lucky enough to have sufficient real addresses for your needs, you might still choose to use IP masquerading. There are certain security advantages to using private addressing on your internal network. Think about it: You can't make prank phone calls to someone without a phone number, right? Similarly, it's much harder to mount an attack on a machine with a private address, since (certain conditions aside) you can't tell the Internet to send packets to such a machine.

We intend to show you how to build such a box, since the technology adds a fundamental level of security to your network, and it is very easy to add masquerading support to a packet filtering firewall.

There are, however, some disadvantages to IP masquerading. The principal one comes from that step we glossed over above, the step where the IP masquerading box receives the response back from the Internet and then works out the real recipient of the packet on your internal network. Recall that the responses all have the IP address of the masquerading router. How does the masquerading box know which private machine the packets are intended for? There's no other information in the packets that would give the router any clue.

The solution is to look a layer deeper, at the TCP or UDP port to which the application is binding. The masquerading router uses a trick called *port mapping* to help it route responses to the right internal machine. Every TCP or UDP packet has both a source and destination port specified in its header (see Chapter 2, "Fundamental Internet Security Issues"). When the masquerading router gets a packet from an internal machine, it replaces the source port number with one of its own, chosen from a range that few applications ever use. It then stores the old source port number and the new source port number in a table, along with the private address of the machine that sent the packet. When the response comes back to the masquerading machine, it should arrive on a port that corresponds to one of the new source ports. By looking that port number up in a table, the router can obtain the private address and the original source port for the internal machine that should receive the packet in question. An example:

Outbound Packet from Internal Machine: Source IP: 10.0.0.6, Destination IP: 18.69.0.5, source port: 1200, destination port: 514.

Outbound Packet from Masquerading Router (209.21.210.49): Source IP: 209.21.210.49, Destination IP: 18.69.0.5, source port: 22005, destination port: 514.

Inbound Packet from Internet: Source IP: 18.69.0.5, Destination IP: 209.21.210.49, source port: 514, destination port: 22005.

Inbound Packet from Masquerading Router (10.0.0.1—the "private address of the router"): Source IP: 209.21.210.49, Destination IP: 10.0.0.6 source port: 514, destination port: 1200.

This works really well for many applications, but there are some cases where problems arise. The classic problem child is FTP, the *file transfer protocol*. Some FTP clients use what is known as *active-mode FTP*, where the server opens a brand new connection with the client for the data stream on a new, randomly selected port. This is a major problem for the masquerading router, because the return connection won't be in the port-map. The result is that the router can't figure out where to send the packets, so it just drops them.

There are few effective solutions to this problem. The easiest way to cope is denial, which means only supporting *passive mode FTP*. In passive mode FTP, the client opens up two connections to the server on two different ports. Because both connections originate from behind the firewall, this works perfectly well with a masquerading firewall. For longer explanations of how active and passive FTP work, see the *Problems Associated with FTP* section later in this chapter.

Another option for handling active-mode FTP is to obtain a kernel patch that special-cases this particular issue as well as a few other types of problematic services (including Real Audio). This patch is available for Linux only, and has some drawbacks. It works by noting when an internal client starts an active-mode FTP session. It then looks for a return connection from the FTP server (identifying it by IP address). It port-maps this return connection and allows it through the firewall. The problem is that the return connection may not be the expected FTP connection. While this case is rare, it could create problems by blindly forwarding the wrong packets to a waiting FTP client on the internal network. We'll deal with FTP in greater detail later in this chapter.

If you must provide services like active mode FTP, a potential solution is to use a *proxy server* in conjunction with the masquerading firewall. A proxy server acts as a gateway to a particular Internet service. Machines on your LAN ask the proxy server for information from the Internet. The proxy server then retrieves the data from the Internet and passes it back to the machine that requested it. For example, with a Web proxy server the user's Web browser asks the proxy server for the Web page it wants. The proxy server retrieves the page from the Internet and sends it to the user's machine. The machine doesn't need to have any direct connection to the Internet—it simply needs to be capable of reaching the proxy server. There are many freeware and commercial proxy server packages. There are proxies for every major network protocol, and some proxy packages can be customized to handle new protocols. Sadly, the more dynamically customizable the proxy, the more intelligent the client has to be in order to deal with this configurability. This in turn restricts the clients that can be used. For example, one such dynamically reconfigurable proxy protocol is called SOCKS. Most major browsers are SOCKSified—that is, they know how to talk to a SOCKS proxy and tell it that they want it to proxy HTTP requests—but few command-line FTP clients are. Command-line FTP won't work through a SOCKS proxy because the FTP command isn't bright enough.

In the case where you're using both a proxy and a firewall, the firewall can be configured such that all communications between the internal network and the Internet pass through the proxy server. This adds to the complexity of the firewall system and requires careful configuration. Nonetheless, it is a viable solution and, done properly, can significantly improve the security of your network. Do not, however, run the proxy on your firewall itself. Doing so adds a lot of complexity to your firewall, which in turn increases the likelihood of your firewall being compromised.

A last caveat about IP Masquerading relates to port starvation. The firewall has a finite number of ports—large, but finite—with which to rebadge outgoing connections. If you have too many hosts inside your network, each of which is making a large number of connections to the outside world—downloading many Web pages with large numbers of images, and running a number of streaming media applications—you could conceivably run out of ports. It's not likely, but it is a possibility. If you do, you can increase the range with techniques that are outside of the scope of this book, including black magic. As a rule of thumb, this is *extremely* unlikely to be a problem with less than 25–30 machines on your internal network, but it's something to keep filed under cursory knowledge.

Now that we've explained IP Masquerading, it's safe to start looking at some network topologies.

Network Topologies

Figure 3.1 shows the simplest, and possibly most common, way to use a firewall. The Internet comes into the firewall directly via a modem. You can't have a DMZ in the traditional sense. The firewall takes care of passing packets that pass its filtering rules between the internal network and the Internet, and vice versa. It may use IP masquerading and that's all it does. This is known as a *dual-homed* host. The two "homes" refer to the two networks that the machine is part of—one interface connected to the outside home, and the other connected to the inside home.

This setup has the advantage of simplicity, and if your Internet connection is via a modem and you have only one IP address, it's what you're probably going to have to live with, unless you create a more complex network as described next. The simple dual-homed host is great for home networks and small to midsize companies, but at some point your network is going to get more complex. You may ultimately have to deal with a network design with requirements that a single dual-homed host can't handle alone.

In the more advanced configuration shown in Figure 3.2, the router that connects to the outside world is connected to a hub. Machines that want direct access to the outside world, unfiltered by the firewall, connect to this hub. One

A Simple Dual-Homed Firewall

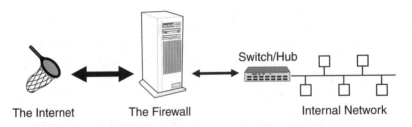

The Internet   The Firewall   Internal Network

Figure 3.1   A simple dual-homed firewall network.

An Exposed DMZ Firewall

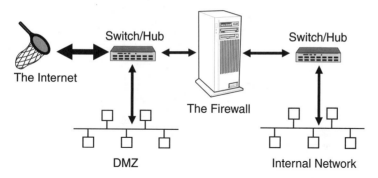

Figure 3.2   A two-legged network with a fully exposed DMZ.

of the firewall's network adapters also connects to this hub. The other network adapter connects to the internal hub. Machines that need to be protected by the firewall need to connect to this hub. Any of these hubs could be replaced with switches for added security, in particular it would be most effective (and recommended) to use a switch for the internal hub.

There are good things about the *exposed DMZ* configuration. The firewall needs only two network cards. This simplifies the configuration of the firewall. Additionally, if you control the router you have access to a second set of packet-filtering capabilities. Using these, you can give your DMZ some limited protection completely separate from your firewall.

On the other hand, if you don't control the router, your DMZ is totally exposed to the Net. Hardening a machine enough to live in the DMZ without getting regularly compromised can be tricky.

The exposed DMZ configuration depends on two key factors: 1) an external router, and 2) multiple IP addresses. If you connect via PPP, or you don't control your external router, or you want to masquerade your DMZ, or you have only 1 IP address, you'll need to do something else. There are two straightforward solutions to this, depending on your particular problem. One solution is to build a second router/firewall. This is useful if you're connecting via PPP. One machine is the exterior router/firewall. This machine is responsible for creating the PPP connection. The other firewall is a standard dual-homed host, and its job is to protect the internal network. This is identical to the situation described in Figure 3.1; your PPP machine is the local exterior router.

The other solution is to create a *three-legged firewall*, as illustrated in Figure 3.3. This means you have an additional adapter in your firewall box for your DMZ. The firewall is then configured to route packets between the outside

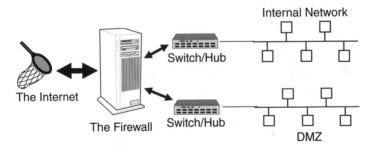

Figure 3.3   A three-legged firewall.

world and the DMZ differently than between the outside world and the internal network. This is a useful configuration, enough so that we've included installation and configuration instructions for three-legged systems.

The three-legged setup can also give you the ability to have a DMZ if you're stuck with the simple topology we outlined first. Replace "router" with "modem," and you can see how this is similar to the simple topology, but with a third leg stuck on the side. If you're being forced (by poverty of IP address space), or have chosen to IP masquerade, you can masquerade the machine or machines in the DMZ too, while keeping them functionally separate from protected internal machines. People who have cable modems or static PPP connections can use this system to run numerous servers within a DMZ as well as an entire internal network off a single IP address. It's a very economical solution for small businesses or home offices.

The primary disadvantage to the three-legged firewall is the additional complexity. Access to and from the DMZ and to and from the internal network is controlled by one large set of rules. It's pretty easy to get these rules wrong if you don't take particular care.

On the other hand, if you don't have any control over the Internet router, you can exert a lot more control over traffic to and from the DMZ this way. It's good to prevent access into the DMZ if you can.

Subnetting the DMZ

If you plan on masquerading within your DMZ, then you've got nothing to worry about. Simply follow the instructions in our installation and configuration chapters and you'll have a nice three-legged network in no time.

On the other hand, if you want to use public IP addresses in your DMZ, you'll need to make sure that the DMZ is part of a separate subnet from any other external IP addresses not in the DMZ, including that of the *firewall/exterior router*.

As an example, let's say you have the IP address range in the subnet 209.21.10.0/27 (this translates to 209.21.10.0-209.21.10.31—if the slashes are confusing you, see the sidebar titled *Masking*). You have public access servers that need to have real IP addresses, but you want to be able to apply filtering rules to packets before they get to the public servers. The problem is, your firewall and/or exterior router are in the 209.21.10.0/27 subnet. You need to break the subnet down further in order to create a separate subnet for the DMZ. The easiest way to do this is to subnet as follows: 209.21.10.0/28 (0–15) and 209.21.10.16/28 (16–32).

There are two problems with this approach. The first is that each time you subnet, you effectively lose two addresses. In the preceding example, 209.21.10.15 becomes the broadcast address for the 209.21.10.0/28 subnet, and 209.21.10.16 becomes the network address for the 209.21.10.16/28 subnet. These addresses are no longer assignable to external machines.

The other problem is that you really only need two addresses in one of the subnets: one for your firewall and one for your external router. That means you have 12 extra IP addresses that will probably be wasted, in addition to the four unassignable network and broadcast addresses that resulted from subnetting. One solution to this is to further subnet one of the two subnets. Break the 209.21.10.0/28 subnet into 209.21.10.0/29 and 209.21.10.8/29. Now you can assign the router and firewall to one of the six addresses in the first subnet. You can also set up the DMZ interface to receive packets for both the 209.21.10.16/28 subnet AND the 209.21.10.8/27 subnet. This means you now have 20 usable addresses in your DMZ, and you've lost six to subnetting. There are now only four extra fully exposed addresses. This is a bit more complicated, but potentially worth it if you're short on address space.

There is a way to get around the different subnet issue by *bridging* between the two interfaces. Bridging involves having the firewall take an active role in detecting packets on one network and forwarding them to another network. This can create all sorts of problems, and makes understanding what's happening on the network a lot more difficult. This technique is way beyond the scope of the book, and flat out not recommended.

These are the simplest network topologies, but think of them as building blocks. It's possible to use a combination of dual-homed hosts and multi-legged firewalls to make much more complex networks. There's also the issue of proxy servers—where do they fit into the picture? The answer requires too much theory for this book. The Chapman and Zwicky book *Building Internet Firewalls* (O'Reilly 1995) deals with these topics in much greater depth. Past that, you'll want to look at various archived firewall discussion lists (Chapter 12 will tell you where to find them). There's bound to be plenty of chat about optimal configurations for proxy servers, as well as tons of other useful information about firewalling in general.

Masking

Subnets and address ranges are identified by a value known as the *subnet mask*, or more commonly, the *netmask*. This is a value with the same form as an IP address, but with a different meaning. They often look very similar, all starting with 255, or some other high number. To understand the subnet mask, let's first define a *mask* in general.

In the art world, a mask is used when spray painting to cover up portions of a work that shouldn't be altered. Thus the true purpose of "masking tape." In the computer world, a mask also covers up portions of a number that shouldn't be changed. Let's look at an IP address and a netmask. In decimal these are 169.69.6.9 and 255.255.255.0, respectively; in binary, these are:

The address: 10101001.01000101.00000110.00001001
The mask: 11111111.11111111.11111111.00000000

The 1's in the mask "cover up" the parts of the address that should stay the same. The 0's allow the "paint" to alter the address. This particular mask says that the last eight bits (each 0 or 1 is a bit) can be any value. Or to put it another way, any address that matches the first 24 bits of the first address belongs to the subnet. Valid addresses for the subnet specified by this mask range from:

10101001.01000101.00000110.00000000

to:

10101001.01000101.00000110.11111111

Converting from binary to base 10 does not come naturally to those who don't program for a living, so an alternate method is to count the number of 1's in the mask from the left to the right. In the preceding example, there are 24 1's. The subnet mask is then expressed as the IP address/number of ones. For this example, it's '/24'. As we increase the number after the slash (up to /32), we decrease the number of free bits. 169.69.6.9/32 means 169.69.6.9 and no other IP addresses at all (all 32 bits are fixed). As we decrease the number after the slash (down to /0) we increase the number of free bits. 0.0.0.0/0 matches any IP address.

If you think about it, you'll also see that 169.69.6.9/0 matches any IP address—it too has no fixed bits (all 32 bits are free). It is traditional, however, when using this form to force to zero any bits that are not fixed by the mask. For example, the subnet containing the addresses 169.69.6.0-169.69.6.255 can be represented equally well as "169.69.6.9/24" and "169.69.6.0/24", but the convention suggests that the latter is better as all the free bits—the last eight—are set to zero.

Our last bit of advice on the topic: Stay simple for now. Use the basic dual-homed host until you're comfortable with it. Then you can approach the more complex topologies with skill and confidence.

Other Thoughts on Security

The classic clueless-user damage comes from viruses. If a virus makes its way into your network (and it's not the job of a firewall to stop a virus), the damage can be disastrous, and can potentially open up significant security holes to boot. There are three ways in which a virus can get onto your network:

- A user deliberately creates it on a local machine
- It comes in on a disk
- It comes in from the Internet

Nothing can protect you from the first situation. A good desktop virus scanner can protect you from the second, as well as some strong policies about installing software (must be checked by system administration first, etc.). The third is the hardest to protect against. Most Internet-based viruses do the bulk of their damage before the major virus protection companies can update their software to recognize the virus.

After desktop virus scanning, good internal host security is your best general defense against virus damage, because it minimizes the damage a virus can cause. Not letting ordinary users edit system files, a policy Unix applies by default and NT can be made to apply, helps an awful lot here. Discretionary control on network resources does much of the rest. A recent popular virus attempted to delete any files it could find on any local or network-attached file stores; a Certain Large Company, which set up its file store for documentation so that any doc writer could read and write any doc file, lost the lot when hit by that virus.

User Management

One holy grail often sought by firewall managers, as opposed to firewall administrators, is to limit access by certain people to certain network services. Before you allow anyone to convince you to do this, you need to realize that user-level restriction is a huge can filled with many fat and slimy worms. Don't open it if it's not absolutely necessary.

If you must offer different Internet services to different users, there are a few ways of accomplishing the task. One of the most common (yet least secure) methods is filtering based on internal IP address. This method assumes that the user logs into only one particular machine and no other users can access that machine or that IP address. This is a bad assumption. It's hard to enforce, and requires updating the filters any time someone changes desks or moves machines about. This approach is totally useless if you also are using a dynamic IP assignment system within your network.

Another approach is to set up proxy servers with user authentication. If you're really lucky, you may be able to tie your central authentication system into the proxy authentication. This means that a user would only have to log in once—the proxy server would be able to authenticate the user automatically using some sort of token or ticket framework. Good luck pulling that off—maybe in a few years if Kerberos (a highly secure authentication system developed at MIT) becomes the Windows standard. Until then, your users will probably have to log into the proxy server every time they wish to access a proxied service. Said users will be much happier about this if their client software fully supports proxy servers. This means the client software can cache the authentication information so that the user only has to log in the first time they connect, or after an extended idle period. Note that this means authentication information is stored in a retrievable format on the user's machine. This is a significant security concern. If the client software can read the authentication information, a hacker can also.

The advantage to the proxy server approach is that it gives you fine-grained, user level control over Internet access. It is also an application-level firewalling tool, which offers added security. Some proxy servers may be able to perform useful services such as automatic virus detection. The disadvantage is that the access list needs to be maintained independently, which just adds another item to the system administrator's workload. It also makes accessing the Internet very complicated for the people who are authorized so to do. One of the best ways to persuade management not to try to enforce such complex restrictions is to show them just how complex it will make their lives.

Back Orifice: A Worst-Case Illustration

An important point to keep in mind throughout all of this is that *any* form of Internet access creates considerable security risk, regardless of how tightly you think you've secured your network. We'll illustrate with a hack that will blow through every security measure you can build.

Joe User is browsing the Web using a Windows-based machine and goes to Sam Evil User's site. Sam's site contains a browser-based exploit (Web code that takes advantage of flaws in popular browsers), which causes a buffer overflow on Joe's machine. The code that Sam executes installs a program called Back Orifice onto Joe's machine. Once installed, Sam's version of Back Orifice (BO) is undetectable by any existing virus detection program. This is because BO runs in the background, and Windows has no way of detecting programs that are running in the background. Furthermore, the BO program file can go by any name. It can even be faked to look like some other important program. Sam also has the source code to BO (it's freely available) and has altered the program such that existing BO detectors can't see his version.

BO looks at Joe's machine and sees that it's connected behind an IP masquerading firewall. The only service Joe can access is the Web. BO tries to contact Sam's server through the Web, but is stopped by the proxy server, which asks it for authentication. This doesn't deter BO, which has been programmed to handle this situation. It simply waits for Joe to log into the Web again and captures the keystrokes as he types in the password (on Windows machines BO has access to absolutely everything that is happening). Now BO can access Sam's machine whenever it wants via HTTP, because it has the authentication information it needs to pass through the proxy server. HTTP provides more than enough two-way communication flexibility for Sam, who can obtain full control of Joe's machine across the network, even though theoretically there is no direct route from Sam's machine to Joe's machine. Lest you think this is only a Web-based attack, BO can be delivered via email, either as a Trojan attachment or as a direct exploit (meaning that you don't even have to read the mail for the exploit to work) for any of the common mail clients. Social engineering can always be used to get BO installed if all else fails.

How could this have been avoided? The only real way is to *not* run Windows on machines that have direct or proxied access to the Internet. Only allow this sort of access through a DMZ machine. If the DMZ machine is "owned" by a hacker, it shouldn't make it any easier to access your internal network. Keeping Windows off the DMZ machines will help protect you against BO-style attacks, though it's no magic bullet either.

If you must provide full network access, make sure that the user's machines are running only the minimum services necessary. Log all traffic to and from proxy servers. Inspect the logs by hand once a week. Soon you'll recognize patterns, and you'll be able to spot any anomalies that could indicate hacker activity.

You also need to make sure that users are running the most recent versions of their Internet clients. Do not use Internet Explorer as a Web browser—it has many security flaws both in the design and in the implementation. Instead, we recommend using an open source browser such as Mozilla. If you must go with a commercial browser, then use the latest versions of Netscape or Opera, because you'll cut down on a large number of security risks. Likewise, do not use Active desktop or any other type of unnecessary Web-frill technology such as ActiveX, Java, Shockwave, Flash, Splash, etc. JavaScript is heavily used throughout the Internet—disabling it will break a number of important Web sites. It's best to turn it off by default and enable it only when necessary.

A Word on Java

It is true that malicious Java applets can be created. Newer Java virtual machines (VM—the system that enables Java programs to run) protect against these malicious applets. Unfortunately, the VM's integrated into older versions of Netscape and IE are susceptible to certain malicious applets. Because of this, we recommend disabling the browser's internal Java VM support.

On the other hand, we do feel that Java is an important tool for dynamic content. You can have the best of both worlds by using the Java Plug-in. This is a browser plug-in from Sun Microsystems (the makers of Java) that enables you to use the VM of your choice with the browser of your choice. The result is that you can always run the latest Java VM without having to wait for the browser manufacturer to upgrade their system.

Of course, the Java Plug-in may have some security problems itself, but as a plug-in it's fairly easy to upgrade. Thus far, the plug-in has been fairly stable.

Finally, there's always the option of not running Windows at all on machines inside your LAN. Linux is slowly becoming a viable desktop system, and it's far less susceptible to these types of attacks. You owe it to yourself at least to see what alternatives are available.

The moral of our story: Don't assume that you can outsmart a determined hacker. The skilled and determined hacker can find a way to compromise almost any system. In fact, there is some value in not going overboard with your security. There are two levels of hackers: recreational and professional. The recreational hackers should be stopped by a well-designed firewall. The professional hacker will blast through anything you can dream up. The goal is to keep your site from being a professional hacker's target. Often pros break into very secure sites just to prove that they can. By not bragging about your ultra-secure site, you will reduce the likelihood of being a target of this sort of attack. On the other hand, if someone hires a pro to hack your site for a specific reason, there's little you can do. Just hope that your security measures will buy you enough time to detect the intrusion and find a way to shut out the hacker. In the worst-case scenario, just think about deep sea diving. Good divers always carry a knife on them in case they get tangled in a cord or net and need to cut themselves free. Likewise, you should always keep a pair of wire cutters handy.

Network Services

We've finally reached the heart of the security policy—identifying and controlling the services that will be provided to your users. This is most relevant to the rest of the book, as the decisions made here will directly affect the design of your firewall.

Our first step into the world of network services brings us to a fork in the road. The sign pointing to the left reads: *permit everything that is not explicitly denied*. The road leading in this direction looks well paved and easy to travel along. There appears to be a small, dark storm cloud in the far distance. The sign pointing to the right says: *deny everything that is not explicitly permitted*. This pathway is overgrown with tangled vegetation and red-tape hangs off of every limb. You have a machete, but it looks like a lot of hard work to get down the road to the right. The only encouragement is the large rainbow that appears to end somewhere in that direction.

Should you take the path that looks easy but might lead to trouble, or should you put in the intense effort now for the possibility of a pot of gold? If this were an adventure game, you'd probably hit the Save key right now. If you chose the wrong path, you could always re-start. Here, the wrong path could mean serious trouble for your network or possibly your job.

It should be apparent by now which path we are going to recommend for this book. But the reasoning might not be as apparent, so let's take a look at each of these roads.

Permit Everything That Is Not Explicitly Denied

The general concept here is to select a few things that you know to be troublesome and protect against them. Everything else is fair game. The advantage to this method is that you can be immediately fully functional. It takes very little time to create policy that enforces this rule, because you can always add to the denied list whenever a problem arises.

Users and bosses will love you because if you didn't deny something explicitly, then they have the authority to go ahead and do it. There's always a way around anything that's denied—that is, until you spot it and plug the hole. And therein lies the rub. You're always playing catch-up. Sure, you might put in some work and block off all the known security holes (which would take a *long* time to accomplish), but at some point someone is going to find a new way in that you didn't block off. By the time you realize what happened, the damage may have already been done.

Maintaining security with this policy requires constant intense monitoring of your network and of the various security advisories. Which begs the question: What should you be monitoring? It's not possible to scan every incoming and outgoing packet, and monitoring ports is equally futile. The range of potential services is unbounded—which makes effective monitoring very difficult, if at all possible. What looked like an easy path in the beginning will turn out to be a stormy road to hell. This path is getting rather hyperbolic, so let's try the other one.

Deny Everything That Is Not Explicitly Permitted

In order to travel down this path, you need to decide what is permitted. This means that you have to evaluate all the networking needs and desires of your users. It may help to break your users into groups based on needs. Only then can you make an informed and defensible (without doubt you will be attacked by a boss or user at some point) decision as to the software, services, and access needed by each group of users.

Along this road you're sure to meet many of the denizens of the ether. With names such as TCP/IP, UDP, FTP, ICMP, ARP/RARP, BOOTP/DHCP, and HTTP, they may look gnomish and foreboding. Have no fear—in this chapter we will be your guide, showing you the good and bad sides of all the ones you're likely to be dealing with on your network.

The advantage to this road is that it forces you to have an understanding of everything that happens on your network. Things that you don't understand are denied and there's no workaround unless you explicitly make one. Except for security holes in the services you've permitted, you don't have to worry about your network being compromised through a service that you don't know about.

One corollary to this policy is that you shouldn't permit anything without knowing as much as possible about its effects on your network. This chapter gives you some tools that you can use to properly evaluate new services.

Problems with this route are that your users will not like being restricted. You will get a lot of resistance, especially when you decide *not* to permit a service or access that a user has been enjoying for any period of time. Many of these problems can be avoided if the policy is created and enforced at a very early stage in your network's development. If you're not lucky enough to be at that point, you can look forward to some serious struggles ahead.

From here on we'll assume you've sharpened your machete and have rolled up your sleeves. Hack your way through a few vines and meet us in the next section. We're about to get technical. We're going to dissect the common protocols and services that are built upon TCP and UDP. For each one we'll look at what they do and which programs are standard components. Then we'll look at the various networking requirements. Finally, we'll look at the insecurities presented by these protocols and services, with an eye toward how hackers can use them to compromise your network.

Domain Name Translation

Life on the Internet would be pretty dull if every site was only accessible by its IP address. It's hard to imagine Yahoo! becoming popular if they had to advertise as "204.200.71.68!" This section will describe the system that allows your Web browser to translate a domain name like www.yahoo.com into an IP address such as 204.200.71.68.

DNS: The Domain Name Service

The DNS is what turns names like www.yourcompany.com, which humans can read, into numbers like 127.145.13.68, which routers can route. It's pretty hard to function on the Internet without it. In the simplest form, your ISP will tell you the IP addresses of their DNS server or servers, you will plug this into all your clients, and name resolution will just happen. In a more complex form, you can run a caching name server on your local network, which does exactly what the ISP's name servers do, but remembers the result. If a second client on your network asks for the same name to be resolved shortly after the first client, the caching name server can produce the answer from its own memory without having to go out on the Internet and ask. In the most complex case, you run your own name server which lets the outside world resolve names inside your domain; this will usually act as a caching name server for your internal clients as well.

DNS is also responsible for *reverse-resolution*—taking the question "what host has the IP address 127.145.13.68?" and answering "www.yourcompany.com."

It's not the job of this book to tell you how to set up a DNS server. If you want to know more, a very good book on the subject is *DNS and BIND* by Paul Albitz and Cricket Liu (O'Reilly, 1998). Suffice it to say that to permit simple DNS through a firewall, you need to permit UDP packets either to or from port 53 on the machines that you use at your provider to resolve DNS requests. If you run a name server for your own domain and you have secondary servers outside your internal network, you need to permit TCP to and from port 53 between your name server and your secondary name servers as well.

Problems Associated with DNS

DNS, like all services, is subject to the usual round of buffer overflows and denial-of-service attacks. Keeping an eye out for your DNS server in CERT (the Computer Emergency Response Team) advisories (see Chapter 12) is prudent. DNS also suffers from a more serious vulnerability in that it can be lied to. When your client asks DNS to resolve, say, "www.cert.org" to an IP address, your system tends to believe the answer it gets. It is possible, although cumbersome, to generate false replies to DNS requests, which may be believed. Because this requires some skill as well as non trivial control over your upstream ISP service, it's not common. If it were to happen, though, someone would have almost arbitrary control over your access to the Internet—mail could be redirected, Web requests could be sent to the oddest places; in general, bad things could happen.

How to Make DNS Secure

If this possibility worries you, you can always hard code really important IP addresses in your local /etc/hosts file. This has unpleasant consequences if, for example, your ISP decides to change the IP address of their mail server, which you have hard coded. Alternatively, read RFC (Request For Comments) 2065, which deals with authenticated, verified DNS using public-key cryptography. You can find RFC 2065 at, inter alia, www.isi.edu/in-notes/rfc2065.txt. Support for secure DNS exists in BIND 8, which can be found at www.isc.org/. Most of us, however, just tend to hope no one hacks the DNS.

Email

Email is, in many ways, the Internet's herald. Even totally paranoid companies, who fear an Internet connection as they fear little else of human origin, tend to make arrangements to get email in and out of the company. One of your authors has worked at a bank where email was sent to a central server machine, which dialed up the outside world using a 9600 baud modem and used UUCP (the venerable and inscrutable Unix-to-Unix Copy Program) to copy big tarfiles full of mail in and out of the company, which were then unpacked and sent on to the recipients. The latency on this was enough to make grown men weep; it was almost unusably slow. And yet, it was faster than snail mail, and you could send things without printing them out, so it was used. Email gets everywhere.

POP: The Post Office Protocol

Back in the interesting old days, everyone who wanted to connect to the Internet used a Unix machine, or a VAX, or a similar multiuser system. This system was permanently connected to the Net and permanently up, so it got mail as and when mail felt like arriving. The mail was collected in some central location, and users then read it with mail clients that often operated on the mail files directly.

This solution doesn't work very well with modern desktop machines, and with PCs in particular. People tend to turn them off, move them around buildings—around continents, in the case of laptops—and still expect to collect mail. POP—the Post Office Protocol—was designed to cope with your need to collect mail from a central mail repository without making you run a full-blown mail server on each desktop. POP-2, which is now of primarily historical interest, ran on TCP port 109, and POP-3, the more modern variant, runs on TCP port 110.

Problems Associated with POP

For a widely-used protocol, POP leaves a lot to be desired. Because email is supposed to be private, POP has an authentication step. In this step, the username and password are transmitted from the client to the POP server in plain text. This isn't so bad on an internal network (as long as you don't mind nosy employees reading your mail). But when you let passwords go outside your network in cleartext (unencrypted), things get hairy. If passwords are only going to your ISP's POP server, and you have a direct connection to that server (not always the case), it's *probably* not a terrible security risk. But if you're using something like a cable modem to connect to the outside world, where your neighbors may see your traffic, it's bad. And if you're sending passwords way across the Internet in cleartext, you're asking for trouble.

How to Make POP Secure

For secure access from your site to remote POP servers, a limited number of POP clients support APOP, which enables authentication without actually exchanging the password at all. You will need to ensure that both client and server support this, if you wish to use it. More details can be found in RFC 1939 at www.isi.edu/in-notes/rfc1939.txt. You should also read the sidebar on secure tunneling, because this technique can be usefully applied to POP.

For secure access from remote clients to your POP servers, you should not let outsiders have access to any POP servers you are running inside your network. If people want to read mail from offsite, you need a proper remote access solution. Letting POP in is a bad idea.

Secure Tunneling

Suppose you had set up a secure connection between a trusted local machine, and a trusted remote machine, over the insecure untrusted Internet. Suppose the connection were authenticated, so that the remote machine knew that it was talking to the real you, and you knew that you were talking to the right remote machine. If you were clever, you could use that connection to have a logon session on the remote machine without anyone eavesdropping or changing your communications. You could open up another connection to exchange mail with the remote machine, without anyone seeing your POP password. You could do more things. If you were really clever, you could write a protocol that allows a single secure connection to negotiate on a packet-by-packet basis what remote service each particular packet is intended for. One packet could be part of a login session, another part of a mail message, yet another part of a chat session. Fortunately, such protocols already exist. This technique of making connections to multiple services through the one pipe is called *secure tunneling* or *secure port forwarding*. You can find more about secure tunneling in the *ssh* section later in this chapter.

IMAP: The Internet Message Access Protocol

POP-3 has several disadvantages as a mail collection protocol, so IMAP was created as a more sophisticated replacement. It runs on TCP port 143.

However, as a network protocol, it has the same essential problems as POP; passwords are sent in cleartext. Like POP, it supports more secure authentication methods. If you connect to an IMAP server outside your own network, your best option is to create a secure tunnel to the IMAP server. This way you don't have to worry about the quality or nature of the encryption scheme. Additionally, it's recommended that external passwords be different from those used internally, especially if you don't have exclusive control over the IMAP server (for example, if the IMAP server is run by an ISP). If you're running your own IMAP server, don't allow direct connections to your server from outside your network. If you need to provide remote access to the IMAP server, have your users create a secure tunnel to the IMAP server. To the server it will appear as if the connections are coming from within the network.

SMTP: The Simple Mail Transport Protocol

POP-3 and IMAP are protocols for getting mail from its final resting place to a mail reader on the recipient's own computer. They do not, however, deal with getting mail from the sender to the recipient's POP or IMAP server, nor do they handle sending any replies or original mail. The sending and transmission of mail is the responsibility of a *Mail Transport Agent* (MTA). The protocol behind nearly all MTAs is SMTP, and its extension, ESMTP, the *Extended Simple Mail Transport Protocol*. The following discussion applies to both.

The reference implementation of SMTP is sendmail (www.sendmail.org/). By default, SMTP servers run on TCP port 25. If you read all incoming mail for your site using POP, and send all outgoing mail using an SMTP server at the ISP, you won't need to run your own local SMTP server. You'll only need to deal with outbound access to your ISP's SMTP server. On the other hand, if you want to run your own local SMTP server—be it sendmail, qmail, Exchange, and so forth—you will need to allow inbound connections to TCP port 25 on your mail server.

Should you run your own SMTP server? Good question. The decision may not be yours—you may already have a fully fledged mail server running at your site, or there may be a higher-level management refusal to accept the time and expense of running one. If the question is still open for discussion, here are some thoughts.

The pros to running your own mail server are the vast increases in functionality you can get from email. Instead of merely receiving and sending individual emails, you can set up mailing lists—both static (you add new users) and dynamic (they add themselves). You can run auto-responders, which automatically generate replies to new sales leads, for example. Email can be used to initiate many more things than simple written responses from human beings. It is possible to do all these things while fetching mail from a POP mailbox, but you end up trying to rewrite your MTA to have a POP interface, and it's probably not worth the trouble.

The drawbacks to running your own mail server are security and complexity. It takes time, effort, and knowledge to run a mail server properly. If you don't invest that time and effort, you will be running an invitation to crackers.

Problems Associated with SMTP

The classic abuse of SMTP is the relaying of UCE (unsolicited commercial email), more popularly known as spam. We're fairly certain that there isn't anyone on the Internet who hasn't at some time or another received mail offering, well, let's just call them unwanted business or entertainment opportunities. If you ever try to trace these emails back to their source, the trail almost invariably leads to somebody who had nothing to do with sending the message.

How does spam work? It takes advantage of the fact that SMTP passes on messages blindly. The program that connects to a SMTP server tells the server where the message is going, and who/where it came from. SMTP never checks to see if the messenger is telling the truth. When a spammer connects to an open SMTP server, he or she forges the details of the message origin and sends it off en masse to millions of frustrated souls. Clever spammers will use a variety of techniques to cover their traces even more completely. They will also choose intelligent From: and To: addresses to circumvent standard email filters.

System administrators everywhere have been striving to solve the spam problem. Like various types of Denial of Service attacks, you can't completely prevent spam, but you *can* avoid being the cause of more spam. We'll discuss this in the section *Making SMTP Secure* later in this chapter, along with some techniques for getting rid of spam.

As we have said, running your own SMTP server vastly increases the power of email. It allows email to initiate all sort of things other than replies from your mail server. Sadly, not all these things may be what you wanted. By way of example, consider a mailing-list subscription engine. Most of us have used them—you send mail saying "subscribe me@mysite.com RedHotIce" to a remote server, and then you get lots of interesting email about serving strawberry sorbet at lip-scalding temperatures. Of course, if the subscription engine were badly written, you might be able to send an email that fooled the remote server into executing code instead of adding you to a list. You'd suddenly have a lot of control over someone else's mail server. This is not a fantasy example. Many free and commercial mail servers have been susceptible to problems like this in the past. Some still are.

Another interesting point about subscription services: Forging a From: address is exceedingly trivial. Often people are subscribed to high-volume mailing lists as a Denial of Service attack. If you're running such a list, make sure there is some sort of sign-on verification process. On a verified list, after sending the subscribe message, you receive an email saying: "reply to this message if you REALLY want to subscribe." There should also be an easy way to unsubscribe. This mechanism should be noted at the top or bottom of every message sent across the list. This helps to prevent the incredibly annoying "Please unsubscribe me" messages that are guaranteed to appear on any unmoderated mailing lists.

In summary, if you decide to run any of these interesting services at your site, you need to be careful about which ones you run. Generally, any program that's open source, has been around for a few years, and is reasonably common is likely to have had most of its blatant holes found. Anything that's brand-new, or closed source, or unheard-of will cause problems sooner or later. Sendmail is a perfect example of a good open-source mail server. It used to be considered very insecure. Through extensive use and debugging by the Internet community, all of the known holes were closed up. Now it is very rare that a security hole is found in sendmail.

How to Make SMTP Secure

If you do decide to run your own mail server, you would be well advised to ensure that it doesn't relay what it shouldn't. In other words, you need to prevent your SMTP server from acting as a spam server. The easiest way to do this is to ensure that your SMTP server only allows outbound mail to originate from within your network. This will foil most spammers, unless they can trick your SMTP server into believing that they are within your network.

Some spam prevention technical assistance for a variety of mail transport agents can be found at Glenn Fleishman's site, currently at www.glenns.org/spam/sendmail.antispam.html. You don't want to be a spam relay. Trust us. People you don't know will hate you. Organizations like the Mail Abuse Prevention System (http://maps.vix.com/) and the Open-Relay Behavior Modification System (www.orbs.org/) will ensure that a lot of other people all refuse to accept mail from you. It can also cost you a lot of money paying for the bandwidth required to relay mail. Make no mistake, if someone finds you running an open relay on a good connection, it's perfectly normal to find yourself sending on a quarter of a million pieces of somebody else's junk mail. That's quite the denial-of-service attack.

You should also take advantage of your MTA's ability to limit the size of incoming messages. 1Mb is enough for most low-bandwidth sites, and 10 Mb is enough for nearly anyone. There are better ways than mail to send 600 Mb files around, and not every 600 Mb file someone tries to send you is something you want.

You could run your SMTP server within your DMZ or in your internal network. Putting it inside your firewall has pros and cons. An advantage is that you don't have to spend time securing nonmail functions of the machine against attack, because your firewall protects it. The problem is that if the machine is compromised due to a security hole in the SMTP server, the Bad Guy has a direct connection inside your firewall. Whatever you do, don't run your SMTP server on the firewall itself. The section *Should Your Firewall Provide Services?*, later in the chapter, will explain why this is a bad idea.

The Web

What on earth could we say about the World Wide Web that hasn't already been said, or better yet, posted on the Web itself? Fire up a browser and go look. However, for this book, the Web server protocols are our concern. It must be stressed that this section is in no way an attempt to tell you how to set up a Web server.

HTTP: The HyperText Transfer Protocol

HTTP servers normally run on TCP port 80. We've used the phrase *normally* in most of the protocol sections in this chapter when discussing port bindings, but in most cases it's pretty much mandatory. There's nothing to prevent you from compiling a mail server that runs on port 5037, but don't expect to get too much mail—no one else will know how to find your server. HTTP, however, can genuinely run on any port because the general format of an HTTP URL allows a server port to be specified. Ever seen a URL that looked like "www.company.com:81/page.html?" It's the 81 after the colon that specifies the port number. If none is specified, as is usual, then the default is port 80. But there's nothing to stop you running a Web server on port 81, or 1999, or 8080, or 60003 for that matter. If the URL a browser follows contains your server and its port number, your server will be found.

Problems Associated with HTTP

The HTTP protocol by definition is an *insecure protocol*, that is, there is no authentication, and no encryption of data. HTTPS, described next, provides for an encrypted data stream and authentication of the server, but it's up to the HTTP client and server to figure out how to authenticate the client. This is often done via an HTTP form that collects a username and password from the client. On the back end, either the Web server or a program processes the data.

Dynamic pages are the most prolific source of web server security problems. Back-end form processing scripts are notoriously riddled with buffer overflow problems. Hidden HTML tags are also occasionally used as a shortcut when building dynamic pages. This can create significant security problems by revealing crucial access data to hackers. A poorly written form handling script can give a hacker all they need to compromise an entire network.

There are no known major flaws in HTTP itself, although there are plenty of problems with any particular HTTP server implementation. Each day it seems as if another teenager finds a new way to break into Microsoft Web servers. Netscape server security holes are found less often. This doesn't mean

Netscape servers have fewer holes though. Many hackers are looking for bugs in Microsoft products with the sole intention of discrediting Microsoft. Hackers tend to feel sympathetic to Netscape and generally don't look for holes in Netscape products—unless they're trying to break into a system.

So your choice is a system with lots of highly published security holes, or a system that may or may not have security holes that only hackers know about. Not too appealing, is it? Luckily, there's a better option. It's called Apache (www.apache.org/), and it's the most commonly used Web server on the Internet for some very good reasons: It's free, it's open source, and it does everything a Microsoft or Netscape server can do and more—but faster, better, and with less security holes. Tough sell, huh?

How to Make HTTP Secure

Hopefully you're running Apache as your Web server. If for some reason you're not allowed to run Apache, lie to management and run it anyway. They'll never notice the difference. Actually, if they notice anything, they'll be complimenting you on the increase in stability and faster performance. Okay, we're done pushing Apache.

There are some general steps you can take to improve the security of any Web server, especially servers other than Apache. The first step is to make sure you're running the latest version of the Web server. The second step is to make sure your Web server has no more access to the system than it absolutely needs. Under Unix systems, you can prevent the Web server from accessing critical resources by running it as if it were a user with very low privileges. Essentially, the Web server only needs to be able to view a few files in a limited selection of directories. There is no reason for it to be able to execute arbitrary user programs. Finally, you should turn off every feature you can. Turn each feature back on only after you know what it does. Let's take a look at a few of these features.

If you configure your server to permit it, client Web browsers can activate executables on your server via the *Common Gateway Interface* (CGI). This feature can lead to major problems. Any CGI script you allow to run on your server must be carefully checked for potential security holes—buffer overflows, loose file permissions, and the like. A security hole in a CGI script could compromise your entire sever. It makes sense to keep all your CGI scripts and executables outside the Web document hierarchy. This is because any file inside the document tree that can be read by the HTTP server process can and will be served to a browser on request (barring separate security precautions). If your CGI scripts live inside your document tree, people can retrieve them, read them, and look for security holes at their leisure.

There are now numerous alternatives to using CGI for dynamic content. One popular alternative is pre-processed HTML, used by tools such as Java Server Pages (jsp), php, Cold Fusion, and Microsoft Internet Information Server. Instead of loading a plain HTML page, the Web server is reconfigured to load more complex pages that include programs within them. For example, a jsp page might be mostly Java code. The output of the Java program creates the HTML that is sent to the end user.

The advantage to pre-processed HTML is that arbitrary programs are not executed at the system level. Instead, the pre-processor is responsible for interpreting the programs directly from the source code. Since the pages reside on the server in source code form, an administrator can always look at the code to see if any security violations are occurring. Furthermore, a well-written pre-processor will not let poorly written pages do bad things to the system.

If you run a Web server, you will need to allow the Internet to access TCP port 80 on your server. While it's possible to choose another port, it's not a great idea if you want your site to be easily accessible. On the other hand, don't assume that using an obscure port number will make the site private or secure. It is trivial to determine what ports are running Web servers given an IP address. Ensuring that no publicly accessible pages link to the private URLs adds a marginal degree of security against the casual surfer, but this technique is mostly worthless against a professional hacker. You can gain far greater security by password protecting your private pages or running a private Web server inside the firewall.

HTTPS: Secure Web Service

This is probably a bit of a misnomer in a book on network security. There exists a subsidiary protocol called HTTPS, or Secure HTTP. This normally runs on TCP port 443, and provides for secure, authenticated connections between browser and client. Authentication is one-way—the client browser is sure the server is who it says it is, but the server still knows very little about the client. The security here merely means that both client and server can be sure that nobody is eavesdropping on or changing the data being sent across the network. From a network security viewpoint, exactly the same concerns apply to HTTPS servers and the content they serve as apply to HTTP servers.

Web Clients

To make people feel more comfortable about using the Web, Microsoft and Netscape have both spent a lot of advertising dollars on convincing the public of their product's security.

When the makers of a Web browser tout their strong security features, they're invariably referring to the level of encryption used when communicating over HTTPS. For the time being, most of this talk is meaningless chest beating. While it *is* possible to crack the encryption used in Netscape's standard browser (the one that is legal to export), it requires an amount of computing power that is simply unavailable for amateur hacking. This may not be the case in as little as a year, but for now it's *highly* unlikely that anyone is intercepting credit card orders over HTTPS. Why bother? A simple radio receiver can capture hundreds of credit card orders made over cordless phones.

This isn't to say that we think encryption is pointless. On the contrary, encryption is of the utmost importance. But it has nothing to do with this section. We're concerned about the security of the browser itself. In this area, both Microsoft and Netscape have shown a consistent inability to deliver. It is all too easy to construct a Web page that can exploit security flaws within either browser to gain full control over the visitor's machine.

The World Wide Web began as a simple mechanism for document sharing and turned into a multimedia menagerie. In order to "enliven" the Web, Netscape and Microsoft have piled all sorts of additional features into their Web browsers. Unfortunately, the race to come up with the flashiest new technology first meant a lot of sloppy code writing, which means a lot of bugs and security holes.

Most people are totally unaware of what their Web browser can do. This is especially true for Microsoft's Internet Explorer (IE), which has been built into the operating system of Windows 95/98. Both browsers can read, write, and delete any file on the user's hard disk. This would be fine if the browsers were totally secure and all access had to be authorized by the user. Obviously, this isn't the case.

Every version of every Web browser put out by Netscape and Microsoft has numerous security holes that range from the relatively innocent (unauthorized access to user information) to the obscene (allowing any Web site to execute arbitrary commands on a user's machine). Many of these holes can be activated without any knowledge or action on the user's part—simply visiting a malicious Web site is enough. To make matters worse, most people don't know how to upgrade their browsers, or simply don't realize that they need to upgrade. This means that old, well-known exploits are still effective on a large number of machines. Let's take a look at a few particularly nasty holes.

Problems Associated with Web Clients

The biggest problems with IE and Netscape stem from their default settings. Java, ActiveX, JavaScript, and many other features are usually turned on by default in most Web browsers. This opens up the browsers to a range of exploits that go beyond the problems inherent in the browsers themselves. People are constantly finding insecurities in these "extra" technologies. Luckily, most of the dangerous technologies can be disabled. We're not going to deal with JavaScript, Java, or ActiveX exploits here since they're too numerous and can be easily fixed by disabling the feature. Some sites will no longer work properly, but this is a small price to pay for significantly better security. Java can always be reactivated through the Java plug-in, as previously mentioned.

There are other settings within the browsers that deal with convenience features, such as the caching of form data and cookies. By default, many of these features are set to on. It is your responsibility to go through the entire configuration program and learn about each feature. Many of the features have downsides that are not immediately obvious. For example, one feature in IE5 is to allow paste operations via script. This probably means nothing to the average user in the context of the configuration program. But if they knew that this feature allows any Web site to download the contents of their Windows clipboard, they'd turn it off immediately.

Then there are the high-tech variations on the social engineering theme. One such attack is *frame spoofing*, in which under certain conditions it's possible to alter the browser window so that it appears as if you're browsing a site such as Amazon.com (the URL seems to say "www.amazon.com," and the page looks similar), but in reality you're still browsing the malicious site. This could be used to trick people out of credit card information or other personal information (username, password, and so forth). These attacks are often detectable by careful observation. Unfortunately, the victims of social engineers are those who don't pay careful attention to reality.

The other major browser security holes involve buffer overflows. As more features are added, each browser needs to be able to handle other resources besides HTTP and to be able to understand content other than HTML. As handler software is added for these new features, the probability increases that at least one of the handler packages contains a buffer overflow condition. These overflows often take the form of a URL that is too long. When the browser tries to load the URL, it chokes. The process described at the end of Chapter 2, "Fundamental Internet Security Issues," enables the malicious Web site to execute arbitrary code by placing the code at the end of the URL. Just when you'd think the browser makers would have figured out how to write a good browser, another buffer overflow hole is discovered. Remember our earlier discussion about chrome and security.

One example of a new feature that immediately led to a buffer overflow is the IE5 "favicon.ico" bookmarking bug. As you may or may not know, IE5 notifies Web sites when a user adds the site to their list of favorites. It does this by asking the

Cookies and Privacy

Since version 4 for both IE and Navigator, cookies are turned "on" during an install or upgrade. Should you turn them off? We can't answer that question for you, but we can help you better understand the main issues.

The good: Cookies are an important way for Web servers to provide targeted or personalized content to visitors. Many popular sites simply won't work without cookies. Furthermore, major sites need cookies to track their visitors. Analyzing visitor patterns helps the Web developers to make better sites. It also helps them get better ad revenues. Web sites are expensive to run and maintain—someone needs to pay for it.

For the most part, cookies are secure. Each cookie can only be read by a Web server from the same domain as the server that created the cookie. This means that go.com can't read the information that yahoo.com stored in the cookie file. Furthermore, the information stored in the cookie file is usually an ID number that maps to an internal database connected to the remote Web server. Even if another site could read the cookie, the ID number would be meaningless. Used properly, cookies can only reveal personal information that has been voluntarily given by the user to the site that is being visited.

The bad: Nonetheless, cookies can be used improperly. One major company sells a very popular product for managing advertisements and dynamic content. When a Web site using this product collects detailed demographic information about a user, the information is associated with a cookie. That's pretty straightforward. What is scary is that this cookie is stored in a global database along with the profile. When the visitor goes to another site that uses the same product, all of their profile information is immediately available.

The company that offers this product ensures that no personally identifiable information is associated with the global profile. Assuming that this is really the case, there's a more significant problem. Someone may be willing to give demographic information to a medical site under the belief that not entering their name and address anywhere on the site protects their privacy. They then might give their name and address to a different site in order to make a purchase. If both sites used the aforementioned product, this latter site would have the ability to correlate the visitor's name and address with the demographic profile gathered on the medical site.

The ugly: If you think that was bad, look at what's around the corner. At the time of this writing, one of the largest online advertisers, and one of the largest direct market data companies, announced a merger. If you have cookies enabled, chances are you have a cookie from this online advertiser. They have one of the largest cookie databases on the Net. The traditional marketing company has a vast database linking names, addresses,

Cookies and Privacy *(Continued)*

and other personal information to purchasing patterns. Most mail-order purchases go through this company. Their intentions are not secret: They plan on merging the two databases. Ultimately, any site with a banner ad will know your name, address, and demographic profile. If you browse through an auto manufacturer's Web site, don't be surprised when you receive a catalog in the mail shortly thereafter from that auto manufacturer. Of course, that's only if your credit rating is good enough. Goodbye privacy, hello Big Brother.

A compromise: New products are starting to appear that recognize the positive benefits of cookies but also protect the user against the negative aspects. For example, Zero-Knowledge (www.zeroknowledge.com) is a company that offers a privacy program called Freedom. Their software allows a user to create multiple identities when using the Internet. Cookies associated with each identity are stored separately. Thus, you can create a purchasing identity for when you make your online purchases, a medical identity for medical information surfing, and any other identities you want. You can ensure that the profile information obtained from filling out an online form can't be used to track you when you're looking at more sensitive types of pages.

Other companies are creating tools that block banner ads altogether, along with any cookies they might try to send. With products like these becoming more common, your users can maintain their privacy while continuing to take advantage of dynamic sites and providing useful feedback to Web sites.

Web site to provide a customized icon for the entry in the favorites folder. Putting aside the privacy issues inherent in this system, there's a more serious buffer overflow problem. If the icon file is not properly formatted, IE5 crashes. A skillfully crafted icon file could actually execute arbitrary code on the client's machine. While this attack does require a user to actively bookmark a site, there are plenty of social engineering methods for getting a user to bookmark a site.

Of course, there's always the threat of Back Orifice and its descendents. If one of your users browses to the wrong Web page, a hacker could own every Windows machine on your network within a few hours. We're not kidding. Back Orifice is *far* more dangerous than most of the industry realizes. The original release proved the concept. It is relatively easy to modify it in such a way that it is not detectable under Windows. Furthermore, it can communicate through HTTP, so firewalls and proxy servers won't stop it. Once it's on a machine, it provides complete access to everything imaginable. BO also makes it very easy to mount attacks on other machines from an owned machine. A hacker can then delete the BO executable and any other trace of their presence on the intermediary machine. Awake yet?

How to Make Web Clients Secure

You would think that upgrading to the latest version of your chosen browser would fix the security holes. To some extent, you'd be right. The most publicized holes are usually plugged up with the next release. Of course, each release has also introduced numerous other security holes. Furthermore, there are many holes that hackers have *not* published. Back when browser exploits received significant press, it was worthwhile for hackers to publish a few holes. Now that the media is completely ignoring browser security issues, hackers have little incentive to publish holes they find. Instead, they keep the holes private within the hacking community. End users now have a false sense of security—the lack of media attention would lead one to believe that browsers have become more secure. Nothing could be further from the truth.

So what can you do? A firewall won't protect your users against many of the browser exploits, especially the most dangerous ones like Back Orifice. Using a proxy server, forbidding plug-ins, and turning off Java, JavaScript, and ActiveX will help to some extent, but it still leaves more than enough holes.

The most secure solution is to *not* use either Netscape or Internet Explorer. Instead give your users an open source browser such as Mozilla. Since it's true open source, you can fix any security holes that you find. More to the point, you can fix any holes that anyone can find, as soon as you hear about them.

Another solution is to allow only Web access from machines in the DMZ. This definitely reduces convenience, but it's a major boon for security. If Back Orifice compromises a DMZ machine, it won't compromise your internal network, although your DMZ might be a stepping stone for future attacks.

Back Orifice and similar exploits are only undetectable on operating systems that don't log processes. Operating systems like Linux and OpenBSD keep a record of every running process. A good suite of intrusion detection software will be able to detect unauthorized processes. Windows and Mac machines are much more susceptible to Back Orifice-type attacks because background processes cannot be detected. This means there's no way to tell if Back Orifice has compromised a machine just by examining the machine alone. Some intrusion detection programs, such as the Network Flight Recorder (NFR) tools released by the l0pht, are capable of detecting communications between a standard BO client and server. Unfortunately, the open source nature of both Back Orifice and the detection tool means that a skilled hacker could easily create a variant of BO that is not detectable by the NFR tool. Nonetheless, the l0pht tool will definitely catch recreational Back Orifice use by script kiddies.

We don't recommend using email programs integrated within a browser (Netscape, IE/Outlook) because it's too easy for a Web page to use an exploit that gathers the user's email address. Additionally, HTML mail is a bad thing, and both Netscape and IE encourage its creation. HTML mail is bad because it means that any of the Web-based exploits we're talking about can be sent as an email message and activated immediately upon opening the message. If your users don't have HTML mail, they can't get hurt as easily through email.

Transferring Files between Machines

Sometimes, you just need to move a file from point A to point B. It might be a zip file full of images, or an archive file containing the source of the FSF's (Free Software Foundation) latest masterpiece, or you might just be moving data off to a backup site for storage.

FTP: The File Transfer Protocol

FTP is the most common method of moving files around the Internet. Traditionally, it was the first protocol for file transfer across the Internet, and as such is the system best understood by the bulk of serious Internet users (those users who realize that the Internet is more than just Web and email access).

Like many of the major TCP/IP protocols, FTP was not designed with security in mind. In fact, its very design creates numerous security problems. Combine this with its immense popularity and you'll quickly see why it poses one of the firewall administrator's bigger problems.

Problems Associated with FTP

We talked about how FTP can be a real pain briefly in the earlier section *IP Masquerading*. Now let's take a look at it in greater detail.

Some people say that bad things come in pairs. Others say that bad things come in threes. FTP covers all the bases by having three pairs of bad things: (1) it communicates with the server on two separate ports—one for commands and the other for data; (2) it operates in two different modes (active and passive); and (3) it will give you headaches twice—first from trying to understand it, then again when you realize the implications. We'll now look at why two channels and two modes are bad things. If you don't understand why headaches are bad, you should repeatedly hit yourself on the head with a brick. If you still don't get it, then you'll have years of happiness ahead of you as a system administrator.

The two-channel structure deals with separating requests for data from the data itself. Each FTP server has a *command channel*, where the requests for data and directory listings are issued; and a *data channel*, over which the requested data is delivered. All other control information, such as authentication exchanges, is sent over the command channel.

Active Mode

In active mode, an FTP server receives commands on TCP port 21, but uses a strange mechanism to exchange data with the client. When a client contacts an FTP server in active mode and wants to send or receive data, the *client* picks an unused local TCP port between 1024 and 65535, tells the server over the command channel, and listens for the server to connect on the chosen port. The server opens a connection from TCP port 20 to the specified port on the client machine. Once the connection is established, the data are passed across. The important point here is that *the server initiates the data connection*. Most command-line FTP programs use active mode by default, though some of them can be configured to use passive mode.

Active mode FTP is good for FTP servers behind firewalls, because the firewall only has to permit access to one predetermined port on the server. Unfortunately, it's terrible for clients behind firewalls for two reasons. First, the server is communicating with the client on some arbitrary port between 1024 and 65535. This means the firewall needs to permit any computer on the Internet to access any port between 1024 and 65535. For a network security administrator, that's very bad news indeed.

The other problem with active mode FTP is a technical hurdle for masquerading firewalls: When the client picks a port for the data connection, it sends it across the command channel. The server initiates a return connection to the firewall on the port chosen by the client. The server expects the client to be waiting for that inbound connection, and indeed, the client is waiting—but the firewall isn't. Most standard portmappers have no way of knowing that the incoming connection is part of an active mode FTP session. Additionally, the information present in the inbound packets doesn't tell the firewall which internal machine is the intended recipient.

One attempt to address the port mapping issue is called *adaptive firewalling* and is described in detail later in this chapter in the section *Commercial Firewalls*. As you'll see, adaptive firewalling is not really a great solution.

To be brief: Unless you want to blow large, swiss-cheese type holes in your firewall, you have to say no to active-mode FTP clients.

Passive Mode

In passive mode, the command channel is still port 21 on the server, but the traditional data channel on port 20 is not used. Instead, when the client requests passive mode, the *server* picks an unused local TCP port between 1024 and 65535 and tells the client. The client opens a connection to that port on the server. The server is listening on that port for the inbound connection from the client. Once the connection is established, the data flow across. Most modern browsers use passive mode for accessing *ftp://* URLs.

It's easy to have your firewall support passive mode FTP clients because the client is initiating both the command and data channel connections to the server. The portmapper sees the outbound connection from the client and sets up the proper mapping. The server can then communicate back with the firewall through the new channel.

The trouble with passive mode begins if you're running an FTP server. The nature of passive mode requires you to permit any machine to open a connection to any port between 1024 and 65535 on your FTP server. If your FTP server is on your internal network and is meant for internal access only, this may not be a terrible problem. It is an issue if you're concerned about attacks from within the network, since it creates some opportunities for hackers who already are within your internal network. In such a scenario, you might consider making an internal-only active mode FTP server. Of course, the best solution is to use a non-FTP alternative for internal-only access.

The real problem with passive mode occurs if you need your FTP server to be externally accessible. It's an extremely poor idea to allow this sort of access to your internal network, and it's very hard to do with port forwarding anyhow. Therefore, servers that can be accessed from the Internet in general should always be in a DMZ. To your internal machines, the DMZ server should look like any other outside machine—that is, they'll have to use passive mode to get past the firewall. Even if servicing your own users is not a priority, the general trend on the Internet is strongly toward passive mode since most Web browsers use it when connecting to FTP sites.

By and large, if you can hide under a rock, do it. This means not having a local FTP server, and only allowing users to use passive mode FTP across the firewall.

More Problems: Anonymous FTP

Many FTP servers support *anonymous FTP*. While FTP once required a valid username and password on the FTP server, it eventually became clear that there were some files the server administrator would wish to make available to everyone, regardless of whether they had an account on the server. Anonymous FTP was the solution to this problem. You can talk to an anonymous FTP server by logging in as user "anonymous" (or as user "FTP" on more recent servers—for those of us who can't type so quickly). By tradition, the password you pass back should be your full email address. Many FTP servers will grumble at you if you provide a junk password, but they'll still let you in. A few rather fascist FTP servers will refuse you access unless you provide a real (or correctly formatted) email address, but they have no way of checking if it's really your address.

Any half-decent FTP server will make use of the *chroot* system call, or OS-specific equivalent, for anonymous access. This is a system call that hides most of the file system from the FTP server process. It works by constraining the server to a specific subdirectory and all of its sub-subdirectories. As far as the server is concerned, there are no other directories outside of the chosen subdirectory. It thinks that the chosen subdirectory is the root, or top-level directory, of the file system. This isn't perfect security, but it makes it very hard for a user to abuse an anonymous FTP session and get to parts of the FTP server that the client should not see. If you must run an FTP server, make liberal use of this feature. One well-known, open source FTP server is the wu-ftpd (originally the Washington University archive FTP server), current details of which can be found at www.landfield.com/wu-ftpd/.

Now for a word on incoming FTP: If you must run an FTP server, and it must support anonymous FTP, fight as hard as you can to avoid having incoming anonymous FTP. This is an area on your FTP server to which the anonymous FTP user can write. Not only are these glaring targets for denial-of-service attacks, but also you will end up being used for *wareshousing*. This is when some random punk uploads a whole pile of pirated software (usually Windows games) to your incoming FTP area, and then tells about half a million "friends" of his where they can download cool "warez." Not only does this bog down your Internet connection, but it may have unpleasant legal liabilities for you, depending on your location.

One of your authors worked for a company that insisted on having incoming FTP, and in consequence made it on to several lists of "open" sites maintained by the warez community. When we discovered the problem, our first thought was to control it by monitoring uploads and rapidly deleting anything suspicious that was uploaded. We wrote a perl script that relayed all new upload information to our beepers. The theory was that the wareshousers would wise up in a couple of days and move on.

It turns out that our theory had no correlation with reality. We found out that we could rapidly get fed up with being woken at 4.30 A.M. because someone uploaded his latest junk to our FTP site. The wareshousers didn't pay any attention, they just continued uploading stuff. After three weeks of this, we turned off incoming FTP with an axe, and threatened to give our beepers to anyone who wanted it turned back on. It's still off.

Nonanonymous FTP

Running an FTP server that requires a username and password is *only* a good idea if the usernames and passwords have nothing to do with internal network logins. The entire FTP session is unencrypted—passwords are sent over the network in plain text. The only way to protect the login process is to encrypt the entire network session between the client and the server. If you have the capability to create a secure tunnel, then you also have available far better mechanisms of file transfer available to you. Read on to see what we're talking about.

Other File Transfer Options

FTP isn't the only method of moving files around the Internet. *TFTP*, the Trivial File Transfer Protocol, is mostly used for booting diskless workstations, configuring network equipment, and the like. It should not be allowed in through a firewall; it runs on UDP port 69. *RCP*, the *Unix Remote Copy Program*, is so insecure that it is scary, and under no circumstance should it ever be allowed in through a firewall (along with all the other r commands, *q.v.* below). If you wish to use a Unix style copy command, use *SCP*, the Secure Copy Program. This is part of the ssh (secure shell) suite which we praise fervently in a few pages' time.

Filesharing (mounting a file system from one computer onto another across a network) should not be allowed across the Internet unless done securely (i.e., with a proper Virtual Private Network solution, discussion of which is outside the scope of this book but touched upon in a few pages). This translates to no *NFS* (Network File System), a Unix filesharing technology; or *SMB* (Server Message Block), a Windows filesharing technology, across a firewall.

NFS runs on UDP (and, in some modern implementations, TCP). The port it runs on is less tightly defined than with normal TCP and UDP services; clients coming to connect to NFS do so by asking a service called the *RPC portmapper* (Remote Procedure Call) to tell them which UDP or TCP ports the NFS service is running on today. Note that RPC is distinctly different from RCP, the Remote Copy Program. The RPC portmapper runs on TCP and UDP ports 111; access to this port number should never be allowed through a firewall because it can give a hacker tons of useful information. With most standard versions of NFS, it's also a good idea to block TCP and UDP access to port 2049, because this is the default port number on which the NFS server usually ends up running.

SMB uses TCP ports 137, 138, and 139. Access to these should be blocked incoming through a firewall, and in our opinion it should be blocked outgoing as well, especially if you have any Windows boxes on your internal network.

More than one small network administrator has found himself or herself sharing more than he or she wanted with the neighbors.

Newsgroups

If you've been using the Internet for a few years, you have probably looked at newsgroups. Newer users have also probably seen some part of the system without even realizing it. It generally takes Internet newbies a while to realize that there's more to the Net than email and the Web. A first encounter with the newsgroups is likely to be through a Web-based interface to a particular newsgroup or through an organization whose Web page explains how to participate in their newsgroup. Regardless of how you learn about the newsgroups, invariably you will be blown away by the sheer amount of information being exchanged.

Newsgroups are basically bulletin boards. The difference between a newsgroup and some Web-based discussion boards is that the postings to a public newsgroup are sent all over the Internet. A posting to a Web board is only available on that particular Web site.

The framework of the newsgroups is a giant hierarchy, much like the way the Web is set up. Top-level groups have names like "alt," "rec," "comp," "us," and so forth. These are conceptually equivalent to the "com," "net," and "org" domains on the Web, although it's possible to create new top-level newsgroup domains by running your own server. Underneath these top level names there are thousands of specialization topics. For example, under "comp" there are "sys," "os," "mail," "lang," and others. These topics break down many more times, resulting in group names like: "comp.unix.bsd.openbsd" and "comp .security.unix." Each level has numerous branches, and sometimes the topic is very vague until you get down past the third branch; but looking for keywords within the tree of newsgroup names is an effective way to find a group that discusses a particular topic.

NNTP: The Network News Transfer Protocol

Unlike email, netnews has a single protocol that deals with reading, posting and transmitting news. It's called the *Network News Transfer Protocol* (NNTP). An NNTP server normally runs on TCP port 119. The modern reference implementation is "inn."

Problems Associated with NNTP

NNTP has precisely one responsibility, the transmission of news. Nearly all modern enhancements to NNTP servers are concerned with performance improvements and keeping up with the flood of news. This tends to make NNTP servers efficient and short on security holes.

The real issue with NNTP is practicality. Do you really want to run an NNTP server within your organization? Is your primary goal to allow people within your organization to access public newsgroups, or are you planning on running your own news hierarchies?

Taking a full news feed creates significant bandwidth problems. At the time of this writing, the average daily volume of news traffic can easily exceed the full capacity of a T-1 leased line, which is about 15 Gb per day. You might notice that supporting a full news feed is an expensive proposition of limited value, especially given that a significant amount of this volume is composed of pornography and spam.

If you just want internal access to public news groups, the easiest solution is to point your users at one of a number of Web-based interfaces to Usenet such as Deja.com and remarQ.com. The next best solution is to find an ISP that runs a news server and to let your users connect to the ISP's news server directly.

If you want to run public discussions on specific topics, there are better ways to accomplish this than by using a news server. You can set up a Web-based discussion list, or you can use a commercial site that lets you create your own on their server.

How to Make NNTP Secure

With all that said, we hope we've managed to communicate that you probably don't want to run a public NNTP server. Nonetheless, you might be considering an application for which it is necessary and worthwhile. If you do, you'll need to open up access to TCP port 119 from the outside world. As with any other server, pick any common, reliable, open source implementation, keep an eye on the developers' mailing list, and you'll hear about the few holes as soon as they're known. Keep up with your patches.

If you just want to provide access to an outside news server, you merely need to let machines at your site access port 119 on the external NNTP server of your choice.

Streaming Services

Until now, we've discussed communications protocols that are based around the concept of request and response. The client or server requests information, and the other party sends it. Data are sent across in chunks and are processed upon the complete receipt of the information. There is another type of communication where the data flow is continuous and processed immediately. This is known as *streaming communications* because there is a constant stream of data.

The first types of streaming communications were very basic. Programs like *talk* enabled two users to type messages to each other in real-time across a network connection. Each letter would appear on the other user's terminal as soon as it was typed. This gave a sense of immediacy to the communication that could not be obtained through email.

Initially, video and audio were downloaded in bulk form—only after the client had received a large data chunk could it play the result to the user. It wasn't long before somebody figured out how to send very small chunks of information that could be processed and played immediately. If the connection between two machines was very fast and very stable, real-time audio or video could be sent across the network. It was a short leap to then enable two-way communications over the Net.

Somewhere along the line, some over-eager developers slipped and let a marketroid look at the technology. Immediately things like Internet phones, voice chat, and video conferencing were being hyped as "the next big thing." The marketroids didn't understand that the fundamental framework of the Internet simply couldn't fulfill the promises they were making. Unfortunately, their hype was creating a large demand for the technology. Kicked out of the house at an early age by the marketing hype, streaming technology had to do a lot of growing up, and quickly.

The problems facing real-time streaming services are numerous. A minute of video or audio results in several megabytes of data. Without compression technology, it's not possible to transfer that much data in real time, especially considering the fact that most users connect to the Internet over modems. But existing compression technology required the entire data file ahead of time. Furthermore, the decompressing of the data took significant processing time. New compression technologies were invented to reduce the amount of data sent by a significant factor.

On the network side, TCP requires too much overhead to deliver streaming services quickly enough. Remember that TCP was designed to provide reliability at the expense of redundancy. Thus, UDP was used for data and TCP was reserved for command information. Since UDP is completely unreliable, parts of the data stream might be missing or out of order at any given time. The real trick was finding compression formats that could still be decompressed with missing data. Over the past few years, major strides have been accomplished in delivering streaming content. Nonetheless, there's a long way to go. Issues like latency, lag, and computing resources still greatly influence the performance of streaming communications, especially the more recent variants.

We'll address two of the most common types of streaming services here, but be aware that all of the following sections deal with sending data in real time across the network and have many of the same underlying problems from a network design standpoint.

Internet Relay Chat

In late 1988, Jarkko Oikarinen wrote *Internet Relay Chat* (IRC) to enable multiple users on multiple servers across the world to communicate in real time. Other multiuser environments existed prior to this, but were limited to smaller networks or individual computers. Since then, IRC has grown to become the most popular mechanism for real-time communication. Many of the Web-based and proprietary chat networks also use IRC as the underlying technology.

Problems Associated with IRC

IRC is not a secure communications framework. Everything is sent cleartext over the network, including private messages. Given the size and nature of the IRC network, this means a lot of computers will see your message, unless you're running a private IRC server.

The biggest problem with IRC is that tons of wanna-be hackers are roaming the public networks, looking for targets. They start probing your IP addresses for standard vulnerabilities. Some popular IRC clients (mIRC in particular) have notable insecurities that allow these hackers to directly attack the machines of your users, completely bypassing any network security measures you have in place. They'll also try to use various social engineering techniques to get your users to download trojan programs such as Back Orifice.

Once a hacker has penetrated your network, they may decide to brag about their accomplishment by setting up an IRC server on your network. When other immature hackers see this, they are filled with envy and rush out to try and hack somebody else's network. If you see an IRC server running on your network filled with users named k'nG 3g1, g0d, phr33k d00d, etc., you can bet that you've been hacked by a bunch of 100z3rZ (for an explanation, see the Jargon file entry on lamer-speak: www.tuxedo.org/~esr/jargon/jargon.html#Lamer-speak).

How to Make IRC Secure

The first question you need to ask yourself is, "Do I need IRC?" If you just want to participate in IRC discussions, you can use a Web-based interface to IRC or some other chat network. Virtually every portal site offers some form of real-time chat. Talkcity.com is one of the major Web chat providers. Linux.com offers a Java applet interface to a number of Linux discussion channels. Undernet.org, Webmaster.com, and others offer full Web-based interfaces to IRC.

If you still want to use a traditional IRC client to connect to IRC networks, be aware that many popular IRC clients are also notoriously full of security holes. The most popular Windows client, mIRC, is continually being exploited. Even worse, mIRC is not open source. As popular as this client is, we recommend you avoid it. In general, Windows IRC clients are not very secure. The best IRC clients are those that have been around for a while and are open source such as "ircii." These open source clients are only available for Unix platforms. You can find links to them on www.irchelp.org.

It's hard to imagine any situation in which users within your private internal network need direct IRC access. You're far better off providing this service on a DMZ machine, preferably one running Linux or some other relatively secure OS. You should also pick a set of IRC servers that will be allowed. Some servers will use nonstandard ports, and this will just require punching more holes in your firewall. As it is, you'll need to allow outbound connections to TCP port 6667 and possibly a few others. There are also SOCKS proxy servers for IRC.

Running a publicly accessible IRC server is also not recommended. There are plenty of alternative solutions to providing real-time chat that are easier to access and interact with. Many IRC users want to run a server simply to gain server operator access. These users feel that operator status is impressive. Real server operators know that it's just a time-consuming job.

If you're set on running an IRC server, you need to make sure your server software is open source and actively being developed. Like newsgroups, running a full IRC server is an expensive proposition. The bandwidth requirements are very high—you won't be allowed to link your server to many of the public networks without *at least* a T-1 connection.

A great starting place to learn more about IRC is www.irchelp.org/.

Streaming Media

There are numerous variations on the streaming audio/video theme. Broadcast video/audio, canned video/audio clips, Internet telephony, and even video games fall into this category. As bandwidth increases, more and more applications are using streaming technology to deliver real-time interactivity to their users.

The demands of streaming media are closely tied with the level of interactivity. The lowest demands are from one-way broadcast audio, such as Internet radio. Usually the broadcast source has a good connection to the Internet, so the quality of your connection is greatly influenced by the quality of your network. Two-way broadcast audio requires that both parties have a decent connection. Video is far more demanding, and video conferencing is absolutely meaningless on anything less than a T1 connection.

There are two methods generally used for optimizing conferencing-type applications (which can include multiplayer video games). With the first method, each client application connects to a central server. The central server processes the data and sends them out to each client. In the case of an audio conference, the server needs to handle the case where multiple people are speaking at the same. This is a very difficult task, and slows down the conferencing to the point of unusability. Nonetheless, for less-demanding applications such as videogames, this method is easier to implement. From a firewalling standpoint, it means you only have to open up a hole to a particular server's IP address.

The second method is used by newer conferencing packages and by high-performance networked games. A central server is used as a matching service, identifying the IP addresses of all the participants. Each client application then establishes connections with each of the other clients in the conference. The burden of processing the incoming data is on the client's end. If a particular client can't keep up, only that client will suffer. From a firewalling standpoint, this method is a total nightmare—any computer on the Internet needs to be able to connect to one or more ports on your firewall.

Problems Associated with Streaming Media

Streaming media applications are very complex. Companies compete based on the quality of their application's performance, which is determined by their compression algorithms and networking tricks. The only way to keep this information out of competitors' hands is to keep their software closed source. This means that the applications may have numerous security vulnerabilities. On the Windows platform, a security hole can quickly lead to a compromised machine.

The plethora of streaming media products available also creates an opportunity for trojan programs. A user might go to a Web site that offers exciting streaming media, but requires a special plug-in. Users often download this plug-in and install it without any thought as to whether the plug-in is doing what it claims. Because of the high bandwidth requirements, a user won't notice if the site is downloading the contents of their hard drive in the background.

Even the official tools might be sending private information to third parties without your knowledge. Nonetheless, one can reasonably trust the Real Player, from Real Networks (www.real.com). They do give you options to turn off certain types of tracking that they perform (although it's still possible that other data are gathered without your consent).

Privacy issues notwithstanding, there's also the possibility that a hostile site could send back data to your client that exploit a security hole in the client software, allowing the hostile site to take control of your machine. Microsoft NetMeeting has been notorious for containing numerous insecurities of this nature. The fact that it is installed by default on Windows-based machines and can be launched (and compromised) from an email message should cause some concern. NetMeeting is a scary program when you realize what it's capable of and how many problems have been found in it. Check out NetMeeting vulnerabilities on bugtraq (www.geek-girl.com/bugtraq).

Conferencing software (not just NetMeeting) is very dangerous in general for a number of reasons. For speed reasons, the transmissions are almost never encrypted. This means numerous people on the Internet can eavesdrop on an entire conversation very easily. It's like talking on an old radio-based cordless phone. Anyone in the neighborhood can listen in with an AM/FM radio. Most conferencing packages also have tools such as file exchange and remote desktop control. A hacker doesn't even have to cause a buffer overflow to use the software to attack your machine if they can find a flaw in the client's access control (assuming it has some). We explore this further in the *Remote Window Interface Control* section later in this chapter.

Another problem with any type of multiuser networking software is that it can involve broadcasting your IP address to the world as a user of said software. For example, many conferencing tools allow you to be listed in a directory so that others can contact you. These directories often contain all sorts of information useful to a hacker—from the version of the software you're using to other personal information (such as your name), which can help them if they decide to use social engineering.

Games are notorious targets for hacking. Game release cycles are very short, and there's a lot of pressure to get games out the door. This results in poorly coded games with numerous bugs that take a while to fix. Sometimes the game has security bugs that allow hackers to invade the machine of a gamer while they're connected to the game network. Hackers simply wait on the game networks for victims and then strike when they get a vulnerable IP address.

Another popular attack is the simple denial of service. In combative multiplayer games, players often are ranked based on their in-game performance. Many gamers take these rankings *very* seriously. Sore losers may sometimes resort to DoS attacks if they fear they might lose a match. By launching a DoS at their opponent they'll either paralyze the opponent, allowing a win for the attacker, or they'll disrupt the match, invalidating the match score. This is a reason for not allowing highly popular multiplayer games through the firewall—your entire network may get disrupted by an external disgruntled player who decides to ping flood in retaliation.

How to Make Streaming Media Secure

Getting multiuser software (conferencing and games) to run through a firewall is simply not recommended. If you need to conference between branch offices of the same company, or with other trusted companies, you can set up a secure tunnel for the conferencing application. Either way, running the conferencing software in the DMZ is a better alternative.

In general, the more the client software tells you, the better. Systems that only require connecting to one machine with a fixed IP address are far easier to handle than those that make arbitrary connections to machines all over the Internet. For example, you could allow Real Player content from a set of trusted servers, or a CuSeeMe connection to a specific list of machines. This reduces the risk of opening up holes on the firewall, but IP address spoofing could still gain undue entry.

How well can you trust that a software package is doing what it claims? Here's an experiment you can run. Take a streaming client like Real Player. Punch a hole through the firewall on the necessary ports to one trusted Real Server (it helps if this server is controlled by you or someone you know that isn't affiliated with Real Networks). Look at your firewall logs and see if the client attempted to make connections to unauthorized sites. If you are running the server, check to see if the server is trying to communicate with other sites as well. This would be an indication that some information about your connection is being sent to a third party such as Real Networks for tracking purposes. If nothing appears, it's not conclusively safe—the data may be transferred in batches later. As you can see, it's not easy to figure out if software is truly operating in a safe manner unless you have the source code and can compile your own binaries directly from that source.

Some companies are well aware of the security risks that their software poses. They have gone to great lengths to provide numerous alternatives for accessing their content from protected networks. For example, Real Networks is well aware of the problems with firewalls. They offer three solutions to the network administrator:

- Instructions on how to accept standard connections by punching TCP and UDP holes

- A client-side option for TCP only connections
- A proxy server for even better security that works with numerous popular proxy solutions

This doesn't mean that their software is secure, but it's far better than other packages that tell you the only choice is to open massive holes on your firewall.

As with everything else in this book, open source client/server software is the preferred route. With any sort of complex multimachine communication tool, it's critical to know as much as possible about whom you're communicating with. Nonetheless, it's also important not to base security solely on trust relationships. The server you trusted yesterday may have been compromised today.

Providing Command Level Access

Often, there's no substitute for logging onto a remote machine and issuing commands. Anytime this happens over the Internet in a manner that requires a username and password to be sent, there's a good chance of them being intercepted. If they've been sent in cleartext, there's a very good chance you'll have unexpected visitors soon thereafter.

Telnet

Telnet, the classic remote access application, runs on TCP port 23. It runs completely in the open - no encryption, no authentication other than the username and password that are transmitted in clear. We think anyone who allows telnet access in this day and age is foolish as someone who bungie jumps off of a 200-ft bridge with a 200-ft cord, but if your users need to telnet out that's fine. Let them know, very clearly, that they're going to get intercepted. Let them know, very clearly, that they should not use the same passwords for these remote systems that they use for internal systems. Let them know why. Do not allow incoming connections on port 23 to any machine inside your network; if people must have remote, interactive access, try ssh.

How to Make Telnet Secure

There exist versions of telnet designed to work with Kerberos. If the remote system supports this, and you can get hold of kerberised telnet, that will adequately secure your entire telnet session. Otherwise, it's pretty much impossible to make telnet secure. More information about Kerberos can be found in Chapter 12.

Rlogin

Rlogin and rsh (the noninteractive version of rlogin) allow you to avoid sending a password in cleartext across a network by pre-instructing the remote system to allow any requests that claim to come from a particular user at a particular IP address. Needless to say, forging the username is trivial, and forging the IP address is just as easy. The r-command servers (rexecd, rlogind, rshd (which also provides RCP service), and rwhod) run on TCP ports 512, 513, 514, and UDP port 513, respectively. None of these services should be allowed to enter your network.

How to Make Rlogin Secure

Don't bother trying. Use ssh. Ssh does everything rlogin does and more. Making rlogin secure would involve using ssh anyhow, so just keep reading and pretend that rlogin doesn't exist.

ssh

ssh is an application whose time had definitely come. It descended on the world from Helsinki University of Technology in Finland, and answered the prayers of many an administrator. In its basic form, it uses encryption to protect an interactive session between two computers. The protection ensures that: You are talking to the same machine you talked to last time you accessed that IP address; no one is eavesdropping on your conversation; no one is modifying your conversation; and no one can hijack your conversation midstream. The protection is not useful if either the local or the remote machine have been compromised; it protects the channel, not the endpoints. The ssh server runs on TCP port 22.

As we discussed in the earlier sidebar on secure tunneling, ssh can do much more than provide a secure shell. Having established an ssh connection to a remote server, you can (configuration permitting) tunnel connections from your local machine to arbitrary ports on the remote server (the POP port, for example). If you invest some time in configuration, *all* TCP conversations between you and the remote server can benefit from ssh's protection. UDP tunneling is unfortunately *not* part of the standard ssh distribution, but there's no reason why this feature couldn't be built into a GPL'd version of ssh by some kind individuals (hint hint).

Configuration of an ssh server is outside the scope of this book. The reference implementation is available from SSH Communications Security (www.ssh.fi).

NOTE

This implementation is not covered by the GPL, and you may find that you need a license in order to use it. Kinder-hearted souls, bless them, are working on a GPL'd implementation called lsh, more of which can currently be found at ftp://ftp.lysator.liu.se/pub/security/lsh/. There is also mindtunnel, a Java ssh server from Mindbright Technologies, which has been released under the GPL. It's pretty rudimentary, but you could easily enhance it.

If you feel you have set up ssh correctly, then you will need to open up access through your firewall to port 22 on your ssh server. Outgoing ssh can be permitted with little or no worry.

For your internal and external workstations, you'll want to obtain a decent ssh client. If the workstations are running a Unix variant, you'll find that the ssh package comes with a perfectly reasonable client. Windows users are in a bit more of a bind. A number of good ssh clients are either commercial and/or closed source. SSH Communications Security (www.ssh.fi) is the commercial entity that sprung up from the original development effort. They provide the latest version of ssh on a license basis. It's still open source, but it's no longer freeware. Datafellows (www.datafellows.com) offers a full-featured set of Windows ssh tools, but at a price. Cedomir Igaly's ssh program (www.doc.ic.ac.uk/~ci2/ssh) is free, but is closed source.

The best open source ssh client that is fully featured is the Mindbright Java client (www.mindbright.com/english/technology/products/mindterm/) The advantage of Mindterm is that you can run the same client on any platform. It has all the features you'll need, and it's GPL'd. Programmers will love that the core ssh client functionality was designed as a library. This makes it very easy to embed ssh functionality into your applications. The only downside is that Java is still somewhat slow on Windows. The code has been extended to make it easier to tunnel. The Mindterm code and its extensions are available on the companion Web site.

Problems Associated with ssh

Attacks on ssh rely on cryptographic techniques. Every once in a while, someone finds out that an encryption algorithm thought to be secure has some problem that allows it to be cracked in some way other than brute force. Alternatively, a couple thousand hackers link their computers together over the net and decide to crack a few weakly encrypted keys. Things like this do happen; keep up with your patches and watch for unusual gatherings of nerds.

You might be thinking, most forgivably, that ssh makes a great basis for a *Virtual Private Network* (VPN). Well, put such thoughts aside. While it's very good for securing most access between a *machine* and a *network*, it's not so good between a *network* and a *network*. There aren't any technological bars to it, per se, but it's not really what it was designed for. If you need a VPN, build a VPN. One excellent free tool is *CIPE* (Crypto IP Extensions), written by Olaf Titz. You can find more about it at http://sites.inka.de/~bigred/devel/cipe.html.

While on the topic of VPNs, it's worth mentioning *IPSec*—the *IP Security Protocol*. This is actually a pair of protocols: the *Authentication Header* (AH) and the *Encapsulating Security Payload* (ESP). It is used to create a secure IP level tunnel between two networks. This is a relatively new protocol, is governed by an official standardization board, and is quite a hot area of development. There are open source implementations for both Linux and OpenBSD. OpenBSD actually contains a built-in VPN solution that uses IPSec. It's still in development, but it's pretty cool nonetheless. For more information, check out www.ietf.org/html.charters/ipsec-charter.html A free Linux implementation can be found at www.xs4all.nl/~freeswan, and the OpenBSD implementation is documented under the ipsec man page. We also should note that IPSec does have some problems with masqueraded networks.

Remote Window Interface Control

We touched on the concept of Remote Window Interface Control a little bit ago when we initially examined Microsoft NetMeeting. This is more of a concern for Windows than Unix because many Windows applications only have Window level access.

The X Window System

In a nondescript building deep in the heart of Cambridge, Massachusetts, a group of computer wizards were trying to make their computer network easier to use. They wanted to be able to run graphical applications on one computer and view them on another. A techie could walk over to another workstation and gain full graphical access to his own workstation. If software only ran on one type of machine, it could run on that machine yet still be controlled from a different type of computer. Their ideal system would make it possible to use powerful central machines as application servers and less expensive machines as terminals. Multiple users could connect to these powerful servers and work on different applications at the same time.

There was an existing graphic window interface system called W, but it was too slow, didn't have all the features they needed, and worst of all it came from California. So they improved it and, following a long-standing tradition of one-upmanship, called it X. It was first conceived in 1984. Over the years, it would be expanded, improved, standardized, and ported to every platform under the sun.

X is, in the words of the Jargon File, "An over-sized, over-featured, over-engineered and incredibly over-complicated window system developed at MIT and widely used on Unix systems." X is so complex that it can take a highly skilled programmer years to understand. Go to a book shop and look at the O'Reilly series on X programming (assuming you can find a computer-specific book shop that doesn't mind devoting a full third of their shelf space to this particular series).

X is even confusing from an end-user standpoint. Envision the following scenario: You are sitting at Computer A. You want to display an application running on Computer B on Computer A's screen. Guess which computer is running the X server? If you guessed Computer B, you'd be wrong. Here's an explanation *from The Free On-line Dictionary of Computing* (http://wombat.doc.ic.ac.uk/, Editor Denis Howe):

> X uses a client-server protocol, the X protocol. The server is the computer or X terminal with the screen, keyboard, mouse and server program and the clients are application programs. Clients may run on the same computer as the server or on a different computer, communicating over Ethernet via TCP/IP protocols. This is confusing because X clients often run on what people usually think of as their server (e.g., a file server) but in X, it is the screen and keyboard, etc. which is being "served out" to the applications.

X runs on TCP port 6000; if you have more than one display on a machine, other displays run on 6001, 6002, and so on. You are strongly advised to block TCP from port 6000 to about port 6010 in both directions through your firewall.

Problems Associated with X

X is not encrypted, and its authentication system can be compromised. A hacker could easily hijack an X session, creating all sorts of mischief. Particular versions of X clients and servers may also have inherent insecurities. Running an X session across the firewall is a very bad idea.

How to Make X Secure

You can use ssh to create a secure tunnel for X. Part of the ssh standard implementation includes a facility for creating secure X connections. The ssh client automatically sets the DISPLAY environment variable on the server, telling it to forward all connections through the ssh tunnel. The ssh client also uses a secure authorization scheme (X has its own authentication mechanism separate from the login authentication).

Another option is to use *VNC* (Virtual Network Computing). While VNC is not more secure than X on the protocol level, the source code is GPL'd. This means you have full access to the source used to compile your client and server binaries.

VNC

In a nondescript building deep in the heart of Cambridge, England, a group of computer wizards were trying to make their computer network easier to use. They wanted to be able to run graphical applications on one computer and view them on another. A techie could walk over to another lab rat's workstation and gain full graphical access to his own workstation. If software only ran on one type of machine, it could run on that machine yet still be controlled from a different type of computer. Their ideal system would make it possible to use powerful central machines as application servers and less expensive machines as terminals. Multiple users could connect to these powerful servers and work on different applications at the same time.

There was an existing graphic window interface system called X, but it was too slow, didn't have all the features they needed, and worst of all it came from the United States. So they improved it and, in an effort to avoid undue stigmatism, called it something other than Y. Over the years, it would be expanded, improved, standardized, and ported to every platform, including Sun's Java.

VNC uses a more understandable client/server model: The server is the machine that you want to access, the client is the machine that displays the desktop. The protocol is very simple, as opposed to the complexity that is X.

Some other advantages are stated on the VNC site itself (www.uk.research .att.com/vnc). We've paraphrased a few as follows:

With X, if your machine crashes or is restarted, all the remote applications will die. With VNC they go on running. This means you can leave your desk, go to another machine, whether next door or several hundred miles away, reconnect to your desktop from there and finish the sentence you were typing. Even the cursor will be in the same place.

VNC is small and simple. The Win32 viewer, for example, is about 150 K in size and can be run directly from a floppy. There is no installation needed.

VNC is sharable. One desktop can be displayed and used by several viewers at once.

VNC is truly platform independent. Any viewer can connect to any server. A desktop running on a Linux machine may be displayed on a PC, a Solaris machine, or any number of architectures. The simplicity of the protocol makes it easy to port to new platforms. There is a Java viewer, which will

The Cambridge Conspiracy

Sometimes it seems as if the town of Cambridge has a doppelganger across the pond. To prove it, we have created a feature comparison chart for the two cities.

CAMBRIDGE, U.K.	CAMBRIDGE, MASS.
Academic Mecca	Academic Medina
Old, historic buildings	Old, historic buildings
High-tech capital of UK	High-tech capital of US
Lots of Indian food	Lots of Indian food
People drive on wrong side of road	People drive on wrong side of road
Takes an hour to get to London	Takes an hour to get to Boston (locals that have waited for the Red Line or sat in Harvard Bridge/Big Dig traffic should understand)
Lousy weather for most of the year	Lousy weather for most of the year
Funny accents (cor blimey, guv'nor, strike a light)	Funny accents (pahked my cah neyah Havahud Yahrd)
Left-of-centre politics	Left-of-left-of-center politics
VNC	X Windows

run in any Java-capable browser. There is a Windows NT server, allowing you to view the desktop of a remote NT machine on any of these platforms using exactly the same viewer.

Problems Associated with VNC

Like X, VNC is not a secure protocol. All of the caveats about X apply.

How to Make VNC Secure

Unlike X, it's true open source, so you can get the source code without a license. This means you can plug in any type of encryption system you'd like, but we don't recommend it. Instead, simply forward the VNC TCP connection through an ssh tunnel.

Forwarding VNC is easy to do: Let's say your VNC server is running on port 5900 (the default for display 0). Tell your client program to communicate with local port 5901. Then, use ssh on the client side to forward local port 5901 to port 5900 on the server end.

Another option is to use the Mindbright variant of the Java VNC client. Upon a suggestion by one of the authors, Mindbright plugged their Mindterm ssh library into the Java VNC client (it involved changing less than 10 lines of code). The result is automated ssh tunneling with VNC. Very cool.

Regardless of how you do it, you should definitely run VNC through ssh. Ssh has built-in compression that will significantly reduce network traffic and improve the speed of the connection.

NOTE

VNC has a number of different encoding formats for communicating between client and server. The client defaults to sending raw data if it sees that the server is on the local machine. This results in much more data being sent across the connection, but gives better performance for local use. By using ssh to tunnel the connection, the client will think that the VNC server is local and will send raw data. To reduce the bandwidth usage, you should run the client with the "–hextiles" option. This uses an encoding system that's more efficient for network transmissions.

Microsoft Windows-Based Products

There are numerous products on the market that allow you to remotely control a Windows machine from another machine somewhere on the network. Fundamentally, this is the most dangerous type of service you could possibly offer—full control over a machine. Thus, it's absolutely critical that the system used is as secure as possible.

Problems Associated with Windows Remote Control Products

The Windows platform was never built with security in mind; security was added as an afterthought. There are fundamental weaknesses in the operating system that can't be cured with a bandage. For example, background processes can run in a way such that they cannot be detected. This is just the tip of the iceberg—point your browser at bugtraq's archive (www.securityfocus.com—look under "forums" or use the search tool) and search for "win" or "windows" to see what we're talking about. Part of the problem stems from the fact that the vast majority of Windows packages are closed source. This means that only the original developers can identify and fix bugs in the software. Most Windows-based software products that aren't compiled directly from GNU licensed Unix source code are security disasters.

To make matters worse, companies confuse issues by claiming security through strong encryption. While the data in transit might be secure, that has nothing to do with whether the program is secure on a fundamental level. For example, often encryption keys and passwords are stored on disk so users don't have to type them in every time. Regardless of how complex the scheme, the original information can always be recovered if the password is stored on disk and can be recovered by the program without user input.

Many Windows applications are developed using common development libraries, most of which come from Microsoft. Hackers have repeatedly found insecurities such as buffer overflow conditions in these libraries. It becomes trivial to determine if an application has been built using such a library. For example, many Windows applications are susceptible to buffer overflow attacks due to weakness in a core Microsoft development library. These libraries have provided hackers with a reliable and consistent set of exploits.

Because of this, you must assume that while the data *may* be secure in transit, the client and server applications themselves are fundamentally insecure and can often be easily compromised. As for the security of the data in transit, your trust should also be reserved. You simply can't trust an encryption algorithm unless you can view the source code that implements the algorithm.

Laplink, NetMeeting, PC Anywhere, and other remote session control systems for Windows all rely on proprietary unpublished transport mechanisms to create an aura of security. While you may be unable to determine what these programs are doing with your data, rest assured that hackers know exactly how the data are being transported and how to compromise the data stream. Since nobody can see the source code, and since only the vendor can create and distribute fixes, these programs are a hacker's dream.

How to Make Windows Remote Control Products Secure

Drop the machine off a cliff. Okay, so that's not always an option. Sadly, you can do very little to secure most of these programs. If you're able to determine the exact transport mechanism, you may be able to use ssh port forwarding to create a secure tunnel that the applications can then use for their insecure communications. Besides that, our best recommendation is VNC or X through ssh. These are well-understood packages that many rely upon.

There is one other open source remote control program available for the Windows platform that's worth mentioning: Back Orifice. It can be very useful as a remote control tool, but you need to read every line of the source code and compile it yourself. Putting the effort into understanding how Back Orifice works at this level could also help you avoid future BO attacks. Because it's open source, you can figure out a way to encrypt the communications through ssh. The downside to running BO as a network tool is that it may make it more difficult to detect hostile BO attacks on your network.

Distributed Computing

Most of computer science research and development is directed toward distributed computing. The Internet is essentially a giant distributed computing network. The Web is a perfect example. Documents are stored on computers all over the world, but can be easily retrieved on any other machine via a simple protocol (HTTP). Over the past few years, the Web has moved even more toward true distributed computing. Many Web servers now present content dynamically to users based on various input parameters—all sent over the simple HTTP protocol.

Of course, HTTP is far from the best mechanism for distributed computing. Most of the computing world has settled on the object-oriented paradigm of software development. A good distributed computing architecture should be able to work with objects directly. There are numerous architectures that do this, and they have created a confusing landscape of acronyms, many of which are almost pronounceable. The common goal for all of these architectures is that an object on one machine can use an object on another machine.

In this section we'll deal with two of the most common distributed computing frameworks: *Remote Method Invocation* (RMI) and the *Common Object Request Broker Architecture* (CORBA). Each framework has its own protocol for communicating over the network. RMI uses the *Java Remote Method Protocol* (*JRMP*) while CORBA uses the *Internet Inter-ORB Protocol* (IIOP). Recently, Sun added support for RMI to communicate over IIOP in addition to JRMP.

Before we get into any of this, we'll take a moment to sort out a few terms. One of the most daunting aspects of distributed computing is the plethora of acronyms found in every sentence. Some writers don't even bother to explain what any of the acronyms mean, expecting you to already know their meanings and their relationships. We'll give you a road map that will hopefully help you when you next encounter these technologies.

Object. A small program. Each object performs a specific task. The goal of object-oriented programming is to make the task performed by the object as simple as possible, so that it is easily reusable in any other program. Combining lots of little objects together can create complex systems. For example, a "car" program might be composed of an engine object, a few wheel objects, some seat objects, etc. Objects can also contain other objects. For example, an engine object would be made up of spark plug objects, a carburetor object, a radiator object, etc. Any one of those objects might be composed of even smaller objects.

The key to object-oriented programming is that the smaller parts are "abstracted" away from the larger program. The car object doesn't need to know how the spark plug object fits into the engine object. It just knows that it needs an engine, and it needs to be able to turn on the engine. The engine object takes care of asking the spark plug object to "fire." The car object also can link other objects together; for example, the accelerator pedal would be linked to the engine object.

The functionality of a given object is described by its *methods*. For example, the engine object would have a method called "ignition" and another called "throttle." When the car object wants to tell the engine object to turn on, it would call the engine's "ignition" method and pass it a value such as "on."

The benefit to this system is that it becomes very easy to build complex systems. Once a programmer is familiar with the object-oriented approach, it becomes easy to see programs as a collection of objects communicating. Often, many of these objects have already been designed. For example, the *Java Developers Kit* (JDK) comes with thousands of pre-made objects that handle many common tasks. There are also third-party vendors that sell objects, and many objects have been made freely available on the Internet. Even if the object needed doesn't exist, it is often made up of smaller objects that are available.

The object-oriented program often starts of as a collection of *interfaces*. These are descriptions of how the various *components* (objects used together in a program they are often referred to as components) will communicate with one another. Looking at a well-designed set of interfaces should quickly reveal exactly what a program does and how it functions. As long as an object conforms to the interface specified, it should work in the program. A major advantage to this system is that different programmers can work on different components and the system will still integrate easily as long as everyone adheres to the interface descriptions.

Some types of object communications are so common that the interfaces have become standardized. For example, the JavaMail specification defines interfaces for objects that handle email. When programmers need to incorporate email functionality, they can use the JavaMail interface and then choose from a number of objects that implement the standardized interface. As long as the object is JavaMail compliant, it will work with the programmer's application.

These concepts are important to understand, because all of the technologies we're about to discuss attempt to extend these concepts into a networked environment.

Distributed Computing. Machines networked together share resources (files, processor time, databases, programs, and so forth) to perform a given task.

Going back to our car example: What if you wanted to build a car that used somebody else's engine? Wouldn't it be cool to see how your car might run using the latest engine from Ferrari? With distributed computing, it's possible! You would use one of the frameworks we'll describe shortly to interact with an engine object that actually resides on a server at the Ferrari research labs in Fiorano. The car would run as if all the parts were on your machine, but in reality the engine would be running off of the high-performance racing server in Italy.

Remote Method Invocation (RMI). If your car is a Java object, and the Ferrari engine is also a Java object, then you would probably use RMI to connect the two. RMI is Java's own way of letting one object reference the method of another object located somewhere else on the network. It uses its own protocol for communicating, and is not very useful for anything other than pure Java environments. It is possible to use RMI to access non-Java objects through the use of *Native Method wrappers* (a system that allows you to run non-Java programs from within Java) but there are better ways of accomplishing the same goal.

Object Request Broker (ORB). The problem with our car example is while you might speak English and Java, the paisani at Ferrari speak Italiano. How does your program communicate with the Ferrari server? The answer is that you use an Object Request Broker. This is a special type of program known as *middleware*, because it sits in the middle (like a translator) and doesn't really care what the transaction is about. Its job is to figure out how to make the transaction happen.

Interface Definition Language (IDL). Each language has its own way of providing access to methods and data. Not every language provides adequate facilities for an ORB to figure out which methods are available and what data types they support. The ORB's IDL is a common way to specify the methods that each object has available, along with the types of data the methods can receive as parameters. When a programmer creates an object, they also create an interface definition file written in the ORB's IDL. Every programming language uses the same interface definition language. Using the IDL files, the ORB can figure out how to make a Java object seem like a C++ object to the C++ programmer and vice versa.

Common Object Request Broker Architecture (CORBA). The problem with our story so far is that every ORB vendor could specify a different interface. If that were the case, a programmer would have to decide on an ORB ahead of time. If they ever wanted to use a different ORB they might have to rewrite their program. That's where CORBA comes in. CORBA is a specification for how ORBs should interface with various programming languages. This is mostly accomplished through the CORBA IDL—an interface definition language standard that all CORBA compliant ORBs use. It is an open standard managed by the *Object Management Group* (OMG). If the programmer uses the CORBA interface for their language, they can be sure that their program will work with any CORBA-compliant ORB on the market.

General Inter-ORB Protocol (GIOP). It's also important that ORBs from different vendors can intercommunicate. While I might run one vendor's CORBA-compliant ORB on my network, the Ferrari team might use a different ORB. GIOP is part of the CORBA framework. As long as both ORBs are CORBA compliant, they'll be able to intercommunicate via GIOP.

Internet Inter-ORB Protocol (IIOP). CORBA-compliant ORBs use IIOP to communicate between one another over the Internet. IIOP is an Internet-specific implementation of the GIOP.

Distributed Component Object Model (DCOM). Microsoft's attempt to make the rest of the world use its proprietary standards. DCOM has the same goals as CORBA. Most CORBA-compliant ORBs will treat DCOM objects as CORBA objects without much effort. Because of this, it's safe to ignore DCOM and assume the world is CORBA compliant.

Did you notice what happened? With each definition, the ratio of acronyms to English grew. And we were trying to keep it as readable as possible. Try looking at some of the technical documents on the Object Management Group's Web site (www.omg.org). Some documents manage to have entire pages of nothing but acronyms. At least that's behind us. Now we can look at how this will affect network security.

RMI

Your RMI-through-the-firewall experience is going to be heavily influenced by whether you control both endpoints or not. If you control both the client and the server, then you'll have little trouble making RMI work. If the server is behind your firewall, then you have some flexibility. If the client is behind the firewall and you don't control the server, you may have some trouble, especially if the remote server is behind a firewall. Finally, if you don't control either the client or the server, you're in for a fun ride.

Let's start with the easy scenario: you control both the client and the server. The best thing to do is use ssh to tunnel between the client and the server. This makes everything else easy. Unfortunately, you rarely have the luxury of having that much control over your environment.

The next best situation is if you can control the server, and it's behind your firewall. The first thing to do is to try to force all of the clients to tunnel via ssh. If that doesn't work, things get difficult. You'll probably have to put the server in the DMZ. If you do, you might want to consider running RMI on port 80—more on this in a bit.

Under no circumstances should you ever use the HTTP hack that is suggested in the RMI FAQ. This involves setting up a Web server inside the firewall and running a CGI program that turns the Web server into an RMI server. The RMI client sends an HTTP request to the standard HTTP port 80. The request is an HTTP POST request with the real RMI server port in the URL. The CGI program then directs the rest of the RMI request to the correct port.

The HTTP hole places the security onus on the application programmer. If a hacker figures out what has been done and knows the RMI interface, they can easily impersonate a client and potentially compromise your network. They might also find a vulnerability in the RMI CGI program, or in the Java VM. If you want to play with this hack put the RMI server in the DMZ.

If you decide to put the RMI server in the DMZ but still need access to internal resources, such as a database, then you'll need to create an application level proxy. What you do is create a tiny Java program that communicates over a secure tunnel through the firewall. This program acts as a proxy on a method by method basis for the specific RMI object/application. You must make sure that this proxy can't be abused to gain access to the internal network. Once again, the security onus is on the application programmer, but now the risky application is much smaller and easier to audit. In order for a hacker to break in, they'd have to first compromise the external application, then compromise the proxy. Compromising the DMZ machine won't help because the only channel between the DMZ machine and the internal network will be the application level tunnel.

That's pretty hairy. Let's back up a bit and assume we only have to deal with RMI clients that wish to get out to a server somewhere on the Net. The HTTP server trick has two sides. RMI clients can send out requests that appear to be standard HTTP requests, but where the port number is the RMI port on the target RMI server. The RMI server doesn't need to be running a Web server—it can just strip away the extra HTTP information. On your end, if outbound HTTP requests go through a proxy server, you'll have no problem—unless your proxy doesn't like non-standard port numbers. If the RMI server is running on port 80 you won't have to worry about that (this is the reason we suggest running the RMI server on port 80—other clients will appreciate it). Of course, the administrator of the remote server might be foolish enough to run the CGI/RMI hack. If so, then you can send out HTTP from port 80 regardless of what port the RMI server is running on.

If you don't have any control over the client or server parameters, or if the other party is also behind a firewall, you can pretty much forget about letting RMI across the network. It's unlikely that either party will agree to a common strategy without a lot of head banging. Your policy should be firmly against punching holes in the firewall for RMI. Explain your position clearly and firmly. Let the people who want RMI access argue among themselves as to how they're going to get through the firewall, but stay out of it until they provide you with an acceptable solution (such as VPN tunneling).

CORBA/IIOP

There are three critical aspects to a security model for networked applications. The first is a secure user access system that can limit the access a particular user has to a particular set of resources. An unauthorized user should not be able to access restricted data. This is invariably the responsibility of the application programmer. The second aspect is a secure method of user authentication. In the CORBA framework, this is the responsibility of the ORB, which either provides its own authentication system or uses an external system such as the operating system's own authentication scheme. Finally, the data that pass across the network need to be made secure. This is the part that we're most concerned about.

The problem with securing the communications channel is that both endpoints need to agree on an encryption system. The CORBA security model deals with providing security within a single security technology domain. This means that the security policy and framework for the entire environment is consistent—for example, within a large, well-organized company. The CORBA specification does not deal with connecting two or more domains with different security policies. It suggests using a security gateway technology, which translates to a VPN solution.

Using a VPN solution is great, but requires the remote administrator to support ssh and not some other VPN solution. This also limits the usefulness of CORBA, since only trusted systems will be able to securely connect. Ideally, CORBA can let any system on the network access a resource securely.

The current trend toward this end is to build SSL support into IIOP. The advantage to SSL is that if it becomes part of the CORBA specification, then all ORBs will support it and the channel can be considered secure without tweaking the firewall. The problem with SSL is that you're locked into a particular technology for encryption. With secure tunneling, you achieve the same goal but with the flexibility of switching your method of tunneling at any point.

Technically, it should be possible to use ssh to tunnel between two ORBs, but this requires coordination on both ends of the connection. Of course, any other existing security measure requires just as much communication at the moment.

The key to making ssh work is that both ends think they're communicating with "localhost." The result is that the address of the foreign objects is always at localhost, which will be valid. The trick is coordinating port numbers and supporting callbacks—where the server requests objects from the client. It appears that very few people have tried playing around with securing the CORBA communications channel with ssh.

The one thing to be wary of are hacked solutions such as HTTP tunneling. If you can't get a real secure solution such as a VPN to work, then you're better off putting the server in the DMZ, as suggested in the *RMI* section.

Other Services

There are some services that don't fit into any of the above categories, but need to be mentioned as well.

NTP

The *Network Time Protocol* (NTP) is one of life's great boons, at least if you need to know what time it is. Using NTP, you can keep the clocks on your systems slaved to Real Time, often to within millisecond accuracy. A discussion of NTP is outside the scope of this book, but more information can be found at www.eecis.udel.edu/~ntp/ and on the newsgroup comp.protocols.time.ntp.

NTP uses TCP and UDP ports123; you will have to allow some of this through your firewall if you wish to synchronize one or more of your machines to one or more external NTP servers. Access to these services on any of your internal servers should be limited to packets *coming from* trusted NTP servers (such as those run by your ISP) and *going to* those internal machines that synchronize externally. The nature of NTP is such that you only need to synchronize one or two internal machines to external sources, then your other machines synchronize to those one or two.

Yes, you can synchronize everything internal directly to external servers, but it's pretty rude to load NTP servers down like that. Especially public servers. Using your firewall to prevent any internal machines other than your internal NTP servers from synchronizing to external NTP servers is a good way of forcing most local machines to sync to your local NTP servers.

NOTE NTP wants to talk to its servers every couple of minutes or so. It's not a good protocol to run if you're on a dialup line of any sort, because the line will be off the hook a lot more than you would like. It's okay on a line charged by bandwidth, because NTP packets are small.

NIS

The ubiquitous *Network Information System* (NIS) allows information about user accounts and the like to be centrally administered. Should you run NIS, denying access to the portmapper (see earlier discussion of NFS in *File Transfer Options*) is even more important. This won't stop someone from guessing what UDP port the NIS server might be running on, but it does stop them from cribbing off the portmapper. Blocking inbound UDP except on certain ports that you choose to accept, rather than accepting all UDP packets save those you choose to deny, is the other main weapon in your fight to keep the cracker from having a chat with your NIS server.

Yet Other Services

This book will turn into a telephone directory if we try to list all the protocols available on the modern Internet. However, we've covered the most common. When someone comes to you and asks "can you open up port xxxx so I can access the squiddleprotz server at Notta University?," you'll have some idea what the question means. You can then make some kind of rational decision about the consequences. Services that require you to open up all UDP ports between 40000 and 55000 for inbound traffic, for example, are Not Good. Services that require you to open inbound TCP service on port 4638 from one external server run by some institution you have reasonable confidence in might be acceptable—if there's a demonstrable need for the service, if the implementation is open source and in regular use at other sites, and/or if there are no horror stories from any of the major security advisory channels relating to the service.

Should Your Firewall Provide Services?

The simple and idealistic answer to this question is no. Anything that your firewall does besides packet filtering reduces the level of security. It also increases the load on the machine, and may require more powerful hardware than we're recommending.

The real answer to this question depends on your resources. If you have limited resources, then you may not be able to afford additional machines for your other services. In that case, your firewall may end up providing Web, mail, news, and proxy services.

The problem with services is that each added service weakens the security of the machine dramatically. Programs such as Web servers and mail servers are very complex and notoriously riddled with security holes. Sendmail had a particularly bad reputation due to some incredibly nasty holes. If sendmail is running on your firewall and a hacker exploits a security hole, they gain access to the firewall. Once that happens, your entire network has been completely compromised.

Another problem with the one-box-does-all solution is that each additional service increases the chance that an error could occur. If a Web server crashes your firewall, you lose your network. Web, email, and news servers can also become overloaded with heavy traffic. This will slow down the machine, which will cause your network to slow down noticeably.

Services also publicly expose your firewall to a greater degree. Someone may try to hack your Web server without realizing it's also your firewall. You don't want to explicitly invite users to your firewall.

Commercial Firewall Systems

Up to this point, we've treated the firewall as an abstract box. As we close this chapter, it's time to see what's inside the box. If you work through this book, your box will be a standard PC system, from a hardware point of view. Less-enlightened system administrators might go out and spend a lot of money on a commercial firewall box. These sound great in the advertisements, and we won't argue: They are wonderful solutions. But in general, they offer nothing more than what you'll get if you follow the instructions in this book.

How could something that's mostly free be just as good as an expensive commercial product? Believe it or not, there are very few practical differences between firewall boxes and what you're going to build. Many commercial firewalls run an operating system internally that is derived from BSD, one of the OS's we use in this book. The software that is layered on top frequently uses the same freely available core tools that we'll use. You're paying for a nice interface and support. The hardware used is sometimes optimized for packet routing and filtering (all firewalls are filtering routers by definition), but you're unlikely to notice the difference this makes unless your connection to the outside world is fatter than a T1, and especially if the PC you're using is powered by a Pentium/Pentium II class processor.

Of course, when you factor in the time you'll spend building and configuring your own firewall, the real price gap between your box and a commercial solution narrows considerably. But the knowledge you'll gain from building the firewall with your own hands will have a far greater value in the long run.

"But what about security?" you might ask. All of the commercial firewall vendors now claim that their firewall can do things that no ordinary packet filtering firewall can accomplish. Yet we just said that the firewall we're building *is* an ordinary packet filtering firewall, and *isn't* very different from a commercial firewall. So what's going on?

The competition among commercial firewall vendors is intense. To help differentiate their products, vendors have been expanding the scope of what a firewall is and does by adding features. One of the standard additions is something called *stateful inspection*. With this technology, the firewall keeps track of connection details in a table. It constantly verifies each connection against the table and cuts the connection if something doesn't match up. Sounds great, but in practice it offers a very marginal increase in security. Stateful inspection *might* be able to stop a handful of attacks, but hackers have an almost limitless supply of attacks that won't be stopped by stateful inspection. These include attacks directed specifically at the firewall system itself, social engineering attacks, denial-of-service attacks, client exploits, and many others.

Another hot feature is *adaptive filtering*. Here, the firewall gets involved at the application level by analyzing packets. If it recognizes the application it can dynamically adjust the firewall. The most common example is active mode FTP. Adaptive firewalls recognize the outbound FTP command packets from the client. When the client tells the FTP server which port it wants to use, the firewall interΔcepts the command packet and records the port number and the server's IP address. The firewall then knows what to do when it sees an incoming connection from the FTP server's IP address to the specified port on the client machine. Numerous other communications protocols, such as Real Audio/Video, work better using this technology.

Adaptive firewalling sounds like a great solution, but it can have some nasty side effects. Do you really want your firewall automatically opening and closing ports based on client requests? Crafty users within the network can take advantage of such a technology to open arbitrary ports on the firewall simply by "faking" a few packets. Furthermore, it's an unnecessary technology. Most applications will work through a normal firewall. Even Real Audio/Video provides numerous alternatives for those users behind a firewall. Proxy servers are basically adaptive technology, except the technology is placed outside the firewall, where it belongs. Most applications that have trouble with firewalls tend to have some sort of support for a proxy server.

Finally, most commercial firewall vendors have rolled some form of intrusion detection into their firewall product. While this makes for easy one-stop shopping, it doesn't significantly improve security. The quality of the intrusion detection product may not be as good as some of the other products available on the market. But if your firewall comes with an intrusion detection package, it's unlikely that you'll shop around for another one that might be better. The all-in-one approach might also lead you to believe that the intrusion detection software can be set up and forgotten about. In reality, the biggest component of any intrusion detection system is *you*. Don't expect any product to provide adequate intrusion detection on its own. If you go through the process of selecting and configuring an intrusion detection system yourself, you'll have a better understanding of why the human factor is such a critical component of a good detection system.

As you can see, features that look good on paper may not really add that much value to your firewall. Add some simple filtering rules on top of Network Address Translation and you're most of the way there. This book will get you at least that far and hopefully a bit farther. The rest of the features provided by commercial vendors are just icing on the cake.

Creating Your Policy

Now that we've looked at all of the issues behind your security policy, it's time to sit down and write. Let's review the key issues first:

- Evaluating your current network design and planning for future growth
- Evaluating the services needed by your users

Even if you're the only user at the moment, you can still plan for the future. If you provide any external services, you already have two groups of users: administrators (yourself) and guests (Web visitors, etc.). This is a good start. You might also want to create a third group for people who physically visit your home or office and wish to access the network. Call these "local guests." If you have a larger network, you will want to group users by business needs. It's a good idea to work on this with a manager. By nature, managers love to group people. There are already group structures set up throughout any large organization—by latching onto these structures, your own network structure will be easier for the end users to understand.

Once you have groups of users, you'll need to figure out how your grouping can best be implemented. Try to keep your implementation options in mind while creating the groups. If you're using a proxy server to control outbound access, check to see if it has user-level access control. The last thing you want to do is decide on a policy that is too complex to actually implement and maintain. Simple is good. A lot can be accomplished with creative subnetting, which brings us to network design.

Is your network currently a computer and a modem? Or is it 20 workstations and a router all connected to a single hub? However your network is set up now, building a firewall will give you a lot more flexibility for the future.

Do you want a DMZ? What types of machines do you want to put in your DMZ? We recommend putting servers in the DMZ and tunneling to services inside the protected network. For example, you could put your Web server in the DMZ, but all of the content could come from a database or file server within the internal network. An ssh tunnel could connect the DMZ to the internal network in a controlled, secure fashion. You might decide to create three zones: a DMZ, a server zone, and the internal network. The server zone could be made significantly more secure than the DMZ, both from a firewall level and by hardening the actual servers themselves. With this setup, the DMZ has no privileged means of communication with the internal network.

The final step is to look over the entire list of resources that we've mentioned in this chapter. Did we leave any out that your company uses? The process of reading through our list of protocols and resources should help you analyze other protocols in a similar manner. Once you've figured out the set of tools your company uses, you'll need to sit down with the manager again and determine the sets of tools that each group should be able to access. The manager will love you for this. It gives them power to say "No secretary should ever need to access FTP resources." It will give you great pleasure when they call you a few months later and request FTP access for their own secretary so that she can get a "critical" file. You can then politely suggest that the manager use the appropriate channels for requesting a change to the security policy.

And that's our final point for this chapter: Make sure this policy is well documented. Make sure you've got a clearly defined procedure for making changes to the policy. It should be nontrivial for anyone in the organization to change the policy. It also should be *very* clear that the policy can't be changed in a short period of time. Forcing at least a week or two of review before any changes are accepted will help prevent managers from blowing holes in the security framework to meet deadlines. Make sure that management understands and signs off on the procedures for requesting changes. If someone complains later, management can't do anything about it. Follow the policy to the letter of the law—any leeway you create will shatter the usefulness of your policy.

Summary

Now that you understand what you're trying to protect, it's time to start building a firewall to protect it. The first step along this path is choosing the platform on which you'll build your opus primum. This book offers a step-by-step guide for two excellent open source platforms: Linux and OpenBSD. The next chapter will help you decide which of the two operating systems is better for you.

4

Choosing an OS: Linux versus OpenBSD

C ontroversy sells. Don't believe us? Try to *avoid* reading this chapter. You won't be able to resist. It's too compelling, too seductive. We hope people will use this chapter as kindling for the age-old "my flavor of Unix is superior" flame war. That'll really boost sales of the book, since there are only a few hundred pages and modern-day book paper burns fast.

If you're like a large portion of the population, you've never heard of OpenBSD. Frankly, you're probably confused by its prominent position in the title of this book. You might ask, why would anyone choose some unknown system over Linux? You'd be asking a good question.

You also might be rather confused about the terminology—a lot of words in this section of the bookstore look the same: Unix, Linux, POSIX, BSD, NetBSD, OpenBSD, BSDI, FreeBSD, etc. Some of these words refer to specific operating systems. Others refer to standards or conceptual frameworks. The reasons why the Unix world is so confusing are rooted in history, politics, and law. In fact, many of the technical differences among the various systems are prompted by legal and political reasons, rather than by pure technical merit. Therefore, in order to understand the Unix world a bit better, we need to take a quick look at its history.

The Abridged History of Unix

A concise description of the early days of Unix can be found on the Unix Work-station Support Group Website at Indiana University. (www.uwsg.indiana .edu/usail/concepts/unixhx.html). Here's an accuracy enhanced extract:

> The Unix operating system found its beginnings in MULTICS, which stands for Multiplexed [Information] and Computing Service. The MULTICS project began in the mid 1960s as a joint effort by General Electric, Massachusetts Institute for Technology and Bell Laboratories. In 1969 Bell Laboratories pulled out of the project.
>
> One of Bell Laboratories people involved in the project was Ken Thompson. He liked the potential MULTICS had, but felt it was too complex and that the same thing could be done in simpler way. In 1969 he wrote the first version of Unix, called UNICS. UNICS stood for Uniplexed [Information] and Computing System. Although the operating system has changed, the name stuck and was eventually shortened to Unix.

Ken Thompson, Dennis Ritchie, and others at the labs were able to originally justify continuation of the Unix project as a documentation system. The functionality of the system evolved and by 1974 the system was significant enough to warrant use outside of Bell Labs. Bell decided to license the system and its source code to a number of universities. Little did they realize that this decision would change computing forever.

The Berkeley Bunch

One of the universities that embraced Unix was UC Berkeley. This was partially due to the fact that Ken Thompson spent a year's sabbatical there in 1976. Several people at Berkeley began to develop Unix by adding such features as true virtual memory and TCP/IP networking. Many programmers from AT&T- licensed institutions all over the world contributed to this project, and the result was known as the Berkeley Software Distribution (BSD). This was great, but as it contained original Unix code, it could only be used under the terms of the Bell Labs license. During the 1980s, the people at Berkeley rewrote so much of the Unix code that little of the original Bell Labs code was left in the BSD. A group of programmers decided to try to replace all of the Bell Labs code, creating a version of Unix that was free of the Bell Labs licensing restrictions. A few of these programmers decided to capitalize on the work and formed a company called Berkeley Software Design, Inc. BSD/386 emerged from this effort in the early 1990s.

At the same time, AT&T/Bell Labs had not given up on Unix. Development continued, ultimately producing a system now commonly known as System V. When BSD/386 was released, AT&T was not too happy about it. Their commercial Unix subdivision, Unix System Laboratories, sued BSDI for violating the AT&T license. Unfortunately for BSDI, they had not effectively removed all traces of the original Bell Labs code. The result was that BSD/386 was withdrawn from circulation. Eventually, an agreement was reached, and an incomplete Unix system called BSD4.4-Lite was released. BSD4.4-Lite contained none of the original AT&T code.

While all of this legal maneuvering was occurring, another license-free BSD system was being developed for the Intel platform. It was called 386BSD and it had the same goal of replacing any leftover Bell Labs code. 386BSD was released in 1993. Two groups independently used this code base to create their own versions of the BSD framework. The two groups never merged due to ideological differences. The NetBSD group wanted to make the BSD framework available for every piece of hardware under the sun. The FreeBSD group wanted to make a freeware, highly reliable, commercial-grade BSD system, but only for the Intel platform. Both groups succeeded at their goals—NetBSD is one of the most widely available operating systems. FreeBSD is highly optimized for the Intel platform (and is now available on a few others) and is considered powerful enough for use in high-load commercial environments. For example, Yahoo's Web servers run FreeBSD.

BSDI didn't give up—they continued to work toward their goal and released yet another BSD-derived Unix system, this time based on BSD4.4-Lite. They decided to commercialize their system and have created a fairly successful and reliable product line.

So where does OpenBSD fit into all of this? The OpenBSD project was founded by Theo de Raadt in 1996. Theo's goal was to create the most secure operating system in the world. He started with the NetBSD codebase and began what is most likely the largest software security audit ever. The following is an excerpt from the OpenBSD site:

> Our security auditing team typically has between six and twelve members who continue to search for and fix new security holes. We have been auditing since the summer of 1996. The process we follow to increase security is simply a comprehensive file-by-file analysis of every critical software component. Flaws have been found in just about every area of the system. Entire new classes of security problems have been found during our audit, and often source code which had been audited earlier needs re-auditing with these new flaws in mind. Code often gets audited multiple times, and by multiple people with different auditing skills.

No other operating system can boast this level of security analysis. While all three free BSD flavors have open source code that can be inspected by users for bugs and security holes, none has a team of volunteer security experts constantly checking all of the code. The result of this process is that OpenBSD is proactively secure. When a security hole is discovered on another operating system, more often than not the issue has already been identified and fixed on OpenBSD. We'll talk more about the impressiveness of OpenBSD's security later in this chapter.

The BSD community has rallied around the major three BSD projects: NetBSD, FreeBSD, and OpenBSD. They all happily coexist because they address different ideological concerns. Each can run code written for the others by way of emulators (a program that converts binary code from another operating system into a format the host OS can understand) or by way of direct binary compatibility (the kernel can directly process the binary code from the other operating systems).

The Finnish Upstart

Unlike the BSD bunch, Linux did not evolve from the original Unix source code. It evolved from an entirely different starting point: Minix. Andrew Tannenbaum created Minix as a teaching tool to illustrate his approach to operating system design. His book, *Operating Systems: Design and Implementation* (Prentice-Hall, 1997), used Minix for its examples. The publisher of the book allowed Minix to be freely downloaded and used for educational purposes. At the time, it was the only freely available Unix-like system, since it was built from scratch and did not include any of the AT&T codeset. It also ran on numerous platforms, making it an easy system for non-PC users to obtain.

Tannenbaum had only intended on creating a supplement to his book—he had never planned on making Minix into a fully fleshed out Operating System. But many students who took courses based on his book were hooked on Minix. They wanted Unix for their home machines, and Minix was the only option. Unfortunately, Minix needed quite a bit of work. It didn't even come close to approaching the standard Unix feature set. Frustrated, Minix users added the tools they needed themselves. A community formed around the software. The Minix community added functionality to the system and fixed bugs, ultimately creating a freely available Unix-like operating system, albeit one that was a bit rough around the edges. It attracted a large user base of hackers, including one student at the University of Helsinki by the name of Linus Torvalds.

Linus had just purchased a 386 and was very excited about learning how it worked. He installed Minix on his machine and started playing around. Soon, he was experimenting with concepts that were core to any operating system's design. He decided to try to build "a better Minix than Minix." After a few months of work, he was able to create a barely functional new operating system. It was purely a hacker's concept, and it contained even less functionality than Minix. One of the people he was in email correspondance with offered to give the source code a home on his ftp server. This person effectively named Linus's new system by naming the main directory *Linux*.

The defining moment in the history of Linux was the sending of this message to a newsgroup of Minix users:

```
From: torvalds@klaava.Helsinki.FI (Linus Benedict Torvalds)
Newsgroups: comp.os.minix
Subject: Free minix-like kernel sources for 386-AT
Message-ID: <1991Oct5.054106.4647@klaava.Helsinki.FI>
Date: 5 Oct 91 05:41:06 GMT
Organization: University of Helsinki
```

Do you pine for the nice days of minix-1.1, when men were men and wrote their own device drivers? Are you without a nice project and just dying to cut your teeth on a OS you can try to modify for your needs? Are you finding it frustrating when everything works on minix? No more all-nighters to get a nifty program working? Then this post might be just for you :-)

As I mentioned a month(?) ago, I'm working on a free version of a minix-lookalike for AT-386 computers. It has finally reached the stage where it's even usable (though may not be depending on what you want), and I am willing to put out the sources for wider distribution. It is just version 0.02 (+1 (very small) patch already), but I've successfully run bash/gcc/gnu-make/gnu-sed/compress etc under it.

Sources for this pet project of mine can be found at nic.funet.fi (128.214.6.100) in the directory /pub/OS/Linux. The directory also contains some README-file and a couple of binaries to work under Linux (bash, update and gcc, what more can you ask for :-). Full kernel source is provided, as no minix code has been used. Library sources are only partially free, so that cannot be distributed currently. The system is able to compile "as-is" and has been known to work. Heh. Sources to the binaries (bash and gcc) can be found at the same place in /pub/gnu.

ALERT! WARNING! NOTE! These sources still need minix-386 to be compiled (and gcc-1.40, possibly 1.37.1, haven't tested), and you need minix to set it up if you want to run it, so it is not yet a standalone system for those of you without minix. I'm working on it. You also need to be something of a hacker to set it up (?), so for those hoping for an alternative to minix-386, please ignore me. It is currently meant for hackers interested in operating systems and 386's with access to minix. The system needs an AT-compatible harddisk (IDE is fine) and EGA/VGA. If you are still interested, please ftp the README/RELNOTES, and/or mail me for additional info.

I can (well, almost) hear you asking yourselves "why?". Hurd will be out in a year (or two, or next month, who knows), and I've already got minix. This is a program for hackers by a hacker. I've enjouyed doing it, and somebody might enjoy looking at it and even modifying it for their own needs. It is still small enough to understand, use and modify, and I'm looking forward to any comments you might have.

I'm also interested in hearing from anybody who has written any of the utilities/library functions for minix. If your efforts are freely distributable (under copyright or even public domain), I'd like to hear from you, so I can add them to the system. I'm using Earl Chews estdio right now (thanks for a nice and working system Earl), and similar works

```
will be very wellcome. Your ©'s will of course be left intact. Drop me
a line if you are willing to let me use your code.
Linus
```

At this point, Linus doubted that Linux would amount to much. There was no ideology, there were no plans for glory. He simply was hacking for fun, and wanted to know if anyone else was interested in the project. At best, he hoped to have a slightly better Minix. In other newsgroup postings he repeatedly mentioned that Linux would never be a full-blown kernel, also frequently referencing "The Hurd" as a freeware kernel that was just around the corner. The Hurd has only recently rounded the corner, and it is a very different beast. More on that later.

The responses to Linux grew over the course of many months. The pace of development was very fast, aided by the enthusiastic support of the Minix community. Initially, Linux required Minix to run (it didn't contain enough to stand alone). By December 1991, less than two months after his initial posting, Linux worked on its own and was usable. Linus would release new versions of the kernel frequently, most of the releases were daily, some were even more frequent!

Today, Linux is a full-scale operating system, with features that rival or surpass many of the other Unix variants, including those that are commercial. It has its weak spots too, but those are rapidly disappearing. It has grown so popular that there are several thousand developers contributing to various aspects of the project. There are also a number of *distributions* of Linux. Distributions differ in the supporting software they provide. Some emphasize ease of installation. Others emphasize flexibility. All distributions use Linus's kernel and the same central Unix programs. Linus still coordinates the development of the kernel, and updates are still very frequent (although the pace has dropped to weekly or occasionally monthly releases).

Why Free Software Exists

Throughout the course of Linux's development, there have been numerous factors that would have probably killed many other similar projects. For example, when Linux first started, Minix was reaching a moderately usable state. There was also a highly anticipated free Unix project based out of MIT called "The Hurd." that was scheduled to be released within a short amount of time. BSD already had a fairly significant community forming. There was little incentive to start work on yet another project, or was there?

Linux made it through its early years because its users were hackers. They weren't trying to make something that the whole world would adopt. They weren't trying to make a profit. They were building Linux because it was fun. Their reward was the appreciation from their peers. They didn't care that they were mostly reinventing the wheel. The Hurd took another five years to materialize, and ended up being something rather different anyway by focusing on a different approach to kernel design.

The release of 386BSD could have derailed the Linux project, but it didn't. 386BSD was built on a much more solid code base, and drew from a stronger following. One would think that the more advanced technology would woo the Linux contributors to jump ship, but they didn't. Something unusual happened within the Linux community. What at first had been simply a hacker's toy transformed into an ideological rallying point. The hobby became a religion—the religion of Free Software.

The Laws and Politics of Free Software

Everybody is talking about it. Large computer companies like IBM, HP, and Oracle are trying to embrace it. Microsoft is scared to death of it. But only a handful of programmers truly understand it. Welcome to the world of free software.

What Is Free?

The word *free* in free software is often horribly misunderstood. To quote Richard Stallman, the Free Software Foundation's leading light, "to understand the concept, you should think of 'free speech', not 'free beer.'" It refers to the freedom to see what's going on under the hood of software, and to tamper with it, and to pass the resulting code around without restrictions. If you charge someone for passing free software to them, that's OK, but it has to be a charge for distribution and not for the software itself. You can find out more at www.fsf.org/philosophy/free-sw.html.

The concept of free software is not new. In the early days of computer science, computer companies facilitated the free exchange of software among their users by maintaining user groups. The hardware manufacturer provided basic software and the end users or contractors often wrote the rest. The manufacturers were content to make their money by selling hardware systems.

In the mid-50s, a few companies began to realize that the software they were being contracted to write could be packaged and sold as a product. Computer Usage Company was one of the first companies to begin selling software products. In the early 60s *Applied Data Research* (ADR) became the first software-only company. They sold a flowcharting package that, ironically, did not do very well because IBM provided a free alternative.

With the birth of proprietary software came organized efforts for promoting non-proprietary software. Academia was a haven for software released to the public domain or with very open licensing. Certain universities contributed heavily to free software and became central clearinghouses for many free software projects. Berkeley, MIT, and Carnegie Mellon were three major bastions of free software development projects. Each university had its own licenses, which also often accompanied all of the externally developed software found in their repositories. Two license models have risen above the rest in recent years, the Berkeley license (based on the UC Berkeley software license) and the GNU General Public License (as created by the Free Software Foundation, based at MIT).

The GNU General Public License

One of the major differences between BSD and Linux is the licensing policy. When Linus first created Linux, he stipulated that the program was free, and that it could not be commercially sold. His initial license was very simple. After a few months, he was persuaded to switch to a different license framework, the *GNU Public License* (GPL). This was probably the single most important event in Linux history.

The GPL is one of the most unusual and powerful software license models ever. While it espouses "free" software, it has a very precise definition of freedom. The bulk of the license deals with how the program is to be distributed and what happens if somebody modifies or uses the program in a future work. For example, one key part of GPL ensures that if an author wants to improve/modify/include existing GPL code in his or her product, the entire resulting software package must be GPL'd. We'll get back to this in a short bit.

How the GPL Launched Linux

When Linux converted to the GPL, all of the existing GNU software became available for direct inclusion. This was a massive repertoire of well-designed free software, worthy in its own right. But more importantly, Linux was able to draw from the extensive talent found in the GNU community. Hackers began to develop for Linux because it aligned with their ideological beliefs. The license was also appropriate for academic environments that wanted to keep their developments open and freely available. It prevented corporations from exploiting code developed by academia for their own products. Hackers similarly enjoy the fact that their work could be viewed by everyone as it improved.

The Berkeley License

The BSD family has been released under what is now called the Berkeley license. Historically, the Berkeley license came first—it was the license that BSD was initially released under. Programmers who developed software for the BSD platform also chose to use the Berkeley license for their software. It is a short license that is easy to understand. The article "Choosing a Software License" in the April issue of Dæmon News (www.daemonnews.org/199904/licensing.html) summarizes the license's main points:

- This is copyrighted material and I own it.
- This material is free.
- You can use it however you want, including selling it for a profit, as long as you include a credit to me, and do not claim you wrote it.
- Whatever happens to you because of this material is your own responsibility, and I'm not liable. There are no warranties, guarantees, or refunds.

The Great Divide

There is a core ideological difference between the Berkeley license and the GNU Public License. The Berkeley license was designed to make software freely available. The GPL was designed to keep software freely available. Under the GPL, derivative works (software based on, or including any portion of, the original) must be also licensed under the GPL unless used internally. This ensures that someone doesn't take an existing GPL work, improve it, and then distribute the result as proprietary software. The Berkeley license has no such provisions.

The best way to understand the concerns of the Free Software Foundation is through example. Joe Hacker releases some cool code under the Berkeley license. Jim Corporation uses the code for their proprietary project. Jim Corporation just took advantage of free software without contributing anything to the community. Now Joe Hacker releases another cool software package under the GPL. Jim Corporation uses the code as part of their software. Jim Corporation is forced by the GPL to in-turn GPL their software and make the source code publicly available. Jim Corporation can still charge for the distribution of the software or for support. Now Jim Corporation has contributed to the free software community, and Stallman is happy.

While the above is a compelling argument for the GPL, it doesn't really show the whole picture. The GPL raises the barrier to entry for non-free competition by forcing "clean room" (starting from scratch) redesigns. Clean room designs are difficult to achieve, especially those that need to be fully compatible with the original. Furthermore, similar bugs to those that were worked out of the GPL'd product are likely to occur again.

The goal of the BSD community is to make a well-understood and secure code-base available under the BSD license. The BSD license lowers the barrier to entry for a new company that wants to compete in commercial marketplace. Commercial vendors that build on this base end up developing software that is of a higher quality than those that need to re-invent everything because the codebase is GPL'd. Of course, they could do just as well by building on top of the GPL codebase and releasing it as a GPL product.

As said by Theo de Raadt, founder of OpenBSD and a proponent of the BSD model:

> Reimplementations have bugs. Our idea is to stop that by making sure that complete reimplementations are not required.

The success of this philosophy can be seen in the immense popularity of BSD-licensed systems such as the Apache web server, much of the Internet's core software infrastructure, The X Window System, and OpenBSD. In addition, many proprietary commercial products are based on BSD licensed code. Commercial vendors that incorporate code from the BSD codebase automatically obtain a high degree of interoperability and compatibility with many other products.

The success of the GPL philosophy can be seen in the immense popularity of GPL licensed systems such as perl, the GNU c compiler and GNU emacs. As said by Richard Stallman:

> Free software packages do not always compete commercially, but they still compete for a good reputation, and a program which is unsatisfactory will not achieve the popularity that developers hope for. What's more, an author who makes the source code available for all to see puts his reputation on the line, and had better make the software clean and clear, on pain of the community's disapproval.

Choosing the Right OS

So what does all of this history have to do with picking an operating system? Well, you could do without it, but then you wouldn't understand why there's a choice in the first place. It might also be of interest if you are the type to be swayed by ideological beliefs, as opposed to raw utilitarian practicality. It's also critical to understand the background behind both systems if you decide to turn to the communities for help. You will find that the background knowledge will help you avoid common newbie pitfalls.

There are many other factors that will affect your choice of operating system. The rest of this chapter aims to help you pick the best operating system for your needs.

The Core Issues

There are a number of critical factors to consider when deciding between the various operating systems. One of the goals of this book is to minimize the differences by providing an easy to follow path from start to finish for each system. Nonetheless, you may find yourself outside the scope of this book occasionally. For example, you may decide to use an old 486 as your firewall. In this case you most definitely will want to read the hardware compatibility section. You also might decide to work with a different distribution or version of an operating system. In such a situation, the installation, configuration, and documentation issues may affect your choice.

Hardware Compatibility

We're assuming that you wish to run your firewall on a PC platform. If you choose another platform, you will almost certainly go with OpenBSD as a solution. OpenBSD supports many diverse platforms, but the hardware selection and installation chapters of this book do not. The chapters on firewall configuration should still apply though, and all other chapters will still be relevant. If you wish to run your firewall on such a system, be sure that you have a supply of spare parts. Keeping a machine running all the time is taxing, and most of the other obscure platforms supported by OpenBSD are old. As much as we'd love to get use out of our Amigas, we'd have a tough time getting a new power supply on short order.

Both OS's offer a rich array of supported hardware on the PC platform. They support most existing Pentium-based hardware, and a lot of 486 hardware. If you have old hardware or very new hardware, then you'll probably have better luck with Linux. The Linux community has done a great job of coming up with drivers for obscure hardware. OpenBSD supports most of the NetBSD repertoire, which is quite a bit. This is a smaller development community, so the newest and the more obscure hardware components are less likely to be supported.

On the other hand, this doesn't mean you'll necessarily have better luck with Red Hat Linux. While Linux has more support for older hardware, not all of the older hardware is supported in the standard Red Hat distribution. You may have to search elsewhere for the proper drivers. This will take you outside of the scope of the standard Red Hat installation and our detailed instructions. Chapter 5, "Getting the Right Hardware" covers the hardware selection issue in much greater detail.

Red Hat is incredibly friendly as long as you travel along the beaten path. Once you veer off the path, the friendly installer turns demonically hostile. It barks, it bites, it even takes candy from babies. By the time you've figured out how to get the installer to happily work with your drivers, you might as well have rewritten the installer by hand. In fact, that's often the solution anyhow. We've made the point clear enough: make sure you're working with Red Hat compatible hardware.

Software Availability

With earlier releases of OpenBSD, there were some software compatibility issues. The current release of OpenBSD can run Linux binaries directly, as well as NetBSD and FreeBSD binaries. This takes care of most software issues.

The only pertinent software system that is really different between OpenBSD and Linux is the packet handling system used by the kernel. OpenBSD uses IPFilter, a tried and true packet filter package. Starting with version 2.2 of the kernel (included with Red Hat 6), Linux supports IPChains, the new system for packet filtering. This is why we have two chapters for each operating system—an installation chapter and then a chapter on the firewalling system used by each operating system. Chapter 6, "Installing Linux" deals with installing Linux and Chapter 7, "Configuring the Firewall under Linux" discusses the technical details of configuring IPChains. Likewise, Chapter 8, "Installing OpenBSD" walks you through the OpenBSD install process and Chapter 9, "Firewall Rules under OpenBSD: IPFilter," explains how IPFilter works.

Ease of Installation

For our readers, both systems will be equally easy to install. Our installation chapters will step you through any difficult configuration steps. If you deviate from the prescribed path, then things get hairy. If the deviation is not too far from the "Red Hat Way," then you should have little trouble. The moment you deviate beyond what Red Hat can handle, you're in hot water, as mentioned in the hardware compatibility section. At this point, OpenBSD may prove to be a better option.

In general, the Red Hat installer will be easier and faster to work with. The OpenBSD installer still needs a bit of work. The single biggest stumbling block for any new user is the hard disk configuration. The interface used to partition the hard drive is not very intuitive. There is an obscure bug in the 2.5 installer (it has already been fixed for the 2.6 release) that could potentially corrupt the master boot record of the hard drive, requiring you to perform a nonobvious task to fix the problem. Don't worry—we'll tell you about all of the crucial gotchas in the install and how to deal with them in Chapter 8.

Ease of Configuration

Once the OS is installed, there are a few things that need to be done in order to tighten up the security of the system. Under Red Hat Linux, the Red Hat Package Management System (RPMS) makes it easy to install and uninstall complex software packages. The system is well documented and even contains a graphical interface. With OpenBSD, there is also a package management system, but it is more primitive than the RPM system and not as well documented.

You'll have to strip a larger number of packages from the standard Red Hat install than you will for the standard OpenBSD install. This actually will mean nothing if you use the script we provide on the companion Web site. The script will automatically remove all excess packages from your installation. You can edit the script (we'll tell you how in the configuration chapter for each OS) to leave certain programs on the system or remove additional packages.

Aside from removing excess software, there are few differences between the configuration of an OpenBSD and a Linux box. Both require modifications to several startup files. Wherever possible, we've provided scripts on the companion Web site that will simplify common administration tasks.

Documentation

The popularity of Linux has led to an abundance of both online and printed documentation. Red Hat 6 comes with a thorough installation guide, and for the first time also comes with a basic Unix primer. Go to http://metalab.unc.edu/LDP/ and the sheer number of HOW-TO documents and MINI HOW-TO's that cover every conceivable topic will amaze you. What isn't in a how-to usually is lurking within a FAQ or Newsgroup archive. Many of the GNU packages now come with their own separate form of documentation. When this happens, it's usually referred to in the man page.

The documentation for an OpenBSD topic is almost entirely based around man pages (online documentation accessed by typing "man *program-name*" at a command prompt). As of OpenBSD 2.5, the man pages have been significantly enhanced. In the past, the man pages on many Unix systems appeared to be written under the assumption that the user already knew how to use the program. It was very difficult to figure out what a program did or how it worked via the man page. They were mostly useful as reference if you already knew how it worked but just forgot how to access a particular feature. Now, the OpenBSD man pages for many critical programs are finally useful to the first-time user. For example, the PPP man page will tell you everything from how PPP works to how it gets configured and run. It's even color coded for easier reading. Additionally, there are several man pages (afterboot, Section 8, in particular) that contain generic information about the system. These man pages can be accessed from the OpenBSD Web site.

There is a FAQ provided on the CD and on the Web site. This is more of a series of mini-how-to documents-waiting-to-happen than a FAQ. It contains a wealth of information not found elsewhere. We recommend reading it a number of times—even the parts that don't seem like they're relevant.

Additionally, the OpenBSD CD comes with a cover insert that contains useful install information—specifically a printout from a complete installation session. The session was carefully crafted to point out certain undocumented features that make the installation process much easier. The only problem is that the user is left to figure out how these features work, what they mean, and what other features are present. We do our best to correct this issue by providing a more thorough explanation in Chapter 8.

Outside of installation and core program issues, OpenBSD users will frequently find that they can get the answers to many questions by studying the FreeBSD and Linux documentation.

Nonetheless, there are many people who want to use OpenBSD because of its security features, yet can't deal with the lack of centralized, Web-based or printed documentation. If you're one of those people, then you've finally found some real documentation. One goal of this book is to help alleviate the lack of documentation that the OpenBSD community faces. The companion Web site has been designed partly as a resource for OpenBSD users. We have even placed the text of the OpenBSD installation and configuration chapters on the Web site as a "HOW-TO" document. We hope that this starts a trend.

General Security

OpenBSD is inherently more secure than Red Hat. As mentioned earlier, security experts have reviewed each line of code in the OpenBSD system many times. While this is impressive in-and-of itself, OpenBSD's security goes farther than just auditing, giving teeth to their motto "Secure by Default."

The basic installation automatically performs security tasks that no other operating system does out of the box. For example, it is configured to send an email out if any system configuration files have changed. The email contains a full run-down of every change that was made. This makes it very hard for someone to compromise the system without your knowledge. This capability can be added to other Unix systems (see our discussion of the "tripwire" program in Chapter 12, "Loose Notes," for more information).

Another major security benefit for the time being is that OpenBSD's level of security has discouraged many script kiddies (people, often teenagers, who run scripts to exploit known vulnerabilities in popular operating systems) from creating OpenBSD exploits. While this is bordering on security through obscurity, it has value because OpenBSD is often not targeted in the publicly available collections of exploits. Linux, on the other hand, is frequently the target of such exploits. One of the biggest reasons for this is that many of the popular exploits are based on security vulnerabilities found by the OpenBSD audit team. When the patch appears on OpenBSD's site, script kiddies know it's too late to exploit the OpenBSD platform, so the unaware Linux community becomes a ripe target.

Encryption and Other Cryptographic Issues

Encryption has always been a sticky issue for U.S. companies. Thanks to some completely inane laws, U.S. companies are not allowed to export products that contain encryption too powerful for the government to crack. The idea is that this will prevent criminals from communicating with uncrackable encryption. Typical of the U.S. government, the underlying assumption is that the only people capable of creating software with strong encryption reside within the United States. That products with strong encryption are commercially and freely available outside the United States hasn't seemed to change this viewpoint. As a result, U.S. companies can't compete in the global marketplace for products with strong encryption.

The OpenBSD product centralizes its development in Canada. Thus, it is immune to U.S. export regulations. All versions of OpenBSD include very strong cryptography throughout the core of the system. For example, the /etc/passwd file is strongly encrypted.

OpenBSD is also distributed with encryption solutions. KerberosIV and Pretty Good Privacy (PGP) are two encryption systems that are included with the standard distribution of OpenBSD. They both provide mechanisms for secure authentication and secure communication between client and server programs.

This is one of the greatest pillars of strength for OpenBSD—anyone in the world can use it and have strong encryption without any restrictions.

Red Hat, on the other hand, is not distributed with strong encryption because Red Hat is a U.S. company. While you can download strong encryption packages from international sites, this requires significantly more work, especially if you are trying to enhance core components of the system.

Support

Hands down, Linux takes the cake for support. For starters, basic support is provided for users who purchase the Red Hat package. Hewlett Packard is now offering support to Linux users, and IBM also supports it to a certain extent. For those willing to go to the net for support, there's a wealth of information available. The URLs www.linux.org and www.linux.com provide impressive online resources for every imaginable aspect of Linux. There are also many people who will respond to a desperate newsgroup posting. There are online chat rooms devoted to helping out Linux users. Some of the best chat rooms can be accessed from the Linux.com Web site, under the "chat" section. The larger Linux community has resulted in a very strong support system.

OpenBSD support is more difficult to find, although those who respond to your questions will often be *very* knowledgeable. There are a number of active newsgroups pertaining to OpenBSD. Daemonnews.org is an online magazine that talks about NetBSD, FreeBSD, and OpenBSD issues each month. This brings us to the next point: OpenBSD is similar enough to NetBSD and FreeBSD that you may find the needed support within these communities.

This book should contain enough information to get most people past the difficult issues for either OS. We're building a pretty limited system with very specific functionality. If you follow the instructions in the book closely, there should be little need for support.

Patches and Updates

OpenBSD updates on a regular, infrequent basis (twice a year). Patches (an efficient way of updating large or complex programs) are provided from a central location. Patches always address specific security concerns and occur infrequently. This is due to the incredible strength of the current release's security.

On the other hand, the Linux kernel constantly updates. Continuous development creates new security holes all the time. Keeping up with the latest Linux kernel release is very difficult and not always worthwhile. Release goals are primarily features and stability, whereas security is less of a concern. However, most updates are kernel level and you won't need to do most of them.

Sometimes, only source code patches are provided. This is actually a good thing—if you study the patch you will be able to learn more about the security hole. The inconvenient side to this is that you'll need to recompile affected programs when patches are released. The catch is that we'll be recommending the removal of the compiler from your firewall as an added security measure. This means installing a patch requires re-installing the compiler, recompiling some software, and then de-installing the compiler again. This will usually be an issue for either system, although binary patches and/or new RPM releases are often quick to appear in the Linux community.

Performance

For firewalling, both Linux and OpenBSD will offer very similar performance profiles. Various benchmarks show both systems to be nearly identical in execution speed. In general, it appears that OpenBSD has somewhat better heavy load stability. OpenBSD machines also tend to have somewhat longer uptimes (elapsed time before having to reboot) than Linux—notice the use of "somewhat." Both systems are very close in performance, and under certain configurations Linux may outperform OpenBSD.

Both operating systems provide significantly faster and more stable performance than Windows NT (benchmarked on the same machine). Linux and OpenBSD also fare favorably when compared to commercial Unix flavors. For example, one benchmark pits OpenBSD against Solaris, a commercial operating system from Sun Microsystems, and shows that OpenBSD is actually faster than Solaris for certain types of calculations.

Rumor has it that the fastest performance on a PC comes from FreeBSD, which has been specifically optimized for the PC architecture. It is for this reason that Yahoo! and cdrom.com (a high-traffic FTP server) are primarily run on FreeBSD.

Miscellaneous Issues

Beyond the various considerations outlined above, we will touch on three other issues that one might want to consider. The first deal with the security implications of the differing development philosophies. The second is applicable if you plan on working with OpenBSD or Linux for other projects in the future. The third deals with the large amount of "my operating system is better" conversation that appears on the Internet.

Development Philosophy

There is a significant difference between the development philosophies for Linux and OpenBSD. Jason Downs, an OpenBSD developer, describes these differing philosophies in an article for ComputerBits magazine (www .computerbits.com/archive/19990300/bsd.htm):

> Linux itself is actually only a kernel: the portion of an operating system that handles devices, manages memory, runs programs and does other things like provide an interface between the computer and its network. Everything else that makes up the Linux operating system is contained in separate programs, usually written by different programmers than those who work on the kernel. The entire system

is integrated and packaged by yet another person or company and sold or given to users as a distribution. The distributor has little or nothing to do with the actual development of the kernel or of the other programs that they're packaging: they just make a few changes, compile everything and create installation tools.

OpenBSD and the other BSD systems are not developed like this. All user programs are developed in conjunction with the kernel, from the same collective source tree . . . . This allows a much higher level of system quality control and better overall integration: If an internal API [Application Programming Interface] is added or changed, all programs using it will be changed at the same time, without the system having to remain compatible with previous interfaces. When a security feature is added to the kernel, all of the user programs that should be using it will be modified at the same time. Conversely, no single person or organization has complete oversight of every program that makes up what is considered the Linux operating system.

What does this philosophical difference mean in real terms? For example, consider buffer overflows. We covered those briefly at the end of Chapter 2, "Fundamental Internet Security Issues."

The concept of a buffer overflow has been around for a very long time, and exploits have been around nearly as long. Nevertheless, new exploits are constantly turning up. Since the beginning of 1998, the Computer Emergency Response Team, (CERT; see Chapter 12) has issued 17 general advisories. Of these, about a third involved overt buffer overflow exploits.

Once the concept of a buffer overflow was understood, the OpenBSD team went through the OS code and ripped out every potential buffer overflow. That's not to say that the same thing hasn't also happened to Linux, but the OpenBSD team have a clear mandate to do that sort of thing—even if it means they can't do new features that people want.

We don't want to scare anyone. There haven't been any CERT advisories regarding Linux kernel holes in that same period, either. But there's clear added value in an OS that makes security a formal requirement across the *entire* distribution base, even at the expense of chrome.

If you want to avail yourself of this, it will mean learning to live without that chrome—and indeed functionality. Your firewall is your machine, so you have to make the call. One author uses Red Hat, the other uses OpenBSD, so even we can't quite make up our minds.

Suitability Outside the Scope of This Book

After reading through this book, you might decide to embark on other projects with either Linux or OpenBSD. The factors affecting your decision will be different depending on the application you are developing.

OpenBSD makes a great platform for highly sensitive or exposed servers, such as Web servers, FTP servers, or internal NFS servers. It is important to remember that OpenBSD's security will only protect you against operating system level attacks. There are plenty of opportunities for security holes in Web server software and FTP software. NFS might be secure from buffer overflows, but that won't protect you if you make a configuration error that allows anyone to read/write all of your files. With either OS, you'll still have to monitor your application's security closely.

Linux is definitely a better choice for machines that need extended features, rather than security. This includes desktops, development machines, and file/application/database servers. While OpenBSD can run Linux software, the lack of support and thorough documentation makes it more difficult to use. As an example, the Red Hat 6 distribution makes it easy to run a nice desktop environment such as KDE or GNOME. With OpenBSD, you just get X Windows with the distribution. It's up to you to get GNOME or KDE running.

Flame War

Both Linux and BSD have advocates. Some of these advocates are intelligent people. Others consider the opposing camp to be the enemy and are constantly trying to convince everyone that *their* operating system is superior. Initially, there was an understandably strong resistance to Linux among the BSD community. They were worried that it would pull developers away from their own operating system, resulting in fewer software packages for the BSD platform. The intelligent developers quickly found an intelligent solution to the problem: They made their systems compatible with Linux. Now, BSD organizers tell developers to write for the Linux platform first, then port to BSD if desired. Their logic is that Linux has a larger user base, so the developer will find a larger population of interested beta-testers and codevelopers. Because BSD can run Linux programs, the amount of available software will still increase. Eventually, if high performance on a BSD platform is desired, someone will port the software to BSD.

Summary

OpenBSD is a remarkable endeavor. Its existence almost illustrates its value, given the saturated marketplace for free Unix-based operating systems. When OpenBSD began, Linux was already gaining popularity, and NetBSD and FreeBSD were well established. OpenBSD was able to convince many users from both camps to switch over on the basis of its heightened security alone.

That said, OpenBSD is not for everyone. A portion of the security was obtained by removing unnecessary programs from the core distribution. This can make it less user friendly than Red Hat. It is often used as the foundation for firewalls and other systems where the emphasis is on security rather than features. It does not make a very good desktop system, and isn't the easiest system to configure. Most of its users are very competent at Unix administration. There is *very little* in the way of documentation. This can be especially frustrating for Linux users, who have long been spoiled by the vast wealth of well-organized and easily accessible documentation.

Linux is the Operating System juggernaut of the 1990s, and one of the largest distributed software projects ever. It's poised to lead a revolution in the way software is developed. Red Hat provides a convenient package with lots of helpful features for beginners and expert users alike. It is constantly in development, with components undergoing daily to weekly updates.

That said, Linux is not for everybody. If security is of high concern, you'll want to go with OpenBSD. Linux machines are high-profile targets in the script-kiddie community. Security problems are often discovered only after they have been exploited.

From here, you are now ready to choose the hardware for your system. The next chapter will steer you through the treacherous waters of hardware compatibility issues.

## CHAPTER 5

Getting the Right Hardware

I n the previous chapter, we helped you select an operating system for your firewall. This chapter assumes you've made your choice and are now ready to take decisive action. If you haven't yet made up your mind, you should find a rock garden somewhere and contemplate matters before continuing.

In this chapter, we'll help you choose appropriate hardware for each operating system. We'll discuss where you might get it. We'll think about the pros and cons of putting your own system together from components, versus buying it off the shelf. The performance of your system will be important, so we'll discuss what makes a system good for the job. Finally, we'll talk about putting your machine together.

After this chapter, you should have a few boxes sitting in front of you. Some will be cardboard. One should be heavy, metallic, and probably beige. If all goes well, the metal one will become a critical part of your network and the others will go into storage. If you find that the reverse has occurred, you'll probably also find this book more useful as a doorstop. At any rate, from here on in when we refer to a *box* we're talking about the expensive whirring gadget with blinking lights.

When you've worked through this chapter, your box should contain hardware you believe to be compatible with the OS of your choice, and in working order.

If you turn the box on, it should make some noise and attempt to read the floppy/CD-ROM drive. It should even show a few lines of boot information on the screen. If you can get to that point, you'll be ready to go ahead to the next chapter and install the OS.

Hardware Overview

What we're trying to build here is a pretty simple machine with the following components:

- A CPU on a motherboard
- Some memory
- A graphics card, monitor, keyboard, hard and floppy disc drives, a CD-ROM drive, and a mouse
- A modem, ethernet card, or other device to connect to the outside world
- One or two ethernet cards to connect to your internal network

This isn't rocket science. The system is performing a relatively simple and highly repetitive task. Therefore, the design should be as simple as possible. There's a maxim about this: KISS (it stands for keep it simple, stupid). The more complex this machine, the more that can go wrong with it. Therefore, we'll keep it as basic and boring as we can.

Lest you think we're belaboring the point, take a look at the Linux Router Project. You can find these people at www.linuxrouter.org. They're serving humanity by making a router so simple that it can fit on a single 1.44Mb floppy—the OS, the routing code, everything. Take an empty box, stick the floppy in, boot it up, and hey presto!—it's a router. That's terse. That's simple. We're not going to go that far. Being that terse has some design implications that we don't want here. For example, instead of just editing a configuration file, you need to remake the boot floppy using special tools. You'll need another machine configured to work with these special tools, since the floppy doesn't have room for anything other than the essentials. Simplicity in configuration is sacrificed for simplicity in operation. Not that this is a bad thing—it's just not what we're writing about. But it's impressive stuff, and it should bring home to you the idea that *simple is good*.

Intel, or What?

Both Linux and OpenBSD run on Intel processors—the heart of your typical PC computer. They've also been ported to a whole lot of other platforms as well. In the mainstream, Linux also runs on Alpha processors (Digital's 64-bit super-fast chip) and Sparc processors (Sun Microsystems' industrially-robust chip). OpenBSD is even more widely ported—it runs on alpha chips, Amiga, old HP workstations, old Macintosh systems, newer Macintosh systems, Sparc systems, and a few other really esoteric systems you'd have a tough job finding. If you want to get really crazy with it, Linux has even been ported to 3Com's Personal Digital Assistant, the Palm. If you were of such a mind, you could run your firewall on a PDA.

But please don't.

We think that Intel-type hardware is your best choice. It's easy to find. It's cheap enough. The variety of network cards, graphics cards, and other cards supported for Intel systems is much greater than for any of the other systems. But the real clincher, the reason that makes us head straight for our Intel hardware cupboard, is that the majority of people are using Linux and OpenBSD with Intel hardware. Another maxim applies: Go with the flow. A larger user base tends to expose problems rapidly. More people than just you will have had trouble getting your preferred network card to work. More people than just you will have wondered exactly what kind of cable they need to connect that particular disc to that particular interface card. And more people than just you will be testing their firewalls in production. The Linux community responds rapidly to software problems and tends to fix most problems within days, if not hours. If something's not right with the code, it's likely to be found and fixed within a short period of time.

Let's be clear about the moral, there: Don't get too adventurous with this. Trailblazing is great: It's educational, and it's good for the soul. But it's not right for your firewall. When it comes to your firewall, do what other people are doing. Build a nice robust firewall like they're building. Then take off for a holiday and blaze trails in the backcountry. Meanwhile your firewall can stay home and tick merrily along, doing exactly what it's supposed to do.

A final note before we continue. When we talk of Intel hardware, note that we're not advocating Intel's processors in particular. More companies than just Intel make CPUs for PCs. The others have their good points too, and we'll come back to them shortly.

Buying the System

Now you have to get the hardware. There are basically two ways of doing this. You can buy the system prebuilt, or you can buy the components and assemble the system yourself.

You already know what we're going to say, right? You're groaning already at the thought of having to assemble your own system, with your own screwdriver, aren't you? Well, you're absolutely right. We suggest you build from parts. The real problem with prebuilt systems is their tendency to have strange, unlabelled hardware in them. This strange, unlabelled hardware is designed to work with Microsoft Windows, so it usually does. But with Linux or OpenBSD, you're taking a lot of system responsibility from the vendor's hands into your own. You need a much clearer idea about what's happening under the hood.

Recently, some companies have appeared on the market selling Linux-oriented PC systems—systems that are either designed to run Linux, or even have it pre-installed. These don't tend to suffer from the 'unlabelled hardware' effect mentioned above. However, we'd still advise making your system from components if you feel that you can. One day, this box will go wrong. All computers do. On that day, you will have to open it up and fix it. That day will be much less traumatic if it isn't your first time inside the box. If you really don't feel comfortable building your own box, contact your system vendor and ask if they can build a box specifically for a Linux or OpenBSD installation. If they seem happy to do that, read the rest of this chapter and work out exactly what you'll need, and tell them. See what they say.

Many people who build their own systems from components do so to save money. We aren't advising you to do it on the cheap. If you choose a reputable hardware supplier, they'll be willing to work with you. They'll help to make sure that the motherboard you're buying supports the memory you want to put in it, and the processor you plan to get, and that it's got enough PCI or ISA slots for the interface cards you're getting. They'll check that the case you're buying fits the motherboard, and that it'll hold all the discs you want to put in it, and that you don't forget the floppy drive. They'll understand that when you specify that the network card should be a 5e309, you mean a 5e309, not something 5e309-compliant or a 5e309b. They'll probably charge a little more than J. Random Weasel's House of Honest Hardware, but it's worth it.

We're not suggesting that you build your system from scratch to save money, or to indulge masochistic tendencies. We suggest you do it because then you'll know *exactly* what's inside the box.

In case we've not made this clear, we also suggest that you buy the distribution of the operating system. Firstly, you get a fresh copy of your very own on CD, which makes installation significantly easier. You also need both the CD and the documentation on a fairly frequent basis. Borrowing the disk from a friend might seem like a wise move at first, but a few weeks later the daily "visits" prompted solely by your need to borrow the CD may begin to tax your friendship.

There are quite a few other reasons for buying a distribution: With Red Hat Linux, you qualify for installation help if you're running tier one hardware and you purchased your own copy (check Red Hat's Web site, currently at www.redhat.com/support/index.html). You also get the excellent Red Hat installation guide book, which is about as horse's mouth as you can get for good installation advice. With OpenBSD you help to fund the project, which is more than just a warm, fuzzy glow. If you're running OpenBSD, and you appreciate that level of security, you really need all those code auditors to keep on auditing that code and finding, and fixing, every little hole they can locate. Neither distribution is expensive. Buy your own copy.

NOTE

■■■■■ Needless to say, check www.openbsd.org and www.redhat.com for precise details.

The Components

Now we're going to dive right into the exact details of hardware. There are a few points that we hope this section will make clear.

Branded hardware is good. In case we weren't successful at communicating the point about *unlabelled hardware* earlier, let's belabor it: Some suppliers will try and tell you that their card is just the same as the card you were asking for, or that it's "100 percent compatible" with what you really want. Ignore them. They have no idea what they're talking about. You need to get the exact part you requested.

Expensive branded hardware is generally better. This is a bit of a shame, but generally true. The more reputable manufacturers tend to be happier about releasing their specifications to the volunteers who develop Linux device drivers, and these same manufacturers tend to charge more for their products. This is, of course, a broadsweeping generalization, but there's truth in it.

Recommended branded hardware is best. Sounds like a truism? In short, hardware that is widely accepted and known by other people to work is the best. Which other people? Recommended by whom? Well, the best of all is hardware recommended by the people who release the operating systems. Red Hat and OpenBSD both maintain lists of compatible hardware.

NOTE

■■■■■ At the time of writing, Red Hat and OpenBSD hardware compatibility guides can be found at www.redhat.com/corp/support/hardware/index.html, and www.openbsd.org/i386.html, respectively. If these or any other URLs in this book have changed, check the companion Web site for updated references.

Red Hat divides hardware into several classes: *tier-one supported, tier-two supported, compatible* (tier-three), and *unsupported*. They describe tier-one hardware as "hardware that the Linux kernel can detect and use. It is known to be reliable in-house and in the field." They describe tier-two hardware as "hardware that should be detected and usable with the Linux kernel. However, some users have reported problems with some versions of this hardware, or with the hardware's interaction with other hardware." We would strongly recommend going for tier-one supported hardware.

OpenBSD's hardware list doesn't subdivide in this manner, so anything on their supported list should be fine.

Hardware recommended by the community is also good, particularly if it helps you decide between two otherwise equally favored cards. Ask around. Listen to people's horror stories and happy endings, and learn from them. Assuming that you don't live next door to a hardware guru, the community can be found on the USENet newsgroups, particularly comp.os.linux.hardware and linux.redhat. Nothing on USENet should be taken as gospel, but you can learn from other people's mistakes, even when the people are unfriendly.

Keep your hands away from the cutting edge. Another truism, this time pointing the other way. Open source operating systems are dependent on volunteer labor to make things work. Commercial OS vendors, particularly ones based in Washington state, get the people who make the hardware to write the drivers. Those hardware manufacturers make very sure that their drivers are compatible with the commercial OS in question. OK, OK, they make fairly sure. Now we'd guess that four times out of five the volunteers who write the open-source drivers are better programmers than the ones who write the commercial drivers. If you doubt such an assertion, judge them by their products; read www.fsf.org/software/reliability.html. These volunteers probably write substantially better drivers than the commercial coders, not least because they have total access to the OS source. But the commercial coders have a huge advantage: They get access not only to all the technical data while the hardware's being developed, but also access to the testing facilities. Although vendors are beginning to clue-in that not all of us who buy their hardware go home and run a commercial OS on it, they're still pretty reluctant to let the volunteer coders into their development process early on.

This all means that driver development for open-source systems often lags a little way behind the release of the hardware. It's the nature of things. Even when a driver is released, the nature of the open-source development model means that the early adopters are beta-testing. We know that many of you think early adopters of commercial code are beta-testing too. This may be true. Be that as it may, the open-source beta testers are aware that they're beta-testing. You don't want to be a beta-tester on your firewall. Sure, beta-test on your development machine; the more feedback and fast testing these developers can get, the more robust the code is, and we all benefit. But don't do it on your firewall.

Tried and trusted hardware is what we want. Not too old. Not too new. Not too cheap. We want well-known hardware that a lot of people have used and found to be up to the job.

Processors (a.k.a. CPUs)

We need to talk about performance a little here, so get a fresh cup of tea (or, if you insist, coffee) and sit back.

The PC world has historically had a strange fascination with processor clock speed (what is really important is system performance, but that's a hard thing to measure and a very hard thing to benchmark). A fast CPU, however, doesn't guarantee a fast system. To build a really fast system you should invest in system components other than the processor. For example, fast memory in quantity, fast discs correctly laid out, well-chosen network cards, and so forth. All of these components can make at least as much difference in the speed of your system as the fastest processor you can buy.

Performance is also application specific; a system that's optimized for intensely mathematical work like cryptography may well not make a good games machine. If you work on it until it's a good games machine, you may well find it still doesn't make a good router. Once you've turned it into a good router, you may well find that it's no longer so good for the mathematical work. It will certainly have absorbed more money than if you'd just set out to make it good for routing. So, let's set out to build a good firewall.

Firewalling can be processor intensive, if the firewall's *ruleset*—the list of instructions about what to allow through and what to turn away—is adequately long and complex, or if the bandwidth of the slowest link to which the firewall is attached is sufficiently high. (Why the slowest link? Well, it doesn't matter if you can't keep up with your very fast internal network's attempts to reach the outside world. As long as you can keep up with the responses coming down the slow link from the outside world, the performance of the system as a whole will not be hindered by the presence of the firewall. In other words, your firewall won't be the bottleneck.)

Unless you are lucky enough to have a T-3 (this is network-person-speak for "an awful lot of bandwidth") coming into your house, however, your firewalling needs are unlikely to be processor intensive. One of the authors has an internal network of four machines, of which two are always extremely busy, all IP-Masqueraded and firewalled behind a system that's well over five years old. It's based around a 66 MHz 486, with 32 Mb of memory and an ISA network card. It's quite enough for the 56k modem that makes the connection to the Internet. In fact, the firewall hardly even turns a sweat. Another of the authors has a 256 kb leased-line, which ends up in an OpenBSD box. This box acts as a router and DMZ firewall for four systems, and another 15 are IP-Masqueraded and firewalled behind it. It's a 333 MHz Pentium-clone system with 32 Mb of memory. It, too, doesn't break a sweat.

What I hope we're getting across is that being a firewall doesn't require the latest, greatest hardware. It won't benefit from it. It may make more economic sense for you to get a bright, shiny new desktop system and turn your oldest, saddest machine into the firewall, providing the rest of the hardware in it is compatible with your operating system of choice.

CPU Vendors

The two major manufacturers of clone chips have historically been AMD and Cyrix. Recently Cyrix decided that it no longer wished to play catch-up to Intel, and has withdrawn from the CPU rat race. AMD has also decided to stop playing catch-up, but they've chosen the other route. Their K7 chip promises to leap-frog the Pentium III technology by a significant factor. You can find more about both AMD and Cyrix at www.amd.com/ and www.cyrix.com/, respectively.

Recall, also, what we said earlier about our not requiring Intel hardware. Several companies make Intel-clone processors. They fit in the same hole on the motherboard that Intel processors do. They look very similar, but they cost a lot less. OpenBSD explicitly permits all the major clones chips in their supported hardware page. Red Hat is more cautious, and only have Intel processors included in tier one. However, one of the authors is writing this on a Red Hat 5.2 system with an AMD K6 processor inside. Another of the authors works for a company where every desktop box is a K6-based Red Hat machine. Bottom line: *your mileage may vary*.

If you're nervous about a clone, but would like the speed, try to find an old Pentium—100 or 133 MHz Pentium chips are pretty common. Get a motherboard that will support both the old Pentium, and something faster, like a high-end Cyrix or K6. If you have any trouble, you can keep every part of the system except the fast processor. You'll still have a working system, and you'll be out a very small sum of money. You can probably even resell the processor.

A Pentium-II is probably more power than you need. A Pentium-III is definitely more power than you need. These chips are expensive, too. We suggest that you avoid them.

As a closing comment on processors, let's just consider the number 1. One is a good number. One is a friendly number. One is also an excellent number of processors to have in your system. Hopefully, you've taken the hint from our diatribe on performance that the usual problem with building a firewall box is getting a slow-enough processor. Hopefully, you weren't thinking of trying to build a multiprocessor box. Well, please don't. Red Hat 6 supports that, but OpenBSD doesn't. Don't try it.

Memory

The amount of memory is not likely to be your limiting requirement. Both OSes will run quite happily in 8 Mb of memory. However, you might wish to do something wild like start up X (Linux and OpenBSD's windowing system) on the console, which will benefit from a little more memory. The author with the 486/66-32 Mb firewall often uses it as a 'guest' console, allowing trusted visitors to the office access to an email and Web terminal. We wouldn't recommend that, for security reasons which we covered at the end of Chapter 3, "How Secure Should your Network Be?" but it just goes to show how little memory is needed. 32 Mb is enough for most of us. You might go to 64 Mb if you're firewalling a T-1.

Speed of memory is always worth maximizing. Memory is used by the OS as buffer space for all sorts of data involved in firewalling. If you're putting together a new system, it's probably worth getting the fastest memory you can. For most modern systems, that means 100 MHz synchronous memory (SDRAM), often known as *PC100 memory*. Check with your trusted vendor.

If possible, use ECC or parity memory. Parity adds some functionality to see if the data in RAM have been corrupted. ECC extends this functionality and attempts to correct some bit corruption errors on the fly. If you aren't using ECC/parity memory, you may get data corruption and other abnormalities. This can occur due to power fluctuations and radiation related issues. Unix workstation manufacturers have been using parity (and now ECC) memory for several years in all of their product lines. Take the hint.

If, despite our best advice, you decided to build a Pentium-II system, bear in mind that the memory may need to come in pairs of matched SIMMs. Check with your vendor.

Motherboards

At first glance, there doesn't seem to be a lot to choose between motherboards. You will need one that supports the kind of processor you intend to get, at the clock speed that the processor supports. It will need to support the memory you intend to put in it, and have enough PCI/ISA slots for the network cards you intend to use. Your trusted vendor on this will most likely get you what you need.

Nevertheless, some motherboards can have problems. Red Hat lists the ones known to be incompatible on their hardware compatibility page. OpenBSD aren't officially forbidding anything, but they note that "custom servers" can present problems due to specialized BIOS code. It's not completely clear what they mean by 'custom' servers, but our best guess is very large, multiprocessor boxes or other ultra-high-end PCs. You shouldn't be looking at that kind of system for your firewall. If you have that much money to burn, go and buy 50 more copies of this book instead.

Our recommendation is to get the most generic, middle-of-the-road motherboard you can. Both of the authors have had a lot of success with Gigabyte (www.gigabyte.com.tw/) motherboards, though again your mileage may vary. Keep away from anything that looks interesting and you should be fine.

Laptops are not a good choice for firewalls. They tend to have lots of strange hardware tweaks, like custom graphics cards or strange BIOSes, that present problems to open-source operating systems. They don't deal well with multiple network cards, since they tend not to have PCI or ISA slots, and you can run out of PCMCIA slots very quickly. Admittedly, some laptops are mainstream enough that Linux or OpenBSD may have been adapted to them; you can find the Linux Laptop Project at www.cs.utexas.edu/users/kharker/linux-laptop/ if you're interested.

Hopefully, you weren't thinking of running your firewall on a laptop. A laptop isn't an appropriate platform for the job. If you do have a laptop that you want to dedicate to the cause, consider using it as part of your network analysis/intrusion detection arsenal. The portability of the laptop will come in particularly handy when you need to track down a hacker on your network. We'll talk more about this in Chapter 11, "Intrusion Detection and Response."

Network Cards

Take another look at the OS hardware compatibility information available at the URLs presented earlier in the chapter. It's a good idea to bookmark these sites.

Generally, for Linux, nearly every card from a particular vendor is supported, instead of the three most recent cards from every vendor under the sun. As we have intimated, this is because some vendors are more cooperative about releasing inside information on their cards to the people who write the Linux drivers. You might think that vendors would be delighted to have extremely competent people writing drivers for their hardware—that make it more saleable, for free. Sadly, many vendors still haven't caught on. Reward those that have by buying their stuff. Tier-one supported cards listed on the Red Hat site are best, but those tier-two supported cards that we have tried work just fine.

At this point, we're going to give a quick plug for CESDIS, Goddard Space Flight Centre's "Centre of Excellence in Space Data and Information Sciences." Why? Not because they invented BEOWULF clusters, one of the more successful attempts to build a massive parallel computer using commodity hardware and Linux. They did invent that, and it's very cool, and well worth a look, but that's not why we'll praise them here. We will praise them because, in the process of building BEOWULF, they found out an awful lot about Linux networking and network drivers, and they make this information available to the public. At the time of this writing, it can be found at http://cesdis.gsfc .nasa.gov/linux/drivers/. You can find drivers for all sorts of weird and wonderful cards here. If you are absolutely forced to use an odd network card, you can go to CESDIS to find out why that was a bad idea and how you can still make it work.

For OpenBSD, all sorts of cards are supported, as they were in its parent, NetBSD. Our guess is that this points to BSD's roots in the halls of academia, where connecting computers together was the main point of having them. Pick one of the many permitted cards and go with it.

A quick word on cards that support *plug-and-play* (or, as the cynics call it, "plug-and-pray"): This technology is not well supported under either Linux or OpenBSD. If you buy a card that might support plug-and-play, make sure the plug-and-play features can be disabled. Plug-and-play is a concept that is tightly linked to Microsoft Windows. Some hardware expects to interact with Windows and gets rather upset when it finds something else. Most cards will let you disable PnP, but you often have to use a DOS program to do it. At least one of the authors doesn't have DOS, but he has found that some hardware suppliers would do it for him if asked nicely. Needless to say, he buys a lot more hardware from them than from vendors who look blank when asked about disabling plug-and-play.

In the beginning of the chapter, we mentioned that you might want several network cards. This is in case you decide to build a three-legged firewall, as described in Chapter 3, or in case your Internet connection is presented to you as a 10-baseT network connection instead of a modem. Linux requires some special boot instructions to recognize two network cards. We will come back to that in Chapter 6, "Installing Linux." If you do plan to buy several network cards, buy them all now, and get the same model for all of them. Linux users should initially only install one card. It will be much easier to get the others installed and recognized *after* you've finished installing the Linux operating system. OpenBSD users should take exactly the opposite advice. The OpenBSD installer will make configuring multiple cards a simple task, so install them all in the machine now.

Graphics Card

Sadly, you have to have a graphics card (unless you're using an Amiga or Mac as your firewalling platform). Your PC won't boot without it. However, you're not going to be doing much graphically intensive work on this machine. Find the cheapest card you can that's approved for your OS and go with that.

In both Linux and OpenBSD's cases, approval for graphics cards relates to their performance with Xfree86, the publicly available Intel hardware port of the X window system. Because you're not going to be running X on your firewall, this isn't likely to be a consideration. So whether you can only get a horrendously old card, or a blindingly new cutting-edge card, you should still be able to get the system working well (the old card will be cheaper, though).

It's worth noting that there are AGP, PCI, and ISA graphic cards on the market (although ISA cards are quite rare). We recommend AGP cards if your motherboard supports AGP, because it saves you a PCI slot that may be needed for a network card. An ISA card would also help free up a PCI slot, but we recommend against using technology that old in your firewall system. It could create numerous conflicts that would be very difficult to fix.

Hard Discs

Since we've decided against the Linux Router Project's approach of keeping the entire OS on a single floppy, you need a hard disc. You don't need a particularly big one, however, and you don't need a blindingly fast one.

The two main contender technologies are IDE and SCSI. SCSI discs come in narrow, wide, and ultra-wide flavors, but they're all a lot more expensive than IDE discs. We would go with an IDE disc, and we'd be happy with 1 Gb. You're not going to be keeping much data on this machine. However, we haven't seen a 1 Gb IDE disc for sale since Richard got back from the crusades, so it's our guess that you'll end up with a 3 Gb disc at the very least. Oh well.

CD-ROM Drives

We can't see any good reason not to use a stock IDE CD-ROM drive. We will suggest avoiding Mitsumi models, since they are notorious for being problematic.

Cases

Provided you get a case that fits the motherboard you're buying, there's really not much that can go wrong with the case. However, some cases will make you regret the purchase a lot more than others. You're going to be fiddling around inside this case quite a lot, however, and you'll be trying to fit your own motherboard. A case with good ergonomics and easy access will eventually be worth its weight in gold. Some cases have sides that swing out with the motherboard attached. Some have power supply units (PSUs) that slide in and out on rails. Some have easily removable and reinstallable covers. All these features are good. Others have sharp or unfinished internal edges that will cut you, or require 47 screws to attach the cover, or come with eight odd little plastic widgets that hold the motherboard in place very permanently indeed. All these features are bad. Spend a little time and money to get a case that will be your friend.

NOTE

Blood is bad for circuit boards. Plus, you don't want them to get a taste for it. Trust us on this.

A word on failure: It's pretty annoying for a desktop machine to fail, but you can live with that. However, if your firewall is providing Internet access for all your machines, failure of the firewall constitutes failure of your entire Internet connection. Incidentally, if your firewall is not the only thing providing Internet access to all your machines, then your firewall might not be worthwhile.

Unfortunately, PSUs tend to fail with monotonous regularity. Discs are about the only thing that we think fail more often, and we'll come to them in a minute. Some cases, particularly those intended for server-class systems, come with dual PSUs. The idea here is that both run normally, but either is powerful enough to power the box alone. This keeps them less stressed in normal operation, and they therefore run cooler. If one ever fails, the machine doesn't die on the spot. These cases are usually quite a lot more expensive than regular cases, but they may be worth it. Another slightly cheaper option is to buy a second PSU at the time you buy the case and the other parts—you'll probably get it at a good discount—then keep it on a shelf until it's needed. Label it well.

When you buy your case, you may also wish to buy an anti-static wrist strap and some cable ties. The anti-static strap prevents you from frying your expensive electronics the moment you first touch it, and you shouldn't touch any parts of your machine unless one end of the strap is attached to the case and you're wearing the other end. We personally also like to have the case plugged into the wall socket (and turned off!) to improve the grounding, but we can't comment on the safety of this because we're not electricians. The cable ties are to let you make the spaghetti cabling inside the case behave itself after it's all correctly connected. Use them extensively.

Modems

If your needs are basic, your connection to the Internet will be a modem. We recommend using an external modem because it's more modularized—the modules being separated by a serial cable. Additionally, all the blinking lights on the modem can be very useful for diagnosing problems. Some internal modems do have blinking lights, but they're generally at the back of the machine where they're a lot harder to monitor.

If you do go with an internal modem, you might wish to disable the second external serial port in the motherboard's BIOS; it can help to minimize internal conflicts. See the following section on BIOSes for details.

Other Considerations

Again, failure in the firewall can be a *bad thing*. Although failure in the PSU is annoying—your firewall's going to be dead until you get a new PSU—failure in the disc can be catastrophic. If you don't have backups, your whole firewall will vanish. You can replace the disc, but you're going to have to rebuild the system from scratch. If you do have backups, you're still going to have to install enough of an OS to be able to read and then restore the tapes, but you're going to be down for a while.

An alternative is hardware *RAID* (Redundant Array of Inexpensive Discs), although it's usually done with high-end SCSI drives and might better be called a Redundant Array of Particularly Expensive Discs. An in-depth discussion of the nature of RAID is somewhat beyond the scope of this paragraph, but information can be found at many places, www.repairsite .com/info.htm among others. One particular aspect of RAID, known as RAID-1 or "disc mirroring," is of interest here. Instead of having one disc with everything on it, you have two. Both of them have everything on. Every change made to one disc is automatically made to the other as well. If one disc fails, the other is still there and will run the system. When the first is replaced, the contents of the second are automatically copied onto it, and life continues sanely.

RAID software is built into Linux, but it can be pretty hairy to configure, and we would not recommend it. However, you can do cheap and cheerful hardware RAID with two IDE drives and a small piece of dedicated hardware that does writes to both discs. The system thinks that it has only one disc. Such hardware can be obtained from ARCO (www.arcoide.com), and doubtless from other places, too. Ask your favorite Web search engine about "IDE," "RAID," and "mirroring." See what happens.

One other item worth considering is an additional case fan. Many cases have a place for a second fan. Installing one can significantly improve airflow through the case. This will keep your components cool and will extend their life. When you install the fan, first determine which way the primary case fan blows (usually on the power supply and it usually blows outwards). Hook up the second fan so it creates an air corridor through the case (if the power supply fan blows outward, the other fan should be on the other side of the case blowing inward). Another useful item is cheesecloth. Use it to cover all of the intake vents. This will prevent dust from collecting within your machine. Make sure you clean it regularly or you may end up cutting off the air supply.

Building the Box

This can be pretty traumatic if you let yourself think about it. The bravest of us have received a big box in the mail, unpacked a motherboard and 38 little anti-static bags, spread them all over the floor, and burst out crying.

Well, don't think about it.

Firstly, your vendor manuals are your new friends. You're going to grow to love them. Read them and inwardly digest them. The motherboard manual, in particular, will take you gently through the details of setting all the motherboard jumpers correctly. These jumpers control such things as processor speed and board clock rates. Most motherboard manuals will have lookup tables that show you the settings for all relevant jumpers on a processor-by-processor basis. The trickiest part is connecting the tiny led and power wires from the case to the appropriate pins on the motherboard. Often a flashlight can help in reading the pin labels. Just take it slowly and gently, and think logically.

Try building the box in stages. The aim of the game is to get the box to recognize the floppy drive. You'll need some memory, the graphics card, the motherboard, the floppy drive, the processor and the keyboard, but that's all. Get it to the boot stage with this limited kit, then add in pieces one at a time and keep trying to boot. Maybe add the rest of the memory, then try one network card, and then try a hard disc.

TIP

Place the CD-ROM on the secondary IDE controller as "MASTER." Do not try to use it as a slave to the primary controller.

If you have two hard drives in a RAID array, use a separate power lead for each drive.

Take a moment to determine which motherboard socket is for the Primary IDE controller and which is for the Secondary controller. Also note the order of the PCI sockets—is PCI 0 the leftmost socket or the rightmost on the motherboard?

Building a system from components can be very frustrating, but as we said earlier, you'll have it back in pieces one day when it goes wrong. Better now than then. It's also a completely logical process. The motherboard does not hate you—yet (the hate circuitry doesn't kick in until the operating system has been installed). If something's wrong, it can be discovered and solved. Keep re-reading the documentation. Experiment with moving parts around— maybe you have the memory in the wrong slot, or the processor settings don't match the motherboard jumpers.

Your life will be much easier if your machine is capable of booting off of the CD-ROM drive. Setting up the machine to boot off of the CD-ROM drive now will also help you determine if the drive is connected properly. This involves making some changes to the BIOS settings and potentially a bit of troubleshooting. After the OS is installed and the firewall is setup, you should make sure to change the settings back so that the machine DOESN'T boot off the CD-ROM. Otherwise, if someone leaves a CD in the CD-ROM drive, which is pretty common, then when your firewall reboots it will either sit there forever (bad) or try to boot off the CD-ROM in the drive (worse).

BIOS Tweaking

The BIOS, or Basic Input/Output System, is the chip on the motherboard that serves as a repository for all sorts of settings relating to the low-level hardware configuration. It provides access to the floppy, CD-ROM and hard drives and enables the operating system to communicate with other peripherals, such as the keyboard, mouse and printer. It is responsible for everything that happens up to the point where an OS is loaded from either the floppy, CD-ROM or hard-drive. As such, you will need to work with it in order to enable booting off of the CD-ROM. We'll give you a general overview here; you can learn more about BIOS at www.sysopt.com/biosdef.html.

When you first boot a PC, hitting the delete key will usually bring you into the BIOS configuration screen (your motherboard may use a different key—check the manual). There are two BIOS configuration settings necessary to enable CD-ROM booting. First you need to let the BIOS know that you have a CD-ROM drive in the system. This is often accomplished from a configuration screen with a title that's something along the lines of "Standard CMOS Setup." If you don't see this option, look for "IDE," "HDD," or "Hard Disk/Drive." The screen you want should have a table with four rows (sometimes this is on the initial screen and the menu is across the top or bottom). The first column should read: Primary Master, Primary Slave, Secondary Master, Secondary Slave.

If your CD-ROM is connected as Primary Slave, then you need to make sure the value for the TYPE column is set to either "CD-ROM" or "AUTO" if there is no "CD-ROM" value. Every BIOS interface is designed differently, so please refer to your motherboard manual if your BIOS configuration screen doesn't match this description, or if you're excessively confused.

NOTE

While you're on the IDE controller screen, you should also check to see if the hard drive is properly configured—if in doubt, setting the TYPE value to "AUTO" for the Primary Master drive won't hurt. If the AUTO setting isn't available, there may be another BIOS configuration screen for "IDE HDD auto detection." This process will try to determine the proper drive configuration automatically. If all else fails, you may need to input your hard drive geometry information by hand.

The other necessary configuration involves telling the BIOS to try booting off of the CD before booting from the hard disk. This is often done from a screen titled "BIOS FEATURES SELECTION." The setting you're looking for says something like "boot sequence: A, C, SCSI." You want to change this to read: "CD-ROM, A, C", "CD-ROM, C, A" or something of the sort. Refer to your motherboard manual for instructions on how to accomplish this.

If you've configured everything properly, when you boot the system it should access the CD-ROM drive first and then either the floppy drive or the hard drive. If nothing happens, try rebooting. If you still are having no luck, check to see if the system is detecting the drive. Often, the BIOS will print out status messages, including drive detection messages. It should say something about finding a CD-ROM drive within the first few seconds of booting (after testing the memory), assuming your BIOS provides this type of information.

If the BIOS is properly detecting the drive, then your particular configuration might be incapable of booting from the CD-ROM. If the BIOS can't see the drive, the only explanation is that it hates you—just kidding. Read on to figure out what might be wrong.

CD-ROM Troubleshooting

If the BIOS isn't detecting the drive, you first should review all of your BIOS settings. Sometimes your changes might not get properly saved if you exit the BIOS configuration program the wrong way.

If everything is properly configured in the BIOS, then it's time to open up the case again. First step is to check those ribbon cables. Did you align the red stripe with pin one on both the drive and the mainboard? Try a different ribbon cable—sometimes they are defective. Another common problem is the master/slave setting on the CD-ROM drive. If it's connected to the primary IDE controller along with the hard drive, the jumper on the CD-ROM should be set to slave. If the drive is alone on the secondary controller, then the jumper should be set to the master position. If you're using two hard drives without an IDE RAID controller, place the CD-ROM drive on the primary controller as a slave and the second hard drive on the secondary controller.

One of the authors had a bit of trouble getting OpenBSD to find his CD-ROM drive. It turns out that with his particular combination of hardware, OpenBSD could only see the CD-ROM drive under certain conditions. It worked perfectly if it was connected as a slave to the primary IDE controller. But, it would only work as master on the secondary controller IF the BIOS were configured to boot from the CD before booting from the C drive. Since you want to boot off of the CD (the author was experimenting), you need to use that configuration setting anyhow. However, if you do have problems getting RedHat or OpenBSD to recognize your CD-ROM drive, you should switch from primary/slave to secondary/master or vice-versa as the case may be.

What to Do if Your CD Still Isn't Working

If after all the troubleshooting your CD still isn't being detected and/or doesn't autoboot, there's a pretty good chance that the boot floppy installer won't be able to find your CD-ROM drive either. This doesn't necessarily mean that you should run out immediately and buy another CD-ROM drive, or that you wasted your money by purchasing a CD. Since you are installing a firewall, you probably have at least one other computer that you wish to protect. Chances are, that computer has a CD-ROM drive. If it doesn't, you might want to install the problematic CD-ROM drive into your other computer. Either way, you can place the installer CD in the other machine and perform the install over the local network. It's a lot faster than FTPing the files from the Internet!

Burn-In (or Burning?)

Once it boots from the floppy drive or the CD-ROM drive, everything is fine. Put the rest of the hardware in, check that it still boots, and leave it running over night (it doesn't have to be doing anything, it just has to be switched on). A god idea is to put a smoke detector above the machine and make sure someone's in the house/office overnight. If you've accidentally misconfigured a jumper setting, you might cause your processor to overheat. Leave the case open so that the chance of a fire is reduced. Use the sniff test frequently.

Now you've got a working box. Proceed to the next chapter!

Summary

You started this chapter having decided which OS to run on your firewall, but precious little else. You have now obtained the hardware that will be your firewall. You have made sure this hardware will support the OS you intend to use. You have put the hardware together, and got it as far as booting from the floppy or CD-ROM.

In Chapters 6 and 8 we discuss the installation of the operating system. Chapter 6 deals with installing Linux, and Chapter 8 deals with installing OpenBSD. You're now ready to turn the page to the appropriate chapter and start the business of building software.

## CHAPTER 6

Installing Linux

There are many good books on how to install Linux, which proves two things: It's possible to write a whole book about installing and configuring Linux, and it's been done already. We wanted to be a little more original. Our first thought was: *Installing Linux Whilst Bungie Jumping In The Nude,* but logistical problems prevented us from completing the necessary research. We settled for the mundane but slightly more relevant topic of building a firewall with Linux.

For reasons described in the introduction, this is a book that specifically targets Red Hat Linux 6.0. You should therefore have access to the appropriate RedHat distribution (CD-ROM highly recommended). If you've got the boxed version, you'll find that the rather hefty nature of the box is due in part to the inclusion of their excellent book entitled "Installation Guide." This guide is so well written you'll forgive them for not including a section on nude bungie jumping.

However, the Installation Guide doesn't know you're trying to set up a firewall. To be general, it leaves open some questions that shouldn't be left open for a firewall. It doesn't require you to install certain things that we will, and (equally importantly) it doesn't tell you not to install certain things that we're going to forbid.

This chapter will walk alongside the installation process. We'll offer helpful suggestions when the choices get too wide. We'll try to ensure that you don't leave anything out that you'll need. We'll try even harder to ensure you don't accept anything you really shouldn't have. Once you've got a working system, we'll go through stripping out things you don't need on a firewall. Finally, we'll direct you to and help you install and configure tools you'll need that don't come on the stock CD. By the end of this chapter, you should have gone from a pile of hardware, a CD, and a boot disc to a bootable system, stripped and ready for action.

The Red Hat Install

The best way to learn about installing Linux is to install it. All of us do it, and we do it often. Every time we set up a new box, even though we've installed Linux maybe 50 or 100 times before, we usually end up doing it two or three times to get the best-tuned system.

The Red Hat installation guide recommends that you read the entire guide before trying to install. There is some wisdom in this, particularly if you've never done a Red Hat install before. It would be even wiser to read the rest of this chapter before actually performing the install as well.

If you're at all worried about the basic install, we suggest that you go through one. Accept all the defaults. Let the install script make all the hard decisions. Watch and learn—it doesn't take more than an hour to do an install. It can take less than ten minutes. When you've seen it all go through once or twice, and you think you know which bits go where, try taking matters into your own hands. Explore your options. Ask it to do weird things. You can't damage anything, so don't be afraid to get complicated. We'll re-install anyway, so nothing you can do at this point can carry forward into your final firewall configuration.

At some point, however, you will be comfortable with the installation process, and you will need to start installing properly. You should do this by stepping through the installation guide, the installation process, and the rest of this chapter at the same time. The following sections correspond to chapters in the Red Hat Installation Guide (or, to be precise, with reference to the Red Hat 6 installation guide "Inst-6.0-Print-RHS (04/99)").

We will not discuss every section of the Red Hat Installation Guide. Some sections don't apply to the hardware configuration we've specified; some are not necessary to do an install; and some are so well written that no comment is necessary.

Chapter 2

It isn't strictly necessary to read this chapter in order to perform the firewall install, but there's a lot of useful information in it.

Section 2.3

Read this to find out what you should know about your hardware in order to install without problems. You should be able to find out all the information it says you should know from the documentation that came with the parts of your firewall system.

Chapter 3

Chapter 3 is the first chapter to really get started on an install.

Section 3.1

This section discusses how dialogue boxes are handled, and is worth reading if you have never done an install.

Section 3.2

Here, you insert the boot floppy and really start cooking. The first thing you'll see after the system tries to read the boot floppy is a line of text that starts "SYSLINUX 1.43" and disappears before you've had a chance to read the rest of it. It's a good sign and is followed by a better one—the boot screen. The boot screen starts "Welcome to Red Hat Linux," probably in an interesting combination of colors, and ends with a "boot:" prompt in the bottom left-hand corner of the screen.

When you've read it, hit <CR> (or wait 60 seconds and it'll continue by itself). You'll see two lines of text appear over the next 60 seconds or so, telling you that initrd.img and (later) vmlinuz are loading. If nothing has happened after a minute, you've got a problem and will want to consult the Red Hat manual for troubleshooting aid and, if necessary, technical support contact information (see Appendix A on p. 229 of the Installation Guide).

NOTE

There are more ways of denoting the <CR> key on a computer keyboard than there are packets on the Internet. Some call it "Enter," some call it "Return," some label it "arrow pointing down and to the left." We're calling it <CR>, which is short for "Carriage Return," because we're traditionalists.

What you are more likely to see after a couple of lines of dots is an awful lot of text flashing by. This is what a Linux kernel spits out as it boots for the first time. To borrow one of the best descriptions of this sequence we've read, "you get a long telegram printed in stark white letters on a black screen…Most of the telegram has the semi-inscrutable menace of graffiti tags (Neal Stephenson's

'In The Beginning Was The Command Line')." Like a telegram, it's terse and densely information packed. It's also extremely useful for working out whether the operating system is seeing your hardware or not. Assuming you've got nice, sane hardware as we recommended, however, this shouldn't be an issue. Very shortly thereafter, the "Welcome to Red Hat Linux" screen pops up. This is a lot less telegram-like.

We're in Section 3.3, now. Read the introductory screen if you're so minded, and hit <CR>. Choose your language, and hit <CR>. Hopefully, you chose English. If you're reading this book, your English is definitely good enough to complete the installation in English, and we can't write about the other languages since we don't understand most of them. Red Hat did once offer "Redneck" as an installation option, which let you perform the whole installation with a Southeastern U.S. drawl and optional chewing tobacco. That option seems to have disappeared in Red Hat 6. We think that's a shame.

Choose your keyboard appropriately, and hit <CR>. We're now moving into Chapter 4.

Chapter 4

Chapter 4 of the Red Hat Installation Guide deals with the main part of the installation, when performed from "local media." Since CD-ROM is "local media," this means us. It is worth noting, though, that Red Hat Linux can be installed in a whole variety of other ways—from an FTP server with the CD-ROM on it, from an NFS server with the CD-ROM on it, even from a Web server. Chapter 5 of the Red Hat guide deals with how to perform such installs; we mention them just in case you ever need to know that the possibility exists.

Section 4.1

This section asks you about installation method. The installation method should be "Local CD-ROM." We advised you to buy one, because they're not very expensive. Select "Local CD-ROM," hit <CR>, put the CD in the drive (if it's not already there) and hit <CR> again to confirm that the disc is loaded.

If you need to do the install any other way, it's perfectly possible, but you'll have to work out the differences yourself. The Red Hat Installation Guide will be very useful in this respect.

Section 4.4

We're moving into Section 4.4. There will be a short pause while your computer spins up the CD-ROM drive. You will be asked whether you wish to install or upgrade a Red Hat system. Choose "Install" and hit <CR>.

Section 4.5

We're really coasting now. Next you'll be asked whether you wish to do one of the two stock installations—"Workstation" and "Server" or "Custom." Select "Custom" and hit <CR>.

Section 4.6

This section wants to know about SCSI, the ubiquitous Small Computer Systems Interface. SCSI adapters are used to drive disc drives and tape drives, and more recently, scanners, CD-ROM/R/RW drives and a whole variety of other peripherals that you absolutely don't need on a firewall. Hopefully, you haven't got any SCSI adapters in this machine, so if the dialogue about SCSI adapters appears, you can tell it NO and pass on. If you have put one in for some reason, or if your motherboard has a built-in SCSI adapter, the installation process will identify it and install drivers accordingly. You can answer "NO" to the question about having any more SCSI adapters, since you definitely don't need two SCSI adapters on a firewall.

Section 4.7

This is where things start to get complex. Because we've chosen the Custom installation, we have to make some decisions about disc layout. You'll be asked which tool you want to use to do the disc layouts. For now, Disk Druid is probably the best tool. The alternative is fdisk, which is terse and powerful but does absolutely no checking of the information you give it. Let's stick with Disk Druid. Select that, and hit <CR>.

Now would be a good time to read Section 4.7.1, which tells you about Disk Druid. Once you've done that, look at the top of the Disk Druid screen, "Current Disk Partitions." If any are defined, use F4 to delete them. This is a brand-new disc, and you aren't planning on having any other operating systems on your firewall, right? If at any point in this section you feel you have just confused things too badly, then *don't* press F12 or try to leave Disk Druid. Instead, you can press F5 and (after you confirm the reset) things will be returned to how they were when you entered Disk Druid.

Now, we'll need to create three partitions. If you're wondering what a partition is, Appendix C of the Red Hat Installation Guide has a very good explanation, and you should read it before going on.

The first partition to create is /boot. For technical reasons connected with the eldritch relationship between the Linux boot loader, LILO, and your computer's BIOS, we need to separate off the code that's run at boot time into its own small partition at the beginning of the disc. Press F1 to add a new partition. In the Edit New Partition screen add the following information:

- Mount Point: /boot
- Size (Megs): 15
- Grow to fill disk: UNchecked
- Type: Linux native
- Allowable drives: check only hda

Select OK and hit <CR>. If the partition has been added successfully, it should appear in the section at the top of the screen.

Next, we'll add a swap partition. Press F1 to add a new partition, and enter the following information:

- Mount Point: leave blank
- Size (Megs): 127
- Grow to fill disk: UNchecked
- Type: Linux swap
- Allowable drives: check only hda

Now we'll add a root (/) partition. This is where everything else in the entire filesystem will live. Now, we are well aware that wars have been fought over partitioning schemes. The Red Hat manual makes explicit reference to this, in the last paragraph on p. 29. Our preference, based on years of UNIX sysadmin experience and a distinct fondness for good single malt scotch, is to enter the following information:

- Mount Point: /
- Size (Megs): 1
- Grow to fill disk: CHECKED
- Type: Linux native
- Allowable drives: check only hda

At this point, the top of the screen should list three partitions currently defined. A 15 Mb partition, probably called mounted on /boot; a 127 Mb partition with no mount point, but of type "Linux Swap," probably called hda5; and a large partition, probably called hda6, mounted on / . If the size of this last partition (as listed in the "Actual" column, not the "Requested" column) isn't very nearly the size of the whole disc drive, try deleting and re-creating it. We don't want to waste any space on this disc.

NOTE

Don't worry that the hda numbers are not sequential (hda1, hda2, hda3, and so forth). Conversely, don't try to make Disk Druid create them sequentially—it doesn't work.

Select F12 to leave Disk Druid, and confirm that you want to save the changes we have made.

Section 4.8

Since we have created precisely one swap partition, when the install process asks you what partition you would like to use for swap space, it should give you exactly one choice. Check that one choice, and check the option "Check for bad blocks during format." Select OK. Hit <CR>.

Section 4.9 relates to hard-drive installations only. Since we're installing from CD-ROM, not from a hard drive, we can pass over this section.

Section 4.10

You'll now be asked about which of the recently created partitions you wish to format. Formatting, in this context, means laying out a blank, prototype file system on each partition so that data (i.e., files) can be placed on the partition in a meaningful way. The swap partition isn't included in the list; that doesn't need formatting in this sense. All the other Linux partitions will appear here, and (as the Red Hat instructions recommend), you should format all of them.

In addition to formatting / and /boot, you should also opt to check for bad blocks during format. While checking for bad blocks can take a long time (possibly an hour or so for a 3 Gb disk), it's worth doing it once. If it seems to be causing problems, it's OK not to do it. If you've done it in a previous install, it's OK not to do it this time. It's never OK to skip the format option, however—if you do, the file system will not be properly set up and the installation will crash in flames.

Section 4.11

Now we have to select components to install. We would recommend installing the following—and only the following—components:

- Networked workstation
- Dialup workstation
- C development

- Development libraries
- C++ development
- Kernel development
- Extra documentation

Anything else you install puts more tools on the system. More tools can have more bugs, and require more maintenance. There are some other individual packages we'll need, but we'll be installing those after the main install is complete.

We would advise against checking "Select individual packages," since it will get you into a very lengthy dialogue about the installation of every single package that makes up the OS. Not only is this time consuming, but some of the questions are pretty inscrutable. Now, select OK and hit <CR>.

At this point, you'll be told about the installation log. Read the information, select OK and hit <CR>. At this point, the install process will start to format the file systems / and /boot. If you didn't check "Check for bad blocks" up in Section 4.10, this should take no more than a few minutes. If you did, it can take a long time, but if it goes over two hours, something is wrong and you should reboot the computer.

NOTE
If anything seems to be dramatically wrong during the installation, use your reset button to reboot the computer. The current install will be irrevocably trashed, but you can always start again from scratch.

Once the formatting is over, the package installation dialogue will start up. This is an essentially read-only process, but it gives you an idea of how long it's going to take, and how far it's gotten. It is detailed very well in Red Hat's subsection 4.11.4. For the tiny subset of a full-blown installation that we're doing, installation doesn't take very long. Even on a 66 MHz 486, it only takes about 20 minutes; on a 300 MHz K-6 system, it takes about five minutes.

NOTE
Sometimes the Red Hat installer will say "signal X" where X is some low number. This is installer death. The first solution is to reboot and try again. If the problem is chronic it can be an indication that some critical piece of hardware in your system is either damaged or incompatible.

Have a quick cup of coffee/tea/juice/water (although the effects of the coffee will probably be most useful a few hours from now). Turn to Chapter 6 of the Red

Hat Installation Guide (p. 91), and let's finish up the installation. Chapter 5 deals with other forms of install than the "Local CD-ROM" and "Hard drive" varieties.

Chapter 6

Red Hat's Chapter 6 discusses how to complete the Red Hat installation and reboot the system into its new configuration. This will conclude the Red Hat-managed phase of the firewall installation. We'll then proceed to our phase of the installation.

Section 6.1

At this point, you need to configure a mouse. Assuming you have a supported one and that it's attached, the system should find it. If you only have a two-button mouse, you might wish to check "Emulate 3 Buttons" before selecting OK and hitting <CR>.

Section 6.2

The networking configuration refers to your ethernet card, not to any dial-up networking you might be using. If you're going to be using a two (or more) ethernet card configurations, the discussion refers to the interior interface of the firewall, rather than the interface to the DMZ and/or the interface to the outside world. We'll be putting the other ethernet cards in later.

If you're using private ethernet addresses with a view to masquerading (see the *IP Masquerading* section in Chapter 3, "How Secure Should Your Network Be?"), you should pick an ethernet address for your firewall's interior interface from that range. Pick one that suits your numbering plan. We often use the 192.168.1.0 subnet, and use 192.168.1.1 or 192.168.1.254, depending on site policy, for the firewall itself. You could use these addresses, or you could use others (see Chapter 3). If you plan to use real IP addresses for your network, you'll need to pick one of these to assign to the ethernet card.

If your internal network is using DHCP (Dynamic Host Configuration Protocol), you need to find an address in your local subnet that isn't going to be assigned by your DHCP server. Unless you want to run routing protocols on your internal network, having your firewall continuously changing internal addresses is Not A Good Idea. If your external address is assigned by way of DHCP, that's OK.

If you've used a particularly old network card, Red Hat may ask you to tell it about what kind of card it is, in which case, do so. Red Hat will then ask if you want to configure LAN networking. Select YES and hit <CR>.

Next, you'll be asked to choose a method of assigning host addresses. Select Static and hit <CR>. Give the IP address you've selected, and the appropriate netmask. If you've decided to do masquerading, and to use the 192.168.1.1 address for your firewall's internal interface, the appropriate values for these two are 192.168.1.1 and 255.255.255.0. Since this machine is your default gateway, you need to leave the "default gateway" box here blank, but when you set up other machines on your internal network, you'll tell them that 192.168.1.1 (or, if you've picked another address, the address you chose) is their default gateway. If you have an internal nameserver already, enter its IP address in the "primary nameserver" box; otherwise, enter the IP address of your ISP's name server (DNS server).

Select OK and hit <CR>. This takes us to screen two of the network parameters setup. If you are lucky enough to have a real domain name, enter it in the first box. If not, leave the first box blank. Your hostname goes in the second box. If you have a real domain name, you will need to talk to the person who administers your DNS to get the hostname assigned properly. If, as is the case for most of us, you don't have a real domain name, think of a catchy host name and enter it in this box.

If you entered a domain name in the first box, it will be automatically pasted into the second box. The cursor will be put at the beginning of the domain name in the hostname box. This is OK. As a brief example, if you enter the domain name "foo.bar" in the first box, when you leave the box ".foo.bar" will be automatically pasted into box two, and the cursor will appear before the leading dot. If you decide that "fnord" makes a catchy host name (well, there's no accounting for taste), you would type "fnord" in here, so the second box reads "fnord.foo.bar".

Should you have more than one internal DNS server already, or should your ISP have more than one DNS server, you can enter secondary and (if available) tertiary DNS servers in boxes three and four. Again, enter them by IP address, not by name. Select OK and hit <CR>.

Section 6.3

Now, you need to select your time zone from the list provided. The box at the top, regarding whether your machine clock keeps GMT, is a little more confusing. The terse answer seems to be that most modern motherboards observe local time, and the time shifts in autumn and spring, and thus do not keep GMT. So don't select "Hardware Clock set to GMT" at this time. If this assumption turns out to be wrong, you can change it later by editing the file /etc/sysconfig/clock and changing the line "UTC=false" to read "UTC=true".

Select OK and hit <CR>. (We're not going to say this any more, by the way.)

Section 6.4

Choosing services to start on reboot is a bit like partitioning discs; you can have holy wars about it. Our opinion is that you should select the following, and deselect all other, services: atd, crond, gpm, inet, keytable, network, random, syslog. You need these to get things running properly; the other services provide only potential security holes.

Section 6.5

Don't configure a printer. This is a firewall, not a print server.

Section 6.6

It's worth taking a few minutes to think about setting a root password. The usual rules apply: No words from any language, no variants on any such words—don't think that mixing a couple of numbers into a word makes it secure. Our recommendation would be to take a book down off your bookshelf, pick a sentence at random, and use the initial letters of that sentence. Don't pick a famous sentence. Don't open the book at page one. Don't use the book you're currently reading (this book!) and don't leave this book next to the one you do choose, either. If you need to highlight or underline the sentence as an emergency reference if you forget the root password, that's OK (well, it's better than writing the root password down on a piece of paper, anyway). Pick a good one and spend a little time fixing it in your memory.

Section 6.7

We would strongly recommend enabling "Use Shadow Passwords" and "Enable MD5 Passwords," and disabling "NIS." Shadow passwords help security by storing the encrypted passwords away from public view, and MD5 passwords help frustrate dictionary attacks by allowing you to pick passwords of more than eight characters (conventional Unix permits passwords of more than eight characters, but ignores every character from the ninth onwards). Enabling NIS, the Network Information Service, would delegate authority about who can and can't log in to the firewall to some other server. Nobody but you should be logging in to the firewall. Since NIS is so insecure, enabling it is not a good idea.

Section 6.8

If you have a spare preformatted floppy, we would also recommend creating a boot diskette. The floppy doesn't need to be blank, but anything on it will be erased. Don't overwrite the Red Hat boot floppy by mistake (as we often do).

Section 6.9

Install LILO on the MBR of /dev/hda. It is unlikely that you'll need to add options to LILO, but follow Red Hat's advice about checking "Use linear mode" (first paragraph on p. 107).

Section 6.11

That's the end of the Red Hat phase of the install. Your computer will now reboot into a fully fledged Linux system. Remove the Red Hat boot floppy, or the boot diskette you created in Section 6.8 if you've been following our advice.

NOTE

If your system is set up to boot from CD-ROM in preference to the hard disc, the computer is going to start trying to reinstall the OS again. The Right Thing would be take the CD out of the drive before you reboot, but most modern CD drives will allow the operating system to lock the drive shut (i.e., disable the eject button) if the OS considers it necessary. Since that is necessary when the CD is mounted, as it has been throughout the installation, it is unlikely that you will be able to eject the CD before rebooting. So, if your computer tries to reboot off the CD, the "Welcome to Red Hat Linux" screen you remember from the section earlier comes up, and it starts looking a lot like you're about to reinstall the OS, don't panic! Just grab your towel, press the reset button on your computer, and then hold the eject button down on your CD-ROM. As soon as the computer has reinitialized the CD-ROM drive, the drive should obey the button and pop the CD tray out. Remove the CD, and close the drive.

You might want to consider tweaking the BIOS so that the system no longer boots off the CD-ROM. This isn't a bad idea, as you may be using the CD later to install packages and might forget about the CD's presence. If the system reboots for any reason, you could be stuck on the CD's install screen for a while.

Now we're ready to start doing some real customisation work. We're not going to configure the firewall yet, (that's in Chapter 7, "Configuring the Firewall Under Linux"), but we're going to install the tools that make a firewall possible.

The Firewall Install

Assuming your system came back up fine, log in as root with the root password you picked in Section 6.6. If it didn't come back up, consult the Red Hat Installation Guide for troubleshooting information and support details. Not that you need us to remind you of this, but Unix is case-sensitive nearly everywhere.

Not only is this not a book on installing Red Hat, it's also not a book on getting packets to flow between you and the outside world. The job of the firewall is to stop packets flowing between anywhere and you, and the job of this book is to help you build a firewall. However, we think it would be a good idea to dwell briefly on the basics of setting up Internet connectivity, and above all to include new ideas and pointers to reference sources.

You do need to get your network set up before you can firewall. One of the beauties of Unix is that things are modular—you can separate the networking setup from that of the firewall, and set up the network utilities separate from the network, and so on. Take advantage of this modularity, and don't try and do everything in one giant stage. It's easier to correctly and verifiably manage a small part of the setup than it is to get the whole thing right. Few people can accomplish this, and fewer still would ever want to do it that way a second time. We are not among the few, the proud, and the soon to be regretful. There's no reason you should be, either.

Installing Extra Packages

The first thing to do is to install a few more Red Hat packages. If you installed from local CD-ROM, Red Hat will have automatically set up your system so you can mount your CD-ROM by popping the Red Hat CD-ROM into the drive, and typing "mount /mnt/cdrom". If you get an answer like "mount: can't find /mnt/cdrom in /etc/mtab or /etc/fstab", try "mount -t iso9660 -o ro /dev/cdrom /mnt/cdrom".

Once you've got the CD mounted, type "cd /mnt/cdrom/RedHat/RPMS". You're now in the directory where all the software packages live, including all those that were installed a few minutes ago when you built your system. We want a few more of them. Type the following commands:

```
rpm -ivh ipchains-*.i386.rpm
rpm -ivh tcpdump-*.i386.rpm
```

RPM is the RedHat Package Manager, the tool that manipulates the packages that make up the OS and applications. -ivh is the combination of, and is equivalent to, the three flags -i, -v, and -h. The first means "install the package file specified at the end of the line," the second means "be verbose about problems you encounter," and the third means "print some hash marks while you install the package." When you hit <CR>, you will install two packages. The first, ipchains, is the firewall manipulation tool. The second, tcpdump, is an application for monitoring traffic on a network, packet by packet. It is very useful for debugging network problems, so we're likely to want it. The third, minicom, is a terminal emulator package. It allows us to talk to devices such as modems, and have the results of the conversation appear on the screen in a recognizable manner.

Unmount the CD-ROM by typing "cd /", then "umount /mnt/cdrom" (that's "umount" and not "unmount"). The first command is necessary since the kernel won't let you unmount a file system if it's busy. The fact that your current directory is within the CD-ROM's path constitutes a "busy" CD-ROM device. Even though you're not technically accessing any files, unmounting the device would leave you with an invalid current directory. The kernel would like to avoid this unpleasant situation and so would we.

Removing Unwanted Packages

We don't want to turn this into a manual on RPM any more than we wanted to rewrite the installation manual. However, RPM lies at the heart of software management on a pure Red Hat system, so it's worth discussing.

To list the packages you've currently got installed, type "rpm –qa". To remove any one of these, type "rpm -e PACKAGENAME", substituting the name of the package for PACKAGENAME. For example, to remove the C compiler, you'd type "rpm -e egcs-1.1.2-12", but don't do that yet. We'll need it for a while, but we will remove it before the firewall goes into production.

Modem-Based Firewalls

This section is particularly relevant if your connection to the Internet is through a serial connection. By serial connection, we mean something that attaches to a serial port, rather than a network port, on your computer.

It is true that leased lines (such as the ubiquitous T1) are serial in a sense, as well. However, they're rather beyond the remit of this book. They usually require special equipment that ends up giving you a standard network (ethernet) connection to the leased line anyhow.

Finding Your Modem

The first thing to do is work out which serial port the modem is on. If you don't find this challenging, please skip to the next section. It occurred to us that we've hardly ever been able to look at the back of a PC and know which serial port is which. While it's true that some machines externally label the ports as "1" and "2," these labels don't necessarily correspond with the internal designations. Since the black art of identification is rather badly documented elsewhere, we'll dwell on it a little here.

There are only two serial ports on most modern PCs (don't confuse them with the parallel, or LPT, port), and they are accessed through the device files /dev/ttyS0 and /dev/ttyS1, and they correspond to COM1 and COM2, respectively. These can also be known as COMA and COMB, also respectively. If your modem's connected to a serial port on the back of your firewall, it can be talked to through /dev/ttyS0 or /dev/ttyS1.

But which one? Well, your best guide is your motherboard manual. If it makes it clear which of the serial ports is COM1 and which is COM2, then you know which port your modem is connected to. If it's on COM1 or COMA, you will use device file /dev/ttyS0 to talk to your modem; if your modem is on COM2 or COMB, then talk to it through /dev/ttyS1. If your motherboard manual isn't helpful, then read on.

If you have a serial mouse, life's easy—the modem's on the other port from the mouse You can find out which port the mouse is on by doing "ls -al /dev/mouse". /dev/mouse is a soft link which points to the real device the mouse is on. On the machine I have with a serial mouse, the output from the above command looks like this:

```
lrwxrwxrwx    1 root      root            5 May 15 14:22 /dev/mouse
    -> /dev/ttyS1
```

which means that the mouse is on /dev/ttyS1, so the modem must be on /dev/ttyS0. You may find that the "/dev/" is missing from before the "ttyS1"; don't worry, it's not important. If you get something like this:

```
lrwxrwxrwx    1 root      root           10 Nov 18  1998 /dev/mouse
    -> /dev/psaux
```

then you have a PS/2 mouse, and will have to think harder.

If you don't have a serial mouse, then it's a good thing you have an external modem with status lights (you did follow our suggestion in Chapter 5, "Getting the Right Hardware," right?). Try doing "echo AT > /dev/ttyS0 &" and watching the lights on the modem. If the lights flicker, you've just had a very short conversation with your modem. If the lights don't flicker, try it with /dev/ttyS1 instead. The "&" was used to run the command in the background, because doing this has a tendency to wedge the serial ports—you certainly can't do it twice in a row unless you're lucky.

The other thing that can go wrong is to have the wrong type of cable. Assuming the ends are the right size and gender to connect your modem to your computer, there are still two types of cables: One is intended to connect modems to computers, and the other is intended to connect computers to computers (or modems to modems). If you have the wrong type (they're very difficult to tell apart), no signals will get through. If you suspect that might be the case, a device called a *null modem adaptor*, which plugs into one end of either type of cable and turns it into the other, can be extremely helpful in testing. They don't cost very much, and most computer stores should carry them. If you're really unlucky, you may even have a dud cable, or something that looks like a serial cable, but isn't. If you suspect the worst, buy a new cable.

After You've Found the Modem

Once you've worked out which port the modem is on, it will save a lot of time in the future if we put in a link—much like the mouse link we already mentioned—to point to the modem, and refer to the modem through that.

If your modem turned out to be on /dev/ttyS0, issue the following commands:

```
cd /dev
ln -s ttyS0 modem
```

If the modem turned out to be on /dev/ttyS1, change the ttyS0 in the preceding command to ttyS1. Once this link is made, every time you refer to /dev/modem, you'll automatically be talking to your modem. The rest of the modem section assumes that you have done this.

Firing Up Minicom

Now we want to have a serious talk with the modem. To talk to a device on a serial port, we need some kind of software to mediate the conversation. Minicom comes with Red Hat 6, and we installed it a few sections ago. If you have a preferred package, by all means use that, and skip ahead to the section below on PPP.

To set it up, as root, run "minicom –s". The parameters that need to be changed are "Serial port setup" and "Modem and dialing"—the rest of the parameters will already be set sanely.

Use the arrow keys to move to "Serial port setup" and press <CR>. Press "A" to edit the device, and change the text there to read "/dev/modem"(if it doesn't already say that). Hit <CR> to confirm that. If you need to change the speed, or data/parity/stop bit settings, press "E" and choose from the menu that appears. Our experience has been that most speeds are fine, as modern modems will adjust automatically (and this speed doesn't represent the speed that you want to drive the modem at when talking to the Internet, anyway); 8N1, which is short for 8 data bits, no parity bit, one stop bit, is usually fine for the latter setting.

Use the Escape key to get back to the main menu, and the arrow keys to move the cursor to "Modem and dialing," and hit <CR> to enter this menu. You will want to edit strings A and B back to the null string (i.e., nothing). The default values probably do wonderful things to modems, but unless you know what it is that they do, and that they are the right strings to do it to *your* modem, you're better off without them. Hit "A" to select the first string, use delete to prune it, and hit <CR> to accept it once it's gone. Repeat for string "B."

Again, use the Escape key to get you back to the main menu, and choose "Save setup as...". Select this with <CR>, and give the name "modem", hitting <CR> to confirm. Once back to the main menu (which will happen automatically) select "Exit from Minicom" to get back to the shell prompt.

From now on, you need only type "minicom modem" to have a conversation with your modem (the "modem" after "minicom" tells it the name of the configuration file we just saved). So, try it. What we're looking for, at least for most modern ("Hayes-compatible") modems, is that you should be able to type "at" to your modem, hit <CR>, and have it reply "OK" to you. If you can get that far, you're definitely talking to your modem.

To exit minicom, press CTRL-A, then Q, and hit <CR> to accept "Leave without reset".

If things aren't working, watch the blinking lights on your modem while you try typing at it with minicom. If you're seeing lights, but gibberish (or nothing) is coming back from the modem, you probably need to play around with the speed and data/stop/parity settings. If you're not seeing blinking lights, you should go right back to the beginning and start with "Finding your modem" again.

Point-to-Point Protocol

Given that your modem and computer are talking to each other, we now have to get them talking to the Internet. This involves transmitting *IP* (Internet Protocol) signals down a serial cable. In the early days of the Internet, the first protocol to try to do this was called SLIP, the Serial Line Internet Protocol. This had limitations, and was replaced nearly everywhere by *PPP*, the Point-to-Point Protocol.

PPP is what you will very likely be running over your modem line, between your Linux box and your ISP, in order to talk to the Internet. A full discussion of how to set up PPP is beyond the scope of this book, and moreover it is unnecessary, since you have just installed an excellent HOWTO on the subject. If you look in /usr/doc/ppp-2.3.7, you will find an excellent README.linux file which discusses the theory and application of PPP. It gets to the application section around line 400 (try "less +398 README.linux"). If you read this along with the manual page for pppd, the PPP dæmon (man pppd), it should be possible to get a basic PPP conversation set up between you and your ISP. Eventually, the PPP daemon (pppd) can take care of the dialing and logging in as well as the PPP connection itself.

Nevertheless, if you want to reduce things to the lowest common denominator, you can use minicom to set up the connection between you and your ISP, then hand over to pppd. This isn't great for regular use, but it's the best way, for example, to debug your connection or check exactly who says what.

To do this, fire up minicom with "minicom modem". Say "AT" to your modem to check that it's listening (it'll say OK back if it is). Then say "ATM1DT08451234567" (M is for speaker, 1 turns the speaker on, D is for dial, T is for tone dialing, and you should replace 08451234567 with your ISP's dialup number). You will hear the modem pick up, dial your ISP, and connect. Hopefully, some text will be displayed on the screen welcoming you to your ISP (or, more likely these days, threatening you with horrendous penalties if you're unauthorized), and inviting you to log in. If your ISP only supports CHAP (the Challenge Handshake Authentication Protocol) or PAP (the Password Authentication Protocol), you won't be able to log in manually; these are authentication protocols designed to let pppd handle the authentication. Assuming you can log in manually, enter your username and password when requested. If you've entered them correctly, the screen will light up with gibberish as your ISP tries to talk PPP to you. At this point, quit minicom with CTRL-A then Q, and type at the command line "pppd /dev/modem defaultroute". This starts pppd, which will set up your Internet connection. You need to type this before your ISP drops the line, otherwise you will need to restart the paragraph.

Wait. After about 10 seconds, pppd should have had a nice chat with your ISPs PPP server, and should know what IP address it will be using for the session, what IP address is at the other end of the modem, and packets should be beginning to flow. If you were to type "ifconfig ppp0", you should see something rather like:

```
ppp0      Link encap:Point-to-Point Protocol
          inet addr:12.34.56.78  P-t-P:23.45.67.89  Mask:255.255.255.255
          UP POINTOPOINT RUNNING NOARP MULTICAST  MTU:1500  Metric:1
          RX packets:10 errors:0 dropped:0 overruns:0 frame:0
          TX packets:23 errors:0 dropped:0 overruns:0 carrier:0
          collisions:0 txqueuelen:10
```

The key parameters are "inet addr", which says what your IP address is, and "P-t-P", which states your ISPs address. You should be able to ping your own external IP address (in this example, 12.34.56.78); since that's attached to your machine, that's not much of an achievement. You should be able to ping your ISP address (in this example, 23.45.67.89), which is more of an achievement. You should actually be able to get anywhere from here, since you're now a fully fledged member of the Internet.

To bring pppd down and release the telephone line, type "killall pppd".

Diald

Chatting to your modem with minicom can be very enjoyable (we have no lives), but it's not too good for day-to-day Internet access. The PPP README.linux file gives some good suggestions for doing it all with a single command, but you may not want to have to type the command in every time you want to bring up the network. In particular, you may not want to have to manually bring the link up every time you want to go out to the Internet, and you may not want to have to bring it down each time you're finished.

If you don't, you should take a look at diald. This is an extremely neat utility that pretends to be a route to the Internet all the time, but isn't. When you try and send packets over this fake link, diald nips round the back of your computer, taps the modem on the shoulder, and brings up the link to the Internet for real. When you've finished doing stuff, and the link goes idle, diald nips round the back again and shuts the link down. If you live in a country that charges by the minute for ISP access, this can be extremely useful. If you don't have to pay by the minute when your modem's off the hook, but you have several providers you want to dial up, under different circumstances (say, your university for work and your ISP for fun), diald can also be very handy.

You can find more out about diald at http://diald.Unix.ch/. If you want to ask questions and/or find help, there's a very active user's mailing list that you can learn more about at the Web site.

Ethernet-Based Firewalls

Some people are lucky enough to have semipermanent links to the Internet (cable modem, or leased-line) or they're planning on hanging a network off somebody else's network. In any case, their prospective connection to the Internet appears to them as a piece of network cable instead of a modem's serial cable. This section also makes useful reading for those people planning to have three-legged firewalls: one internal network, one Internet connection of any kind, and a DMZ as described in Chapter 3, "How Secure Should Your Network Be?."

The first task is fitting the extra ethernet cards, and making sure they're recognized in the right order. The second task is acquiring an IP address.

Fitting Extra Network Cards

If you are using a three-legged confguration, or your Internet presentation is Ethernet, or you just fancy fitting more than one ethernet card, you'll need to fit a second ethernet card, or maybe even more. This isn't necessarily a production, but it can be. One good guide is the Ethernet-HOWTO, which you can find at /usr/doc/HOWTO/Ethernet-HOWTO on your new firewall; you're looking for Section 3.2, "Using More than one Ethernet Card per Machine." However, since this is something you are likely to need to do, we'll give it some time here as well.

Kernel Recognition

You'll have the easiest time of it if you've bought several identical PCI cards, as we strongly recommended. The one driver installed at installation time will detect all the cards on each boot. All you'll need to do is provide enough configuration files to go around (one per card). Well, nearly all. The trickiest bit about this configuration is working out which card is which. This is motherboard dependent; the network card in the lowest-numbered PCI slot will be eth0, the card in the next-lowest-numbered PCI slot will be eth1, and so on. Your motherboard manual will be of great assistance to you here. If it isn't, roundly curse your motherboard manufacturer and start looking on the board itself for some indication of which slot is the lowest numbered.

If you didn't go for multiple identical PCI cards, you're in undersupported territory . We don't want to leave you totally in the dark, so we'll throw you a few measly paragraphs just to tease you into thinking that there is hope for you. We'll mention two dismal situations: multiple PCI cards from different vendors, and multiple ISA cards in general. If you're mixing PCI and ISA cards, you deserve to be sandwiched between two large circuit boards with lots of pointy solder-spikes pressing into your skin.

The easiest of these scenarios is if you have several PCI cards from different vendors. There exists a file in /etc called conf.modules. This file controls which driver modules are loaded when various devices are initialized. If you look in it, you'll notice a line that starts "alias eth0". The word after this will be something like "3c509," or "3c59x," or "tulip," or "ne2k-pci;" the precise word depends on what brand of network card you bought. To force your second card to be recognized, you need to add a line that says "alias eth1 xxxx". In place of "xxxx" you need the driver appropriate to your network card. To find out which driver that is, your best bet is to go to Donald Becker's Linux Network Drivers page at http://cesdis.gsfc.nasa.gov/linux/drivers/. Look through for your card, then cross-reference it to the driver (they're all called something.c—just chop off the .c).

You win this week's star cauliflower if you have several ISA cards, whether from the same vendor or from multiple vendors. Your life will not be fun, at least not until you get this sorted out. Read the Ethernet-HOWTO in some detail. The key points are getting separate I/O base addresses for each card, to make them logically distinct, then getting the kernel to probe for them in the right order. It's not pretty, and with PCI network cards so cheap, we would recommend just getting several identical PCI cards instead. If you place any value on your time, then heed this warning!

Card Configuration

In /etc/sysconfig/network-scripts lives a file called ifcfg-eth0. This file contains, in very simple language, the parameters required to configure the first ethernet card: eth0. The mere presence of this file is enough to trigger the card's configuration at boot time. Here's an example file.

```
DEVICE=eth0
IPADDR=192.168.1.2
NETMASK=255.255.255.0
NETWORK=192.168.1.0
BROADCAST=192.168.1.255
ONBOOT=yes
```

This file is fairly straightforward, and makes minimal use of deep magic. To configure a second card, cd into /etc/sysconfig/network-scripts and issue the command "cp ifcfg-eth0 ifcfg-eth1". Then edit the new file, "ifcfg-eth1". The DEVICE parameter must be changed to "eth1"; ONBOOT should stay as "yes" unless you really don't want this network card to do much. The other four parameters are a function of the IP address you need this card to have in real life, and we can't help you with them because they'll be particular to your network.

DHCP

Unless you are great friends with your ISP, it is likely that your IP address is assigned dynamically. Talk to your service provider and ask them if this is so, and if so, how they assign addresses. The usual way of dynamically assigning addresses for ethernet-based connections is DHCP.

To install the DHCP client, you should revisit the section earlier *Installing Extra Packages*. This time, mount the cdrom, cd to the RPMS directory, and use rpm as follows: "rpm -ivh dhcpcd-*.i386.rpm". Return to the root directory with "cd /" and unmount the cdrom.

The problem with dynamically assigned IP addresses is that working with the port forwarder becomes very difficult. Each time your address changes, you'll need to tweak the port forwarding configuration. The only way around this is to write fairly complex scripts. Frankly, there are very few reasons why you would want to run publicly available services if you have dynamically assigned IP addresses. Most ISPs (especially cable modem ISPs) scan ports for public FTP and HTTP servers. If they find you running something, they'll kill your account faster than you can say "hey guys, I just set up this really cool warez site!" If you want to run externally accessible services, please ask your ISP for a static IP address.

The actual configuration of DHCP as a client is beyond the scope of this book. However, useful help can be found in the client setup section of the DHCP mini-HOWTO. The version on the Red Hat 6.0 CD-ROM is a little dated; you can find the up-to-date version at http://metalab.unc.edu/LDP/HOWTO/mini/DHCP.html. Since you don't have X on your firewall, and hence you don't have control-panel either, you may find the instructions for Red Hat 4 more useful.

One more thing: Do not plan on running a DHCP server on your firewall. There's no reason for doing this. If your internal network is already running on DHCP, that's fine, but the firewall shouldn't be the server.

Other Important Information

Ah, here's the catch-all section. There are a couple of things we need to catch here before moving on to the summary: the mandatory kernel patch (for a vulnerability that was discovered after the release of Red Hat 6 but before printing) and a discussion of a tool called TCP wrappers.

Kernel Upgrade Patch

At the time of writing, a vulnerability had just been discovered in all 2.2.x Linux kernels, across all distributors, that affected IP packet handling. The precise details are a little abstruse, but the essence is that certain badly constructed packets will cause memory to be freed up twice. If this happens enough, either over a long enough time or because someone's firing these packets at you deliberately, your kernel will panic and your machine will reboot. Since we are building a firewall, blocking known holes for denial of service attacks is a good idea. You should fix this problem.

Red Hat has their security advisories relating to the kernel at www.redhat .com/corp/support/errata/rh60-errata-general.html#kernel; if they've moved this page in the interim, start at www.redhat.com/support/ and look for errata. In any case, we're after a section relating to the June 3, 1999 kernel security problem. There should be a pointer to new kernel and kernel source packages at this page. It is important that you get both kernel and kernel source, or if you ever do rebuild your kernel manually (it's not very hard to do) you'll put the bug straight back in.

Upgrading the kernel is slightly less trivial than applying most Red Hat packages. Forutnately, Red Hat has an excellent guide available at www.redhat.com/corp/support/docs/kernel-upgrade/.

This should be a pretty good illustration of the value of keeping up with your patches and advisories, in case we haven't beaten that horse to death already. Again, see Chapter 12 for pointers. Kernel patches to fix this problem were out within about 24 hours of the problem becoming known. That's the sort of thing to bear in mind next time someone says "we can't use free software, it's unsupported."

TCP Wrappers

TCP wrappers is an excellent package, originally written by Wietse Venema, that contributes to network security on many well-configured machines throughout the world. It allows connections to network services to be screened with respect to the host requesting connection.

Hang on a minute, we hear you cry, that sounds just like a firewall. Well, it is. TCP wrappers does many of the things a packet-filtering firewall does, but the configuration files are a lot simpler. Why, then, do we propose to make you write large, hairy, and complex ipchains code instead of short, friendly, TCP wrappers code?

TCP wrappers can only control access to TCP services—no UDP or ICMP control—and then only to TCP services started through the inet dæmon, inetd (if you want to know more about the inet daemon, we'll be turning most of his functions off in Chapter 7). No TCP service that 's started at boot time instead of through inetd, such as sendmail, or a Web server, can generally be protected by TCP wrappers.

It is true that a few other services, such as the new and improved RPC portmapper, have been modified to check the TCP wrappers control files and honor them, but an awful lot of applications haven't.

TCP wrappers can, however, do some things that ipchains can't do so well. For example, you can use hostnames instead of IP addresses to narrow down who can connect to services, and you can use wildcards in those names. For example, you could bar any machine in the mit.edu domain by denying the host *.mit.edu. Clearly, this makes for pleasant, readable code. Sadly, it also makes for a gaping security hole. If someone can compromise your DNS server, or any DNS server that's trusted by your DNS server, they can disarm your TCP wrapper protection by lying to you about which IP addresses are and are not in the domains you've chosen to permit.

So why do we mention it? Well, it's cool, for one thing. For host-based, rather than firewall-based security, it's an excellent thing for administrators to know about. Remember when we said that host security should not be neglected just because you have a firewall? We also felt we needed to point out why it wasn't very suitable for a firewall, since the tools you need to secure a firewall are somewhat more powerful than the tools needed to secure a desktop host. To find out more about TCP wrappers, do a "man tcpd".

Summary

Where are we now? Well, we started this chapter with a collection of hardware that could boot from a floppy or CD-ROM. Now, we have a fully installed Red Hat Linux system. We have not only installed Linux, but configured additional hardware and network services, installed the software that will be used to create the firewall rules, and already fixed one major security hole (isn't open source wonderful?). We've also connected to your ISP, and made packets flow.

Now, you can go on to Chapter 7, "Configuring the Firewall under Linux," where we'll actually build the firewall.

## CHAPTER 7

Configuring the Firewall under Linux

So far, you've decided to install Linux, you've acquired and assembled compatible hardware, and if you're still reading you've also installed the OS without any major loss of life or limb. In this chapter, we'll start by discussing the theory behind the firewall tool and the underlying concepts. Then, we'll practice making a few trivial rules, and testing them to see that they work. We're *not* going to make too many important decisions regarding the services your firewall allows—that's the job of Chapter 10, "Configuring the Firewall." The goal is to end the chapter with a basic functional firewall. If necessary, we'll also help you set up IP Masqerading.

The tool in Linux 2.2 kernels for configuring firewalls (and masquerading) is called *ipchains*. Until version 2.2 was released, the tool was called 'ipfwadm', and was a rewrite of BSD's "ipfw." Rusty Russell and friends completely overhauled the packet filtering code for the 2.2 kernel.

Before we do anything else, we must make sure you've got ipchains installed in the OS. Issue the command "rpm -qa | grep ipchains". This lists all packages and from that list, extracts any that contain the word 'ipchains'. If you see something like 'ipchains-1.3.8-3', you're clear to proceed. If you don't get anything except a prompt, you'll need to go back to Chapter 6, "Installing Linux," and revisit installing ipchains.

Rules and Chains

Recognizing that this heading may cause deviant thoughts, we'd like to immediately refocus your attention on firewalls. Two concepts are key to the correct use of ipchains: rules and chains. *Chains* are what packets must pass through to enter or leave a network interface, or to move from one interface to another; *rules* control the passage of the packets through those chains.

Chains

When packets travel through a network interface, they are sent through one or more chains. Specifically, when a packet attempts to enter a network interface, it passes through the *input* chain; when a packet attempts to leave a network interface, it passes through the *output* chain; when a packet tries to travel between one interface and another, it passes through the *forward* chain. These chains are applied sequentially. If a packet enters one network interface with a destination that requires it to be routed out another interface, it must pass through the input chain to decide if it's allowed in, through the forward chain to decide if it's allowed to be forwarded, and through the output chain to decide if it's allowed to leave. This point is particularly important in the case of a firewall router, since its job is to move packets selectively from one interface to another.

The forward chain is where masquerading will be included if we decide to use it. Recalling the *IP Masquerading* section from Chapter 3, "How Secure Should Your Network Be?," you will need to use IP Masquerading if you have less public IP addresses assigned to you than you have machines on your internal network. As we also pointed out back then, you may choose to use masquerading for security even if you have enough addresses to go around.

NOTE

Chains do not make decisions about *how* to route packets; that's handled by the routing tables. The only decision made by the chains is *whether* to route packets. We will cover routing tables in more depth in Chapter 10.

Chains have a default policy, which is defined by you. If a chain contains nothing else except a default policy, every packet that passes through that chain will be treated similarly. The possible policies are ACCEPT, DENY, and REJECT. ACCEPT means "allow to pass through the chain;" DENY and REJECT both mean "do not allow to pass through the chain." There is a subtle difference between DENY and REJECT, which we cover next. To make this concrete, consider chains with no rules: if the default policy of the input chain is ACCEPT, then any packet will be allowed to enter any network interface; if the default policy of the output chain is DENY or REJECT, then no packet will ever be allowed out of any network interface.

DENY or REJECT?

DENY and REJECT both mean to refuse passage through a chain to a packet. However, in the case of DENY, the kernel silently discards the packet. Drops it on the floor, as it were. This is the most resource-efficient way of refusing a packet, but it can be unhelpful to the sender—the message just disappears into the void, without any trace that it was dropped. REJECT, on the other hand, tells the kernel to discard the packet and to send an ICMP message back to the sender to advise it that the connection failed. This is much more helpful, but it costs resources, particularly processing power. REJECT also opens you up to being probed for information. If you send ICMP rejections to packets you don't want, then any packet that doesn't trigger one is being accepted. An attacker might not know where a packet has gone, but he or she knows that it wasn't dropped on the floor. The attacker can then concentrate on sending more packets like the one that got through. It's generally better to have attackers sending you stuff you can cheaply drop on the floor. In consequence, it's usually much better to DENY a packet you don't want than to REJECT it. There are a few situations, however, where REJECT is useful, and we will cover those later in the chapter. To avoid ICMP messages bouncing back and forth, REJECT means the same as DENY when applied to ICMP packets.

We will use the term *refusal* or *refusing a packet* to cover the use of either DENY or REJECT to prevent a packet from passing through a chain. When we speak of packets being refused, they may be either denied or rejected. It's your choice, but bear in mind our comments above on which is preferable.

If the only thing you could set about a chain was the default policy, an ipchains-based firewall would be a sorry sort of beast, able only either to route every packet or to route none. A good firewall has the ability to discriminate: allowing some kinds of packets, and denying others. To get this functionality, we add rules to our chains. Rules are what allow you to turn your chains into the core of a useful and usable firewall.

Rules

Rules control the progress of packets through chains. A rule consists of two elements: a *set of conditions* and a *target*. The conditions allow the rule only to be applied to certain packets; the target says what should happen when a packet matches all those conditions. A packet passing through a chain will be tested against each rule in turn, until the packet matches the conditions relating to a particular rule. Then, the target of that particular rule will be invoked to determine the fate of that packet.

It is legal to define a rule that has no target; if a packet matches the rule, nothing will happen. Since the kernel keeps count of the number of packets that have matched every rule, this is a good way of counting packets without acting on them. Unless you're passionately interested in the nature of the traffic through your firewall this is probably a waste of resources.

Conditions

What sort of conditions can you impose upon a rule? You can discriminate based on many different aspects of a packet: where it comes from, where it's going to, what kind of IP protocol it is, what its source or destination port is (in the case of UDP and TCP), or what kind of message it is (if it's ICMP). You can also discriminate based on the particular interface a packet wishes to enter (for the input chain) or leave (for the output chain). Just how discriminating can you get? The ACLU hasn't taken a stand on the issue yet, so you need to use your own judgment. We will cover how to do all these things, and more, in this chapter.

Targets

There are six basic potential targets that can be applied to rules. Three of them we have already discussed: ACCEPT, DENY, and REJECT. Their function as rule targets is just the same as their function as policies. If a rule matches a packet, and the target is ACCEPT, the packet passes through the chain. Congratulations, packet! If a rule matches a packet, and the target is DENY or REJECT, the packet fails to pass through the chain. Try again next week, evil attacking packet.

The other three possible targets are MASQ, REDIRECT, and RETURN. You will probably not use any of these except MASQ (and you might not use that one, either).

MASQ is used only in the forward chain. It is active only if the kernel has been configured with CONFIG_IP_MASQUERADE defined (this is true for the stock Red Hat 6 kernel; if you rebuild the kernel and you use masquerading, you will need to make sure this parameter stays defined). If the target of a rule is MASQ, packets matching the rule will be masqueraded as if they had originated from the interface by which they're about to leave. Replies generated by such packets will be recognized as such and will be automatically demasqueraded and will bypass the forward chain. We'll deal with masquerading in more detail later in this chapter. It is unfortunate that the ipchains tool is also used to administer masquerading, since firewalling and masquerading are rather dissimilar beasts.

REDIRECT is used solely in the input chain. It is won't be effective unless the kernel has been configured with CONFIG_IP_TRANSPARENT_PROXY defined (this is true for the stock Red Hat 6 kernel; if you rebuild the kernel, and you use masquerading, you will need to make sure this parameter stays defined). If the target of a rule is REDIRECT, packets that match this rule will be redirected to a local socket even if they were supposed to be sent to a remote host. This is not something you would usually want to do because it can complicate matters enormously with little consequent benefit for most networks. However, it is cool. It allows you to do things like building transparent Web caches.

Transparent Web Cache

A transparent Web cache is an elegant device for people who run networks with many users all surfing the Web. There's a pretty good chance that many of them will want to go to the same Web site. If people were to satisfy their requests through a central local server, that server would only need to go to the remote site the first time any particular page was requested. Subsequent requests for the same page could be satisfied from the local server, saving access time and Internet bandwidth. Such a local server is called a *Web cache*. To use a standard Web cache requires every user's browser to be configured to go to the central server for Web pages, instead of going out to the Internet. If, however, the firewall through which they had to pass in order to get to the Internet knew that all Web requests should instead be sent to a local Web cache (except requests coming from that Web cache, which must of course be allowed onto the Internet), you could get the benefit of Web caching without having to reconfigure every desktop browser. This is transparent Web caching, and if you've got enough users all going through the one cache, it can cut Internet-bound Web traffic by 50 percent or more.

RETURN is a legal target in any chain, but generally has practical use only in user-defined chains, which we'll discuss later in this chapter. If you use RETURN as a target in either the input, output, or forward chains, the default policy for the chain determines the fate of packets matching the rule. This isn't a good way of accepting or denying packets. Except in user-defined chains, use ACCEPT or DENY as explicit targets, rather than using RETURN.

First Match Wins

The order in which rules are added to a chain is important. To understand this, consider the way chains are evaluated. A packet enters the chain and is tested against the rules in sequence until it matches the conditions of one of them. That rule has a target, which will specify the acceptance or refusal of that packet. Chain processing stops at that point, whether the packet was accepted or refused. Let's reiterate, because this is very important: Once a packet has matched a rule, it goes no further through that chain. The target of the matched rule determines the fate of the matched packet. End of story.

NOTE A rule with no target does not stop chain processing. It's the act of jumping to a target, not merely matching the rule, that stops processing.

How does this affect you? Suppose, for example, you wish to refuse all traffic from a particular IP address, save Web traffic which you wish to permit. There is *no point* in writing the refuse rule first, then the accept rule, since all packets from that IP address will match the first rule and be refused. Web packets will never get to the rule that lets them in; they'll be refused along with the rest.

Specific rules must come before general rules. To put it another way, exceptions must precede rules. English often has this the other way around: The rule is stated, then the exception. What in English is written "none of my cats are allowed inside my house, except the grey one" must be written for ipchains as two rules: "the grey cat may enter my house" followed by "no cats may enter my house."

The second rule did not have to make an explicit exception for the grey cat. She has already matched the first rule and been admitted; cat processing stopped for her after rule one. All my other cats pass through rule one, match rule two, and get shoved unceremoniously out the back door. It is with packets as it is with cats, but quieter.

User-Defined Chains

As we mentioned earlier, you can define your own chains and give them rules just as you would give rules to the three built-in chains (input, output, and forward). You just give your chains different names.

The definition and invocation of user-defined chains are easy. We'll cover how to define them later in the chapter. Once you have defined a chain, you can invoke it as you would any other target. If you have defined a chain called

'Webcheck', Webcheck becomes a valid target for a rule, just like ACCEPT and DENY.

NOTE

You can't set policies for user-defined chains. You also can't invoke the built-in chains as targets for user-defined chains.

User-defined chains constitute the exception to the first-match-wins-and-ends-the-game rule. The previous paragraph told you how a packet passes from one chain to another when a rule in the first chain specifies a second chain as the rule's target. We will call the first chain the *calling chain,* and the second chain the *called chain.* If you call a user-defined chain, and the packet passed doesn't match any of the rules in the user-defined chain, the packet is passed back to the calling chain (remember that there is no policy to be a catch-all, as there would be with a built-in chain). The packet re-enters the calling chain at the rule after the one that sent it to the called chain. If a packet running through a called chain matches a rule inside that chain that has the target RETURN, then the same thing happens—the packet is immediately passed back to the calling chain, returning to the rule following the one that sent it away.

The function of user-defined chains is to allow very complex sets of rules to be moved off into their own chain for clarity and modularity of thought. However, we have rarely come across chains so complex as to benefit from this kind of modularization. On the other hand, user-defined chains do have certain uses in accounting. By and large, we would generally advise you to steer clear of user-defined chains; the examples in this chapter are written entirely with built-in chains.

Practical Chain-Making

We've covered the theory. Now we'll cover the practice. In order to manipulate your kernel's chains, you need to be root. Execute "/bin/su -", give the root password, and away we go.

NOTE

Do everything in this section while logged on at the console. If you're logged in over the network, and you mess with the networking functions of the machine, you're very likely to lock yourself out. Since you will be opening up your server to attack, you may also wish to disconnect any hostile networks while you try these examples. Turn off and unplug the modem, or yank any suspicious-looking ethernet cables.

Flush the Chains

Step one is to get us to a known, good state. Issue these commands:

```
ipchains -F input
ipchains -F output
ipchains -F forward
```

The '-F' flag flushes all rules from the specified chain; the combination of these three commands flushes all of the built-in chains.

Step two is to set the policies. Issue these commands (yes, case is important):

```
ipchains -P input ACCEPT
ipchains -P output ACCEPT
ipchains -P forward ACCEPT
```

The '-P' flag sets policy for the specified chain. We've set all three built-in chains to ACCEPT. This is equivalent to going down the "accept everything that is not explicitly denied" road, described in Chapter 3. When we build the real firewall, we will avoid death and destruction by starting with a more restrictive policy.

Step three is to see what we've done. At any point you can show the state of your rules and chains by typing

```
ipchains -L -n
```

The '-L' flag lists the rules for the specified chain (or all chains if none is specified), the '-n' flag presents all IP addresses as dotted quads instead of trying to reverse-resolve them back to domain names. That distinction isn't important now as we don't have any addresses in our chains, but as we add rules this becomes important. If you omit this flag, it can take a long time to get the output, as you must wait for each DNS reverse-resolve to time out—it's better to get into the habit of using it now. In any case, this is what you should see:

```
Chain input (policy ACCEPT):
Chain forward (policy ACCEPT):
Chain output (policy ACCEPT):
```

Simple, eh? Three chains, three policies, no rules. Just what we asked for. Now it gets tougher. (However tough it gets, you can come back to this section and perform these three steps to return your firewall to sanity.)

Try Out a Rule or Two

We're going to try out a few simple rules, just to get you familiar with using ipchains. It's easier to appreciate what you're doing if you can see the effect that it's having. Seeing the effects is a lot easier if you have another computer to test it from.

We assume that you have at least one other machine on your internal network. When we want you to try something on that other machine, we'll refer to it as the test machine. You will need to know the IP addresses of both the test machine and the firewall. You will also need to move physically to the test machine to try things from it—you are unlikely to be able to keep a network connection up through most of these tests.

Let's try refusing all packets of a certain type, say all TCP packets. Type:

```
ipchains -A input -p tcp -j DENY
```

This is the first real rule we have written. We used the '-A' flag, which appends the rule we're writing to the existing rules already on that chain. There are no rules on that chain, since we flushed the chain in the previous section. This allows us to define rule one. The condition on this rule is specified by the '-p' flag, which specifies a protocol type. We used 'tcp'; we could have used 'udp', or 'icmp', or 'all'—meaning any protocol. The '-j' flag specifies the target for the rule, which in this case is DENY. However long and hairy any rule is, at some point in the ipchains command you'll see the '-j' flag preceding the target (unless the rule has no target as mentioned earlier).

To see what this has done, go to the test machine. Try to telnet to the firewall machine (issue the command "telnet ip.address.of.firewall" from a command prompt). You should find that telnet just sits there, sending requests for a connection, receiving no answer. Since we used the DENY target, the firewall is silently dropping those packets on the ground. To see the difference between DENY and REJECT, try:

```
ipchains -F input
ipchains -A input -p tcp -j REJECT
```

The first line flushes the input rule, to get rid of the DENY rule we just defined. If we didn't do this, the new rule would be appended after the DENY rule, and because the conditions are the same for both rules (-p tcp), the first rule would match any TCP packets, and we would never see the REJECT target in action. The second line defines our new rule with the same conditions as in our original rule, but with a different target.

Again, try to telnet from the test machine to the firewall. This time, you should immediately get a "connection-refused" message. That's the ICMP response telling the test machine that it can't get to the firewall machine—the difference between DENY and REJECT. Try pinging the firewall; you should get an immediate "up" response, since we haven't blocked ICMP traffic, only TCP traffic. If you were to repeat the above steps with '-p icmp', pings would be silently dropped while the telnet connection worked fine. If you wonder why they would be silently dropped even though you specified REJECT, recall what we said about REJECT being equivalent to DENY for icmp traffic.

Now we'll try something a little more ambitious. We will deny TCP traffic just to one particular port, in this case, the telnet port (23). Try:

```
ipchains -F input
ipchains -A input -p tcp--destination-port 23 -j DENY
```

Here, we have added in the new flag '--destination-port' (yes, that is a double dash). Recall that TCP port 23 is the traditional port for interactive telnet access. If you try to telnet to the firewall from the test machine you should get silence, just as you did in the first example. If, instead, you try to connect to port 513 on the firewall with "telnet IP.address.of.firewall 513", you should get an immediate connection (hit return to get your prompt back). TCP port 513 is the rlogin service—one of the dangerous ones we talked about in Chapter 3. We'll be turning it off before the chapter is over. Had we wanted to block a range of ports (say, 99 through 1023 inclusive), we could have said '--destination-port 99:1023'. Had we wanted to block data from a single or range of source ports, we could have used the '--source-port' flag in the same manner.

NOTE

For brevity, '--dport' can be used in place of '--destination-port' and '--sport' can be used in place of '--source-port'. The double dash is still required.

That was also our first rule with two conditions: First, the protocol had to be TCP, and second, the destination port had to be 23. The two conditions must both be satisfied in order to get a match; however many conditions are in a single rule, all conditions must be satisfied in order to match. If you want to apply two conditions and the rule to match when *either* condition is satisfied, write two rules instead.

Now we're going to try specifying a source address. If you have two hosts on your internal network in addition to your firewall and you know all their IP addresses, we can try and filter one out, but not the other. Suppose that the IP address of one of them is 1.2.3.4. Now try:

```
ipchains -F input
ipchains -A input -p tcp -s 1.2.3.4 --destination-port 23 -j DENY
```

The inclusion of the '-s 1.2.3.4' flag requires that the source address be 1.2.3.4 (1.2.3.4 is not the address you will use; you will substitute the IP address of one of your internal machines). The other flags, as we have already discussed, require that the connection be TCP, and that the destination port be 23. The machine with the IP address you have put in place of 1.2.3.4 should now be unable to telnet to the firewall.

Had we wished to specify a source port as well, the '-s' flag allows a second argument for a source port: there is no difference between '-s 1.2.3.4 --source-port 56' and '-s 1.2.3.4 56'. The same holds true for a range of ports: '-s 1.2.3.4 --source-port 56:78' is equivalent to '-s 1.2.3.4 56:78'.

If we want to specify that a condition must *not* apply, all conditions can be negated with the '!' operator. The following will negate the source address condition on the last rule:

```
ipchains -F input
ipchains -A input -p tcp -s ! a.b.c.d--destination-port 23 -j DENY
```

Having negated the source address condition, and no other, we should now find that *only* the machine with IP address a.b.c.d can telnet to the firewall; all *other* machines should fail silently. We could have negated any or all of the other conditions, blocking access to all ports other than 23, or all protocols other than TCP.

Hopefully, you can already see how these few tools will be used together to build a powerful packet-filtering firewall. There are still a few more tools we need to cover, but if you've got your head round everything in this last section, you've got most of what you need under your belt. Practice and experiment until you are comfortable with everything up to this point.

Other Important Flags

If you are matching on ICMP, then the '--destination-port' flag might not seem stunningly useful, as ICMP doesn't have ports. It does, however, have message types, and the '--destination-port' flag is used with ICMP to specify message types. Types you should consider permitting are 0 (echo-reply), if you want to be able to ping outside your network, and 11 (time-exceeded), if you want to be able to use the 'traceroute' tool to check machines outside your network. (If you're not familiar with it, traceroute is an extremely useful tool that can be used to find the path a packet is taking through a network, including the Internet. Do "man traceroute" for more information.)

Do not block ICMP type 3 unless suffering is fun for you. Not only is this used by remote hosts to signify that a firewall or other device has chosen to block your packet (recall the difference between REJECT and DENY), but type 3 ICMP is used by the TCP implementation to negotiate certain parameters. Your network performance will suffer badly if you block type 3 ICMP to the machine you use to connect to the outside world. To allow it, use a line like:

```
ipchains -A input -p icmp-destination-port 3 -j ACCEPT
```

Note that we have now allowed ICMP type 3 packets to enter the firewall, whether they are intended for the firewall or for some machine inside your network.

The '-i' flag allows you to specify only a particular interface. If, for example, your Internet connection is via PPP across a modem, then it is likely that your network interface is ppp0. If this were true, you could apply much more stringent conditions to packets coming in from the Internet by including '-i ppp0' in the conditions or the stringent rules. If your external interface has another name (eth1 or sl0, for example) then just substitute that name for 'ppp0'. Since this is exactly the behavior we require of a firewall—that it should be much meaner to packets coming in from the outside world than to packets leaving from your internal network—we will use this flag a lot in the final firewall.

The '-y' flag allows you to match packets with the 'SYN' flag set on, and the 'ACK' and 'FIN' flags cleared. Any packet trying to initiate a TCP connection must have those three flags set as described; conversely, any packet which has some other set of values for those three flags is not initiating a conversation.

Why is this so helpful? Bear in mind that, behind your firewall, there will be flocks of users all initiating TCP connections to all sorts of ports on all sorts of servers all over the Internet. Packets will be coming back to a variety of local ports from a variety of remote ports on a variety of machines. The only thing all these packets have in common is that they're all responses to connections initiated by users at your sites. You want to let them all in, but you don't want to let everything else in with them.

Consider the following rule:

```
ipchains -A input -i ppp0 -p tcp ! -y -j ACCEPT
```

This rule is part of the input chain. It applies only to packets on interface ppp0, and only those which are TCP packets. It also requires that the '-y' flag *not* apply; that is, it requires that a packet be part of an existing conversation, not a request for a new one. If all three conditions are satisfied, the packet is accepted. Any TCP packet that presents itself on your exterior interface claiming to be part of an existing conversation is one you will want to invite in for a closer look. Combine this with an input policy of DENY and a rule to accept packets originating inside your network, and you've done some highly selective filtering already.

Right now, you may be wondering if the SYN flag can be faked. Well, yes it can. You, as a network nasty person, can put a packet together that says nearly anything. If a packet arrives at a machine claiming to be part of a pre-existing conversation, but the machine has no knowledge of such a conversation, the naughty packet should get dropped on the floor. Using a rule like the above isn't completely safe—what is?—but it can make your filter simpler. A simple filter is much less likely to have unforeseen holes due to rule ordering or poor syntax.

Nevertheless, you may wish to be picky about the source port of such packets. If instead of the one blanket rule you see above, we had several rules which also specified source ports, we could permit only packets that were part of pre-existing telnet conversations, or ssh conversations, or mail conversations. The three rules below do just that, in that order:

```
ipchains -A input -i ppp0 -p tcp ! -y—source-port 23 -j ACCEPT
ipchains -A input -i ppp0 -p tcp ! -y—source-port 22 -j ACCEPT
ipchains -A input -i ppp0 -p tcp ! -y—source-port 25 -j ACCEPT
```

It would be convenient if we could pull this trick with UDP packets, too, but because UDP is connectionless we can't. Filtering UDP packets is harder. If you want to permit replies to DNS requests in, you have to use a rule like:

```
ipchains -A input -i ppp0 -p udp—source-port 53 -j ACCEPT
```

which will permit *all* UDP packets originating from port 53 on remote machines—DNS packets—in the ppp0 interface, *irrespective* of whether they are replies to a request originated by *you*. UDP rules tend to specify source address ranges whenever possible to add more security. For instance, in the above rules, you could permit these DNS packets only from the IP addresses of your ISP's DNS servers.

Masquerading

In Chapter 3, we discussed IP Masquerading, that is, the art of hiding a whole internal network behind one valid IP address. This isn't strictly connected with firewalling, but it's administered with the same tool and it's a common enough need that we're going to cover it here.

Recall from earlier in this chapter that masquerading is achieved by specifying a target of MASQ in the forward rule. Recall also that we only need to masquerade packets going out from our internal network, automatically rebadging them with the IP address of the interface through which they leave. Recall finally that the kernel takes care of automatically tracking replies, demasquerading and redirecting them appropriately, and sneaking them through the forward rule on the return trip. Since that much care is taken on our behalf, all we really have to make sure is that packets which are going to be sent out are pointed at the MASQ target. It's pretty easy. For the sake of argument, let us assume that the internal network is using a subset of one of the private address ranges, 192.168.1.0-192.168.1.255, and that we have no DMZ. Use the lines:

```
ipchains -F forward
ipchains -A forward -s 192.168.1.0/24 -d ! 192.168.1.0/24 -j MASQ
```

The second line matches all packets which have a source IP address inside our network and which have a destination address outside our network, and calls the MASQ target on them. If our internal network were 10.0.0.0-10.254.254.254, we would replace 192.168.1.0/24 with 10.0.0.0/8 throughout; other networks can be similarly specified. Go back and read the sidebar on masking, if needed.

That's really all there is to masquerading.

Forwarding

Red Hat 6, like many modern distributions, is configured not to forward any packets at all. Until this behavior is altered, you can set MASQ targets until you're blue in the face, and nothing will come of it.

You can alter this behavior in several ways. You can have it set on at boot time, by setting 'FORWARD_IPV4=true' in the file /etc/sysconfig/network (have a look at it, you'll see the line there already except that it sets the variable to false). Or, you can switch it on as and when you want, by including code in your firewall startup script that says:

```
echo 1 > /proc/sys/net/ipv4/ip_forward
```

which (interestingly) is exactly what the system does at boot time if you set the flag in /etc/sysconfig/network. You can also switch forwarding off at any time by typing:

```
echo 0 > /proc/sys/net/ipv4/ip_forward
```

Which method is best for you? On the whole, we prefer editing the /etc/sysconfig/network file. There are proper error trapping and sanity checking in the system startup script that implements this method. The downside to doing it that way is that if you don't start the firewall shortly after you start packet forwarding, you'll have a window of opportunity during which time packets you don't want to have forwarded slip through. For more information, refer to the *Starting the Firewall* section later in this chapter.

Practical Firewalling

Enough theorizing, enough practicing—it's time to write a real firewall. We're now going to give a simple example. You could take this script and use it as your own firewall, if your circumstances were right. On the companion Web site (www.wiley.com/compbooks/sonnenreich), you'll find scripts which are more generally valid, in that they use variables to allow you to edit interface names, networks, etc., without editing every rule by hand. If you want to start from a cut-and-dried script, we'd recommend using one of those.

If you were to use the following code, you would type it into a file. Let's assume you call the file /etc/rc.d/init.d/rc.firewall. You would give the file execute permission with "chmod 755 /etc/rc.d/init.d/rc.firewall" and make arrangements to have this file run every time the machine was rebooted. We will cover this further in the *Starting the Firewall* section later in this chapter.

In this example, any line that starts with a "#" (except for the first line) is a comment. Comment blocks precede each section and each substantive line of code where needed. ppp0 is our external network interface, eth0 is our internal network interface, and lo is the loopback interface. You should permit traffic to come in the loopback interface unmolested. Our internal network is masqueraded, and we are using the private subnet 192.168.1.0/24 internally. Our ISP's DNS servers have the IP addresses 1.2.3.1 and 1.2.3.2, and our ISP's NTP server has the IP address 1.3.4.5.

```
#!/bin/bash
##########################################################
# Firewalling rules
##########################################################
#
# flush all rules
#
ipchains -F input
ipchains -F output
ipchains -F forward
#
#
# set policies
#
ipchains -P input DENY
ipchains -P output ACCEPT
```

```
ipchains -P forward ACCEPT
#
#
# allow some packets in but accept all those on the internal interface
#
ipchains -A input -i lo   -j ACCEPT
ipchains -A input -i eth0 -j ACCEPT
#
#
# deny any coming from outside which are illegal
#
ipchains -A input -i ppp0 -s 192.168.0.0/16 -j DENY  # see note 1
ipchains -A input -i ppp0 -s 172.16.0.0/12 -j DENY
ipchains -A input -i ppp0 -s 10.0.0.0/8 -j DENY
#
#
# allow return packets from connections we initiated
#
ipchains -A input -i ppp0 -p tcp ! -y -j ACCEPT
#
#
# allow connections to MAIL and SSH
#
ipchains -A input -i ppp0 -p tcp --dport 25 -j ACCEPT   # see note 2
ipchains -A input -i ppp0 -p tcp --dport 22 -j ACCEPT
#
#
# REJECT auth conections for fast SMTP handshake
#
ipchains -A input -i ppp0 -p tcp --dport 113 -j REJECT   # see note 3
#
#
# allow DNS replies
#
ipchains -A input -i ppp0 -p udp -s 1.2.3.1 53 -j ACCEPT    # see note 4
ipchains -A input -i ppp0 -p udp -s 1.2.3.2 53 -j ACCEPT
ipchains -A input -i ppp0 -p tcp -s 1.2.3.1 53 -j ACCEPT
ipchains -A input -i ppp0 -p tcp -s 1.2.3.2 53 -j ACCEPT
#
#
# allow NTP replies
#
ipchains -A input -i ppp0 -p udp -d 1.3.4.5 123 -j ACCEPT
#
#
# allow certain classes of ICMP
#
ipchains -A input -i ppp0 -p icmp --dport  0 -j ACCEPT
ipchains -A input -i ppp0 -p icmp --dport  3 -j ACCEPT
ipchains -A input -i ppp0 -p icmp --dport 11 -j ACCEPT
#
```

```
#
# finally, deny all other packets to input and LOG them.  let's see
# what's hitting us...
#
ipchains -A input -j DENY -l # see note 5
#
#
###########################################################
# MASQ rules
###########################################################
#
ipchains -A forward -j MASQ -s 192.168.1.0/24 -d ! 192.168.1.0/24
#
# END OF FILE
```

Notes:

1. It's always a good idea to explicitly refuse packets that shouldn't be there anyway. These three networks are the private networks mentioned in Chapter 3. Packets from these networks shouldn't be able to present themselves at your exterior interface, but if they do, reject them. If we were using public address space inside our network, we would also include a line here that explicitly rejected packets coming in from outside that claim to originate from inside the network.

2. We're going to run two TCP services on our firewall, or port-forward them to some server inside. The services are on TCP ports 25 (a mail server) and 22 (an ssh server, for remote administration). We must explicitly allow new connections from the outside world to these services. (Port forwarding is discussed in more detail in the following section.)

3. Recall earlier that we said sometimes it was useful to REJECT instead of DENY, even though it uses more resources. This is one of those cases. When we try to send outgoing mail by way of a well-behaved SMTP server, that server will try to do an ident lookup on us. The "ident" service is an old one, a hangover from the days when everyone trusted each other on the Internet, whereby the machine you're making SMTP connections to will try to call you back on this pre-arranged service to verify a few things about you. This involves an incoming connection to TCP port 113. If this attempt is rejected, the remote server will just shrug, and get on with the SMTP conversation. If the attempt is denied, the remote server will wait until it times out before proceeding with the conversation. The net effect is a delay of a minute or so every time you try to connect to a mail server. If you ever send outgoing mail, rejecting inbound TCP port 113 instead of using DENY will speed up connections substantially. Please note: It's not important that the remote server be allowed to do the ident lookup in order to have mail flow

happily. It's only necessary that it get a prompt and audible NO when it tries to do so.

4. We're explicitly accepting DNS replies—both UDP and TCP—from our DNS servers only. You would replace 1.2.3.1 and 1.2.3.2 with the IP addresses for your ISP's DNS servers. If there are more than two, remember to include a TCP and a UDP line for each of them.

5. Why would we bother with this line when we've already set the policy to DENY for the input list? Isn't this line redundant? Yes, it is—nearly. There's no functional difference to the packet forwarding process between having a policy of DENY, and having the last rule in a chain be an unconditional DENY. However, you can add the '-l' flag to a rule, but you can't add it to a policy. The '-l' flag in a rule causes information about any packet that matches the rule to be logged. The information is logged through the syslog service, with facility "kern" and severity "info." It's a pretty good idea to keep an eye on who's knocking on your door. See the sidebar on logging to learn how to do this.

You've seen your first full-blown firewall. It's short and sweet, but it's usable. What will it do for you?

Logging

All Unix machines come with an excellent tool for centralizing logging called *syslog*. The primary parts are the syslog dæmon syslogd', which we told the system to start at boot time when we installed Linux, and the configuration file /etc/syslog.conf. While the precise operation of syslog is too complex to cover in this book, you can read the full documentation by typing "man syslogd" and "man syslog.conf". For a quick and dirty logging system, add one line to the end of your syslog.conf file which says:

    kern.=info   /var/log/firewall

(and make sure the white space between "info" and "/var" is all TAB characters).

Now, create the file /var/log/firewall by typing "touch /var/log/firewall", and let syslogd know you have changed the configuration file (the fastest way is to run "/etc/rc.d/init.d/syslog restart", though there are more elegant ways). Then, anything your firewall logs will get sent to the file /var/log/firewall. Read this file from time to time. Ponder anything that turns up in it, and read Chapter 11 "Intrusion Detection and Response."

It should also be noted that syslog is itself a network service—it runs on UDP port 514. Although Red Hat Linux distributes syslogd configured to ignore any messages that originate from machines other than the one it's running on, it would be wise to bar packets arriving from the Internet on UDP port 514.

Regarding TCP, any machine on your internal network will be able to establish TCP connections to the outside world, private addresses you use inside (picked from the range 192.168.1.1–192.168.1.254) will be masqueraded behind the real IP address your firewall uses, and replies will be allowed back in and demasqueraded. Inbound, only mail and ssh connections to your firewall will be permitted, and TCP connections from your ISP's DNS servers.

With regard to UDP, only DNS packets from your ISP's DNS servers, and NTP from your ISP's NTP server will be permitted. Any UDP-based Internet service will be inaccessible to your firewall and to machines on your internal network.

Starting the Firewall

The firewall code needs to be embedded in the system startup scripts so that the firewalling happens automatically each time the machine is rebooted. The later in the boot process this happens, the longer the network interfaces are up without firewall protection. If there's enough time, a hacker may be able to compromise the firewall by crashing the machine and then attacking the network before the firewall rules take effect.

We suggest starting the firewall just before the network interfaces are initialized. To do this, look in the directory /etc/rc.d/rc3.d. This contains a lot of files which are executed when the system shuts down (they start with K and a two-digit number) or starts up (they start with S and a two-digit number). They are executed in the order that they appear in a directory listing. S10network is the file responsible for initializing the network interfaces. If you put the firewall startup script in this directory, and call it S09firewall, it will run at startup time just before the network interfaces are brought up. You can put the script in just as it appears above, or you can use a wrapper (a script which in turn calls the firewall start script after doing a few checks) and be somewhat better behaved. A wrapper can be found on the companion Web site– (www.wiley.com/compbooks/sonnenreich). See Chapter 12 for more details.

Remember our earlier section on forwarding and the discussion on how to start IP forwarding in the kernel? If you choose to start the firewall before the network interfaces, the method of starting forwarding by manually writing a "1" to /proc/sys/net/ipv4/ip_forward won't work. If you look more closely at the contents of S10network, you'll see why: this is the startup script that actually starts packet forwarding, if the /etc/sysconfig/network file tells it to do so. If you write a "1" to /proc/sys/net/ipv4/ip_forward at the end of S09firewall, but don't change the value of FORWARD_IPV4 in /etc/sysconfig/network, packet forwarding will be turned off by S10network about half a second after S09firewall turns it on. This is why we prefer the /etc/sysconfig/network method of activating forwarding.

Input, Output, Forward

Almost all of the rules in our example firewall are on the input chain, and we make almost no use of the forward or output chains. You may be wondering about this.

On the whole, we feel it to be safer to use the input chain for control. Any rule in the input chain implicitly protects the firewall as well as all the machines behind the firewall. Since the firewall's your main line of defense against the Internet, protecting it is a *good thing*.

Source Routing

You may recall that we discussed why source routing is bad in Chapter 2, "Fundamental Internet Security Issues." To prevent source routed packets being relayed by your firewall, issue the commands:

```
echo 0 > /proc/sys/net/ipv4/conf/all/accept_source_route
```

and

```
echo 0 > /proc/sys/net/ipv4/conf/default/accept_source_route
```

The first line sets a general policy, the second sets a default which will be explicitly applied to interfaces defined after this line is executed. Putting both lines inside your firewall startup script would be an excellent plan.

No Compiler?

This section's more of an advisory note than a rule. Some people feel that it's a good idea to take cracker-friendly tools off the firewall; others feel that a really good cracker will get by with what he's got. Should you wish to remove the most useful tools, taking the C compiler off the firewall would be a good place to start. You can remove it with:

```
rpm -ev egcs-c++-1.1.2-12
```

and

```
rpm -ev egcs-1.1.2-12
```

If you find you need to put them back later, you can find the packages on the Red Hat CD in the same location as all the other packages.

Port Forwarding

As we've said already, IP Masquerading is great, but it does have a few disadvantages. In particular, if you're using private IP addresses—say 192.168.1.1-254—in your internal network, and masquerading them behind a real IP address on a firewall, the outside world has no way to get to any server other than the firewall. Reminder: running services on your firewall isn't a very good idea. Say you want to run a Web server on an internal machine with the address 192.168.1.17, and your firewall's external address is 203.42.57.2. How will the world get to it?

Enter the port forwarding tool. You can get the RPM from http://juanjox.linuxhq.com/; install it as we described in Chapter 6 then read on. We're not going to cover this in the thorny detail that we gave to ipchains, but we will show you one concrete example and give you pointers—and a warning or two.

The syntax of *ipmasqadm* (the port forwarding tool) is remarkably like that of ipchains, except that some of ipmasqadm's arguments are in lowercase where ipchains's arguments were in uppercase. Give your shift key a half-day off and read on.

To flush the rules (we know you haven't set any up, but it's best to be safe), do an:

```
ipmasqadm portfw -f
```

The '-f' is for flush, just like ipchains (but lowercase). Then, do an:

```
ipmasqadm portfw -l -n
```

to check that there are no rules. The '-l' is for list, and the '-n' is for no-DNS-lookups, again, just like ipchains (but, again, in lowercase). You'll see something like this:

```
prot localaddr        rediraddr           lport   rport pcnt  pref
```

Now, let's add the rule that will let people get to your real Web server by connecting to port 80 on your firewall. Do the following:

```
ipmasqadm portfw -a -P tcp -L 203.42.57.2 80 -R 192.168.1.17 80
ipmasqadm portfw -l -n
```

and you should see this:

```
prot localaddr        rediraddr           lport   rport pcnt  pref
TCP  203.42.57.2       192.168.1.17           80      80   10    10
```

The first field is protocol. Recall that HTTP is a TCP protocol that runs on port 80 (usually). The second field is the local address, that is, the address on the firewall that people will be trying to connect to when they want to get to this service. The third field is the redirect address, that is, the internal network address to which these connection attempts should be sent. The lport and rport are, respectively, the port on the firewall that people will be trying to connect to, and the port on the specified internal address that they should be sent to instead. The last two fields refer to preference; their use is outside the scope of this coverage.

What will this do for you? Well, if you open a hole in your firewall for incoming traffic to port 80, anyone trying to connect to port 80 on your firewall will get magically transported to port 80 on 192.168.1.17, well inside your network. You can run your Web server on this machine, safe in the knowledge that no packet can get to any other port on it, however hard it tries.

We did mention some downsides, right? Here's one: You only have one port 80 on your firewall's external IP address, so you can only redirect port 80 once—only one Web server. There's no way to run multiple internal Web servers, all on port 80, and have them all accessed by the outside world from port 80 (unless your firewall has more than one external IP address, but if you're that lucky, then you can simply write multiple ipmasqadm rules, one for port 80 on each address).

Here's another problem: This technique works for any protocol that has a single channel. HTTP, NTP, DNS—any UDP or TCP protocol that has just one channel is fine. But protocols like IRC or FTP, that have control and data channels, cause particular problems for port forwarding. Consider passive-mode FTP. Sure, you can forward the incoming command requests to port 21, but when the server passes back a random port for the client to open a data channel, how are you going to tell the firewall what port needs forwarding? There's no way to tell, in advance, what port the FTP server is going to pick, so there's no way to write the rule. Doubtless, in the future, a more adaptive ipmasqadm will be developed that deals with these problems, but for now, multiple-channel protocols are out.

A last problem to mention relates to dynamic IP addresses. You will notice that you have to specify your firewall's IP address in the ipmasqadm command; you can't just tell it to forward any old connection request to port 80 that happens to wander in off the Internet. If your external IP address is dynamically assigned, then there's no way of making one rule that will be valid for any IP address you might be given. You'll have to rewrite the rule in real time, as your address is given to you. That's way beyond the scope of this book, so we'll have to discourage you from trying to forward services in this manner unless you have a static address.

IPChains Reference

The following is a listing and description of every single flag that can be used to modify the behavior of the ipchains command. Many of these flags are not needed to build most firewalls, but if you ever find yourself wondering how to do such-and-such a thing, this section may give you food for thought. This information can also be found by typing "man ipchains", but it's ordered differently there—by function, not alphabetically. We hope this is also a useful resource for you.

A: Appends a rule to a chain.

b: A rule with this bidirectional mode flag will match packets in both directions (i.e., swapping source and destination).

C: Checks a given packet against the specified chain. If you're not sure if something would be allowed through, specify the parameters of a test packet with the -s, -d, -i, and -p flags, and other flags if you need them. Ipchains whips up a test packet according to these specifications and runs it past the specified chain, telling you if it would be allowed in or not.

D: Deletes the specified rule. This can be either a rule number (do a listing with -L, and start counting) or the rule itself.

d: Specifies the destination of a packet. The remainder of the argument is an IP address, with an optional mask; the mask is separated from the address by a slash. You may also specify a port or a numerically sequential range of ports; the port information is separated from the address or address/mask combination by a space; if a range of ports is given, the start and end values are separated by colons. Examples are:

- d 1.2.3.4 matches the destination address 1.2.3.4

- d 1.2.3.0/24 matches the destination addresses 1.2.3.0-1.2.3.255 inclusive

- d 1.2.4.6 1:1023 matches the address 1.2.4.6 but only if the destination port is between 1 and 1023 inclusive

Before the address/mask negates the address/mask criterion; before the port or port range, if present, negates the port criterion. These may be combined to negate both criteria. Example:

- -d ! 1.2.3.0/24 56:78 requires that the destination address not be between 1.2.3.0 and 1.2.3.255 inclusive, AND that the destination port be between 56 and 78 inclusive

destination-port, -dport: Specifies only the destination port of a packet. A numerically sequential range may be specified, as shows under -d, in the form start:finish. If used for packets of type ICMP, specifies the message type.

F: Flushes (deletes all the rules on) the specified chain.

f: Requires that the rule be applied only to second and later packets of datagrams which have become fragmented.

h: The help flag gives a brief description of ipchains syntax.

I: Requires a chain and a rule number, and a rule; inserts the specified rule at the specified position in the specified chain. 'ipchains -I input 1 ...' inserts the rule that follows in position 1 (i.e., the first rule) of the input chain.

i: Specifies an interface through which the packet must enter (for an input rule) or leave (for an output rule). '-i ppp0' specifies the interface called ppp0. '-i eth+' specifies all interfaces whose names start with the string 'eth.'

icmp-type: A more convenient and explicit way of specifying ICMP message type.

j: Specifies the target to jump to in the case of a match. The rest of the argument must be any one of the six built-in targets ACCEPT, REJECT, DENY, MASQ, REDIRECT, RETURN, or the name of a user-defined chain.

L: Lists all the rules in the specified chain, or in all chains if no chain is specified.

l: Logs information about any packet that matches this rule, and any target specified.

M: Combined with -L, lists information about the masquerading tables currently in use. This isn't the general masqerading policy, this is live information about how (eg) port A has been remapped to port B for TCP access from machine C to machine D, and the entry in the masquerade tables will expire at time E. Interesting to look at, if you like watching magic at work.

Combined with -S, allows you to manually set entries in the masquerade tables. See -S for further information. Don't do this.

m: Marks matching packets with the specified value. This is analogous to slapping a sticky note on the packet as it goes by. In the words of the man page, "If you are not a kernel hacker, you are unlikely to care about this." Trust them.

N: Creates a user-defined chain by the specified name. Name must be eight letters or less, and must not already exist. You cannot assign rules to a user-defined chain, nor use it as a target, until you have declared it with this flag.

n: In a listing (-L), presents all IP addresses as numbers. Do not attempt to reverse-resolve them back into names. This can be very useful if your link to the Internet is a dial-on-demand link; otherwise, DNS lookups will bring the line up.

o: Copies matching packets to the userspace device. This requires kernel reconfiguration and substantial kernel internal knowledge. Don't use this flag.

P: Sets the policy for the specified chain to the specified target. 'ipchains -P input DENY' sets the policy for the input chain to DENY. Neither built-in nor user-defined chains may be used as policy targets.

p: In a rule, matches the specified protocol. The protocol must be tcp, udp, icmp, or all, a protocol name from /etc/protocols, or the corresponding protocol number. '!' may be used between -p and the protocol name to invert the selection. Example: -p ! icmp specifies all protocols except ICMP.

R: Replaces the specified rule in the specified chain with the rule in this command. The rule is specified by number, starting at 1 for the first rule in each chain.

S: With -M, sets the timeout parameters for masquerading. This is Deep Magic From The Dawn Of Timing, and you shouldn't need to use this flag unless you've a got a lot of very busy clients behind your firewall.

s: Specifies the source address of a packet. Arguments are identical to those of -d.

source-port, -sport: Specifies only the source port of a packet. Arguments are identical to those of—destination-port.

t: Can be used to specify masks for altering the Type Of Service (TOS) field in the packet header. Magic doesn't come much deeper than this. Don't use this flag.

v: Verbose output, when used with -L. A 132-column window is recommended for reading the output this flag produces. It's as overwhelming as it is educational.

X: Deletes the specified user-defined chain. There must be no references to that chain in any other chains, nor must the chain contain any rules, or deletion will fail. If no chain name is given, it will attempt to delete all user-defined chains.

x: Used with -L, displays exact packet counter values, instead of the rounded values that are displayed normally when counts get high enough.

y: When protocol is set to tcp, matches only packets with the SYN flag set, and ACK and FIN cleared. The very first packet, and only the very first packet, in a TCP conversation satisfies these requirements. Often used with "!" to invert the meaning, which allows only packets that form part of an existing conversation.

Z: Zeros the packet and byte counters in the specified chain. If no chain is specified, all chains are cleared. Doesn't clear the policy counters on the chains; we have to reboot or change the policy to clear those.

Summary

You're now able to create a line of firewall code to meet most requirements. If someone asks you to poke a hole in your firewall to allow a service through, you know what sort of line to insert into the firewall startup code, and where to put it. Hopefully, you've already got a simple firewall running on your firewall machine. You're ready to go on to Chapter 10 where we'll go through many of the services discussed in Chapter 3, but this time showing you exactly how to permit or block them.

## CHAPTER 8

Installing OpenBSD

Consider yourself fortunate. You are embarking on an exciting journey of discovery. You will be facing challenges that have brought highly skilled system administrators to their knees, with tears flowing into their pocket protectors. You will tread forward, over the backs of those whom fear has crushed. Your bravery comes from the eternal source that has likewise emboldened the hearts of humanity's most cherished heroes: You have nothing to lose.

Many people embark on the quest to install OpenBSD with the desire to retain an existing operating system on a portion of their hard drive. These poor souls take each tiny step knowing that one wrong move means lengthy recoveries from backup files. Our deepest sympathies go out to the novices, who assume that a recovery from backup is the worst case scenario (if they didn't backup, they're about to win a one way trip to hell). The reality is that Windows has a host of little chicken and egg problems, which means that loading the recovery program can become more difficult that one would expect. This is especially true when the recovery program realizes that the OpenBSD installer has changed the partition table (more on that in a bit).

Not that setting up a dual OS system with Linux is a stroll in the park either unless that park is in Cambodia or Kosovo. Those who are using Linux with LILO (LInux LOader the default boot loader for Linux) are in for a rather harsh surprise when the inevitable wrong move happens. LILO is *very* sensitive to the way the hard disk is set up. Once you've played with the partition table, it can become unbelievably difficult to get LILO to respond to anything short of a shotgun blast to the drive-head. There is a road to recovery, but it's a windy mountain road that's only one car-width wide, has deep potholes everywhere, and a whole convoy of 18-wheeler logging rigs driven by inebriated monkeys coming the other way.

You, on the other hand, couldn't care less if you make a mistake during the install. You can wipe the hard-drive time and time again with reckless abandon each time you splatter your inexperience all over the partition table. You also are working with a very simple system consisting of the most basic hardware. There's little chance of device conflict.

Think you can get the install right the first time through? Don't even bother. You should do a full install at least twice, and walk through the upgrade procedure at least once. Now is the best time to play around and figure out how everything works. The knowledge will really pay off when it's 4:30 A.M. and your network is being torn apart by a bunch of teenagers. Playing with the installer a few times now will ensure that you aren't confused in the future. Take good notes and keep them near the firewall at all times.

But First...

Suggestion number one: Read this chapter once before actually attempting to install OpenBSD. They tried to teach us to do that in school, but we never listened. To this day, we still get bitten in the rump by it. Speaking of rump roast, just last week, one of the authors was making a frittata with sundried tomatoes, asparagus, and porcini mushrooms. At the bottom of the recipe, it said to *immediately* place the pan into a *preheated oven* for a few minutes until the top is golden brown. Two problems became suddenly apparent: 1) the oven hadn't been preheated because there was no earlier mentioning of it, and 2) the handle of the pan chosen for cooking the frittata was plastic. Excessive application of grated pecorino romano cheese saved the frittata (we like romano), and even improved the non-slip grip of the pan by becoming partially embedded in the molten plastic handle. With lessons like that, it's no wonder we never learn.

Suggestion number two: Print out some of the critical online documentation and *read it through* at least once (many potential problems have been documented—if you read it now you'll recognize problems a lot faster later on). It's also really helpful to have it in front of you on paper—plus you can make notes. The key docs are:

INSTALL.i386. located on the CD-ROM in the directory: /2.5/i386/.

The FAQ. most recent version at: www.openbsd.org/faq/index.html.

Some important man pages. You can find them online by going to www.openbsd.org/faq/faq2.html#2.3. In particular, you should print out: afterboot, disklabel, ifconfig, man, and vi (not linked but you can search for it through the Web interface to man). If you're connecting to the net via modem, you might want to print ppp (also not linked).

Preparing Your System

We're assuming that you have a fully assembled computer with a blank or completely sacrificial hard drive installed. To the best of your knowledge, this computer is in working order. If the preceding two sentences describe your present situation, you're ready to begin the installation. If not, we're incredibly proud of you for deciding to read all the instructions first, before doing anything irreversible.

Your life will be *much* easier if your machine is capable of booting off of the CD-ROM drive. This is due to the nature of the installer program. The installer doesn't attempt to detect the CD drive until it needs to copy the files, which is after it has spent numerous minutes formatting your hard drive. Realizing that OpenBSD can't see your CD-ROM at that point can be rather frustrating. If the machine can boot off the CD, then it's almost certainly going to recognize the drive during the installation. Setting up the machine to boot off the CD-ROM drive now will help you avoid this situation. Fore more information, refer to the *BIOS Tweaking* section in Chapter 5, "Getting the Right Hardware."

If you chose this route, you'll need to use a boot floppy, so check out the sidebar titled *Using a Boot Floppy*.

Using a Boot Floppy

Get your hands on a machine that already has an OS installed—any OS will do. Put the OpenBSD CD # 1 into that machine. Next, you'll need to format a couple of floppies—four to be safe. Do a thorough format with bad block checking turned on. If there are any bad blocks, use another floppy.

The next step is to do something useful with the disks. Two of them should be made into bootable DOS disks—this can usually be accomplished by specifying an option in the format program. Onto each disk, copy the program FDISK.EXE, which usually is found in your WINDOWS directory.

Continues

Using a Boot Floppy *(Continued)*

The other two disks will become OpenBSD install floppies. There is a disk image (a special system-independent file that expands onto a floppy disk) on the OpenBSD CD (#1) called floppy25.fs. Under DOS/Windows, you'll extract the image using the rawrite.exe program located in the tools directory of the CD (#1). You can run this program directly off the CD. The program is DOS-based, so when it runs it will open an MS-DOS window. It will ask you for the image file. Type in: floppy25.fs and hit enter. The target drive is the letter of your floppy drive (often A). Perform the same extraction on both remaining floppies so that you'll have a spare copy in the event that one floppy is defective.

Now you're ready to insert the boot floppy and power up the computer. If it works, you're all set—the rest of the install is identical to the CD-ROM installation. If it doesn't work, try the dos floppy . . . did that load up to a dos prompt? If not, try using another machine/floppy to create the dos floppy. If it still doesn't work, you either got two bad floppies in a row or your floppy drive is not installed correctly.

If you can get the dos floppy to work, then the problem could be the physical media for the boot floppy.

Rawrite is really sensitive, and tends to work with about a 50 percent accuracy rate. Try rawriting to a few different floppies. Also, make sure you fully dos-format the floppy first (clears up any bad sectors and will alert you to media defects).

One final note—make sure you're rewriting floppy25.fs, and not the install.i386 file or some other file. In an earlier life, one of the authors wasted two hours trying to figure out why the floppy drive was defective because of a mistake remarkably similar to what was just described.

The Install

Okay, let's say it worked and you see boot stuff happening (as opposed to fire stuff, smoke stuff, or darkness stuff). You will eventually notice a line that says:

```
boot>
```

This brings us to our first lesson in OS installation: the <CR> key. Usually, hitting <CR> will automatically "do the right thing" by picking a reasonably acceptable choice, but occasionally it will format your hard drive, empty your bank account, and run away to Rio with your spouse. By wantonly hitting <CR>, you'll be exuding a cool indifference and total disregard for life or limb that embodies all the badness of "do you feel lucky, punk?" growled out by a 15-year-old in the #acne-sufferers IRC channel.

NOTE

There are more ways of denoting the <CR> key on a computer keyboard than there are packets on the Internet. Some call it "Enter," some call it "Return," some label it "arrow pointing down and to the left." We're calling it <CR>, short for "Carriage Return," because we're traditionalists.

So gather your courage and take the plunge—hit that <CR> key for all it's worth. If you can't muster the inner resolve to take such a leap of faith, the installer will do it for you after about 10 seconds. Either way, you're going over the edge—by jumping you can at least delude yourself into thinking that you had some choice in the matter:

```
Booting fd0a:/bsd:#######
```

where ####### is a number followed by a twirling cursor.

If all goes well, you'll see something like the above line. If you're booting off of a floppy or a slow CD-ROM drive, it will stay this way for a long time. Don't freak out. Soon, another number will be appended to the line, and you'll wait even longer. Stay calm.

With little warning, stuff in blue will start scrolling up the screen (if it's oozing out the side of the screen, run for your life). Reading this stuff carefully can tell an OpenBSD expert a lot about your system, but it won't mean anything to you. So just wait until the screen shows the following:

```
sh: ./etc/rc: No such file or directory
Enter pathname of shell or RETURN for sh:
```

Pull all your money out of your bank account, pray for your hard drive, and keep your spouse out of the room. It's time to hit <CR> again. If all goes well, you should now see:

```
(I)nstall, (U)pgrade or (S)hell?
```

Type "I" and hit <CR>.

Next you'll see a welcome screen with some information on how to restart the install process. Finally, it asks you if you'd like to proceed with the installation. Type "y" and hit <CR>. Hitting just <CR> actually does the WRONG thing here—it quits the installer. Luckily, no harm is done. If you accidentally hit <CR> before typing "y," you can restart the install by typing "install" at the shell prompt followed by <CR>.

The next lines will be:

```
Cool! Let's get to it…
Specify terminal type [pcvt25]:
```

Here, hitting <CR> selects the value in brackets—"pcvt25". <CR> always will select the value in brackets if you don't type anything else. For any standard PC system, pcvt25 will be fine. If you're playing with hardware that requires a different terminal type, you're way out of the scope of this book.

Setting Up the Hard Drive

This part of the install deals with configuring and formatting your hard drive to run OpenBSD. It's a rather tricky part of the install, but we can just reboot and try again if we mess up.

The installer will first ask you about the root disk. It will show a list of all the drives in your system (there should be only one). The name will be something like "wd0". This should also be the default answer in brackets, so just hit <CR> again.

The next question asks if you want to use the *entire* disk for OpenBSD. We can't think of any reason why you should settle for less, so type "yes" and hit <CR>.

Suddenly, the installer tells you that a "BIOS 'A6' ('OpenBSD')" partition has just been created, and proceeds to give you all sorts of confusing information about partition tables, offsets, and disklabels. It then says:

```
Treating sectors 63-### as the OpenBSD portion of the disk.
You can use the 'b' command to change this.
Initial label editor (enter '?' for help at any prompt)
>
```

The ### is the total number of sectors on your hard disk.

So now you're at a > prompt. Unfortunately, here the manual talks about disklabel in a very generic way. It doesn't help your problem, which is that the > prompt won't go away. This is the most complex part of the entire install, so read carefully.

First thing to do is hit ? followed by <CR>. This should give you a list of commands. The first command in the list is 'p' for *print label*. Let's do that to see what the current disk setup looks like. Press "p" and hit <CR>.

You should see a bunch of information about your disk geometry, followed by a list of the currently active partitions. Write down the number next to: bytes/sector. You'll need this later.

If your hard drive was empty prior to this install, you will most likely have a 'c' partition and an 'a' partition. The 'c' partition should never be touched—it spans the total size of the disk. The 'a' partition should now be deleted, so that we can re-size it properly. To do this, type "d a" and hit <CR>. 'd' is the delete partition command. 'd a' says to delete partition 'a'.

Next we'll create our real partitions. We're going to only create two partitions—a root partition that spans most of the disk, and a swap partition of about 200 megs. You could get away with less, but there's really no point unless you're using a very small hard drive. In general, you should have twice as much swap space as you have RAM.

When adding a partition, the installer will ask for the partition size. There are two ways to specify this: 1) in megabytes, or 2) in sectors. Specifying megabytes is slightly easier, but there are some funny issues with drive sizing that we discuss in the sidebar. We're going to show you how to do it both ways, since dealing with sectors is something with which you should be familiar.

When Is 1000 Equal to 1024?

The drive size problem stems from the fact that drive manufacturers often calculate their drive size assuming that 1 meg is equal to 1000 kilobytes (10^3), instead of 1024 kilobytes (2^{10}) Since computers work off of powers of 2, the latter calculation is actually correct.

The result of this game is that the drives appear slightly larger. This difference normally is not too relevant, but the current trend in storage is toward entry-level drives with sizes upwards of 4 gigs. At those sizes, the few extra bytes can add up. Here's an example of what we mean:

If you have a 4 gig drive, you might think you have 4096 megs (4,294,967,296 bytes of space). In reality you may be getting triple whammied. If you're drive manufacturer is playing the game, they probably have not only defined a meg as only 1000 kilobytes, but also a kilobyte as only 1000 bytes, and a gig as only 1000 megs. The short of it is that you're losing 294,967,296 bytes (281 real megs).

If you're going to specify the partition sizes in megabytes, you'll need to create the swap partition first. If you don't, then you need to know the exact size of your drive in real megabytes in order to create the main partition. If you overestimate due to the sidebar problem, you might not leave enough room for swap. It's far easier to start with the swap partition, which is a known size (200 megs) and then use the rest of the drive for the main partition.

Type "a b" and hit <CR>. The 'a' means add a new partition and the 'b' tells it to create partition 'b.' The installer will ask for an offset value. The offset should default to '63'. Hitting <CR> here is fine. Next you will be asked for the size. Enter in "200M" for the size. It will tell you that it's rounding to the nearest cylinder. The FS type should be "swap" (the default; just hit <CR>).

Now it's time to add your main partition. Type "a a" and hit <CR>. This says to add partition 'a'. The default offset value should be set to a large number. Accept the default by hitting <CR>. The default size should be the rest of this disk. Just to be certain, enter "*" as the value—it tells the installer to use the rest of the space for this partition. The default filesystem (FS) type should be "4.2BSD". Hit <CR> again or change it if necessary. The mount point should be "/". For everything else, the default values should be acceptable.

Partitioning by Sectors

If you feel like doing the partitioning by sectors, you'll need to first figure out the size of the swap space in sectors. Look at the bytes per sector number that you wrote down. If the number is 512, that means each sector is half a kilobyte. To get 200 megs, you'll need about 400,000 sectors for your swap space (throw in a few extra for good measure—I used 450,000).

Now you can type "a a" and hit <CR>. This says to add partition 'a'. The installer will ask for an offset value. The offset should default to '63'. One <CR> later you will be asked for the size. The size you want is the total number of sectors, minus the number of sectors of swap space (technically you should also subtract the 63 sector offset, but if you don't it will just come out of the swap space and won't make a difference). The FS type should be 4.2BSD (the default; just hit <CR>). The mount point should be "/". The default values for fragment size, block size, and cpg are fine; just hit <CR> for each of them.

Now you're ready to create your swap partition. Type "a b" and hit <CR>. The default offset should be the size of the root partition plus 63. If it is, hit <CR>. If it isn't, you messed up somewhere. Likewise, the default size should be roughly the size you picked for the swap partition (minus 63 if you didn't subtract it from the size of the root partition). The FS type should be "swap"—this should be the default; if it isn't, just type it in.

Print your disk label again ('p') and you should see partitions a, b, and c properly set up. Now type "w" to write the information to disk, hit <CR>, and then type "q" to quit.

Since you've only got two partitions, the OpenBSD installer knows which ones to use for root and swap. It will give you the opportunity to configure another disk, but since you only have one drive, the default should be [done]. Just hit <CR> to continue. It will ask you if you want to edit using ed. The answer is "n". Finally, it will get ready to wipe your root partition. Hit "y" and wipe away—remember, you have nothing to lose.

Configuring the Network

So you've set up your hard disk. Great. Your next move is to get your network connection up and running. You don't need to get all of your cards running now, but it will really help if at least one card is configured (especially if your CD-ROM isn't working and you need to perform a network install).

The installer makes network configuration very simple. If your card is likely to be supported with the default kernel, then the installer will detect it. The installer also will let you configure multiple cards. Therefore, we recommend connecting your firewall to the network in the configuration you ultimately plan on using. This will give you an early heads-up to potential networking problems, and the lights on the cards/switches/hubs will help provide useful diagnostics.

If you aren't placing your DMZ behind the firewall, then you'll just need to plug one network card into a switch/hub on the internal network, and either another network card plugged into the external network or a modem. If you're using a modem, we'll have to configure it later.

If you are creating a three-legged network with a DMZ, you'll need three network cards or two network cards and a modem. Plug one network card into a switch/hub on the internal network. Plug another network card into a switch/hub in the DMZ. If you're connecting to the Internet via Ethernet, then connect the last network card to your external network router/switch/hub.

Assuming that your network card has diagnostic lights, check to make sure that they're showing a "link." Likewise, the switches/hubs should also show a active links. If the cards aren't lighting up, they may be installed incorrectly or they may be defective. Catching this type of problem now will spare you numerous headaches a few paragraphs later.

It's time to move on with the installation. When the installer asks if you want to configure your network, type "y" and hit <CR>.

You're now asked for the system host name in short form. The system host name is the name you want to give your computer. You might want to call it something other than "firewall"; this makes it a little less obvious to the casual hacking observer. Maybe calling it "pita" or "nostril" would be a better choice. Short form means that you shouldn't put your domain name after the hostname. If your domain name is bread.com, you'd enter just "pita" here, not "pita.bread.com".

The next step asks for the domain name. Here, just enter "bread.com", or whatever your domain name is. If you don't have a domain name, don't worry—just leave it blank. You can change this later if you do decide on getting a domain name.

You'll see a short paragraph about DHCP servers next. If your external IP address is determined by DHCP, then you should pay attention to what it says. We'll remind you again at the appropriate time.

You should now see a list of network interfaces—one for each network card in your system. The list will looks something like:

```
[ ] pn0
[ ] pn1
[ ] pn2
```

It probably won't say "pn" in front of the 0,1,2, and so forth. Instead, you'll see something like: ne, fxp, xl, etc. What you see depends on the type of network card you have. It's totally irrelevant. The only thing that matters is that there are as many interfaces listed as there are network cards in your system. If there aren't, then the installer isn't recognizing one or more of your network cards. The installer should be able to detect 99 percent of the cards that are supported by OpenBSD. If you're card is listed under supported hardware and the installer isn't recognizing it, the problem is most likely on your end. Try using one card at a time—this can help you determine if it's a card problem, or a motherboard problem.

Hopefully everything went smoothly, and you see the proper number of interfaces. If so, it's time to configure them. It's fairly easy to change these settings later, so don't worry if you can't answer some of the questions yet. You can just put in dummy values and move on.

Let's select an interface to configure. The installer will default to the first interface in the list. Hit <CR>. It's going to ask you for the IP address of this interface. Let's make this the internal interface. In order to connect the firewall to the internal network, you'll need know which physical card corresponds to this particular interface. You can figure out which is which by following the techniques in the sidebar. Once you figure this out, you might want to label the cards for easy reference.

The next question asks for the IP address of your machine. Are internal addresses already being allocated by DHCP? If so, you have to request a static address within the subnet for the firewall. If there is no existing network structure, then your choices are wide open. For now, we recommend using the address: '10.0.0.1'. We can always change it, but at least this particular address will give you maximum flexibility later on.

Which Interface Is Which?

If you have more than one network card, it's a bit tricky to figure out which is which, especially if they're all the same type (as they should be).

Technically, the interfaces follow the numbering of the PCI slots. So, if your slots numbers increase as you go left to right along the mainboard, the leftmost network card should be 0, the next one to the right should be 1, and so forth. Skipping a PCI slot won't cause the network interface numbers to skip though. Network interfaces are assigned incrementally from the lowest PCI slot to the highest.

On some mainboards, the slots are numbered from left to right. On others it's right to left. There are two ways to tell:

Open up the case and look on the board. Somewhere around the PCI slot should be a label like 'pci0'. That's the slot number.

Open up your motherboard manual and look for a diagram of the mother-board. Often, the PCI slots are labeled in the diagram.

During the installation, it really doesn't matter which interface gets assigned to which network. In the worst case, you can always reassign them later on. In a later sidebar we'll explain how to positively identify each network card using the 'ping' command.

Once you've determined the internal address of the firewall, enter it at the prompt and hit <CR>. Now pick a host name for this particular IP address. The default will be the hostname you entered a few screens back. Just accept it and move on, unless there's a specific reason why the hostname used for the internal network needs to be something different.

If you entered 10.0.0.1 as your IP address, you should enter in 255.255.255.0 as your net mask. If you entered in something else because of an existing network structure, then you'll need to figure out the netmask for your particular network. For more information, see the *Netmasking* section in Chapter 2, "Fundamental Internet Security Issues."

Now you'll see a bunch of information about media directives. The choice you make here will depend on the nature of your network card. If your card is a 10/100 card that can autodetect the network speed, then type "media autoselect" at the prompt and hit <CR>. Otherwise, choose the setting that is appropriate for your card and hit <CR>.

That's it! You've finished configuring an interface. Now you'll be looking at the interface selection screen again. If you have more than one interface, you should configure the other ones now. Note that the default answer to the "Configure which interface?" question is "done." You'll want to manually enter the interface that needs to be configured. If you have a DMZ, configure that interface next.

Eventually you'll need to make a decision about your DMZ; are you going to be using real IP addresses within the DMZ, or will you use private addresses with NAT and port forwarding, or both? If you plan on using internal addresses, then you'll need to pick one or more real IP addresses to masquerade behind. Unless you know exactly how you'd like your DMZ to work, you should just enter another internal network address. You'll get a chance to reconfigure it properly later on. If you chose 10.0.0.1 for your internal network address, you might want to pick 10.254.0.1 as your DMZ network address. There's no particular reason for this choice, other than the fact that it's unlikely to clash with your subnetting strategy.

The final interface you need to configure is the interface that connects to the outside world. If you're going to be connecting via modem, then you don't have anything to configure yet. But if you're connecting to the outside world via a network card, you'll need to configure this interface with a static, external IP address. If your address is assigned via DHCP, then you'll need to enter 'dhcp' as the IP address.

Once you've finished configuring your interfaces, type "done" at the "Configure which interface" prompt. You'll be asked for the IP address of the default route. If your IP address is assigned dynamically, leave this and the next question blank. If you have a static IP address, you'll need to use IP address of your router, or the ISP's gateway router. Most ISPs will tell you the address of their gateway if you ask. Likewise, they'll give you the IP addresses of their DNS servers. You can leave out the DNS server, but we don't recommend it. When it asks if you'd "like to use the name server now," you should answer yes if you've given it a valid DNS address.

Next it will give you the opportunity to escape to the command shell to perform additional configuration. If everything has worked thus far, then there's no need to go to the command shell. If the network didn't configure properly, don't sweat it yet. You're installing from CD, so you really don't need network access now. You can continue the installation to get a feel for what the rest of the install is like and to identify any other problems. Later you can go back and figure out what went wrong.

The installer will now mount the hard drive onto the file system. When it's finished, it will ask you to set a root password. It's worth taking a few minutes to think about choosing a good password. If someone can guess your password, all the work you've done to make your network secure will be totally wasted.

The last major step is to get the stuff off the CD and onto your freshly lobotomized drive. The installer will tell you as much, and then ask you to select the installation media. Select (C)D-ROM from the "Install from" prompt by typing 'c' followed by <CR>.

Some Thoughts on Passwords

There are standard rules that you should always try and follow when choosing a password: no words from any language, no variants on any such words—don't think that mixing a couple of numbers into a word makes it secure.

Hackers have wonderful tools that crack password files very efficiently. You can and should download these tools and run them on your password files. If you have a sizable number of users, you'll be shocked by the high percentage of passwords that can be cracked by these password cracking programs. If you crack a user's password, they should be instructed to change their password immediately. This should *not* be done through e-mail if you could crack the password, somebody else probably did too and is reading the users e-mail. Pay them a visit, or leave them a voice mail (although first check to see if their voice mailbox code is 12345).

Our recommendation would be to take a book down off your bookshelf, pick a sentence at random, and use the initial letters of that sentence. Don't pick a famous sentence. Don't open the book at page one. Don't use the book you're currently reading (this book!), and don't leave this book next to the one you do choose, either. If you need to highlight or underline the sentence to give you an emergency reference if you forget the root password, that's OK (well, it's better than writing the root password down on a piece of paper, anyway). Pick a good one and spend a little time fixing it in your memory.

You'll now see a list of CD-ROM drives available for use. If this list is empty, then you need to read the sidebar on "what to do if your CD drive isn't being recognized." Assuming it worked properly, you should see one CD-ROM drive. Answer the question "Which is the CD-ROM with the installation media?" by typing in the name of the drive (could be something like "acd0").

When it asks for file system, select cd9660—which should be the default. The directory relative to the mount point that contains the file is /2.5/i386 (which should also be the default).

Now comes the fun part: Selecting the various packages to install. This process is somewhat different from that of RedHat 6.0 and quite different from Microsoftland installs. There are three separate systems for packaging programs under OpenBSD. The first is called the *disk set*, which are the collections of core programs that make up the OpenBSD OS. The installer will let you choose among these sets (although some are required). The second system is called the *package* system, and it consists of a few tools that operate on a directory of precompiled software deemed stable by the OpenBSD crew. When needed, a simple command adds and removes packages from your system. Finally, there's the *ports tree*, which is for programs that are under

What to Do If Your CD Drive Isn't Being Recognized

The easiest way to do a network install is via FTP. Install an FTP server on the other computer (if it's a Windows box, we suggest using one of the many good free FTP servers, such as WAR-FTPD). Make the CD-ROM drive accessible by anonymous FTP login (It's OK to use anonymous FTP, since you're just connecting these two machines to an isolated hub—just make sure you turn off the FTP server when you're finished). Connect the firewall and the FTP server to a hub. Select appropriate internal IP addresses for the FTP server and the firewall. Make sure they're both within the same subnet. Now when you're asked to choose an installation method, select FTP. Specify the FTP server by its IP address. Give the installer the proper path to the CD-ROM drive and it should make the connection.

If the FTP install doesn't seem to work, look at the FTP server. Does the server log show a connection? If not, the server may not be installed properly or the IP address you gave might be incorrect. If it does show a connection, then the problem might be an incorrect path or a bad username/password combination.

After you finish the install and reboot, you should see if OpenBSD detects the CD-ROM drive. If not, you should definitely return the drive and exchange it for a new one. Don't buy Mitsumi drives—they tend to create lots of problems. Once you've installed the new drive, try doing a full install again. If it autoboots and finds the CD-ROM, then you're doing much better!

active development. These programs are distributed as source code and compiled as needed. The unusual aspect of the ports tree is that the source code for a given program is downloaded from its author's Web site during the installation. The tree itself is simply an index of what's available. When you go to a directory in the tree for a program you need, simply typing "make" will cause the ports system to download the necessary source code, compile it, and install it—all automatically.

What we're dealing with here is the disk set method. Disk sets are basically gzipped tarballs (a collection of files archived using the tar program and compressed using gzip) that are extracted in the / directory. The problem with this is that it's an all or nothing approach—you either take all or none of the files in a disk set. To make matters worse, there is no standard method for uninstalling a disk set later on. This is OK because well only be installing core programs that you'll want to leave on the system. For the truly adventurous, your benevolent authors have provided you with a tool for managing disk sets after the installation (you'll find it on the companion Web site). You can send us praise and thanks, but we'd prefer money.

The installer allows you to select the disk sets you want from the following list:

```
[x]  base25.tar.gz
[x]  etc25.tar.gz
[ ]  misc25.tar.gz
[ ]  comp25.tar.gz
[ ]  man25.tar.gz
[ ]  game25.tar.gz
[ ]  xbase25.tar.gz
[ ]  xshare25.tar.gz
[ ]  xfont25.tar.gz
[ ]  xserv25.tar.gz
[x]  bsd
```

Note that base, etc, and bsd are already selected because they are required. We'll also need misc, comp, and man. You can select these additional packages in a number of ways. The easiest is to type in the file names one at a time.

The fastest is to use wildcard matching. Type m*<CR>, followed by c*<CR>. That will select the other three packages. Using * alone will select everything, and -* will deselect everything. You don't need the x packages because you won't be running X on your firewall. The same applies to games.

Type "done<CR>" and hit <CR> again when it asks if you're ready. This will start the installation process. With any luck, the process will finish after a few minutes and will ask you if you want to extract any more sets. The default is [n], so just hit <CR>.

The next step is to set a timezone for your location. This is pretty straight-forward. Just type "?" for a list of valid timezones. You'll notice that some locations in the list have a trailing slash. If you select one of those locations, you'll be prompted to select a more specific region.

Once you've finished selecting a timezone, the installer will go through some gyrations. It will lastly ask you if you plan on running X on this system. Your answer should be "n" followed by <CR>.

That's it! You've finished installing OpenBSD. It will tell you to type halt at the command prompt in order to shut down your machine. Actually, you can pop out the CD-ROM and type: reboot<CR> instead. This will halt the machine and force a reboot.

At this point, you should have a system that boots up to a login prompt. If you do, congratulations. If you don't, then please read over the install.i386 file, look inside the cover booklet for the CD-ROM, and read the FAQ. Somewhere in one of those documents is the answer to the problem you're having, assuming you're using relatively standard hardware. If not, you can always try the OpenBSD news groups for support.

NOTE

If your system is set up to boot from CD-ROM in preference to the hard disc, the computer is going to start trying to reinstall the OS again. The right thing would be take the CD out of the drive before you reboot, but most modern CD drives will allow the operating system to lock the drive shut (in other words, disable the eject button) if the OS considers it necessary. Since that is necessary when the CD is mounted, as it has been throughout the installation, it is unlikely that you will be able to eject the CD before rebooting. So, if your computer tries to reboot off the CD, and it starts looking a lot like you're about to reinstall the OS, don't panic. Press the reset button on your computer, and then hold the eject button down on your CD-ROM. As soon as the computer has reinitialized the CD-ROM drive, the drive should obey the button and pop the CD tray out. Remove the CD, and close the drive.

You might want to consider tweaking the bios so that it doesn't boot off the CD-ROM. This isn't a bad idea, as you may be using the CD later on to install packages and might forget about the CD's presence. If the system reboots for any reason, you could be stuck on the install screen for a while.

Basic System Configuration

Just because your machine boots to a login prompt doesn't mean that it's of much use at the moment. Sorry to break it to you, but you're far from done setting up your OpenBSD system. You've got a lot of work ahead of you in order to configure it properly. There are numerous tasks you'll need to perform to configure and tune the system for use as a firewall. The good news is that we'll keep walking you through the process. Our first configuration task will involve properly setting up your network cards and/or a modem.

Before you do anything, we're going to suggest taking a good look at the *afterboot* man page. Type man afterboot<CR> at a command prompt. Don't worry if you don't understand everything—we're actually going to cover many of these topics in the following pages. Reading afterboot now will help your understanding of the rest of this chapter.

Configuring Network Cards

If you're creating a DMZ you'll need to go beyond the network configuration performed during the installation. Even if you aren't building a DMZ, you'll have occasion to alter the settings of your network cards as your network evolves. This section will describe how to use the 'ifconfig' program as well as describing the few critical configuration files needed to set up your network.

The ifconfig Tool

Let's first work with ifconfig. This program is used to make real-time changes to your interface settings. It's very useful for diagnostics and initial configuration. It's important to note that ifconfig doesn't save the changes you make, but we'll get to that in a little bit.

Log in as root and type "ifconfig –a" and hit <CR>. This tells ifconfig to print out a status report on the current configuration. You should see a list of each network interface in your system, a number of which will look very unfamiliar. Don't worry about those—just look for your ethernet adapters. If you see all of them, then you're in great shape. If you don't an adapter that you know is in the machine, then your system isn't recognizing the adapter. You should make sure the adapter is properly seated in the PCI slot and that the adapter is supported by OpenBSD.

There are two other status options for ifconfig: '-A' does the same thing as '-a', but also prints out alias information for each interface. '-Am' and '-am' cause the list of potential media options for each card to be printed out. These are options such as "100baseTX", "10baseT", and "autoselect".

Of course, the real purpose of ifconfig is to actually tweak your card settings. The format for the ifconfig command is as follows:

```
ifconfig <interface> [<address family>] [<address>] [<parameters>]
```

where <interface> is the name of the interface you want to configure. If your network card appeared as pn0 when you typed "ifconfig –a", then that's your interface name.

The rest of the parameters are somewhat optional, depending on what you're trying to do (throughout this book, optional arguments are surrounded by [brackets]). For example, if you're just trying to turn off an interface, you can skip the <address family> and <address> parameters and simply type:

```
ifconfig eth0 down
```

The <address family> describes the type of network addressing structure on your network. For us, we're going to use the value 'inet,' since we're connecting to the Internet. Other valid options include 'ipx', 'atalk' (appletalk), and a few other more obscure network types. <address> is the IP address you wish to assign to the interface.

If you provide just the address to ifconfig, it will simply set the interface to the given address. If you make a mistake, just run ifconfig again with the correct address and the old one will be overwritten.

The fun happens within the <parameters> part. There are many different parameters that you can set for a given interface. Here's a list of the most important ones. You can figure out the rest by looking at the man page for ifconfig.

Down. Turns the interface off. A useful way of cutting the cable that can be done remotely. Just remember—if you down the interface that you're connecting on, you'll lose your connection. Unless you can get in through another interface, you'll have to bring the interface back up from the console.

Up. Turns the interface back on again.

Netmask. This keyword is followed by the network mask, which can be expressed in dotted quad notation (255.255.255.0) or as a single hexadecimal value (0xffffff00).

Alias. Allows you to directly set alias addresses for the given interface. For example, if the interface pn0 is currently configured with the address 10.9.8.7 and you'd like the interface to accept packets destined for both 10.9.8.7 and 10.9.8.6, you could use the command:

ifconfig eth0 10.9.8.6 alias

delete. Removes the network address specified from the given interface. If you erroneously add an alias to an interface you can use this to remove the bad alias.

Media. Many cards today are 10/100 capable. This means that they can function as 10baseT and 100baseTX cards. Some cards also can handle other network technologies such as 10base2, although you really should avoid having anything to do with those older technologies, if at all possible. To figure out what media is supported by your card, do an 'ifconfig –am'.

Mediaopts. Lets you switch between "full-duplex" and "half-duplex" modes if your card supports it. Don't play with this setting unless you know what you're doing; the results can be unpredictable.

Configuration Files

As we mentioned up front, 'ifconfig' does not save your changes. It's good for making runtime alterations, but when you reboot the computer all of your changes will be lost. In order to make your settings permanent, you'll need to place them in configuration files that are located in the /etc directory. These files are named 'hostname.xxx' where xxx is the name of a network adapter. There should be one such file for each adapter in your system. The format of this file is:

```
<address family> <ipaddress> <netmask> <broadcast address> [<parameters>]
[dest <destination address>]
```

Which Interface Is Which—Revisited

Once you've configured your interfaces with their appropriate addresses, you'll want to make sure you know which card physically corresponds to which interface. 'ifconfig –a' used to give a status line that made it really easy to figure this out, but now it's gone. Here's another way to do it.

Connect one of your network cards to a network with a live computer on it that will respond to a 'ping' request. For each interface, execute the following command:

ping –I 10.0.0.1 10.0.0.2

where '10.0.0.1' should be replaced with the address you gave the interface and 10.0.0.2 should be replaced with the IP address of a machine that is accessible from that network. If you get a response, then you've just matched a card to an interface. If you don't get a response, switch the ethernet cable into the next card over and try it again.

If this interface is configured through DHCP, the file should contain only the word 'dhcp'. Otherwise, this file controls all of the interface attributes that can be set with the program ifconfig. In fact, this file is read at startup (when the script '/etc/netstart' is executed), and the contents are passed almost verbatim to the ifconfig program.

Editing Files

If you've never edited files in a Unix environment, you're in for a bit of a shock. There's no "notepad" equivalent for the Unix command line. Instead, there's 'vi,' a powerful text-editing tool that is easily the most unintuitive program ever created by man. Don't believe us? Type "vi" at a command prompt and hit return. In a few seconds, the screen will fill with a bunch of '~' symbols. You're now in vi. Okay, now try and quit the program. If you can figure this out within 10 minutes, you're doing better than any of the authors did the first time we encountered it. We'll explain how to perform some basic editing tasks (such as quitting) in Chapter 12.

You should be aware that the syntax of this file is not as flexible as the ifconfig syntax. You must give an address family, an address, a netmask, and a broadcast address before specifying extras. For the broadcast address, it's often easiest to put in the value 'NONE', unless you have a specific reason to do otherwise. By using 'NONE', the program simply defaults to the broadcast address implied by the IP address and the netmask. This should be correct unless you're doing something really weird. All of the other fields correspond directly to their 'ifconfig' equivalents.

You can force the system to re-read the hostname.xxx files by running the command:

```
sh /etc/netstart
```

While 'ifconfig' is useful for setting up interfaces, it doesn't tell the OS how to get packets from one interface to another. There is another program called 'route' which is used to alter the kernel's packet routing tables. While it's helpful to know a bit about 'route', we actually don't need to worry about it here, because the proper route commands are automatically executed by the '/etc/netstart' and 'newifaliases' scripts. We suggest looking at the man page for 'route' some day when your firewall is finished, but it's not needed for today.

There's one 'ifconfig' parameter that won't work in the hostname.xxx file: 'alias'. In order to set persistent aliases you'll need to edit the /etc/ifaliases file. Once again, this file is read during start up and the contents are passed to the 'ifconfig' program. The format of this file is very simple. Each alias is on a separate line; there can be as many lines as needed. The format of each line is:

```
<interface> <address> <netmask>
```

All three values must be present. If you have multiple aliases for an interface, place one alias on each line. The 'netstart' script will not activate the changes in this file. Instead, you should use the script we provide called 'newifaliases.' Download the script from the companion Web site (or just type it into your favorite editor). If you don't use our script, there are two other ways to get the aliases to activate: 1) reboot and 2) use the 'ifconfig' program with the 'alias' parameter.

Another important file is /etc/hosts. This file contains mappings of IP addresses to hostnames. The domain name resolver often checks this file first before checking with the DNS system. It's a good idea to have entries for your firewall system here. A typical file might look like this:

```
127.0.0.1        localhost
10.0.0.1         firewall-internal    firewall-internal.mydomain.com
101.112.131.4    firewall-external    firewall-external.mydomain.com
```

The first line makes sure that the system knows what to do with the loopback address. The second line handles the internal network interface, and the third line handles the external interface. On the second and third line, we specify the internal and external hostnames, followed by the host + domain name. All three are different ways of referring to the same machine.

Knowing about these files will enable you to configure any combination of interfaces and networks. If one of the interfaces is connected directly to the Internet via a dedicated line, then you'll be able to skip the next section and move on to the section titled *Fine-Tuning the System*. Otherwise, keep reading to figure out how to get on the net with a modem.

Connecting to the Internet via Modem

If you don't have a dedicated Internet connection through some device such as a T1 multiplexer, an external ISDN modem, or some sort of DSL unit, then you'll probably need to connect to the net with a modem. This is far less trivial a task than connecting via a network card, because there are numerous additional pieces in the puzzle. We'll need to deal with determining the port that the modem is on, creating a dialup script, configuring the modem to auto-dial your ISP, and so forth. If your IP address is dynamically determined by the ISP, then you'll have even more issues to deal with.

Finding Your Modem

The first thing to do is work out which serial port the modem is on. If you don't find this challenging, please skip to the next section. It occurred to us that we've hardly ever been able to look at the back of a PC and know which serial port is which. While it's true that some machines externally label the ports as "1" and "2," these labels don't necessarily correspond with the internal designations. Because the black art of identification is rather badly documented elsewhere, we'll dwell on it a little here.

There are only two serial ports on most modern PCs (don't confuse them with the parallel, or LPT, port), and they are accessed through the device files /dev/cua00 and /dev/cua01, which somewhat correspond to the PC concept of COM1 and COM2. If your modem's connected to a serial port on the back of your firewall, it can be talked to through /dev/cua00 or /dev/cua01.

Theoretically, there should be some way of determining which is COM1 and which is COM2, by looking at the motherboard. But this isn't a great guide, because BIOS and OS issues can move the ports around. For example, if you happen to have a serial card of some sort COM1 may be on the card while COM2 is one of the two ports and the other port is disabled.

The easiest way to locate the modem is to plug it into one of the two serial ports. Then at a prompt type "ppp" followed by <CR>. This brings us into the interactive mode of the ppp program. We'll be in and out of this mode many times over the next several pages.

Before doing anything, look at the modem. Note which lights are on and which are off. Now, at the prompt, type:

```
set device /dev/cua00<CR>
term<CR>
```

If the program hangs for a while, don't panic. After some time one of two things will happen: 1) you get another prompt or 2) one or more new status lights illuminate on your modem, the ppp program tells you to type "~?" for help and then it seems to hang. If the former occurs it simply means your modem is on another device. If the latter occurs, type the following:

```
ATH1<CR>
```

You won't see anything on screen as you type, but when you hit return you should hear a dialtone (assuming you have the modem plugged into a live phone line). Even if you don't hear anything, you should see more status lights on your modem than before. That's a good sign. It means your modem was found on device cua00. Now let's turn off that annoying dialtone:

```
ATH0<CR>
```

If the modem wasn't found, then you'll need to type:

```
set device /dev/cua01
term
```

and try again. If that doesn't work, then you should switch the physical port in back and start again from the top. You can also try the following devices: /dev/cuaa0, /dev/cuaa1, /dev/pccom0, and /dev/pccom1. Just keep repeating the process by changing the device until you find the modem.

If things still aren't working, don't go crazy. The cable connecting the modem to the computer is often another source of problems. Assuming the ends are the right size and gender to connect your modem to your computer, there are still two types of modem cables: one is intended to connect modems to computers, and the other is intended to connect computers to computers (or modems to modems). If you have the wrong type (they're very difficult to tell apart), no signals will get through. If you suspect that might be the case, a device called a *null modem adapter*, which plugs into one end of either type of cable and turns it into the other, can be extremely helpful in testing. They don't cost very much, and most computer stores should carry them. You also might have a defective cable or a cable that has the right gender but is actually meant for something else entirely. (One of the authors has a router that uses a special serial cable for management and spent a while debugging the modem before realizing that he had the wrong cable.)

After You've Found the Modem

Once you've worked out which port the modem is on, it will save a lot of time in the future if we put in a link—much like the mouse link mentioned above—to point to the modem, and refer to the modem through that.

If your modem turned out to be on /dev/cua00, issue the following commands:

```
cd /dev
ln -s cua00 modem
```

If the modem turned out to be on /dev/cua01, change the cua00 in the preceding command to cua01. Once this link is made, every time you refer to "/dev/modem", you'll automatically be talking to your modem. The rest of the modem section assumes you have done this.

Gettin' Jiggy with PPP (Point-to-Point Protocol)

Given that your modem and computer are talking to each other, we now have to get them talking to the Internet. This involves transmitting IP (Internet Protocol) signals down a serial cable. In the early days of the Internet, the first protocol to try to do this was called *SLIP* (Serial Line Internet Protocol). This had limitations, and was replaced nearly everywhere by PPP, the Point-to-Point Protocol.

PPP is what you will very likely be running over your modem line, between your OpenBSD box and your ISP, in order to talk to the Internet. A full discussion on all the aspects of PPP is beyond the scope of this book, and moreover it is unnecessary, because you have just installed an excellent manual on the subject. If you type "man ppp<CR>" at a command prompt, you will find an excellent document that discusses the theory, application, and configuration of PPP. This document, along with every other man page, is available online from www.openbsd.org/cgi-bin/man.cgi.

Nonetheless, we won't leave you to figure it all out on your own. The initial configuration of PPP can be a little bit confusing, so we'll walk you through it here. Before we do that, we need to make an important point: The ppp program in OpenBSD is a very complex piece of software. It's got far more features than its Linux counterpart. For example, it includes the ability to do dial-on-demand, which requires an additional program in Linux (diald). It's also capable of doing its own packet filtering, separate from the filtering we'll be talking about in the next chapter (we do not recommend using PPP's filtering system—it just means you'll have two sets of rules to keep in sync, and that can make your life a living hell when you forget to tweak one or the other). This means that you won't find too much additional help on PPP outside of the BSD community, because Linux users have a much simpler program.

The first step is to dial your ISP from the ppp program. We need to figure out the login procedure for your ISP. Hopefully this will be fairly straightforward. If it isn't, we suggest changing your ISP or calling your ISP's tech support and asking for help. Often changing ISPs is faster and easier. Our example uses MindSpring, which happens to be compatible with the default settings in the ppp.conf file.

Start the ppp program by typing "ppp" at the command line. Once you're in the program, type:

```
set device /dev/modem
term
```

This will put you in terminal mode. To connect with your ISP, type:

```
ATH1M1DT1234567
```

Replace the 1234567 with your ISPs phone number and hit <CR>.

If your modem is connected correctly, after a few seconds you'll hear a bunch of beeping, followed by the sound of a pig in a blender on a pogo stick. This is a good, albeit sick, sound. Shortly the blender will stop and you should see something like:

```
CONNECT 9600
Welcome to MindSpring Dialup Service
arc-1a.bos login:
```

If the prompt doesn't say "login" then write down exactly what it does say (maybe it says "username:"). Type in your username. For MindSpring, it's your e-mail address. After hitting <CR> it will say:

```
Password:
```

Once again, if this says something other than "password" you'll need to write it down. Type in your password and hit <CR>. If both username and password were correct and active, you'll see something like this:

```
Packet mode enabled: PPP session from  168.121.1.1 to  165.247.33.16
beginning..
.~ }#À!}!}!} }8}!}$}%Ü}"}&    }%}&}#+"5}…
```

This means you've successfully established a PPP connection. Exit the term session by typing "~." followed by "close<CR>" at the command prompt. If you had trouble connecting, or it didn't ask for anything remotely like a login and password, you probably have an ISP that uses a different authentication method. The ppp program can connect to these types of ISPs, but we don't cover the process in this chapter. The ppp man page and the ppp.conf.sample file give a detailed explanation of this process. If you can't figure it out, try switching ISPs.

Now let's create a script to automate the connection process. Go into your /etc/ppp directory via the command:

```
cd /etc/ppp
```

In this directory there are numerous sample configuration files. These files can be easily turned into real configuration files by removing the .sample extension from them. What we're going to do is copy one of the files, removing the .extension in the process. We'll then edit the copied file and convert it into a real configuration file. To do this, type:

```
cp ppp.conf.sample ppp.conf
```

Now call up "vi" (refer to the command reference in Chapter 12) and let's edit the ppp.conf file. Use the down arrow on your keyboard (or ctrl-n if that doesn't work) to move the cursor down past the 'default:' to the line that says:

```
set device /dev/cuaa1
```

Move the cursor to the "c" in 'cuaa1' and hit "D" . Now type "a" followed by "modem" and finish by hitting escape. The result should be a line that says:

```
set device /dev/modem
```

Now we need to modify the phone number used to dial our ISP. Move the cursor down past the "pmdemand:" line, to the line that says:

```
set phone 1234567
```

Position the cursor over the 1 and hit "D" . This should delete the phone number. Now type "a" followed by the phone number of your ISP. When done, hit the escape key. The new line should now have the phone number of your ISP after the word "phone" (there should be a space between "phone" and the phone number).

Now let's put in your username and password for your ISP. Move the cursor to the line that says:

```
set login "ABORT NO\\sCARRIER TIMEOUT 5 ogin:—ogin: ppp word: ppp"
```

and position the cursor over the first ppp (after "–login:"). Hit "x" three times to delete the "ppp". Now type "i" followed by your username. Hit escape, move over to the second "ppp", press "D", hit "a", and type in your password. Whack the escape key again.

When you were connecting manually, you might have written down an alternate login or password prompt. If this were the case, you'll need to also edit the part that says "ogin:—ogin:" or "word:" to reflect the prompt given. For example, if your ISP prompted with 'username', you could change the section to read: "name:—name:". Anything more complex and you'll have to check with the man page.

The final step will be to delete the lines that we don't need. Move the cursor down past the pmdemand: section. Place it at the beginning of the line that starts with:

```
# When we want to use PAP or CHAP instead of …
```

Now delete all the stuff from there to the end of the file. This can be done with the command:

```
:.,$d
```

This tells vi to delete ('d') all the lines from the current one ('.') to the end of the file ('$'). At some point in the future you may wish to read the text you deleted—it has some interesting examples of things you can do with ppp. For now, we're satisfied that we've stripped out all the stuff that's not relevant for our firewall.

Once you've finished making the appropriate changes to both files, it's time to run the ppp program again. We'll use it to test whether the changes you made were correct. Type "ppp" at the command prompt to enter the ppp interactive mode. Then type:

```
load pmdemand
open
```

If you did everything properly, you'll hear the modem dialing your ISP. One pureed pig on a pogo later and you should have a running ppp connection to your ISP. If you don't, check back over all of the steps to see if you missed something. With vi, it's often easy to accidentally delete or insert a character in the wrong place. Look through the ppp.conf file and check to make sure everything is there. To do this, you can use the commands: "more /etc/ppp/ppp.conf".

Once you've established an active connection, it's time to finish automating the connection process. The ppp program has an option called "auto", which causes ppp to run in the background and automatically dial up your ISP the moment a program tries to use the Internet.

The auto option is great for networks where you're only concerned about providing outbound access on demand, but it's not good for servers. This is because auto responds to outbound connections only—there's no way for it to know if someone is trying to reach your machine if the PPP connection is down. In fact, due to the very nature of PPP, the inbound packet will never reach your machine. Instead, the ISP will send an ICMP unreachable error whenever someone tries to access your IP address. If you're running important servers on a fixed IP address, you'll want to make sure your PPP connection is *always* active. You don't want a poor phone connection to keep your servers off line for extended periods of time. Luckily, there's an option for this exact situation called "ddial". This option ensures that the PPP connection is always active—if the link goes down it immediately brings it back up again.

We need to ensure that the ppp program is run with either the auto or the ddial option whenever the computer boots. To do this, add the following line to your /etc/rc.local file:

```
ppp -ddial myisp
```

or

```
ppp -auto myisp
```

Fine-Tuning the System

We've got a computer that can connect to the Internet, but it's still not ready to be configured as a firewall. We need to patch up a few things (in order to get rid of known security holes) and optimize the system for use as a firewall. This is a process you'll need to go through once in a while anyhow, so you might as well learn it now while you still have nothing to lose.

Mounting the CD-ROM

Before we can patch anything, we'll need to be able to access some files on the CD-ROM. Unfortunately, you can't just stick a CD in the drive and immediately access it. You'll first need to mount the CD drive onto the file system. This basically means you'll be creating a directory and making the contents of the CD accessible from within that directory.

We like to make the CD accessible from /mnt/cdrom. Therefore, the first step is to make the directory. Type: "mkdir –p /mnt/cdrom" and hit <CR>.

The next step is to figure out what system device represents your CD-ROM drive. The fastest way to do this is to type: "dmesg | more" and scroll through the file. You're looking at the output your system created when it first booted. Somewhere in this file should be a line about your CD-ROM drive, often appearing shortly after the network cards are listed. Look for something like "ATAPI" or "volume levels" somewhere on the line.

Once you've found the right line, look at the beginning. The first thing on the line is the CD-ROM device name. For us, it happens to be "acd0". Tack an "a" on to the end of that device name and you have the device name for your CD-ROM. So, our CD-ROM is "/dev/acd0a".

If you don't see anything that could be a CD-ROM drive in the "dmesg" output, then you should re-read the note on CD-ROM troubleshooting in Chapter 5. Your CD-ROM may need to be connected differently (slave instead of master, and so forth).

Now that we've found the CD-ROM, let's verify that we've got the right drive. Place the OpenBSD CD#1 in the drive and type:

```
mount_cd9660 /dev/acd0a /mnt/cdrom
cd /mnt/cdrom
ls
```

Replace "acd0a" with the appropriate device for your CD-ROM. If all goes well, you should see a listing of the files on the OpenBSD CD. If you see nothing, or something other than the contents of the OpenBSD CD-ROM, then you may have mounted the wrong device. Look more carefully at the "dmesg | more" output.

Let's make our lives a bit easier by making a link to our CD-ROM device, similar to what we did with the modem:

```
ln –s /dev/acc0a /dev/cdrom
```

Once again, replace the "acd0a" with your CD-ROM device name. From here on in, we can access the CD via /dev/cdrom.

Now let's unmount the CD so that we can eject it:

```
cd /
umount /mnt/cdrom
```

Note that the command is "umount" and not "unmount". If it complains that the device is busy, try:

```
umount -f /mnt/cdrom
```

Make sure that you do the "cd /" first—if you're current directory is within the CD-ROM tree when you do this it will complain or cause other problems.

To eject the CD, type:

```
eject /dev/cdrom
```

Finally, lets look at making this process a bit more automatic. Type:

```
vi /etc/fstab
```

Move the cursor to the end of the last line and type "a" followed by <CR>. Now add the following line:

```
/dev/cdrom /mnt/cdrom cd9660 ro 0 0
```

When finished, hit escape, followed by ":wq" which will save the file. To test your settings, place a CD in the drive and type:

```
mount -A
```

at a command prompt (the capital A is important). If it worked, then your system will try and mount the CD-ROM at boot time. You can also easily mount the CD at any time with the command:

```
mount /mnt/cdrom
```

It's not critical that you get this to work—you can always explicitly mount the CD-ROM drive with a command such as:

```
mount_cd9660 /dev/cdrom /mnt/cdrom
```

but "mount /mnt/cdrom" is easier to remember. In case you're wondering, the "mount" command attempts to automatically determine the type of file system that's being mounted. It then calls the appropriate filesystem specific mount command. For CD-ROMs, this is "mount_cd9660". We explicitly state "mount_cd9660" here because sometimes the mount command doesn't recognize the CD filesystem. If you make the suggested addition to /etc/fstab, the mount command will reference that file first before guessing at the file type. Our additional line explicitly states that /dev/cdrom is a cd9660 device.

Optimizing the Kernel

The OpenBSD distribution comes with a fairly generic kernel. This kernel has support for most hardware, but isn't optimized for firewall usage. If your firewall has to process a large number of packets, the stock kernel may run out of memory. Therefore it's necessary to rebuild the kernel with certain memory parameters added. While we're at it, we'll apply a few patches to the system. This may sound like the scariest part of the entire installation, but in reality it's no more difficult than anything else we've already done.

The first step is to locate the source code for the kernel and make it directly accessible to the filesystem. The kernel source code can be found in the sys directory on the CD-ROM, Disk #1. If we didn't need to patch anything, we could just compile it directly from the CD-ROM. But, since we need to change the source code, we'll need to have the source code in a writable directory. Your first inclination might be to copy the entire source code off of the CD-ROM and onto your hard drive. This will take a while, and isn't necessarily the best option. At the least, it's one more thing you'll have to remember to strip out of the system later.

A better thing to do is to use a concept known as a 'union mount'. This is a cool technique—the CD-ROM is mounted as a writable file system. How does this work? It's relatively simple: When you edit a file on the CD, it actually creates a temporary file on the hard drive with the changes. When the edited file is read, the union mount system transparently retrieves the changes from the file on the hard drive. This is a very efficient way of working with the CD—only the files that are changed are copied to the hard drive.

NOTE

There is a downside to the union mount: Your changes are not permanent. When the device is unmounted, all of your changes are lost.

To perform a union mount, type the following:

```
mkdir /mnt/cdrom<CR>
mkdir /usr/src<CR>
mount -t union -o -b /mnt/cdrom /usr/src<CR>
```

Editing the Kernel Configuration File

Configuring the kernel isn't as easy on OpenBSD as it is on Linux, because it doesn't have a neat little graphical interface. Nonetheless, it's a pretty straightforward process that's entirely managed by a single configuration file. The OpenBSD distribution comes with numerous example configuration files, each of which is tailored to a specific purpose. The one that best fits our purposes is the "GENERIC" configuration file. Assuming that you've performed a successful union mount, you'll be able to view this configuration file by typing:

```
more /usr/src/sys/arch/i386/conf/GENERIC
```

Before we edit the file, let's create a copy of it so that we don't have to change the original:

```
cd /usr/src/sys/arch/i386/conf
cp GENERIC MYKERNEL
```

Now let's edit the MYKERNEL file with vi:

```
vi MYKERNEL
```

The goal is to add a few lines that will improve firewalling performance. These lines can be added to the end of the file. Hit ctrl-d until the cursor is at the end of the file. Hit "e" a few times to advance to the end of the line. Hit "a" to append text to the end of the file. Hit <CR> to start a new line and type:

```
option NMBCLUSTERS=8192
option NKMEMCLUSTERS=8192
option MAX_KMAP=120
option MAX_KMAPENT=6000
```

This is pure and unadulterated black magic (okay, maybe a wee bit of adultery was thrown in). If you want to know what's going on here, you'll need to read the OpenBSD FAQ, section 12, and the man page for "options".

You might notice a line that says "include ../../../conf/GENERIC" toward the beginning of the file. There is actually another GENERIC file that contains the options which apply to all platforms on which OpenBSD compiles (the file we've been editing is Intel specific). To view the file, type:

```
more /usr/src/sys/conf/GENERIC
```

Note the two lines that say:

```
option IPFILTER
option IPFILTER_LOG
```

These lines enable the IPFilter code in the kernel. If either of these lines starts with "#" (the comment symbol), you'll need to edit the file and remove the "#". If the lines are not present, you'll need to add them. If you're using the OpenBSD 2.5 CD, these lines should be present and uncommented.

Once you've gotten these changes to successfully compile, you may want to play around with stripping out unnecessary kernel options. The GENERIC configuration file includes everything under the sun—your system needs less than half of the file. The trick is figuring out which half to delete. Slimming down your kernel will improve boot time and the performance of your machine. It will also make it a little more secure—there's less stuff that might be insecure. We're not going to help you much here, but here are some general pointers:

- Instead of deleting lines you don't want (done with 'dd' in vi), you should comment them out by placing a # at the beginning of the line. This turns the line into a comment, which is not processed when the kernel is compiled. The advantage to commenting the line out is that if you accidentally deactivate something critical, it's very easy to re-activate it again. To add a comment to the beginning of a line, simply position the cursor at the start of the line, type "i", followed by "#" and then hit escape.

- Some things you can definitely delete are audio drivers, pcmcia drivers, scsi drivers (assuming you're using IDE), and excess CD-ROM/network drivers for drives/cards other than the ones you have.

Compiling the Kernel

Now is the moment of truth—if we're lucky, a few commands will result in a fully compiled kernel. Type:

```
cd /usr/src/sys/arch/i386/conf
config -s /usr/src/sys -b . MYKERNEL
make clean
make
```

If things are working properly, you should see a lot of compiler messages, and it should not immediately return to a prompt. Instead, the system should crunch away for a few minutes, spewing out chunks of compiler commands. After about 2 to 5 minutes (possibly longer depending on the speed of your machine), you should see the following lines:

```
lots of compiler stuff
...
rm -f bsd
ld -z Ttext F0100000 -e start -x -o bsd $(SYSTEM_OBJ) vers.o
text        data        bss        dec        hex
2023424     143360      1063348    3230132    3149b4
```

This means everything went well and you have a new kernel ready to be installed (your last line of numbers may be different). If you see something else, or the compilation exited with an error message, you've got a problem. Here are a couple of troubleshooting tips:

Is your compiler installed? Did you select the comp25.tar.gz disk set when installing? If you didn't, you'll get a message like: "cc not found" or "gcc not found." You can install it with the following commands (if you're not sure whether the compiler is installed or not, don't worry—doing these commands won't hurt either way):

```
cd /
umount /mnt/cdrom
mount_cd9660 /dev/cdrom /mnt/cdrom
tar xzf /mnt/cdrom/2.5/i386/comp25.tar.gz
```

Make sure you do the "cd /" command first, otherwise bad things will happen (at best you'll have compiler files scattered all over your hard drive, creating a difficult-to-clean mess, and at worst it will cause a kernel panic).

Try compiling the GENERIC kernel directly from the CD-ROM, without any patches or modifications. Here's how:

```
mkdir /tmp/kernel
cd /tmp/kernel
umount /mnt/cdrom
mount_cd9660 /dev/cdrom /mnt/cdrom
cp /mnt/cdrom/sys/arch/i386/conf/GENERIC .
config -s /mnt/cdrom/sys -b . GENERIC
make
```

This will create a temporary directory, mount the CD-ROM normally, and compile the GENERIC kernel in the temporary directory. If it still isn't working, you can try copying the entire source tree over to the hard disk. It's possible there's some problem with your CD-ROM. To do this, try the following:

```
cd /
umount /mnt/cdrom
mount_cd9660 /dev/cdrom /mnt/cdrom
mkdir -p /usr/src/sys
cd /mnt/cdrom/sys
tar cf - . | (cd /usr/src/sys; tar xvf - )
cd /usr/src/sys/arch/i386/conf
config -s /usr/src/sys -b . GENERIC
make
```

This creates a directory on your hard drive called /usr/src/sys and copies the kernel source code into it. It then uses the GENERIC file to compile a kernel directly from the hard drive source.

If you can get the GENERIC kernel to work off of your hard disk or your CD-ROM, then you probably made an error when you modified the MYKERNEL file. If you've patched any system files, you could have a problem with the patches, although it's unlikely. Finally, the union mount code isn't perfect, so try using the full hard drive copy method if all else fails.

If *nothing* works, there's still hope—you can survive without compiling the kernel (although you'll be sacrificing a degree of security). On the companion Web site we've placed a copy of the bsd kernel binary specially tuned for firewall systems. We've also patched security holes in the kernel. We'll try to keep this kernel as up to date as possible, but there will be some lag time between security patches and updates to the Web site. Turn to this option only as a last resort. We can't make any guarantees as to the security or stability of our kernel binary.

NOTE
■■■■■■ From a security standpoint, using our kernel in a production firewall is a *bad idea*. This is because you can't tell if it's been compromised (someone might hack our Web site and place a trojan bsd kernel on the site, or we may have installed a trojan patch, and so forth). It should only be used for experimental purposes.

Installing the New Kernel

Your new kernel is the file called "bsd" sitting in your current directory. Installing this new kernel is relatively easy. First, rename the old kernel to a backup file:

```
mv /bsd /bsd.old
```

Now copy in the new kernel:

```
cp ./bsd /
cd /
```

The next time you reboot you'll be booting from your new kernel (you *must* change to the / directory before rebooting or your computer will crash, due to instabilities in the union mount system). If anything goes wrong, you can use a recovery disk to copy the "bsd.old" file back to "bsd" with the command:

```
cp /mnt/recover/bsd.old /mnt/recover/bsd
```

Use of a recovery disk is beyond the scope of this chapter, but here's a hint: Since the recovery disk is a floppy, your "/" directory with the "bsd" kernel in it is actually on the floppy. You'll need to mount the partition with your root system onto a temporary directory. On our system we'd do this with the following commands:

```
mkdir /mnt/recover
mount /dev/wd0a /mnt/recover
```

Applying Patches

Once you've compiled your kernel for the first time it only gets easier (the same is true of climbing Mount Everest without oxygen, so we hear). We'll take advantage of your newly found kernel-compiling skills to patch some security holes in the kernel. The first step is to obtain the necessary patches from the OpenBSD ftp site. Type "cd /tmp" to change directories to the temporary directory. Then type "ftp ftp.openbsd.org" and hit return. When it asks you for a username, log in as "ftp" with password "ftp@ftp.com" (you should technically give your real e-mail address…). Next, type "cd /pub/OpenBSD/patches/" followed by <CR>.

To download the file, type: "bin" and hit <CR>. This tells the FTP program that you'll be transferring binary files. Finally type: "get 2.5.tar.gz" <CR>. This will download all the 2.5 patches to your home directory. Type "bye" and hit <CR> when you're finished.

To extract the patches, type "tar xzf 2.5.tar.gz" at a command prompt. This will create a directory called "2.5". Type "cd 2.5" to change into the directory. Type "ls" to see a listing of all the files and directories within the 2.5 subdirectory. You should see directories for each architecture supported by OpenBSD. There are two directories here that concern us. The more important is "common," which contains system independent patches. At the time of writing, there are numerous common for 2.5. The other directory of concern is "i386," which contains patches specific to the Intel platform. These are more rare—at the time of this writing there are no Intel-specific security holes. We'll walk through the process of applying a few of the common patches.

For the most part, we're only concerned with kernel level patches and server dæmons that are critical to the firewall's operation (ipf, ipnat, and so forth—all other programs can be deactivated or removed). To get some basic information on a patch, type:

```
head patch_filename
```

This will print out the first few lines of the patch, which often contains installation instructions. For example, the bmap.patch file is installed by doing the following:

```
cd /usr/src/sys
patch -p0 < bmap.patch
```

If you actually try doing this, it won't be able to find the bmap.patch file. That's because our patch files are in the directory "/tmp/2.5/common." So, you should change the second line to:

```
patch -p0 < /tmp/2.5/common/bmap.patch
```

Once the patch has been successfully applied, you need to rebuild your kernel.

If you're patching something other than the kernel, you'll need to pay careful attention to the output of the patch program. For example, when you apply the fts.patch to "/usr/src", it tells you that you'll have to rebuild "libc". Where is "libc?" If you look at the patch output, you can see that it patched files in "lib/libc". If you type "cd lib/libc" followed by "make", the patched "libc" program will be recompiled.

Keeping Your Machine Secure

We'll talk about this in much greater depth in Chapter 10, "Configuring the Firewall" but there are some OpenBSD specific issues we need to address now.

One of the key strengths of OpenBSD is its security audit process. Once a piece of software has passed through this process a few times, it's important to get future patches and upgrades from the OpenBSD site directly; otherwise, you risk introducing code that hasn't been audited.

Apache

One notable exception to this rule is Apache. OpenBSD now includes Apache as part of its default distribution. The version of Apache that comes with OpenBSD has not been fully audited. Therefore, you should consider the most recent stable version of apache to be the most secure. If a security hole is found in apache and posted at apache.org, then you should upgrade your version of apache. This has absolutely no relevance to your firewall, since you won't be running a Web server on your firewall. But after going through this chapter, you might decide to run OpenBSD on a few other machines in your network (such as your Web server). In that case, this will be very relevant.

You should check the OpenBSD site at least once a week for security updates. It's also useful to scan the changelog between revision 2.5 and whatever is current. This will give you some idea of what will be in the next release.

In Chapter 10 we talk about stripping down the firewall, removing anything that is unnecessary. In OpenBSD, this is not nearly as easy as it is with RedHat Linux. The problem is that most of the tools on the system were installed from a disk set. These are tarballs that are unwound in the "/" directory. This means that files get sprinkled all over your drive—in /usr, /etc, /bin, /sbin, and so on. You can't simply delete a directory to uninstall these disk sets. Therefore, we provide a script on our companion Web site that allows you to remove entire disk sets: "dsuninstall". This tool takes a tarball as input and uses it to locate and remove the files that were installed.

The "dsuninstall" program has an additional use: If you pass it a customized tarball, it can be used to strip out a more specific selection of files. How is this useful? Well, there may be a few programs in base.tar.gz that you don't want on your firewall. So create a new tarball that contains just the files you want to remove from your system. Place this tarball on a CD or floppy. To uninstall the files, just run the script on it. To reinstall them for maintenance purposes, just untar it into the '/' directory.

Installing ssh

You need to install ssh. It will make your life much easier. Trust us. ssh is provided as an OpenBSD package, but isn't actually included on the CD-ROM due to patent restrictions. It is, however, provided on the OpenBSD ftp site. To install ssh from the ftp site, type the command:

```
pkg_add ftp://ftp.openbsd.org/pub/OpenBSD/2.5/packages/i386/ssh-1.2.26-intl.gz
```

That's it—the nifty package installer will handle the rest. The sshd daemon will automatically run the next time that you restart the computer. For now, you can activate the daemon by typing: "/usr/local/sbin/sshd" at a command prompt.

Summary

In this chapter you learned how to install OpenBSD. You also learned how to prepare it for use as a firewall. We walked you through configuring PPP, additional network cards, and your kernel. You should go through the process of installing and configuring OpenBSD a number of times. Each time you do it you'll become more comfortable with working in the OpenBSD environment.

Now that you've finished this chapter, we suggest re-reading the afterboot man page again. This time, follow the instructions for tightening up security on the system. You'll notice that we've covered many of the topics already. Once you've finished going through afterboot you'll be ready to start configuring your firewall.

Now it's time to learn how to turn the machine into a packet filtering firewall. The next chapter will explain the ipfilter and ipnat suite of tools in great detail.

9

Configuring the Firewall under OpenBSD

A t this point you should have OpenBSD installed on your equipment. What you don't yet have is a useful firewall. Your machine, if connected to the network properly, will cut off all traffic between your network and the outside world. The firewall can talk to the outside world, and the internal network can talk to the firewall, but nothing will pass between the firewall's external and internal interfaces. This is a *good thing*. This chapter will teach you how to selectively allow data to move between the inside and outside world.

We'll start this chapter by discussing the underlying concepts behind firewalling in OpenBSD. We'll learn how to work with the tools used to implement the firewall. Then, we'll practice making a few trivial rules and we'll run some tests to ensure that they work properly. The goal is to end the chapter with a basic functional firewall. If necessary, we'll also help you set up *Network Address Translation* (known as Masquerading in the Linux world). We're *not* going to make too many important decisions regarding the services your firewall allows—that's the job of Chapter 10, "Tuning Your Firewall."

The tool in OpenBSD for configuring firewalls is called *IPFilter*. IPFilter is actually a suite of programs—ipf, ipnat, and ipstat. *ipf* is used to configure the packet filtering aspects of the firewall. *ipnat* is used to perform Network Address Translation (NAT) and packet redirection (forwarding). *ipfstat* is used to obtain a printout of the rules currently active within the kernel. This is very useful for debugging firewall problems.

The good news is that there's nothing else to install—the IPFilter package is part of the basic OpenBSD installation (everything is in the base disk set). Before we start playing with these programs, let's take a look at the fundamental theory behind IPFilter.

IPFilter Theory

IPFilter is a very simple, yet powerful, filtering system. It can do nearly everything the Linux IPChains system can do. IPFilter even has a few advantages over IPChains, the most notable of which is its easy-to-read syntax. Another advantage of IPFilter is the distinct separation of filtering (ipf) and forwarding/masquerading (ipnat) functions. This makes the rule system much easier to understand, which means you'll be less likely to write incorrect rules that do bad things, which in turn is a *good thing*.

IPF

The bulk of your firewall rules will be crafted with the ipf program. This program is used to add and remove filter rules from the kernel's filter queue. The kernel actually takes care of the filtering, but the rules are set using the ipf program.

NOTE IPFilter does not make decisions about *how* to route packets; that's handled by the routing tables. The only decision made by the filter is *whether* to route packets. We will cover routing tables in more depth in Chapter 10.

The ipf program processes a *rule file*, which is a simple text file that you will create. In this file, each line specifies a *filtering rule*. A filtering rule is a *set of conditions* and an *action* to take when the conditions are met. In general, the action is to either discard the packet (the ipf term for this is *block*) or to allow the packet to pass through the firewall (*pass*). We say "in general" because there are other things rules can do, such as cause packets to be logged (*log*). For the truly adventurous, rules can even trigger the execution of special kernel functions (*call*). For the most part, we're only concerned with the *block* and *pass* actions.

The rules in the rule file are processed in the order they appear. When a packet arrives at an interface, the kernel tests the packet against each rule, in sequence. When a packet matches a rule, the kernel takes note of the action. In some cases it takes immediate action and stops processing the packet. In other cases it will continue processing the packet against more rules.

There are two events that will trigger the kernel to block or pass a packet. The first is when the kernel reaches the last rule in the rule list. It will then perform the action specified in the last matching rule. If no rules match, the packet will be passed by default. The second event is when a matching rule explicitly says to stop processing the packet and take the prescribed action (accomplished via the option keyword *quick*). This is used to short-circuit ipf's rule processing, and can significantly speed up the firewall if there's a large ruleset. We'll talk more about the value of quick rules a little later on.

NOTE

If a packet matches a rule with a *log* or *count* action, the action is immediately taken. The kernel continues to process the packet against the remaining rules. This enables logging and accounting of traffic that is independent from whether a packet is accepted or rejected.

But wait, you say. What happens if more than one rule matches a packet and none have the quick option? What if the first match says to block the packet, the second says to pass the packet, and a third match says to block the packet again? How do we know which action will be performed by the kernel?

Only the Last Match Counts

This is not a philosophical musing by a chain smoker. Instead, it's the key to understanding how IPFilter works. IPFilter processes its rules much like we process rules in English. Let's take a common situation as an example: Selectively allowing certain pets into our apartment. If we want to prohibit all pets from our apartment, we would hang up a sign that says: "No pets allowed." If we later decide that goldfish and iguanas are bearable, we could amend the sign to read: "No pets allowed, except for goldfish and iguanas." It would be somewhat awkward to say it the other way around: "Goldfish and iguanas are allowed in my apartment. No other pets are allowed." Why is this format more awkward? It's because we tend to want to hear the general rule first and then the exceptions, especially when there's a long list of exceptions. There's a good reason for this. Imagine hearing the following:

> "Goldfish, tropical fish, catfish, crayfish, lobsters, crabs, sharks, dolphins, penguins, iguanas, lizards, toads, turtles, scorpions, spiders, caribou, elk, reindeer, moose, gazelles, rabbits, gerbils, ferrets, mice, and hamsters are allowed in my apartment. No other pets are allowed."

After the penguins the average listener is wondering where the heck this list is going. By the time we get to gerbils, their eyes have glazed over. When we finally get to the rule, almost every listener will have forgotten most of the list (with the exception of the landlord, who'll be copying it down verbatim for the eviction notice). This is because the listener doesn't know that it's important to pay attention. We could have just as easily said:

"Goldfish, tropical fish, catfish, crayfish, lobsters, crabs, sharks, dolphins, penguins, iguanas, lizzards, toads, turtles, scorpions, spiders, caribou, elk, reindeer, moose, gazelles, rabbits, gerbils, ferrets, mice, and hamsters are cool pets."

The listener could then respond:

"You've gotta stop watching Wild Kingdom every night."

without actually remembering the contents of the list.

On the other hand, by placing the rule first, the listener knows exactly what we're talking about. It also tells the listener that the subsequent exception list is important. Furthermore, instead of having to remember the whole list, the listener simply has to see if their pet species is one of the exceptions before bringing it into the apartment. This is why placing the rule before the exception makes sense.

If you read the corresponding chapter for Linux (Chapter 7, "Configuring the Firewall under Linux), you'll notice that the Linux tool does the opposite and places exceptions before rules. Why? Well, there's a downside to last-match-wins processing: Every single rule has to be digested for every single packet. With first-match-wins, list processing can stop after a match is found. This leads to less readable rules that can be processed more quickly; power-in-configuration is sacrificed for increased power-in-performance. Performance is unlikely to be an issue for you unless you're using your firewall on a very fast line (a T1 or better, at the very least), but we thought it worth briefly dwelling on the issue so you could see the practical consequences of a design decision.

The pet analogy extends to IPFilter, although IPFilter exceptions appear as rules that contradict an earlier rule. For example, in IPFilter-speak, the above example would appear as the following two rules:

First Rule: "No pets are allowed"

Second Rule: "Goldfish, tropical fish, catfish, crayfish, lobsters, crabs, sharks, dolphins, penguins, iguanas, lizzards, toads, turtles, scorpions, spiders, caribou, elk, reindeer, moose, gazelles, rabbits, gerbils, ferrets, mice, and hamsters are allowed."

Let's suppose that one morning, while we're in the shower, a snapping turtle inadvertently crawls into the trousers we've laid out on the bed. The subsequent bad experience might give us cause to further amend our rule set. We now want to specifically exclude snapping turtles from the list. We could do this by replacing "turtles" in the second Rule with "every type of turtle except for snapping turtles," but this would be awkward. So we'll add a third rule that says:

Third Rule: "No snapping turtles allowed."

The next day Jim and Bob come over to visit. Bob has a caribou with him. He looks at the first rule and gets ready to tie his caribou to the front gate. Then he reads the second rule and sees that caribou are okay. Rule number 3 doesn't apply to him, and since there are no more rules, he and his caribou (named Louise) can come in.

Jim has a snapping turtle named Woody with him. It doesn't matter that Woody is trouser trained. The presence of the third Rule means that Jim has to chuck Woody into a bush somewhere before he can enter the apartment. Rule number three was the last one to match, therefore it's the only one that counts.

NOTE The point here is that the *ordering of the rules* is very important. If the rules are not in the right sequence, the firewall may not work properly.

We've belabored the point more than enough. Now let's look at how rules are written.

Practical Rule Making

In order to manipulate the kernel's rule list, you need to be root. Execute "/bin/su -", give the root password, and away we go.

NOTE Do everything in this section while logged on at the console. If you mess with the networking functions of the machine while logged in over the network, you're very likely to lock yourself out. Since you will be opening up your server to attack, you may also wish to disconnect any hostile networks while you try these examples. Turn off and unplug the modem, or yank any suspicious-looking ethernet cables.

Adding Rules

The most common method for adding rules to the kernel's ruleset is via a script file. This file is usually /etc/ipf.rules. The ipf program will read in the script file whenever the machine boots. Additionally, the following command can be used to flush all of the rules and re-read the contents of the script file:

```
ipf -Fa -vf /etc/ipf.rules -E
```

The '-F' flag flushes all rules from the kernel, and the 'a' says to flush the active ruleset. See the following sidebar, *Active versus Inactive Rulesets*.

Active versus Inactive Rulesets

The kernel has two sets of firewall rules: *active* and *inactive*. The purpose of the inactive ruleset is for debugging. When you load new rules into the inactive ruleset, ipf can notify you if there are any errors in your rule code. If you load buggy rules directly into the active ruleset, your firewall will not function properly until the bugs are fixed. Using the inactive ruleset avoids having to make your network vulnerable during testing and debugging. Once you have a working ruleset, you can swap the active and inactive rules.

The 'v' in the '-vf' flag enables verbose mode, which will print out additional information as the kernel processes each rule in the file. This will help you quickly spot any errors. The 'f' indicates that the rules should be read from the specified file (/etc/ipf.rules). The '–E' says to immediately enable the rules. This command is almost identical to the command executed when the machine first boots up—the only difference is that the boot version doesn't use the verbose flag.

The easiest way to add new rules is to edit the ipf.rules files and then execute the above command. This is what we're going to do as we experiment with different rules in the following sections.

Adding Rules in Production

If your firewall is already in production, you probably don't want to mess with the active ruleset until you know that it works properly. Therefore, you'll want to execute the following:

```
<run test scripts>
ipf –I –Fa –vf /etc/ipf.rules
ipf –s
```

This reads the contents of the ipf.rules file into the inactive ruleset (-I). If all looks good, you can swap the active and inactive sets with the "ipf –s" command to activate your changes.

Why You Shouldn't Do This Remotely, and How You Can Anyhow

We recommend doing all firewall modifications from the console. Nonetheless, you may find it necessary to alter the firewall rules remotely. This creates a major problem: If your rules contain an error, you might find yourself unable to access the machine once the ruleset has been activated.

There is a simple solution to this problem. Instead of just executing "ipf –s", try: "ipf –s; sleep 10; ipf –s". This command sequence will swap the rules, wait ten seconds, and then swap them back.

Once the command has been executed, type a few random commands (change directories, do an ls, and so forth). If your connection is good, then you know the changes haven't broken your ability to remotely administer the machine. If your connection freezes, don't worry—in 10 seconds the rules will revert to their original state and you'll get your connection back. If everything works, you should execute "ipf –s" one final time to fully activate the rules.

NOTE

This technique may give you a false sense of accomplishment if you're using "keep state" within your rules. When you swap rulesets, the state tables are preserved. Packets matching the state table will continue to pass through, even if the new filter rules would otherwise break the connection. To flush the state tables, you'll need to execute "ipf –FS".

We suggest doing all filter modifications from a console login if you're using state.

Some Thoughts on Testing Your Rules

We're going to do all of our testing using the active ruleset, because our firewall isn't hooked up to anything critical yet. Our tests will be real time: We'll connect computers to the inbound and outbound interfaces in order to test the validity of our rules. For example, if we block telnet access, we can test to see if the rule worked by trying to telnet to an internal computer from an external computer.

Eventually, you'll find that real time tests can become tedious. The best way to effectively test your ruleset is to create a test script using the 'ipftest' utility. ipftest lets you create packets with specific attributes. The ipf program then reads in your firewall rules and tests each packet against a simulated firewall. By creating a good set of test packets you can be fairly sure that your firewall is functioning properly. We've created a sample test script for our firewall examples, which you can find on the companion Web site at www.wiley.com/compbooks/sonnenreich.

Once your rules are finalized, you'll occasionally need to make some changes to the ruleset. The best way to test this is to first run the ipftest script on the new rules. If the tests pass, you can place the new rules in the inactive ruleset. You can swap the active and inactive sets to activate your new rules. If there are any errors, you can swap the rulesets back, restoring your original firewall rules.

Set the Default Policies

Now that we have a clean slate, let's open up the /etc/ipf.rules file in vi and get cracking. We're going to create two rules that will form our default policy. Between the two rules, we'll match every packet that passes through the firewall. If no other rules match, then one of these rules will apply. Start your ipf.rules file off with the following lines:

```
pass in all
pass out all
```

This is the simplest possible type of rule. The 'pass' term is the action. The other common action we'll be using is 'block'. The 'in' and 'out' refer to the direction in which packets are traveling, such as coming into the firewall or going out of the firewall. Finally, the 'all' says to match all packets. With these rules we're allowing all packets coming in and out to pass through the firewall. This is equivalent to going down the *accept everything that is not explicitly denied* road, described in Chapter 3, "How Secure Should Your Network Be?" When we build the real firewall, we will avoid death and destruction by starting with a more restrictive policy ('block in all', 'block out all').

To see what this has done, we need to first activate the rules in the ipf.rules file. To do this, save the file, exit vi, and type:

```
ipf -Fa -vf /etc/ipf.rules -E
```

NOTE

If you've already enabled (-E) the ipfilter rules, you'll get an error message when executing this command. The solution is to leave off the '–E' once the firewall rules have been activated.

The verbose output should look something like this:

```
[pass in all]
pass in from any to any
[pass out all]
pass out from any to any
```

What you're seeing is the expansion of the 'any' keyword into its full meaning, *from any to any*. We'll explain what this is all about later on in this chapter. If there are no errors, then your ruleset is active. If there are errors, then you probably have a typo somewhere in your file. Check that each rule appears on a separate line. If you type:

```
cat /etc/ipf.rules
```

on a command line, you should get the following output:

```
pass in all
pass out all
```

If you don't get that exact output, go back into vi and fix up the file.

You can now show the state of your rules by typing:

```
ipfstat -io
```

You should see output similar to the following:

```
pass in from any to any
pass out from any to any
```

Simple, eh? Now it gets tougher. (However tough it gets, you can come back to this section and perform these three steps to return your firewall to sanity.)

Basic Concepts

We're going to test a few simple rules, just to get you familiar with using ipf. It's easier to appreciate what you're doing if you can see the effect that it's having. Seeing the effects is a lot easier if you have another computer to test it from.

We assume that you have at least one other machine on your internal network. When we want you to try something on that other machine, we'll refer to it as the test machine. You will need to know the IP addresses of both the test machine and the firewall. You will also need to move physically to the test machine to try things from it—you are unlikely to be able to keep a network connection up through most of these tests.

Filtering by Protocol

Let's try refusing all packets of a certain type, say all TCP packets. Add the following to your /etc/ipf.rules file:

```
block in proto tcp all
```

This is the first real rule we have written. We're blocking inbound traffic. The 'proto' keyword lets us match on a particular protocol; in this case TCP. The 'all' says to match any source or destination IP address.

Let's see what we've done. First, let's make sure we can telnet to the firewall without the firewall rules being active. If you've followed the instructions in this book so far, you should be able to telnet without a problem. Go to the test machine and telnet to the firewall. You can hit CTRL-d to exit the telnet session. You should see output such as:

```
Connected to 201.201.201.201.
Escape character is '^]'.

OpenBSD/i386 (firemarshall-bill) (ttyp0)
login:
```

There are a few reasons why telnet might not work. If you know something about Unix-type systems, you may have already tried to secure the firewall machine by altering the /etc/inetd.conf file. If you still are having problems, you should go back to Chapter 8, "Installing OpenBSD," and make sure your network cards are properly configured.

Assuming the telnet session worked, let's activate the rules by executing the "ipf –Fa –vf /etc/ipf.rules" command (we've left off the '–E' because we assume your firewall is already enabled). You should see some pretty and verbose output. Once again, go to the test machine and try to telnet to the firewall machine (issue the command "telnet ip.address.of.firewall" from a command prompt). You should find that telnet just sits there, sending requests for a connection, receiving no answer. This means our firewall is working—it's blocking all of the TCP packets being sent by the telnet client.

Giving Some Feedback

Since we just used 'block' without sending any feedback message, the firewall is silently dropping those packets on the ground. Let's try sending back a TCP reset packet to notify the telnet client that the service is unavailable. When the firewall detects a TCP connection, it will send back a Reset packet, which immediately shuts down the connection. Change the last line in the ipf.rules file to read:

```
block return-rst in proto tcp all
```

Activate the ruleset again using the "ipf –Fa –vf /etc/ipf.rules" command (from here on in, when we say "activate the ruleset," you should execute this command). Now try to telnet once again. This time, the telnet client should return immediately with an error message that says "Connection refused." Any other TCP connections to the machine will be likewise rejected.

Another type of message that can be returned is an ICMP error. This is useful for notifying UDP clients such as traceroute that the service is unavailable. If we wanted to send an ICMP port-unreachable error in response to a UDP request, we could change the line to read:

```
block return-icmp(port-unr) in proto udp all
```

Note that there is *no space* between the return-icmp and the (port-unr). If you put a space there, the ipf program will not read in the rule. You can also leave off port-unr and it will send back a generic ICMP destination unreachable (type 3) error.

With TCP connections, you'll find that a TCP reset is faster for the client than an ICMP error. This is because ICMP errors can be caused by other nonfatal factors (someone unplugged the network cable for a second), therefore some clients will not immediately shut down a connection due to an ICMP error. For most cases the difference doesn't matter, but for certain automated services that frequently make connections it can help reduce network traffic and processor usage. Nonetheless, you may have some situations that require an ICMP error instead of a TCP reset.

Let's make sure we've only blocked TCP packets. Try pinging the firewall. You should get an immediate "up" response, since we haven't blocked ICMP traffic. If you were to repeat the above steps with 'proto icmp' instead of 'proto tcp', pings would be silently dropped while the telnet connection worked fine.

Filtering by Port

Now we'll try something a little more ambitious. We will deny TCP traffic just to one particular port, in this case, the telnet port (23). Change the last line of your ipf.rules file to read:

```
block in proto tcp from any to any port = 23
```

Here, we have replaced the 'all' with 'from any to any'. Why did we do this? Because we need to specify a port. The keyword 'all' is synonymous with 'from any port >= 0 to any port >= 0'. The 'port >= 0' means every port between 0 and 65535, inclusive. Since 65535 is the highest possible port number and 0 is the lowest, this is the same as saying "every port." It's pretty unwieldy to type ">= 0" whenever you want to match all ports. Therefore, the kind designers of IPFilter have allowed us to match all ports by just leaving off 'port' altogether. Putting it all together, we can see that saying 'all' really *is* equal to saying 'from any to any'.

What we want for our example rule is 'from any port >= 0 to any port = 23'. Using the shorthand, we leave the first 'port' out, giving us 'from any to any port 23'. Recall that TCP port 23 is the traditional port for interactive telnet access. We could have also put in "port = telnet", since you can use either the port number or the service name, as defined in the file /etc/services.

If you try to telnet to the firewall from the test machine you should get silence, just as you did in the first example. If, instead, you try to connect to port 513 on the firewall with "telnet IP.address.of.firewall 513", you should get an immediate connection (hit return to get your prompt back). TCP port 513 is the rlogin service—one of the dangerous ones we talked about in Chapter 3. We'll be turning it off before the chapter is over. Had we wanted to block a range of ports (say, 99 through 1023 inclusive), we could have said "from any to any port 98><1024". Note again that the range operator is *not* inclusive.

That was also our first rule with two conditions: First, the protocol had to be TCP, and second, the destination port had to be 23. The two conditions must both be satisfied in order to get a match; however many conditions are in a single rule, all conditions must be satisfied in order to match. If you want to apply two conditions and the rule to match when *either* condition is satisfied, write two rules instead.

Now we're going to filter based on a source address. Let's prevent our test machine from being able to telnet to the outside world. Add the following to your /etc/ipf.rules file, replacing the 1.2.3.4 with the internal IP address of your test machine:

```
block in proto tcp from 1.2.3.4 to any port = telnet
```

The machine with the IP address you have put in place of 1.2.3.4 should now be unable to telnet to the firewall, or any machine in the outside world (if you want a telnet host to test this on, try: athena.dialup.mit.edu—you won't be able to get in, but it will at least prompt you for a login if the telnet connection is successful).

Had we wished to specify a source port, or range of ports, we could have written something like "from 1.2.3.4 port > 1024 to any port telnet". This example will block connections from any port greater than 1024 on the machine 1.2.3.4. Only root can execute processes that bind to ports less than 1025, so this will stop all userland applications (those applications that do not run as root) from communicating with the telnet port. This isn't a particularly useful example for a number of reasons, the largest being that Windows and Macintosh boxes don't enforce this privileged port restriction as all users are assumed to be fully privileged.

Filtering by Interface

The 'on' parameter allows you to specify a particular interface. If, for example, your Internet connection is via PPP across a modem, then it is likely that your network interface is ppp0. If this were true, you could apply much more stringent conditions to packets coming in from the Internet by including "on ppp0" in the rule. If your external interface has another name (eth1 or sl0, for example) then just substitute that name for ppp0. Since this is exactly the behavior we require of a firewall—that it should be much meaner to packets coming in from the outside world than to packets leaving from your internal network—we will use this flag frequently in the final firewall. Let's rewrite the prior TCP example above to specifically reference our inbound interface (the example assumes it's ppp0). Note that the 'on' comes after the 'in/out' portion of the rule.

```
block in on ppp0 proto tcp from 1.2.3.4 to any port = telnet
```

Hopefully, you can already see how these few tools will be used together to build a powerful packet-filtering firewall. There are still a few more tools we need to cover, but if you've got your head round everything in this last section, you've got most of what you need under your belt. Practice and experiment until you are comfortable with everything up to this point.

Other Important Concepts

There are a few more things we need to discuss before we're ready to write some real rules. We're going to talk about ICMP, rule optimization, TCP flags, and stateful inspection. These concepts are a little more advanced, but you should be ready to handle them. If you're confused, many of the underlying concepts are explained in Chapter 2, "Fundamental Internet Security Issues."

ICMP

If you are matching on ICMP, then the 'port' parameter might not seem stunningly useful, as ICMP doesn't have ports. It does, however, have message types, and the 'icmp-type' parameter is used with ICMP to specify message types. Types you should consider permitting are 0 (echo-reply), if you want to be able to ping outside your network, and 11 (time-exceeded), if you want to be able to use the traceroute tool to check machines outside your network. (If you're not familiar with it, traceroute is an extremely useful tool that can be used to find the path a packet is taking through a network, including the Internet. Do "man traceroute" for more information.)

Do not block ICMP type 3 unless suffering is fun for you. Not only is this used by remote hosts to signify that a firewall or other device has chosen to block your packet, but type 3 ICMP is used by the TCP implementation to negotiate certain parameters. Your network performance will suffer badly if you block type 3 ICMP to the machine you use to connect to the outside world. To allow it, use a line like:

```
pass in proto icmp all icmp-type 3
```

Note that we have now allowed ICMP type 3 packets to enter the firewall, whether they are intended for the firewall or for some machine inside your network.

There are numerous ways to filter ICMP packets. Some types of ICMP messages contain additional information in the form of *code numbers*.

Quick

One of the most powerful, yet confounding, options is quick. It short-circuits the rule processing system by forcing a matching rule to be the last rule processed. It's a great way to save processing time by quickly throwing away packets that are known to be bad or passing in packets that are known to be good. The problem with quick is that it is *very* order-sensitive. If a quick rule appears in the wrong place, it can cripple your entire firewall.

Recall our earlier point about performance and first-match-wins firewalls. If speed becomes an issue for you, you can use the quick keyword to achieve first-match-wins performance levels for your most commonly blocked or admitted packets. As we've just said, though, this increased performance comes with substantial added complexity in your ruleset. Think carefully before overusing quick.

Let's look at our most recent ICMP example. We know we want to let in all ICMP type-3 packets without exception. Therefore, let's place this rule at the beginning of the file and give it a quickie:

```
pass in quick proto icmp all icmp-type 3
```

Now any ICMP packets will rapidly shoot through the firewall without having to endure repeated prodding by the kernel for mundane conditions such as TCP flags, UDP ports, and so forth.

Only Allowing Established Connections

Bear in mind that, behind your firewall, there will be flocks of users all initiating TCP connections to all sorts of ports on all sorts of servers all over the Internet. Packets will be coming back to a variety of local ports from a variety of remote ports on a variety of machines. The only thing all these packets have in common is that they're all *responses to connections initiated by your users*. If your users start the connection, it's good—if someone outside tries to start the connection, it might not be so good.

Consider the following rule:

```
pass in on ppp0 proto tcp all flags A/SA
```

This rule applies only to packets on interface ppp0, and only those which are TCP packets. So far, so good. But then there's this 'flags A/SA' bit. What does it mean? After consulting the Rosetta Stone of IPF (the man page) we learned that it lets us filter based on the TCP flags present in a packet. There are two parts to the condition: before the / and after the /. The part before the '/' says that we're testing for the presence of the 'ACK' flag. The part after the '/' says that we're only concerned with the state of the 'SYN' and 'ACK' flags. When we put the two together, we see that this rule will match a packet that has the 'ACK' flag set but not the 'SYN' flag. Any of the other TCP flags could be set or not set—this rule doesn't care.

So what does this condition mean, in practical terms? Going back to the three-way handshake model described in Chapter 2, we see that when a client initiates a connection it sends a packet with the 'SYN' flag and the initial client sequence number. When the server responds, it sends a packet with the 'SYN' and 'ACK' flags set, along with the server's initial sequence number and the client's incremented sequence as an acknowledgment. Once the connection is established, neither side will send SYN packets. The only things that get sent are ACKs. Therefore, if we want to only allow established connections, we should not accept any packets with the 'SYN' flag set.

There is an alternate way of implementing this policy that is more explicit: Block the offending packets right up front. To do this, the following line needs to appear at the top of your filter file:

```
block in on ppp0 proto tcp all flags S/SA
```

If you want to add in yet another safety measure, you can block the response that your internal machines would give if an external machine somehow was able to originate a connection.

```
block out on ppp0 proto tcp all flags SA/SA
```

This stops your machines from offering the second handshake. Combine these rules with a default policy of 'block in all' and some rules to accept packets originating inside your network, and you've done some highly selective filtering already.

Stateful Inspection

This is a huge buzzword that every major firewall vendor is sure to have on their glossies. Originally, firewalls had a feature that allowed one to filter TCP connections that were established. This meant that it could tell if a packet was part of an established connection or not and make a filtering decision based on that information. Unfortunately, the mechanism used for this was simply looking at the TCP flags. If the flags contained an 'ACK', but not a 'SYN', then the firewall said, "looks established to me!" (this is the sort of system we've just implemented above in the section on TCP flags).

Of course, any four year old can forge a packet that would pass through such a firewall, so a new mechanism was devised called *stateful inspection*. It basically means that certain bits of information are recorded by the firewall whenever a connection is established. This includes sequence numbers and source/destination addresses. When subsequent packets arrive claiming to be part of the established connection, the firewall verifies their sequence numbers against the recorded numbers. If the inbound sequence numbers fall within a certain range, the packets are considered part of the established connection.

The advantage to stateful inspection is that it is rather difficult to create a packet with the proper sequence numbers. This doesn't mean it's impossible, just that it's more difficult (see the following sidebar *Session Hijacking*). Regardless, it's significantly more secure than just filtering based on TCP flags. Furthermore, it can significantly save processing power—the kernel doesn't have to pass the established packets through the filtering rules. It just applies the initial policy to all of the subsequent packets.

Session Hijacking

We talk about the nature of the TCP session hijacking vulnerability in Chapter 2, "Fundamental Internet Security Issues." Firewalls are not able to effectively stop an attack based on session hijacking. The best security against this is an encrypted data stream—the attacker might be able to get a packet past the firewall, but they won't be able to get the receiving application to respond without the proper encryption algorithm and key.

The good news is that stateful inspection is also implemented in the IPFilter system. Not only can it keep state on TCP sessions, but it can track UDP and ICMP sessions also (although this creates some interesting security issues, since UDP and ICMP are stateless protocols). It's the best way to ensure that only machines inside the network can initiate connections with machines outside of the network.

Stateful inspection is implemented in ipf as the keywords 'keep state.' If you want to allow established connections to come into the firewall, you need to apply the 'keep state' keywords to a rule that spots the outbound request from the client inside your network. Thus, to use stateful inspection on outbound telnet clients, you should write:

```
pass out on ppp0 proto tcp from any to any port = telnet keep state
```

We can generalize this further to allow all outbound TCP connections to benefit from stateful inspection:

```
pass out on ppp0 proto tcp all keep state
```

Likewise, 'keep state' can be used as an additional security measure with inbound connections. A classic example is providing access to a Web server that's inside your network. Assuming you already have the above rule in place with a default policy of denying all inbound traffic, the following code will allow the external web client to make the initial page request. After this request, the Web server sends a response to the client. The response is tracked with 'keep state,' so all future communications between the client and the server are tracked.

```
pass in quick on ppp0 proto tcp from any to any port = 80 flags S/SA keep state
```

State is a good filtering concept for TCP rules, although it should not be used as grounds for passing a packet with no further inspection—do not assume that a packet is your friend merely because its state looks good. In the context of UDP and ICMP, there is no state; trying to invent state for them and use it as a sensible adjunct to other filtering is a bad idea.

Network Address Translation

In Chapter 3, we discussed Network Address Translation (NAT), but we generally referred to it as IP Masquerading. Masquerading refers to the art of hiding a whole internal network behind one valid IP address. NAT is actually a superset of IP Masquerading. The NAT portion of the IP Filter package handles both masquerading *and* port forwarding. You can think of masquerading and port forwarding as two sides of the same coin—masquerading maps the outbound connections from private machines so that they appear to be coming from a public address, where as port forwarding maps inbound connections from external machines to a server running on a private part of the network.

Activating NAT Rules

Before your NAT rules will work, you'll need to make some changes to various configuration files. The first step is to add "net.inet.ip.forwarding=1" to the file /etc/sysctl.conf. NAT requires IP packet forwarding, and this line enables packet forwarding at the kernel level.

In Chapter 8 we ensured that "option IPFILTER" and "option IPFILTER_LOG" were present in the kernel config file when we rebuilt the kernel. If these lines are not present, NAT will not work. Likewise, IPF must be enabled for NAT to work—even if you aren't using it for anything. See the section *Starting the Firewall* for instructions on enabling IPF.

When NAT is activated it needs to have a valid IP address for each interface. If you are using PPP, you have two options for starting NAT:

1. Start up the PPP connection before starting NAT (not a very reliable option)

or

2. Start NAT whenever a PPP connection is established. To do this, add the following line to the /etc/ppp/ip-up shell script:

```
/sbin/ipnat -CF -f /etc/ipnat.rules
```

In IPFilter, NAT rules are stored separately from IPF rules. The NAT rules are read from a file called /etc/ipnat.rules. Don't try and put them in the ipf.rules file—it won't work. Likewise, the NAT rules are injected into the kernel using a different tool. The following line will activate the NAT rules specified in the following /etc/ipnat.rules file:

```
ipnat -f /etc/ipnat.rules
```

Outbound Mapping

We need to map packets going out from our internal network, automatically rebadging them with the IP address of the interface through which they leave. The kernel takes care of automatically tracking replies, mapping them back to the appropriate internal addresses, and redirecting them out the correct interface. Since that much care is taken on our behalf, all we really have to do is tell the kernel which addresses should be mapped. It's pretty easy. For the sake of argument, let us assume that the internal network is using a subset of one of the private address ranges, 192.168.1.0–192.168.1.255, our external network is 210.210.210.0-210.210.210.255, and we connect to the outside world via ppp0. This means we have one IP address for every internal address. We know this probably isn't the case for you; bear with us though, it'll all make sense soon. The above situation can be properly mapped using the rule:

```
map ppp0 192.168.1.0/24 -> 210.210.210.0/24
```

This is will ensure that every internal machine can communicate with the external world.

So what do we do if we only have one IP address? We can't write:

```
map ppp0 192.168.1.0/24 -> 210.210.210.1/32
```

Why won't this work? If two machines on the internal network make a connection to the outside world, they both appear to come from the same IP address. So far so good. But what if both machines are connecting to the same external machine and waiting for a response on the same port number? Now when the responses come back, the NAT system has no idea which packet goes to which internal machine. They both are destined for the same port and IP address. The solution is to use the following two rules:

```
map ppp0 192.168.1.0/24 -> 210.210.210.1/32 portmap tcp/udp 1025:65000
map ppp0 192.168.1.0/24 -> 210.210.210.1/32
```

The first rule invokes the *portmapping* technique for TCP and UDP connections, which works as follows. Internal client 192.168.1.1 sends a TCP packet out to a machine on the Internet. The source port is 4001, the destination port is 80. This means that the internal client is listening on port 4001 for a response. The packet hits the firewall. The NAT system changes the IP address of the packet to 210.210.210.1. The portmapper changes the port from 4001 to 60000 and notes the change, and the originating internal machine, in a table. Now the packet gets sent out of the firewall to the aforementioned machine on the Internet. That machine sends its response back to the firewall (210.210.210.1) port 60000. The portmapper is listening on port 60000 for the inbound connection. It gets the returned packet and looks up port 60000 in its table. It sees that 192.168.1.1 is waiting for this packet on port 4001, so it changes the destination information in the packet appropriately and sends the packet out the internal interface. 192.168.1.1 gets the packet as if nothing unusual had happened. Mission accomplished.

So, how does this help us? While we only have one IP address to work with, we have tens of thousands of ports available. If another internal machine were to make an outbound connection such that it were waiting for a response on port 4001, the portmapper would assign it a different port—maybe 60001. When the connection returns, it's very easy for the portmapper to tell the difference—the different connections simply return on different ports.

One more point: Note that we start our range at port 1025. Why not 0? Because ports under 1025 are special; they can only be accessed by services running as the root user. Therefore most important services tend to run on these ports and they have special meaning. It's a good idea to avoid messing with these ports.

So what on earth does the second line do? Well, what about ICMP? It doesn't have ports to map. We need to do it simply by IP address. If an ICMP packet comes in, the NAT system will try its best to identify the appropriate machine for the packet based on the source and destination IP addresses and previous connection history. If you just have one IP address, this means some ICMP packets may get lost or broadcast to too many machines. This isn't a critical a problem—at the worst it will only affect your network performance.

The really observant readers will note that the order of rules for ipnat appears to contradict the rule order for ipf. According to last match counts theory, TCP and UDP packets would match both the first rule AND the second rule, and would therefore match the second rule. Well, with ipnat, it's the first match that counts. Don't try and rationalize it. Just accept that the rules need to be in the above order and get on with your life.

Some of our readers will have a single IP address that is dynamically assigned by their ISP. Somehow, you need to write the map rule without specifying the exact external IP address. The way to do this is as follows:

```
map ppp0 192.168.1.0/24 -> 0/32 portmap tcp/udp 1025:65000
```

The 0/32 tells IPNAT that the address is being dynamically assigned. It will read the address from the ifconfig system. Whenever the IP address changes, you need to run the command "ipf –y", to notify IPF that it needs to update its NAT tables. This can be automated in your ppp.conf file by adding the following line to your 'pmdemand' section:

```
bg ipf -y
```

Inbound Mapping

Throughout this book we have made reference to a three-legged DMZ structure. This allows you to have a secure internal network and a separate less-secure network (DMZ) behind your firewall. The DMZ can be used to provide security for public servers. It adds another layer through which the hacker must penetrate. If the servers are compromised your internal network will still remain protected (unless your firewall is also compromised).

The servers in your DMZ can either have public or private IP addresses. Either way, all of the traffic to your DMZ will pass through your firewall rules. If you have a number of public IP addresses, you can use some of them for the servers in your DMZ. This can be accomplished by further subnetting your address space and configuring your firewall to appropriately route traffic to the machines in the DMZ subnet. If you only have a small number of IP's to play with you'll probably want to set up static mappings instead of subnetting. At the time of writing this can only be done with OpenBSD. Discussions on setting up routing and choosing an appropriate subnetting strategy are beyond the scope of this book.

If you only have one public IP address, you can *still* use a three-legged firewall. The server would have an internal IP address. The firewall would then redirect connections to a particular port on the external IP address directly to the port of your choice on your internal server machine. For example, if our firewall's IP is 4.3.2.1, we could make 4.3.2.1 port 80 route directly to a Web server running on 192.168.1.2 port 8088. This system ONLY exposes port 8088 of the internal machine yet allows external Web browsers to access the server as if it were running on an external machine with the standard port of 80. The following NAT rule will do just that (assuming our external interface is ppp0):

```
rdr ppp0 4.3.2.1 port 80 -> 192.168.1.2 port 8088
```

Creative use of the redirection rule can allow all sorts of neat tricks.

There are some limitations to inbound port mapping. Here's one: You only have one port 80 on your firewall's external IP address, so you can only redirect port 80 once—only one Web server. There's no way to run multiple internal Web servers, all on port 80, and have them all accessed by the outside world from port 80 (unless your firewall has more than one external IP address, but if you're that lucky, then you can simply write multiple rdr rules, one for port 80 on each address).

Here's another problem: This technique works for any protocol that has a single channel. HTTP, NTP, DNS—any UDP or TCP protocol that has just one channel is fine, but protocols like IRC or FTP, which have control and data channels, cause particular problems for port forwarding. Consider passive-mode FTP. Sure, you can forward the incoming command requests to port 21, but when the server passes back a random port for the client to open a data channel, how are you going to tell the firewall what port needs forwarding? There's no way to tell, in advance, what port the FTP server is going to pick, so there's no way to write the rule. In the future, ipfilter will include proxy support for FTP and possibly other common multi-channel protocols, but for now, multiple-channel protocols are out.

A last problem to mention relates to dynamic IP addresses. You must deal with dynamic IP addresses in the same way that you did for outbound mapping. Wherever you would place the static IP you need to write 0/32 instead. The command "ipf -y" must be run whenever a new IP address is assigned. In most cases you should be able to automate the process. In our section on outbound mapping we gave a sample addition to the ppp.conf file that automates the process for PPP connections.

Practical Firewalling

Enough theorizing, enough practicing—it's time to write a real firewall. We're now going to give a simple example. You could take this script and use it as your own firewall, if your circumstances were right. On the companion Web site at www.wiley.com/compbooks/sonnenreich, you'll find scripts that are more generally valid, in that they use variables to allow you to edit interface names, and networks, for example, without editing every rule by hand. If you want to start from a cut-and-dried script, we'd recommend using one of those.

In this example, any line that starts with a "#"is a comment. Comment blocks precede each section and each substantive line of code where needed. ppp0 is our external network interface, eth0 is our internal network interface, and lo is the loopback interface. You should permit traffic to come in the loopback interface unmolested. Our internal network is masqueraded, and we are using the private subnet 192.168.1.0/24 internally. Our ISP's DNS servers have the IP addresses 1.2.3.1 and 1.2.3.2, and our ISP's NTP server has the IP address 1.3.4.5.

```
###########################################################
# Firewalling rules
###########################################################
# set our default policies: see note 1
block in log all
pass out all

# accept packets coming from the internal interface
pass in on eth0 all
pass in on lo all

# deny any coming from outside which are illegal: see note 2
# first take care of standard unroutables
block in log quick on ppp0 from 0.0.0.0/32 to any
block in log quick on ppp0 from 255.255.255.255/32 to any
block in log quick on ppp0 from 127.0.0.0/8 to any
block in log quick on ppp0 from any to 0.0.0.0/32
block in log quick on ppp0 from any to 255.255.255.255/32
block in log quick on ppp0 from any to 127.0.0.0/8
```

```
# now let's block some more packets we should never see coming inbound
block in log quick on ppp0 from 192.168.0.0/16 to any
block in log quick on ppp0 from 172.16.0.0/12 to any
block in log quick on ppp0 from 10.0.0.0/8 to any

# allow certain classes of ICMP
pass in quick on ppp0 proto icmp all icmp-type 0
pass in quick on ppp0 proto icmp all icmp-type 3
pass in quick on ppp0 proto icmp all icmp-type 11

# Prevent outside machines from initiating TCP connections to machines
# within our network
block in on ppp0 proto tcp all flags S/SA
block out on ppp0 proto tcp all flags SA/SA

# allow inbound ssh and mail connections: see note 3
pass in quick on ppp0 proto tcp from any to any port = 22 flags S/SA keep state
pass in quick on ppp0 proto tcp from any to any port = 25 flags S/SA keep state

# allow return packets from connections we initiated: see note 4
pass out on ppp0 proto tcp all keep state

# REJECT auth conections for fast SMTP handshake: see note 5
block return-rst in on ppp0 proto tcp from any to any port = 113

# allow udp DNS replies from 1.2.3.1 and 1.2.3.2 See note 6
pass in on ppp0 proto udp from 1.2.3.1 port = 53 to any
pass in on ppp0 proto udp from 1.2.3.2 port = 53 to any

# allow NTP replies from 1.3.4.5
pass in on ppp0 proto udp from 1.3.4.5 port 123 to any

# END OF ipf.rules

The following code belongs in /etc/ipnat.rules
##########################################################
# NAT rules
##########################################################
#
# Dynamic PPP mapping - "ipf -y" must be run with each
# new connection
map 192.168.1.0/24 -> 0/32 portmap tcp/udp 1025:65000
map 192.168.1.0/24 -> 0/32          # handle ICMP, etc.
#
# END OF ipnat.rules
```

Notes:

1. The 'log' option on the block policy has the effect of logging any packets which are not matched by one of our other rules. You should inspect the logs frequently during the first few days of operation to see if any particular type

of traffic is being excessively logged by this rule. It may indicate a problem in your rules (for example, your users may be trying to access UDP-based streaming services—the TCP requests make it through, but the UDP responses don't).

Once you're sure the rules are working as intended, the logs will let you know when someone knocked on your door. This doesn't necessarily mean they're trying to hack in, so don't get your feathers ruffled yet—read Chapter 11, "Intrusion Detection and Response" before you call the Feds.

2. It's always a good idea to explicitly refuse packets that shouldn't be there anyway. We should never see packets on our external interface either coming from or going to one of the private networks mentioned in Chapter 3. These rules will reject all such packets. If we were using public address space inside our network, we would also include a line here that explicitly rejected packets coming in from outside that claim to originate from inside the network.

3. This line tells the firewall to track all outgoing TCP connections and allow the return data through the firewall without further processing. This means that the reply to a TCP connection initiated from inside the network (such as a Web page request) will be properly routed back to the intended machine. Inbound TCP packets will only get through if they are replies to requests from inside—nobody will be able to initiate an unsolicited connection to an internal machine.

4. We're going to run two TCP services on our firewall, or port-forward them to some server inside (port forwarding is discussed in more detail in the following section). The services are on TCP ports 25 (a mail server) and 22 (an ssh server, for remote administration). We must explicitly allow new connections from the outside world to these services.

5. Recall our earlier point about how sometimes it's useful to provide feedback to our users, even though it uses more resources. This is one of those cases. When we try to send outgoing mail by way of a well-behaved SMTP server, that server will try and do an ident lookup on us. The ident service is an old one, a hang-over from the days when everyone trusted each other on the Internet, whereby the machine you're making SMTP connections to will try to call you back on this pre-arranged service to verify a few things about you. This involves an incoming connection to TCP port 113. If this attempt is rejected, the remote server will just shrug, and get on with the SMTP conversation. If the attempt is denied, the remote server will wait until it times out before proceeding with the conversation. The net effect is a delay of a minute or so every time you try to connect to a mail server. If you ever send outgoing mail, sending a TCP-Reset for all inbound TCP connections on port 113 instead of just blocking the packets will speed up connections sub-

stantially. Please note: It's not important that the remote server be allowed to do the ident lookup in order to have mail flow happily. It's only necessary that it get a prompt and audible NO when it tries to do so.

6. We're explicitly accepting DNS replies—both UDP and TCP—from our DNS servers only. You would replace 1.2.3.1 and 1.2.3.2 with the IP addresses for your ISP's DNS servers. If there are more than two, remember to include a UDP line for each of them. Note that there are no lines for TCP DNS replies: The TCP replies are already going to make it through the firewall, thanks to the 'keep state' rule.

You've seen your first full-blown firewall. It's short and sweet, but it's usable. What will it do for you?

Regarding TCP, any machine on your internal network will be able to establish TCP connections to the outside world and private addresses you use inside (picked from the range 192.168.1.1–192.168.1.254) will be masqueraded behind the real IP address your firewall uses. Replies to connections initiated by your users will be allowed back in (through the 'keep state' rule) and demasqueraded. Unsolicited TCP connections will not be allowed through the firewall other than inbound mail and ssh connections.

With regard to UDP, only DNS packets from your ISP's DNS servers, and NTP from your ISP's NTP server will be permitted. Any UDP-based Internet service will be inaccessible to your firewall and to machines on your internal network.

Starting the Firewall

The firewall code needs to be embedded in the system startup scripts so that the firewalling happens automatically each time the machine is rebooted. The later in the boot process this happens, the longer the network interfaces are up without firewall protection. If there's enough time, a hacker may be able to compromise the firewall by crashing the machine and then attacking the network before the firewall rules take effect.

Luckily, the OpenBSD team has already thought about this issue and has preconfigured the necessary startup files. All you have to do is activate these configurations by editing the file /etc/rc.conf and changing "ipfilter=NO" to "ipfilter=YES". That's it—the ipf and ipnat rules will now be read in and activated at boot time.

Reboot your system and run a few tests to ensure that your firewall started properly. If everything worked, you're almost ready to move on to Chapter 10. But first, we recommend reading through the following sections. There are many juicy bits of knowledge that we couldn't fit into the main part of this chapter, but will be very useful for your firewall. The following section will also serve to reinforce everything you've learned up to this point.

The (Mostly) Complete Guide to Writing, Testing, and Monitoring Firewall Rules

The rest of this chapter is a fairly thorough guide to the syntax of writing filter rules. It covers both ipf rules and ipnat rules. It also gives a brief overview of ipftest, ipfstat, and ipmon—programs that will help you test and monitor your firewall's performance. While some of this information is a repetition of things said earlier in the chapter, we have presented it in a form that will be easier to use as a future reference. We also have dealt with certain parameters in greater detail. We very much recommend reading this section through—it will help to solidify your understanding of the basics. It also contains details that will be very useful when we build the real firewall in Chapter 10.

IPF

The syntax of a rule follows this general format:

```
[action] [in | out] <options> <protocol> [source/destination] <misc>
```

This somewhat follows the syntax described in the ipf man page, but we've tried to make it easier to understand. For a complete discussion of ipf rule options, see the ipf man page, Section 5. The following paragraphs discuss each parameter in the above rule format. Note that we discuss them in order of importance—not in the sequence they appear above.

There are actually a few more optional parameters that can be squeezed in, but they're not necessary for anything we're going to be doing. If you're curious about all of the possible options, look at the ipf man page.

action

The 'action' parameter is used to determine the fate of packets that matches the given rule. The two most common values for this parameter are block and pass. An action of 'block' means packets matching the rest of the rule will not be allowed through the firewall. Conversely, packets that match the condition of a 'pass' rule may travel through the firewall. Remember though, the only rule that counts is the last one that matches a given packet. For example, a packet can match 20 block rules, but if the last rule it matches is a pass rule then the packet will be allowed through the firewall. Yes, this point was made earlier, but it pays to be redundant. Out-of-sequence rules can render a firewall worthless.

Refusing Politely

When a packet is blocked, the kernel silently discards the packet (drops it on the floor, as it were). This is the most resource-efficient way of refusing a packet, but it can be unhelpful to the sender—the message just disappears into the void, without any trace that it was dropped.

Some applications will benefit from knowing if their communications have been denied. The standard mechanism for doing such is by returning an ICMP "Destination Unreachable" message or a TCP Reset when a packet has been blocked. There are two options to the 'block' action that allow you to send these messages. The options tell the kernel to discard the packet and to send a message back to the sender to advise it that the connection failed. Specifically, the options are: 'block return-rst' and 'block return-icmp(code)'.

The 'return-rst' option is only for TCP connections; it will send back a reset packet, effectively forcing the sender's connection to terminate. The 'return-icmp' option lets you send back an ICMP type 3 (destination unreachable) message to the sender. You can choose the exact type of destination unreachable message by specifying an optional 'code' in parentheses. Note that there is no space between the 'return-icmp' and the '(code)'. Use Table 9.1 to determine the value for the 'code' parameter. You can use either the code name or the code number from the table. Either way, it must be in parentheses.

Table 9.1   'Code' Parameter Values

CODE NAME	CODE NUMBER	MEANING
net-unr	0	Network unreachable
host-unr	1	Host unreachable
proto-unr	2	Protocol unreachable
port-unr	3	Port unreachable
needfrag	4	Needs fragmentation but fragmentation is not allowed
srcfail	5	Source routing failed
net-unk	6	Destination network unknown
host-unk	7	Destination host unknown
isolate	8	Source host isolated (obsolete)
net-prohib	9	Destination network administratively prohibited
host-prohib	10	Destination host administratively prohibited
net-tos	11	Network unreachable for TOS
host-tos	12	Hostunreachable for TOS

Returning ICMP information does open you up to being probed for information. If you send ICMP rejections to packets you don't want, then any packet that doesn't trigger one is being accepted. An attacker might not know where a packet has gone, but he or she knows that it wasn't dropped on the floor. The attacker can then concentrate on sending more packets like the one that got through. It's generally better to have attackers sending you stuff you can cheaply drop on the floor. It's usually much better to block packets outright than to provide excessive feedback.

Logging

Logging can be accomplished in two ways. The first is with the log action, which immediately writes any matching packet to the logging device (a program called ipl, discussed later). The last match counts rule *does not* apply to the log action. This can be used to log certain types of packets, regardless of whether they're actually passed or blocked.

The other way to log packets is with the 'log' option. When 'log' is used as an *option* rather than an *action*, it only logs packets if the rule is the last rule to match. This allows you to see exactly what your firewall blocked or passed. It's especially useful for certain malicious packets that usually occur as part of an attack on your network. A good logging system can be a first warning of an oncoming attack.

With either method of logging, the following qualifiers can be placed after the 'log' keyword. If more than one is used, they should be used in the order shown here.

body. This will write the first 128 bytes of the packet's content to the log file.

first. Used with the 'keep' option and logs only the first packet that triggers a 'keep' rule and allows the rest of the packets to pass without logging.

block. If the logging system can't log the packet for some reason, the action of the rule should be changed to 'block'. This means that if the rule is the last rule to match and the packet can't be logged for some reason, then the packet will be blocked altogether. If a subsequent rule matches, then this will have no effect.

Another action that doesn't follow the last match counts rule is count. The count action causes various accounting information to be written to a system that is separate from the logging system. The accounting data can be seen with the program ipfstat, discussed later.

in | out

An action parameter is required for every rule. Likewise, the action must be followed by either in or out. This refers to the direction in which the packets are flowing. If 'in' is used, the rule will only apply to packets coming in to the firewall. If 'out' is used, the rule only applies to outbound packets. There is no way to write a rule that applies to both inbound *and* outbound packets.

source/destination

After 'in' or 'out', the only other required parameter is the 'source/destination' parameter. This denotes the IP address or range of addresses to which the rule applies. If you want to have the rule apply to all IP addresses, you can use the value all. Some very short, yet valid, rules use the minimum possible notation:

```
block in all
pass out all
```

These particular rules have a practical use: They set a default policy if they're the first rules in your rule file. Every packet will match one of these two rules. These two rules have the effect of setting a policy of denying all inbound traffic and permitting all outbound traffic.

from/to

The IP parameter usually is a bit more specific. The most common form used is the from/to notation. This creates a condition where the packet must be from a particular address or range and heading to another address or range. For example:

```
block in from any to 10.0.0.0/8
```

This rule says to block all inbound packets from any address that are heading for the internal 10.x.x.x network. Packets that match this rule are most likely malicious, since the internal network numbers are not accessible from the outside world. No properly-configured router would ever forward a packet destined for an internal network address.

As you might begin to guess from the example, the from/to parameter can take IP addresses in a number of formats. The format used above is just one way to specify an address range. You could also use a hostname instead of an IP address, but this isn't recommended for performance reasons (resolving the hostname takes time). The network mask can be specified with the /0-32 format used above, or it could be given using hex or dotted quad notation along with the 'mask' keyword. For example:

```
block in from any to 10.0.0.0 mask 0xff000000
```

or

```
block in from any to 10.0.0.0 mask 255.0.0.0
```

Regardless of the format you use, the network mask must be present (unless you use the keyword 'any').

Specifying ports

The source or destination port of the packet can also be specified using the 'from/to' parameters. The format for this is:

```
from src_ip port <op> y to dest_ip port <op> z
```

You can either specify a single port number, or a range of ports with the appropriate operator ('op'). If you leave out the 'port' keyword altogether, it's equivalent to saying 'all ports'. For a single port number, use "=" as the operator. Note that there must be a space before and after the operator. For example, to filter on a destination port of 80, you would write:

```
pass out from any to any port = 80
```

NOTE

'from any to any' is equivalent to the 'all' keyword...almost. The difference is that you can specify a port number with the former. For example, 'pass out from any to any port 80' specifically allows internal machines to access Web servers running on the standard port. This isn't a great way of providing Web access, however.

Table 9.2 contains the possible operators.

Table 9.2   Operators

= or eq	Equal to
!= or ne	Not equal to
< or lt	Less than
<= or le	Less than or equal to
> or gt	Greater than
>= or ge	Greater than or equal to
x <> y	Less than x and greater than y—not inclusive
x >< y	Greater than x and less than y—not inclusive

protocol

You will find that many of your rules are specific to a particular protocol. At the most basic level, you'll find it convenient to deal with TCP, UDP, and ICMP separately. To this extent the protocol parameter is used. This parameter is usually tcp, udp, tcp/udp (specifies both TCP and UDP), or icmp. You could also pass in any transport-level protocol that appears in /etc/protocols. Protocols like ftp and http are notably absent from this file, because these are application-level protocols, which live in /etc/services. Don't edit the protocols file.

options

You have the ability to specify one or more optional parameters that can affect the processing of the packet. Many of your rules will call on at least one of these options.

log

Specifying the log option causes the packet details to be written to the logging system. This will only occur if the rule at hand is the last rule to match for a given packet. See the above discussion of logging in the action section of this reference guide.

quick

The quick option forces the given rule to be the last rule processed for a particular packet. This improves performance by reducing the amount of work that the kernel has to perform when filtering. It is useful when blocking packets that are known to be bad, such as source routed packets.

on [interface name]

By definition, your firewall will have at least two interfaces. This option allows you to apply rules to packets that appear 'on' a particular interface. This rule is most useful when there are more than two interfaces.

dup-to [interface name]:<destination IP>

This option duplicates the packet and sends the copy out from the specified interface. If a destination IP address is given, the kernel will change the packet's original destination to the specified IP.

to [interface]

The to option transparently forwards the packet to the interface specified. The word *fastroute* may be used instead of *to* if you prefer.

If you use more than one of these options, you should make sure they appear in the following order: log, quick, on, dup-to, to/fastroute.

Misc

The following parameters can appear at the end of a rule. They allow you to filter with greater precision, using additional information present in certain types of IP packets.

with [short | frag | opt <ip option>]

The 'with' keyword adds a condition to the rule that pertains to the structure of the packet itself. Multiple with statements can be used in a given rule. The 'and' keyword may be used as a direct synonym for 'with'.

short. If a packet is too short to contain complete IP header information, the kernel flags it as 'short'. The rule, as follows, will block all inbound IP packets that are too short to be legitimate:

```
block in all with short
```

frag. 'with frag' matches packets that are part of a fragmented IP packet.

opt <ip option>. The IP specification allows packets to contain additional options that can be used by routers and applications. These are called *IP options*, and are rarely used by standard Internet applications. To filter based on the presence of specific IP option you'd use 'with opt' followed by the name of the IP option.

Most IP options are harmless, but there are a few (loose and strict source routing) which we'll want to block. An example of a filter that blocks loose and strict source routed packets is:

```
block in all with opt lsrr
block in all with opt ssrr
```

Note that you can specify multiple options by just stringing them on after the first one. You can also filter based on options that are not present: use the 'not' keyword before the option in question.

flags <flag selection>

TCP packets contain special flags that convey additional information about the status of the TCP connection. One such flag is the 'SYN' flag, which is only sent during the handshake process. Another is the 'ACK' flag, which signifies an acknowledgment. See the discussion of TCP's handshake process in Chapter 2 if you're unclear about how the handshake works.

By using the 'flags' parameter, you can filter based on the presence of specific flags and combinations of flags. There are six possible TCP flags, as shown in Table 9.3.

To filter on a particular combination of TCP flags, simply list the first letters of the flags that must be present. For example, 'flags RFAS' will require the 'RST', 'FIN', 'ACK', and 'SYN' flags to all be active in order for the packet to match. If there are any other active flags the packet will not match the rule.

But what if you don't care whether other flags are active? In other words, you want to filter any packet that contains active 'RST', 'FIN', 'ACK', and 'SYN' flags—even if the packets also contain active 'URG' and/or 'PUSH' flags. This is done with the 'flag mask', which involves placing a "/" after the flag list, followed by a second list of flags. The second list contains the flags we're interested in checking. To alter our earlier example, we can use 'flags RFAS/RFAS'. This will accomplish the goal of ignoring whether the 'URG' and 'PUSH' flags are set.

The flag mask notation is also especially useful for denoting flags that must *not* be set. For example, 'flags S/SAP' will match packets with the 'SYN' flag, but not the 'ACK' or 'PUSH' flag. The rest of the flags may or may not be set.

Filtering on TCP flags allows you to prevent external machines from initiating connections to your internal network. An example rule that would accomplish this is:

```
block in proto tcp all flags S/SA
```

Table 9.3 TCP Flags

TCP FLAG	MEANING	LETTER USED FOR "FLAGS"SELECTION
SYN	Synchronize a connection	S
ACK	Acknowledgement	A
FIN	Finishing connection	F
RST	Reset the connection	R
PUSH	No longer used*	P
URG	Urgent packet	U

* The 'PUSH' flag tells the TCP stack to flush its buffers and push all data to the application layer. This is now done automatically by all modern TCP implementations.

The first S indicates that this rule will match TCP packets with only the 'SYN' flag set—not the 'ACK' flag. The '/SA' means we don't care about the status of any other flags—this rule applies only to the 'SYN' and 'ACK' flags.

icmp-type <message-type> [code <code-type>]

This must be used in conjunction with the option proto icmp. It allows you to specify a particular type of icmp message. For example, you could use it to block all echo-request messages:

```
block in proto icmp all icmp-type 8
```

Certain ICMP types have additional information that is conveyed with a code number. For example, ICMP type 3, the "destination unreachable" ICMP message, would use code 1 to signify "host unreachable," or code 0 to show "network unreachable," among others. You could permit only "port unreachable" messages, being code 3, to leave your network with the following code:

```
pass out proto icmp all icmp-type 3 code 3
```

keep [state | frags]

The keep state option can speed up the processing of TCP connections by keeping track of TCP sequence numbers. Once a TCP connection has been established, additional packets with the correct sequence numbers will be allowed through the firewall without passing through the filter. Keeping state does not protect your network against hijacked TCP sessions. In fact, it may be slightly more vulnerable, since the hijacked packets do not ever pass through the filter—once keep state has okayed the data stream it short-cuts all other processing and shoves the packets through. We recommend the judicious use of keep state; it has value, but it is not *secure*.

We do not recommend using 'keep frags', which tracks fragments of an IP packet. If the filter allows the first fragment, it will automatically pass through any other fragments. This can be very dangerous and is not necessary for average operation. In this day and age, IP fragmentation is not all that common, since most TCP/IP stacks are smart enough to avoid creating large IP packets.

head <group id>, group <group id>

The head and group options are used to create *rule groups*. This allows the creation of complex and optimized firewall rules. The 'head' of a group is a generic rule. When you create the generic rule, add 'head' followed by a number. Now you can use the 'group' keyword to further filter packets that only match the generic 'head' rule. For example:

```
block in on eth0 proto tcp all head 100
block in on eth0 proto udp  all head 101
pass in from any to any port = 22 group 100
```

In this example, we create a group (100) from all TCP packets on eth0. We create a second group for all UDP packets on eth0. The third line says to pass in any connections on port 22 (ssh) but *only* for those packets that are part of group 100. This means the TCP packets, but not the UDP packets (which are part of group 101). The example could have also been written as:

```
block in on eth0 proto tcp/udp all
pass in on eth0 proto tcp from any to any port = 22
```

Although rule groups have the potential to make certain rule writing a little more elegant, it can increase your confusion levels dramatically. We'd suggest avoiding this syntax unless your filtering rules are already complex and you need to achieve high degrees of optimization.

IPNAT

Network Address Translation is accomplished via a separate program called *ipnat*. You'll store your NAT code in a separate script file /etc/ipnat.rules. The rule structure for ipnat is similar to, but much simpler than, ipf. There are only two actions that can be performed and very few variations on the matching criteria. The main action we're concerned with is the map action. We'll also touch on the rdr action.

map

The map action is used to cause packets from an internal address to appear to come from an external address.

If the internal address + netmask specifies multiple internal addresses, then all of the addresses will be mapped to the given external address. Likewise, the external address can refer to multiple addresses.

If there are an equal number of internal and external addresses, there will be a 1-to-1 mapping between internal and external addresses. If there are more internal addresses, things can get complicated. See the *portmapping* section for more information.

The general format for the map action is:

```
map [interface] [int_ip+mask] -> [ext_ip+mask] <portmapping>
```

interface

Each rule must specify the interface to which it applies. That's all there is to this parameter.

ip+mask

This is an IP address followed by a netmask. The netmask can be specified using the '/' notation (with the mask either given as a hex value, dotted quad, or as the number of masked bits), or with the 'netmask' keyword followed by a hex or dotted-quad netmask.

The first ip+mask value (int_ip+mask) is the internal network. The ip+mask value after the '->' (ext_ip+mask) is the external network. ipnat will map connections from the internal network to IP addresses on the external network.

portmapping

A problem arises if there are more internal network addresses than external addresses—the extra internal addresses will conflict with existing external addresses that have already been allocated to other machines. Why is this a problem? If multiple machines are using the same IP address and are waiting for connections on the same ports, the NAT system will not be able to determine which packets go to which machine.

To illustrate the problem, let's look at a common situation: You have one IP address that you'd like to share among many machines within your network. Two machines on your network are using Netscape at the same time. Because Netscape uses a very simple algorithm to select a local port for the return connection, there's a high chance that both machines will be waiting for connections on the same port number. When the data packets come back from the external Web servers, they are all addressed to the same IP number and the same port number. There's no way for the NAT system to figure out which internal machine made which request without additional information.

One solution to this problem is to use the *portmapping* technique. When an internal machine makes a request to an external service, it waits for a return connection on a specific port. This information is stored within the packet. The portmapper chooses a new port number that is unique and unused on the firewall's external interface. It then rewrites the packet such that return connections will arrive at the new port number. The portmapper stores the original port, the internal machine address, and the new port number in a table. When the return connection arrives, it looks up the port in its table and can easily determine the internal machine for which the packet is destined.

Why does this work? There are over 60,000 available TCP and UDP ports for a given IP address. By using a portmapper, a single IP address could support over 600 machines making 100 simultaneous connections. Even at peak usage times the average internal machine will probably be making far less than 100 simultaneous connections.

rdr

The rdr action stands for *redirect*. It does precisely what the name implies: It redirects packets destine for one address and port to another address and port. Redirect is the complement to map—while map takes care of outbound packets, rdr takes care of inbound packets.

NAT takes place before filtering. This is important to remember, because a poorly written rdr rule could allow malicious packets to bypass the firewall. If you want to filter packets first and then forward them to other machines, you're in hotly-debated land. Many users are clamoring for finer control over when NAT takes place for this very reason. One possible solution for now involves the use of 'fastroute' and 'quick' options with an ipf pass rule. A more effective solution involves multiple IPFiltering machines, but this adds huge amounts of complexity for minimal gain.

The general format for the rdr action is:

```
rdr [interface] [orig_ip+mask] port [service] -> [new_ip+mask] port [service] <protocol>
```

The rdr action can be used to provide transparent services such as proxy support and web caching. See the sidebar *Transparent Web Cache* for more information.

interface

Packets that arrive on the given interface will be candidates for redirection.

src_ip+mask/dest_ip+mask

This is an IP address followed by a netmask. The netmask can be specified using the "/" notation (with the mask either given as a hex value, dotted quad, or as the number of masked bits), or with the 'netmask' keyword followed by a hex or dotted-quad netmask.

The first ip+mask value (orig_ip+mask) is the incoming IP address that the rdr rule should match. The ip+mask value after the '->' (new_ip+mask) is the new destination address. This address can be inside or outside the internal network. The packet will be rewritten with the new destination and sent out the appropriate interface.

service

Each rdr rule must specify a particular port on which it applies. This can be done with a port number or with the name of a service found in /etc/services. The first port number matches the inbound connection. The second port number

Transparent Web Cache

A *transparent Web cache* is an elegant device for people who run networks with many users all surfing the Web. There's a pretty good chance that many of them will want to go to the same Web site. If one were to satisfy their requests through a central local server, that server would only need to go to the remote site the first time any particular page was requested. Subsequent requests for the same page could be satisfied from the local server, saving access time and Internet bandwidth. Such a local server is called a *Web cache*.

To enable a standard Web cache, every user's browser needs to be configured to go to the central server for Web pages, instead of going out to the Internet. This can be very difficult to maintain in large organizations. If, however, the firewall through which they had to pass in order to get to the Internet knew that all Web requests should instead be sent to a local Web cache (except requests coming from that Web cache, which must of course be allowed onto the Internet), you could get the benefit of Web caching without having to reconfigure every desktop browser. This is transparent Web caching, and if you've got enough users all going through the one cache, it can cut Internet Web traffic by 50 percent or more.

To effect a transparent Web cache with the ipnat and rdr, use the following rules (assumes eth0 is the internal network interface, 10.10.10.1 is the address of the Web cache, and 210.210.210.210 is the external address used by the Web cache):

```
map eth0 10.10.10.1/32 -> 210.210.210.210/32
rdr eth0 0.0.0.0/0 port 80 -> 10.10.10.1 port 80
```

allows you to specify a different port for the destination machine. For example, if you're running a web server on port 8001 of the internal machine 10.10.10.10, but you want it to be accessible to the public on port 80 of 210.210.210.210, then you would use the following rdr rule (assuming your external interface is eth0):

```
rdr ppp0 210.210.210.210/32 port 80 -> 10.10.10.10/32 port 8001
```

protocol

You can optionally specify the protocol of the packet as a further matching criteria. Valid values are 'tcp', 'udp', 'tcp/udp', or 'tcpudp'. The default value is 'tcp'.

IPFTEST

Testing your rules with live tests (for example, trying to access blocked ports) can be time consuming and is to prone to errors of omission. Furthermore it involves placing your new rules in the active ruleset. Any problems with your new rules could immediately disable your firewall.

A better solution is the ipftest program. ipftest reads in a firewall ruleset and some test packets of different shapes and sizes. It then simulates what would happen if the test packets were sent to a firewall that was running the specified ruleset. This lets you test a ruleset without having to make it active.

The beauty of ipftest is that it can read input from many different sources. For example, you can create test packets from the output generated by the tcpdump program. You can use real packets that are captured with the snoop program. You can even use a special ipftest file format to create your own packets by hand.

One easy way to create a test script is to start a packet capture program such as snoop, and then run a series of live tests on the firewall. Do some simple connectivity tests first, then try running nmap, satan, or some other network penetration tool. Stop after every test and save the captured packets to different files. Once you're done, you can create a shell script that executes the ipftest command on each data file. In between files you can print out a status line explaining what the test does. We've included a sample script on the companion web site that uses a series of snoop datafiles with ipftest.

IPFSTAT

The following is adapted, or ripped outright, from the ipfilter-howto document by Brendan Conoboy and Erik Fichtner.

In its simplest form, ipfstat displays a table of interesting data about how your firewall is performing, such as how many packets have been passed or blocked, if they were logged or not, how many state entries have been made, and so on. Here's an example of something you might see from running the tool:

```
# ipfstat
input packets:          blocked 99286 passed 12558609 nomatch 14686
counted 0
output packets:         blocked 4200 passed 12843745 nomatch 14687
counted 0
input packets logged:   blocked 99286 passed 0
output packets logged:  blocked 0 passed 0
packets logged:         input 0 output 0
log failures:           input 3898 output 0
fragment state(in):     kept 0  lost 0
fragment state(out):    kept 0  lost 0
packet state(in):       kept 169364    lost 0
packet state(out):      kept 431395    lost 0
ICMP replies:           0        TCP RSTs sent:  0
Result cache hits(in):  1215208 (out):  1098963
IN Pullups succeeded:   2        failed: 0
```

```
OUT Pullups succeeded:   0      failed: 0
Fastroute successes:     0      failures: 0
TCP cksum fails(in):     0      (out): 0
Packet log flags set:   (0)     none
```

The ipfstat program is also capable of showing you your current rule list. Using the '–i' or the '–o' flag will show the currently loaded rules for in or out, respectively. You can also use both at once. Adding a '-h' to this will provide more useful information at the same time by showing you a "hit count" on each rule. For example:

```
# ipfstat -ho
2451423 pass out on xl0 from any to any
354727 block out on ppp0 from any to any
430918 pass out quick on ppp0 proto tcp/udp from 20.20.20.0/24 to any
keep state keep frags
```

Note that in the example above, there are many blocked packets outbound, even though the filters on outbound traffic are very permissive. From this, we can see that there might be something unusual happening. Something here may warrant further investigation. On the other hand, the firewall may be functioning perfectly. ipfstat can't tell you if your rules are right or wrong; it can only tell you what is happening because of your rules.

To further debug your rules, you may want to use the '-n' flag, which will show the rule number next to each rule.

```
# ipfstat -on
@1 pass out on xl0 from any to any
@2 block out on ppp0 from any to any
@3 pass out quick on ppp0 proto tcp/udp from 20.20.20.0/24 to any keep
state keep frags
```

The final piece of really interesting information that ipfstat can provide us is a dump of the state table. This is done with the '-s' flag:

```
# ipfstat -s
        281458 TCP
        319349 UDP
        0 ICMP
        19780145 hits
        5723648 misses
        0 maximum
        0 no memory
        1 active
        319349 expired
        281419 closed
100.100.100.1 -> 20.20.20.1 ttl 864000 pass 20490 pr 6 state 4/4
```

```
pkts 196 bytes 17394    987 -> 22 585538471:2213225493 16592:16500
pass in log quick keep state
pkt_flags & b = 2,                pkt_options & ffffffff = 0
pkt_security & ffff = 0, pkt_auth & ffff = 0
```

Here we see a single state entry for a TCP connection. The output will vary slightly from version to version, but the basic information is the same. We can see in this connection that we have a fully established connection (state 4/4 is the code for fully established).

We can see that the state entry has a time to live of 240 hours (ttl 864000—the 864000 is in seconds), which is an absurdly long time, but is the default for an established tcp connection. This ttl counter is decremented every second that the state entry is not used, and will finally result in the connection being purged if it has been left idle. The ttl counter is also reset to 864000 whenever the state is used, ensuring that the entry will not time out while it is being actively used.

In the next line we can see that we have passed 196 packets consisting of about 17kB worth of data over this connection. We can see the ports for both end-points, in this case 987 and 22; which means that this state entry represents a connection from 100.100.100.1 port 987 to 20.20.20.1 port 22.

The really big numbers in the second line are the tcp sequence numbers for this connection, which helps to ensure that someone isn't easily able to inject a forged packet into your session. The TCP window is also shown. The third line is a synopsis of the implicit rule that was generated by the 'keep state' code, showing that this connection is an inbound connection.

IPMON

The following is adapted, or ripped outright, from the ipfilter-howto document by Brendan Conoboy and Erik Fichtner.

ipfstat is great for collecting snapshots of what's active on the system, but it's often handy to have some kind of log to look at and watch events as they happen in time. The ipmon tool is capable of watching the packet log (as created with the 'log' keyword in your rules), the state log, or the NAT log, or any combination of the three. This tool can either be run in the foreground or as a daemon which logs to syslog or a file.

Let's use ipmon to watch the state table in action. Run the command "ipmon-o S" and you'll see output such as the following:

```
# ipmon -o S
01/08/1999 15:58:57.836053 STATE:NEW 100.100.100.1,53 ->
   20.20.20.15,53 PR udp
```

```
01/08/1999 15:58:58.030815 STATE:NEW 20.20.20.15,123 -> 128.167.1.69,123
PR udp
01/08/1999 15:59:18.032174 STATE:NEW 20.20.20.15,123 ->
128.173.14.71,123 PR udp
01/08/1999 15:59:24.570107 STATE:EXPIRE 100.100.100.1,53 ->
20.20.20.15,53 PR udp Pkts 4 Bytes 356
01/08/1999 16:03:51.754867 STATE:NEW 20.20.20.13,1019 ->
100.100.100.10,22 PR tcp
01/08/1999 16:04:03.070127 STATE:EXPIRE 20.20.20.13,1019 ->
100.100.100.10,22 PR tcp Pkts 63 Bytes 4604
```

Here we see a state entry for an external dns request off our nameserver, two xntp pings to well-known time servers, and a very short lived outbound ssh connection.

ipmon is also capable of showing us what packets have been logged with the '-o I' option. For example, when using state, you'll often run into packets like this:

```
# ipmon -o I
15:57:33.803147 ppp0 @0:2 b 100.100.100.103,443 -> 20.20.20.10,4923 PR
tcp len 20 1488 -A
```

What does this mean? Table 9.4 explains the meaning of each portion of the output covered in the preceding section.

Table 9.4 Output Descriptions

15:57:33.803147	This is a timestamp.
ppp0	This is the interface that this packet arrived on.
@0:2	This is a reference to the filter rule that triggered this action. The 0:2 notation means group 0, rule 2. You can use the command "ipfstat -in" to figure out exactly which rule is being referenced. Look in the output for rule 2 in rule group 0.
B	This says that this packet was blocked. Passed packets show a little "p" instead.
100.100.100.103,443-> 20.20.20.10,4923	Source address, source port -> destination address, destination port.
PR	Stands for PRotocol, we think. Just a label, like the "->".
TCP	The protocol of the packet.Could be UDP or ICMP.
len 20 1488	The length of the packet header and contents, in bytes. The header of this packet was 20 bytes, the contents were 1488 bytes.
-A	The TCP flags present for the packet. A stands for ACK.

Due to the often laggy nature of the Internet, sometimes packets will be regenerated. In such a situation, it's entirely possible that two copies of the same packet will arrive at your firewall. If you're keeping state, the system which tracks sequence numbers will have already seen and processed the sequence number. It will therefore assume that the packet is part of a different connection and will not automatically allow the packet through. Instead, the packet will continue to be processed through your filter rules. Chances are, this packet will be blocked and logged as suspicious, since it otherwise shouldn't exist. Another related non-malicious reason why packets get logged is when a stateful connection has been closed. You'll often see the last packet of a session being closed get logged because the 'keep state' code has already torn down the connection before the last packet has had a chance to make it to your firewall. Here's another example of a packet that you might see in your logs:

```
12:46:12.470951 xl0 @0:1 S 20.20.20.254 -> 255.255.255.255 PR icmp
    len 20 9216 icmp 9/0
```

The 'icmp 9/0' shown at the end of this line means *ICMP type 9, code 0*. This indicates that we're looking at an ICMP router discovery broadcast message. The point we're trying to make is that you will see strange packets being logged every once in a while—this doesn't mean that your system is under attack.

Finally, ipmon also lets us look at the NAT table in action with the '–o N' option:

```
# ipmon -o N
01/08/1999 05:30:02.466114 @2 NAT:RDR 20.20.20.253,113 <- ->
    20.20.20.253,113 [100.100.100.13,45816]
01/08/1999 05:30:31.990037 @2 NAT:EXPIRE 20.20.20.253,113 <- ->
    20.20.20.253,113 [100.100.100.13,45816] Pkts 10 Bytes 455
```

This example shows a redirection to an identd server. Masquerading hosts are typically unable to provide the identd service for themselves. The server in the example provides ident service for the hosts behind an outbound mapping NAT system.

We've shown you a bunch of examples of normal activity; now lets take a look at an attack in progress. We're going to attack the sample firewall code given in this chapter with the nmap port scanning tool. We ran nmap on a RedHat Linux box using the command: "nmap –v –O fire.wall.ip.address". Here's what the ipmon output looked like (date stamp removed for brevity):

```
#ipmon -o I
03:54:42.526400 fxp0 @0:1 b 209.21.217.50,16644 ->
    209.21.217.53,80 PR tcp len 20 40 -A
03:55:48.487609 fxp0 @0:1 b 209.21.217.50,15558 ->
    209.21.217.53,23 PR tcp len 20 60 -
```

```
03:55:48.496294 fxp0 @0:1 b 209.21.217.50,15560 ->
    209.21.217.53,23 PR tcp len 20 60 -A
03:55:48.504940 fxp0 @0:1 b 209.21.217.50,15562 ->
    209.21.217.53,33658 PR tcp len 20 60 -A
03:55:48.509280 fxp0 @0:1 b 209.21.217.50,15563 ->
    209.21.217.53,33658 PR tcp len 20 60 -FUP
03:55:48.513620 fxp0 @0:1 b 209.21.217.50,15564 ->
    209.21.217.53,33658 PR udp len 20 328
03:55:49.313466 fxp0 @0:1 b 209.21.217.50,15558 ->
    209.21.217.53,23 PR tcp len 20 60 -
03:55:49.313522 fxp0 @0:1 b 209.21.217.50,15560 ->
    209.21.217.53,23 PR tcp len 20 60 -A
03:55:49.313595 fxp0 @0:1 b 209.21.217.50,15562 ->
    209.21.217.53,33658 PR tcp len 20 60 -A
03:55:49.313627 fxp0 @0:1 b 209.21.217.50,15563 ->
    209.21.217.53,33658 PR tcp len 20 60 -FUP
03:55:49.313722 fxp0 @0:1 b 209.21.217.50,15564 ->
    209.21.217.53,33658 PR udp len 20 328
```

A lot is missing from this session due to the way our sample firewall script is written. We don't log the inbound TCP connection packets that are denied by our script. This means we aren't seeing the fact that nmap is scanning every port on the machine. But we do see something else interesting: Two packets to port 23, followed by three to 33658. Then the whole sequence is repeated. This is how nmap attempts to fingerprint the operating system of the machine. If you were to close off the telnet service, you'd see that nmap is incapable of determining the OS of the machine. This is because the telnet service happens to tell any connecting client exactly what OS is running BEFORE asking for identification.

The reason that we're seeing anything at all is because these particular packets have strange flags. Packets with the SYN flag are blocked outright. We're seeing packets without any flags, packets with only the 'ACK' flag set (they appear to be part of an existing connection, but they aren't), and packets with the 'FIN', 'URG', and 'PUSH' flags set. The reason for these weird-flagged packets and the strange port of 33658 is that certain OS's will respond in nonstandard ways to "unusual" packets. This can help nmap determine the type of OS in the absence of any other information. A packet with the 'FUP' flags set should never occur naturally. It's probably the best indication that your network is being scanned.

Summary

You're now able to create a line of firewall code to meet most requirements. If someone asks you to poke a hole in your firewall to allow a service through, you know what sort of line to insert into the firewall startup code, and where to put it. Hopefully, you've already got a simple firewall running on your firewall machine. You're ready to go on to Chapter 10, "Tuning Your Firewall" where we'll go through many of the services discussed in Chapter 3, but this time showing you exactly how to permit or block them.

If you'd like more information on IPFilter, first look at the ipf man pages. They are well written and very useful. At the bottom of these pages you'll find a link to the IPFilter Web site (http://coombs.anu.edu.au/~avalon). From here you can find the IPFilter How-To document, as well as numerous other useful documents. While you're there, give some thought about upgrading to the latest stable version of IPFilter.

## CHAPTER 10

Tuning Your Firewall

You've finally built a working firewall. If you followed the examples in the previous chapters, you even have a few filtering rules in place. Now comes the fun part: Tuning your firewall to suit your own networking needs. This involves:

- Implementing your security policy.
- Tightening up security on your firewall box.
- Ensuring that packets are routed properly.

In Chapter 2, "Fundamental Internet Security Issues," and Chapter 3, "How Secure Should Your Network Be?," we discussed many of the protocols that comprise the Internet. We talked about what they did, how they were insecure, and how they could be made more secure. We also spoke a bit about whether you would want to allow or deny access to such services on your network. Hopefully you've given it some thought and have an idea of what you'd like to allow and disallow. If you haven't finished thinking about it, now would be a good time to take a stab at it. Write your thoughts down, because they're the basis for your Internet security policy.

Implementing Your Security Policy

In this section we're going to look at each of the protocols described in Chapter 2. We'll talk a bit about the issues involved in letting the protocol through the firewall, and then we'll give example code that either permits or explicitly denies the protocol. Each example will contain code for IPChains (Linux) and IPFilter (OpenBSD). But first, we need to set some default policies and stop some blatantly evil traffic.

Basic Policies

We've chosen to start with a default policy of DENY (block) for packets coming in, and ACCEPT (pass) for the other policies. What will this do? It will cut the firewall off from the world. Sure, anything can go out or through the machine, but since nothing can initiate a connection or pass a packet through it, it's dead in the water. This isn't too helpful, so we'll add some short rules that allow machines on your internal network less restricted access to the firewall. We'll also allow the loopback interface access, since that's necessary for the sytem to work properly.

Linux

Flush the chains:

```
ipchains -F input
ipchains -F output
ipchains -F forward
```

Chain policies: deny input, permit output and forward.

```
ipchains -p input DENY
ipchains -p output ACCEPT
ipchains -p forward ACCEPT
```

Accept all packets on the internal interface (eth0) and loopback interface. If your internal interface isn't eth0 change the code accordingly. You can use "ifconfig -a" to check which interface has which address.

```
ipchains -A input -i lo   -j ACCEPT
ipchains -A input -i eth0 -j ACCEPT
```

OpenBSD

Our first three filters will be *blanket* filters that cover all packets. This is equivalent to setting a default policy in IPChains. Add these lines to the /etc/ipf.rules file:

```
block in log all
pass out all
```

The 'log' ensures that any inbound packets that are not matched by any other rules will be logged.

The following lines will accept all packets on the internal interface (eth0) and loopback interface. If your internal interface isn't eth0, change the code accordingly. You can use "ifconfig -a" to check which interface has which address.

```
pass in on lo all
pass in on eth0 all
```

From now on, when we give ipf rules, it is implied that these rules should be added to /etc/ipf.rules. When the ordering of the rules becomes important, we'll make note of the relative position that a rule should have in the file.

Stopping Blatantly Hacked Packets

There are few packets that we should never see on the firewall. These packets do not occur naturally in the wild. They include spoofed packets that pretend to originate from an internal machine, unroutable packets destined for your internal network that should never have made it past the prior router, and various other flavors of evil packets that exist only to cause pain and torment.

The only reason you'd see these packets is if someone were playing naughty games. If you follow these highly suggested rules, the last sound the trespasser will hear before their packets are unceremoniously kicked out the front door is the "Ka-click!" of an eBun-Bun intruder dispatch packet arming itself (see Chapter 12, "Loose Notes," for further explanation and/or new addiction).

Protecting Against Spoofed Internal Packets

You should always forbid inbound packets from the outside world that are intended for the private networks. They should never be routed to you in the first place. Likewise, you should never see packets coming into the external interface that appear to have originated from within your private network. These rules apply to other unroutable IP addresses also—such as the loopback address. If your external interface isn't ppp0, change the code accordingly. Technically, the interface specification isn't required because we've already allowed all packets coming from the internal and loopback interfaces. However, we find it helps focus the mind on the purpose of the rule, and there's no real harm in specifying the interface.

Linux

In the following rules, the '-b' flag stands for *bidirectional*, which means the rule will match packets either from or to the IP address range specified.

```
# first take care of standard unroutables
ipchains -A input -i ppp0 -s 255.255.255.255/32 -b -j DENY
ipchains -A input -i ppp0 -s 127.0.0.0/8 -b -j DENY
# now let's deal with the internal networks
ipchains -A input -i ppp0 -s 10.0.0.0/8 -b -j DENY
ipchains -A input -i ppp0 -s 172.16.0.0/12 -b -j DENY
ipchains -A input -i ppp0 -s 192.168.0.0/16 -b -j DENY
```

OpenBSD

With OpenBSD, NAT takes place before filtering. The filter sees the internal network address as the destination address for all inbound packets that have passed through NAT. This means that at the filtering level there's no way to distinguish between a normal inbound packet that has passed through NAT and an inbound spoofed packet that has been created to have an internal destination address *prior* to going through NAT. This means that a spoofed packet could technically pass through your firewall rules.

This might seem like a major security hole at first, but it really isn't that bad if you're using portmapping properly (although it could be better). When NAT sees the spoofed packet it doesn't know how to deliver the packet because it routes packets internally based on the portmapping table—not the IP address of the inbound packet (which is usually that of the firewall). Therefore when it looks up the spoofed packet's port and source address in the table it finds nothing and just drops the packet. There may be sophisticated ways to gain enhanced access by taking advantage of this issue, but for the most part it's nothing to lose sleep over. Future versions of IPFilter may allow you to specify whether NAT should occur before or after filtering.

```
# first take care of standard unroutables
block in log quick on ppp0 from 0.0.0.0/32 to any
block in log quick on ppp0 from 255.255.255.255/32 to any
block in log quick on ppp0 from 127.0.0.0/8 to any
block in log quick on ppp0 from any to 0.0.0.0/32
block in log quick on ppp0 from any to 255.255.255.255/32
block in log quick on ppp0 from any to 127.0.0.0/8
```

```
# now let's deal with the internal networks
block in log quick on ppp0 from 10.0.0.0/8 to any
block in log quick on ppp0 from 172.16.0.0/12 to any
block in log quick on ppp0 from 192.168.0.0/16 to any
```

Protecting Real IP Addresses behind the Firewall

If you're only using private addresses inside your network that are IP Masqueraded, this covers all the bases. If you have some real IP addresses behind your firewall, then we need to forbid entry for packets that have arrived on our external interface yet claim to originate from real IP's within our internal network.

Suppose that you have some real IP addresses. Let's say you have 209.10.20.32-63, also known as 209.10.20.32/27. If that '/27' isn't obvious, go to Chapter 7, "Configuring the Firewall Under Linux," and reread the *Masking* sidebar. To forbid packets entering your network that claim to originate from your internal IPs, use the following code. If your external interface isn't ppp0, change the code accordingly.

Linux

```
ipchains -A input -i ppp0 -s 209.10.20.32/27 -j DENY
```

OpenBSD

```
block in log quick on ppp0 from 209.10.20.32/27 to any
```

Blocking Packets With IP Options (Source Routed)

IP packets can contain one or more *options*. These are additional parameters in the IP header used by some applications for greater control over the way in which packets are delivered across a network. There are a few options in general that are known to cause serious problems. These are "lsrr" and "ssrr," which stand for *loose source routing* and *strict source routing*, respectively. These are bad and should be killed on sight. Ka-click!

Linux

Linux doesn't do this in the firewalling rules. To remind yourself how to instruct the kernel not to relay source routed packets, re-read the *Source Routing* section in Chapter 7.

OpenBSD

To block all packets with IP options, try the following:

```
block in log quick all with ipopt
```

If your applications find the previous policy too draconian, you might want to just filter out a few of the really bad apples:

```
block in log quick all with opt lsrr
block in log quick all with opt ssrr
```

Filtering by Protocol

For each protocol discussed in Chapter 2, we'll give an example here of one line designed to catch a protocol in general. However, we'll also dwell briefly on certain peculiarities of that protocol, and add a few more lines of firewall code for your consideration.

TCP

To permit an arbitrary TCP packet directed to port nnn, coming from host aaa.bbb.ccc.ddd, the generic forms are shown in the following sections.

Linux

```
ipchains -A input -p tcp --dport nnn -s aaa.bbb.ccc.ddd -j ACCEPT
```

You can add the '--sport' and '-d' flags to control source port and destination IP address, if need be, and several other flags (as documented in Chapter 7).

OpenBSD

```
pass in proto tcp from any to aaa.bbb.ccc.ddd port = nnn
```

Simplifying TCP Filters

One way to simplify your TCP filtering is to permit all external inbound TCP packets which claim to be part of an established connection. Although this is far from tight and won't help with denial-of-service attacks, it's unlikely to allow a Bad Guy to create new connections to your servers. It also has the sterling advantage of simplifying your firewall rules.

Linux

```
ipchains -A input -i ppp0 -p tcp ! -y -j ACCEPT
```

Again, we're specifying the input interface as ppp0, which you should modify to whatever your external interface is called.

OpenBSD

The flag filtering capabilities of IPFilter, combined with the 'keep state' option give us a better and more secure way of handling this situation. We're going to block all inbound requests to initiate a connection (flags S/SA). In the strange event that something manages to get through that rule, we'll block the internal responses to such a connection also (flags SA/SA). Finally, we'll allow all inbound responses to connections initiated from an internal machine (keep state).

```
block in on ppp0 proto tcp flags S/SA
block out on ppp0 proto tcp flags SA/SA
pass out on ppp0 proto tcp keep state
```

Blocking Particular TCP Servers/Services

You may wish to prevent machines on your internal network from accessing certain TCP services on the Internet. Let us suppose you wish to block access to port 80 to prevent Web browsing across the firewall from your internal network. Here's how to do it. In this example, eth0 is taken to be the internal interface; you should modify accordingly.

Linux

```
ipchains -A input -i eth0 -p tcp --dport 80 -j DENY
```

NOTE

If you have used rules such as those in "Basic Policies" above to permit all traffic coming into the firewall from eth0, you will need to put this rule *before* those Basic Policy rules in your firewall script. Otherwise, this rule will never take effect.

OpenBSD

```
block in on eth0 proto tcp from any to any port = 80
```

UDP

To permit an arbitrary UDP packet directed to port nnn, coming from host aaa.bbb.ccc.ddd, the generic forms are shown in the following sections.

Linux

```
ipchains -A input -p udp --dport nnn -s aaa.bbb.ccc.ddd -j ACCEPT
```

You can add the '--sport' and '-d' flags to control source port and destination IP address, if need be, and several other flags (as documented in Chapter 7). To deny the packet and drop it on the floor, replace "-j ACCEPT" with "-j DENY".

OpenBSD

```
pass in proto udp from aaa.bbb.ccc.ddd to any port = nnn
```

ICMP

To permit an arbitrary ICMP packet of message type iii, coming from host aaa.bbb.ccc.ddd, the generic forms are shown in the following sections.

Linux

```
ipchains -A input -p icmp --dport iii -s aaa.bbb.ccc.ddd -j ACCEPT
```

You can add the '-d' flag to control destination IP address, if need be, and several other flags (as documented in Chapter 7). To deny the packet and drop it on the floor, replace "-j ACCEPT" with "-j DENY".

OpenBSD

```
pass in proto icmp from aaa.bbb.ccc.ddd to any icmp-type iii
```

There are certain classes of message type which you would be well advised to permit. At the least you should allow your firewall to receive them. Type 3 should be permitted to enable certain network-level discussions to happen correctly; type 0 should be permitted if you want to be able to use the ping program to check the availability of hosts outside your network, and type 11 should be permitted if you want to be able to use the traceroute program to check similar things. You'll notice that your network cannot be pinged from the outside – we consider this to be a good thing. If you feel differently, you'll also want to allow icmp type 8 through the firewall. Our suggestions can be permitted with the following code; remember to modify ppp0 accordingly.

Linux

```
ipchains -A input -i ppp0 -p icmp --dport  3 -j ACCEPT
ipchains -A input -i ppp0 -p icmp --dport  0 -j ACCEPT
ipchains -A input -i ppp0 -p icmp --dport 11 -j ACCEPT
```

OpenBSD

```
pass in on ppp0 proto icmp all icmp-type 3
pass in on ppp0 proto icmp all icmp-type 0
pass in on ppp0 proto icmp all icmp-type 11
```

Individual Services

In this section, we're going to go through and give examples of individual pieces of code to block and/or permit certain services.

Being the perspicacious type you are, you will have noticed that not every protocol listed in Chapter 3 is covered here. This is because not all of them need to be. We have recommended using a single line of code to permit most of your internal machines to safely have TCP conversations with the outside world. Few other TCP or UDP services need to be permitted into most networks, which sits very well with a general policy of denial. We need to prevent a few services from escaping from your internal network into the unknown, and permit a few special cases in, but other than that, life can be pretty simple. Read on.

DNS

At the very least, you want to be able to talk to your ISP's DNS servers. Since you've used a blanket rule to accept all packets coming from the internal networks, you're only worried about accepting the information coming back from your ISP.

If, when you set up your DNS on machines inside your network you told them your ISP's nameservers by IP address, then you're resolving directly from your ISP's name servers. In the following example code, we've assumed that ppp0 is the external interface, and that 1.2.3.4 and 1.2.3.5 are the IP addresses of your ISP's nameservers. Modify these data accordingly.

Linux

```
ipchains -A input -i ppp0 -p udp -s 1.2.3.4  53 -j ACCEPT
ipchains -A input -i ppp0 -p tcp -s 1.2.3.4  53 -j ACCEPT
ipchains -A input -i ppp0 -p udp -s 1.2.3.5  53 -j ACCEPT
ipchains -A input -i ppp0 -p tcp -s 1.2.3.5  53 -j ACCEPT
```

OpenBSD

```
pass in on ppp0 proto tcp/udp from 1.2.3.4 port = 53 to any
pass in on ppp0 proto tcp/udp from 1.2.3.5 port = 53 to any
```

If you are running a cacheing nameserver inside your network, you can tie the rules down somewhat more tightly. Nameservers communicate with each other on port 53 at both ends of the connection. Actually, as you should be getting used to by now, this isn't strictly true of some more recent name servers; you may need to check your name server's documentation. In particular, if you're running BIND 8.2, you will need to make sure that the line

```
query-source address * port 53;
```

appears in /etc/named.conf. If you have managed to make your name server communicate on port 53, you can tighten up the rules shown in the preceding section as shown in the following subsections.

Linux

```
ipchains -A input -i ppp0 -p udp -s 1.2.3.4  53 --dport 53 -j ACCEPT
ipchains -A input -i ppp0 -p tcp -s 1.2.3.4  53 --dport 53 -j ACCEPT
ipchains -A input -i ppp0 -p udp -s 1.2.3.5  53 --dport 53 -j ACCEPT
ipchains -A input -i ppp0 -p tcp -s 1.2.3.5  53 --dport 53 -j ACCEPT
```

OpenBSD

```
pass in on ppp0 proto tcp/udp from 1.2.3.4 port = 53 to any port = 53
pass in on ppp0 proto tcp/udp from 1.2.3.5 port = 53 to any port = 53
```

Rules for nameservers running other than in forward-only mode are outside the scope of this book, as is a discussion of what "forward-only" means. Still, you should be able to adapt the rules above to suit your needs.

SMTP

If you're running a mail server inside your firewall, you will want to allow connections to it, otherwise you're not going to get any mail. On the other hand, you will want to reject connection attempts to ident, as discussed in Chapter 3. Assuming that your mail server has a real IP address, which is 1.2.3.4, and that your external interface is ppp0, you can do this as shown in the next two subsections.

Linux

```
ipchains -A input -i ppp0 -p tcp -d 1.2.3.4 25 -j ACCEPT
ipchains -A input -i ppp0 -p tcp -d 1.2.3.4 113 -j REJECT
```

OpenBSD

```
pass in on ppp0 proto tcp from any to 1.2.3.4 port = 25
block in quick on ppp0 proto tcp from any to 1.2.3.4 port = 113
```

If you're running a mail server inside your firewall and using IP Masquerading, you will need to permit inbound SMTP, deny inbound ident, and forward the SMTP connection to the appropriate internal private address. Assuming that your internal mail server is 192.168.1.99, that your external interface is ppp0, and your external fixed IP address is 2.3.4.5, you can do this as shown in the following subsections.

Linux

```
ipchains -A input -i ppp0 -p tcp --dport 25 -j ACCEPT
ipchains -A input -i ppp0 -p tcp --dport 113 -j REJECT
```

and a line of ipmasqadm code (you will certainly need to read the *Port Forwarding* section in Chapter 7 before you try to do this) as follows:

```
ipmasqadm portfw -a -P tcp -L 2.3.4.5 25 -R 192.168.1.99 25
```

OpenBSD

```
pass in on ppp0 proto tcp from any to any port = 25
block in quick on ppp0 proto tcp from any to any port = 113
```

and a line of ipnat code (you may first need to refresh yourself by reading the *Port Forwarding* section in Chapter 9, "Configuring the Firewall Under OpenBSD") as follows:

```
rdr ppp0 2.3.4.5/32 port 25 -> 192.168.1.99/32 port 25
```

HTTP

If you're a control freak, and you want to prevent people from making outgoing Web connections, you could do it as follows. In each section the first rule is a blanket restriction on outgoing Web connections. The second rule is a restriction on one particular external address, 1.2.3.4. You would use the second form to interdict one particular Internet site. The third rule, when used with the first rule, will let you selectively allow browsing of approved sites. eth0 is taken to be the internal network interface; modify according to your confguration.

Linux

```
ipchains -i eth0 --dport 80 -j DENY
ipchains -i eth0 -d 1.2.3.4 80 -j DENY
ipchains -i eth0 -d 1.2.3.5 80 -j ACCEPT
```

NOTE

If you have used rules such as those in the *Basic Policies* section above to permit all traffic coming into the firewall from eth0, you will need to put this rule *before* those Basic Policy rules in your firewall script. Otherwise, this rule will never take effect.

OpenBSD

```
block in on eth0 from any to any port = 80
block out on eth0 from any to 1.2.3.4 port = 80
pass in on eth0 from any to 1.2.3.5 port = 80
```

X/VNC/NFS/SMB

Alphabet soup! These are four protocols that it is always wise to block explicitly from going out. Some of these have a tendency to broadcast things that you wouldn't want to release to the outside world, others are just bad news. Assuming eth0 is your internal interface, block them as shown in the code below. The lines are in the same protocol order as in the section heading. Note that the third line, NFS, isn't guaranteed to work. Chapter 3 pointed out that NFS can theoretically run on just about any unused UDP port, and the RPC portmapper mediates the whole scenario. However, nearly all the time nfs ends up on port 2049, so just block it (insert swoosh here).

Linux

```
ipchains -A input -i eth0 -p tcp --dport 6000:6010 -j DENY
ipchains -A input -i eth0 -p tcp --dport 5900:5910 -j DENY
ipchains -A input -i eth0 --dport 2049 -j DENY
ipchains -A input -i eth0 --dport 137:139 -j DENY
```

NOTE If you have used rules such as those in *Basic Policies* above to permit all traffic coming into the firewall from eth0, you will need to put this rule *before* those Basic Policy rules in your firewall script; otherwise, this rule will never take effect.

OpenBSD

Note that there are spaces after the word 'port' and before and after the "><" operator in the following rules. If you don't put in the spaces the rule won't work.

```
block in quick on eth0 proto tcp from any to any port 5999 >< 6011
block in quick on eth0 proto tcp from any to any port 5899 >< 5911
block in quick on eth0 from any to any port = 2049
block in quick on eth0 from any to any port 136 >< 140
```

Masquerading/Network Address Translation

The dictionary defines a masquerade to be *an assembly of persons wearing masks*. We're pretty sure this weird concept originates from the British. Frankly there's no other conceivable explanation. In our particular context, masquerading is hiding one or more IP addresses used on an internal network behind one or more globally valid IP addresses. One of the authors greatly prefers this definition. The other author is galloping around the English countryside screaming "I'm Batman!" and therefore cannot be reached for comment. It must be something in the curry.

In the context of Linux and OpenBSD firewalls, masquerading (also known as *Network Address Translation* in the OpenBSD world) is more precisely the hiding of one or more internal network addresses behind one globally valid IP addresses. If any of this is news, refer to Chapter 3 and reread the *IP Masquerading* section. And please, take that mask off.

Assuming you're using the private range 192.168.1.0/24 on your internal network, IP Masquerading can be achieved with the code in the next section.

Linux

IPChains automatically uses the address assigned to your external interface when masquerading. You only need to specify the addresses on your internal network that should be masqeraded. There is currently only support for masquerading behind one IP address.

```
ipchains -A forward -s 192.168.1.0/24 -d ! 192.168.1.0/24 -j MASQ
```

OpenBSD

Network Address Translation under OpenBSD works somewhat differently than IPMasquerading under Linux. With NAT, you map a range of internal IP addresses to a range of external IP addresses. If the two ranges are not of equal size, you'll need to use the portmapper. The portmapper will map an internal tcp or udp connection to an arbitrary port on an arbitrary IP address within the range specified.

How does this help? Let's say you have 100 internal machines that all have Web browsers. Each Web browser's source port is likely to be the same. Now ipnat has to map each of these requests to an external address and port. Without the port mapper, each request is mapped to a unique IP address and the source port remains the same. This means that you'd need at least 100 real IP addresses to handle all 100 connections simultaneously. On the other hand, if you had just one IP address, the portmapper would change the source port on each outbound connection but would use the same IP address for all of them. Since there are slightly less than 64000 tcp and udp ports available, one IP address could support many simultaneous outbound connections.

The following example shows ipnat mapping all connections from the internal 192.168.1.0 subnet to the external IP address 1.2.3.4. The portmapper is use to map tcp and udp connections. All other protocols (ICMP, IGMP, for example) are mapped directly to the IP address 1.2.3.4.

```
map ppp0 192.168.1.0/24 -> 1.2.3.4/32 portmap tcp/udp 1025:65000
map ppp0 192.168.1.0/24 -> 1.2.3.4/32
```

OpenBSD also allows you to masquerade behind multiple IP addresses. This is particularly useful once your network amasses a large number of machines. To do this, simply use a larger range of IP addresses in the map command. The following example shows our internal subnet being mapped to the real addresses range 1.2.3.1–1.2.3.254.

```
map ppp0 192.168.1.0/24 -> 1.2.3.0/24 portmap tcp/udp 1025:65000
map ppp0 192.168.1.0/24 -> 1.2.3.0/24
```

Now I Can Do Anything

Just don't try to fly out of a 20th story window. At least not until your first real intrusion. You have all the tools you need to create packet-filtering firewalls of arbitrary complexity. You might still be a bit daunted by the precise combination you need, though. To help with this we have put sample firewalls up on the book's companion Web site at www.wiley.com/compbooks/sonnenreich. Our firewall scripts make extensive use of variables which are all assigned at the beginning of the script. But don't worry, we've heavily commented everything, so you should be able to beat them into submission with ease. Just don't get carried away with the beating. Modern-day firewalls are much more sensitive to abuse than the brick ones of yesteryear.

There are three example scripts: One is for moderate security without a DMZ, another is for moderate security with a DMZ, and the third is for high security with a DMZ. There's also a skeleton file which you can use to create your own firewall. Each script is designed to be placed in the appropriate location on your system, as described in Chapters 7 and 9.

Whether you use one of our scripts or you write your own, you'll need to make sure it's executed when the system boots. The following are instructions for ensuring that the firewall code is loaded when the system boots.

Linux

System startup files live in /etc/rc.d/init.d. Your firewall script file should be placed in /etc/rc.d/init.d/firewall. Then, work out which init level you normally run at by doing a "grep initdefault /etc/inittab". You'll get something like this:

```
#    0 - halt (Do NOT set initdefault to this)
#    6 - reboot (Do NOT set initdefault to this)
id:3:initdefault:
```

The last line is the important one (note that the first two are comments—the leading # gives that away). The 'id:3' means that this particular configuration runs at init level 3 by default. The other common init level is 5. Whichever init level is your default, cd to the startup directory /etc/rc.d/rcN.d, where N is your default level, and issue the command:

```
ln -s ../init.d/firewall S09firewall
```

From now on, when you boot, your firewall should start up automatically. You can check this in practice by doing "ipchains -L -n -v" after the system has booted.

OpenBSD

The first step is to place your firewall rules script in the right directory. It needs to be called ipf.rules and should be located in the /etc directory. Likewise, any NAT rules you have should be called ipnat.rules and also should be placed in the /etc directory.

The next step is to tell the system to read the files when it boots. Edit the file /etc/rc.conf and look for the line that starts with 'ipfilter='. Change it to read "ipfilter=YES".

Finally, edit the file /etc/sysctl.conf and make sure there's a line that says "net.inet.ip.forwarding=1". If it's equal to 0, change it to 1. If it's not there, add it. This line enables NAT.

The next time you reboot, your filtering rules will take effect.

Tying Things Down Tighter

You've now got a working firewall. The firewall rules will prevent the outside world from reaching any services that happen to be running on your firewall machine. However, these services will be available to machines on your internal network. We don't want to neglect host security, because a compromise can happen from the inside as well as the outside. Also, there may be moments when you take your firewall code down—it's a good idea not to leave your underwear flapping in the breeze at such moments.

The file that controls most network services is /etc/inetd.conf. If you look at the file, you'll see many lines that begin with #. These lines are comments. Some of the comments are actually valid configuration instructions that have been commented out by default. These lines refer to services that are not necessary for standard operation. The commands are provided as comments to make it easier for system administrators to activate the service (they simply remove the #).

Each line that is not a comment is an active service. This service will get started at boot time. The line contains information about the name of the service (column 0) and what port the service runs on (column 1). You might notice that a number of the port numbers are actually words such as "ftp, " or "smtp" for example. The file /etc/services contains the mappings between protocol names, protocol types, and port numbers. For some good, solid documentation on the format of this file, do a "man inetd.conf".

In any case, what you want to do is to turn off most of the services in /etc/inetd.conf. Do this by inserting a "#" mark at the beginning of any line you don't want to keep. You might want to keep telnet, strictly so you can administer the box locally, but if you choose to administer the firewall via telnet you're going to have your firewall's passwords floating around your internal network in plaintext. This is not, by and large, a good idea. On the whole, we don't think any of the services in /etc/inetd.conf should be running. Administer your firewall from the console, or remotely with SSH. In order to connect to the firewall with SSH, you'll need to make sure that the sshd program is running on you firewall. The best way to ensure that sshd is always running is to start it at boot time.

Once you've commented out all those entries, you need to get inetd to reread the file. On both Linux and OpenBSD, this is done with the command:

```
kill -1 'cat /var/run/inetd.pid' (yes, those are backticks)
```

Linux users can also check what services are still talking to the network with the command "netstat -apn", which should be run as root for maximum effectiveness. The output from this can be a bit verbose, but here are a few representative lines:

```
Active Internet connections (servers and established)
Proto Recv-Q Send-Q Local Address          Foreign Address        State         PID/Program name
tcp      0      0 0.0.0.0:22             0.0.0.0:*              LISTEN        6905/sshd
tcp      1      0 192.168.1.2:3183       206.160.10.5:80        CLOSE_WAIT    5101/netscape-commu
tcp      0      0 192.168.1.2:6000       192.168.1.1:1323       ESTABLISHED   4994/Xwrapper
tcp      0      0 192.168.1.2:1022       192.168.1.1:513        ESTABLISHED   5059/rlogin
tcp      0      0 192.168.1.2:2613       192.168.1.1:143        ESTABLISHED   5018/pine
tcp      0      0 0.0.0.0:25             0.0.0.0:*              LISTEN        3634/sendmail: accep
tcp      0      0 0.0.0.0:111            0.0.0.0:*              LISTEN        249/portmap
tcp      0      0 0.0.0.0:23             0.0.0.0:*              LISTEN        398/inetd
tcp      0      0 0.0.0.0:21             0.0.0.0:*              LISTEN        398/inetd
udp      0      0 0.0.0.0:514            0.0.0.0:*                            1111/syslogd
udp      0      0 0.0.0.0:2049           0.0.0.0:*                            -
udp      0      0 0.0.0.0:111            0.0.0.0:*                            249/portmap
raw      0      0 0.0.0.0:1              0.0.0.0:*              7             -
raw      0      0 0.0.0.0:6              0.0.0.0:*              7             -
Active UNIX domain sockets (servers and established)
Proto RefCnt Flags       Type       State       I-Node PID/Program name   Path
unix  1      [ ]         STREAM     CONNECTED   136114 5074/xterm         @000012d8
unix  1      [ ]         STREAM     CONNECTED   135599 4993/xinit         @000012cf
unix  0      [ ]         STREAM     CONNECTED   836    558/xterm          @00000037
unix  1      [ ]         STREAM     CONNECTED   142058 6813/xmcd          @0000131c
```

Please don't run away shrieking, it's not as bad as it looks. Most of this is a report on the state of currently valid network connections, or on Unix socket (non-network) connections. The lines that concern us are those where the protocol is TCP and the state is LISTEN, and those where the protocol is UDP. These are shown in bold above. The lines represent TCP services that are actively listening for someone to talk to them, and UDP services which are just hanging around waiting. The port, in each case, is the number following "0.0.0.0:" in column four. If you go back to Chapter 3 and the /etc/services file, you should be able to identify each of these services from the protocol and the port number. Find the dæmon that's running that service, and turn it off.

Note that column seven shows you the PID (Process IDentifier) of the listening process, and often the name as well. Some of these listeners don't have PIDs; the listener on UDP port 2049 is an example of this in the above output. These can be harder to turn off. Fortunately, you know that UDP port 2049 is usually NFS, which Linux handles in the kernel. That's why there's no PID or process shown for that entry. Since you are denying UDP port 2049 with your firewall, you can live with that.

OpenBSD users are not as lucky—the netstat command under OpenBSD is a bit more primitive. You'll need to run "netstat –an" (note that there is no 'p'—under OpenBSD the 'p' flag stands for *protocol* and expects to be followed by a protocol name). The output will look something like this:

```
Active Internet connections (including servers)
Proto Recv-Q Send-Q  Local Address          Foreign Address         (state)
tcp       0      0    209.21.217.53.23       209.21.217.50.15161     ESTABLISHED
tcp       0      0    *.37                   *.*                     LISTEN
tcp       0      0    *.13                   *.*                     LISTEN
tcp       0      0    *.113                  *.*                     LISTEN
tcp       0      0    *.79                   *.*                     LISTEN
tcp       0      0    *.513                  *.*                     LISTEN
tcp       0      0    *.23                   *.*                     LISTEN
tcp       0      0    *.21                   *.*                     LISTEN
tcp       0      0    127.0.0.1.111          *.*                     LISTEN
tcp       0      0    *.111                  *.*                     LISTEN
udp       0      0    *.688                  *.*
udp       0      0    *.658                  *.*
udp       0      0    *.518                  *.*
udp       0      0    *.512                  *.*
udp       0      0    127.0.0.1.111          *.*
udp       0      0    *.111                  *.*
udp       0      0    *.514                  *.*
Active UNIX domain sockets
Address     Type   Recv-Q Send-Q    Inode       Conn      Refs    Nextref Addr
0xf0b47100 dgram      0      0     0x0 0xf0ad4440          0x0       0x0
```

Note that there are no service names or PID numbers in this output. The most information you'll get is the list of ports on which services are running (the last part of each number in the Local Addresses column). You need to sleuth around to figure out which services run on which ports—the file /etc/services will be of some help. Once you figure it out, you can use the command "ps auxw | grep *service_name*" to try to figure out what services are running and what are their PIDs.

Keep stopping dæmons by commenting lines out of inetd.conf until there are as few network listeners as possible. This will immunize the machine against network blandishments on nearly all TCP and UDP ports. Packets which somehow make it beyond the firewall rules will find that nothing is waiting for them on the other side. The result is that they'll just get dropped on the floor.

Routing

It would be remiss of us not to dwell on routing tables, at least briefly. You can set up your firewall perfectly (all of your firewall rules correctly in-line, proper masquerading/NAT, FORWARD_IPV4 set to "true," for example) but if your routing tables are wrong, packets won't flow. Before we can claim that our firewall is finished, we'll need to make sure the routing tables are correct.

Generally, you should never have to play directly with the routing tables. Many of the programs used to configure your firewall directly affect the routing tables. The tables are usually set when programs such as pppd, diald, ifconfig, and the like are executed during the boot sequence. Even though we don't recommend modifying this table, it's good to know what one looks like and how it works. Take a look at yours from time to time, it can be instructive.

The command used to interrogate routing tables is "netstat -rn". It produces output similar to the following sample output.

Linux

```
Kernel IP routing table
Destination     Gateway         Genmask         Flags  MSS Window  irtt Iface
192.168.1.2     0.0.0.0         255.255.255.255 UH      0 0           0 eth0
192.168.1.0     0.0.0.0         255.255.255.0   U       0 0           0 eth0
127.0.0.0       0.0.0.0         255.0.0.0       U       0 0           0 lo
0.0.0.0         192.168.1.1     0.0.0.0         UG      0 0           0 eth0
```

OpenBSD

```
Internet:
Destination     Gateway           Flags   Refs    Use    Mtu   Interface
192.168.1.2     0:0a:ce:3e:8f:e7  U       0       0      -     eth0
192.168.1.0/24  link#1            U       0       0      -     eth0
127/8           127.0.0.1         UH      0       0      -     lo0
default         192.168.1.1       UGS     0       0      -     eth0
```

This is an extremely basic routing table, the sort of table you'd find on a machine within your internal network. This particular machine has an IP address of 192.168.1.2. There are a few minor differences between the Linux and OpenBSD versions of netstat. One easy to spot difference is how the network mask is displayed. With OpenBSD, it's displayed using the ip/mask notation on the destination address. Under Linux it's written as a dotted quad in a separate column. The fields we're most interested in are Destination, Gateway, Genmask, (incorporated into Destination for OpenBSD) and Iface/Interface.

The first line has a destination of the machine's own internal IP address, with no gateway (0.0.0.0) under Linux and the Ethernet MAC address of the interface card under OpenBSD. The netmask is 255.255.255.255. You'll recall from the section on masking in Chapter 7 that such a mask refers to the singular, specified IP address. The route ends with the interface of eth0. This route is the kernel's way of reminding itself that it has to use its own ethernet card to get to its own IP address. This entry in the routing table was created during the initialization of the ethernet card.

The second line has a destination of the local subnet, with a genmask of 255.255.255.0 (/24). This is a class C netmask, and comes from the netmask that was given to this interface in /etc/sysconfig/network-scripts/ifcfg-eth0. Again, the gateway is 0 (well, 0.0.0.0) under Linux, but under OpenBSD we see that the gateway is link#1. This tells OpenBSD to send all packets destined for that subnet out of the first interface card. The purpose of the line is to tell the kernel that all hosts on the local broadcast network can be reached directly from the local network interface. This entry was also created during the initialization of the ethernet card.

The third line is a bit weirder. This is an entry for the destination 127.0.0.0 with a class-A netmask (255.0.0.0 or /8)—that is, all addresses that start "127.". Hopefully, you will recall from the *IP Masquerading* section in Chapter 3 that 127. is the loopback network, a way for the kernel to talk to itself via the networking code but without going out on the network. This line tells the kernel that any address starting 127. should be talked to via the loopback interface "lo."

The last line is the only real line here, and the only line where the gateway entry isn't null. This has an entry for destination 0.0.0.0 (default under OpenBSD), with a netmask of 0.0.0.0. A little thought will reveal that this matches absolutely any IP address. What effect will this line have? Well, it sends all outbound packets to the gateway shown, 192.168.1.1, via the interface eth0. This is the line that enables this machine to send packets to the Internet—192.168.1.1 is the local IP masquerading router.

Hang on, we hear you cry, if that last line tells the kernel what to do with any packet whatsoever, what's the point of the other three lines? Come to that, what about the first two lines—packets addressed to myself will match both those lines, as well as the last one. Which line will take precedence? The answer is that routing tables are designed to look for the *most specific* match possible. Packets addressed to myself can match line 1, or line 2, or line 4. However, they and only they can match line 1, so line 1 is applied to them in preference to line 2 or 4. Similarly, packets addressed to, say, 192.168.1.24 could match line 2 or line 4. However, they are a better match for line 2 than line 4 as only packets addressed to the local network can match line 2. Hence, line 2 is applied to them. Strictly, when more than one match is possible for a packet, the match with the most precise mask (that is, the greatest number of 1s and smallest number of 0s in binary form) is the one which is applied.

Hopefully, this is making sense. Routing tables aren't magic, they're just lookup tables that tell the kernel how to get packets to different addresses. Most of the lines in a routing table are usually memos from the kernel to itself. Technically, the kernel can determine this information in other manners, but this makes dealing with special cases faster and more efficient. For example, packets from the machine to the machine itself can be processed through the routing tables like any other packet.

Summary

Now, you've got a running production firewall. Your network is humming along gently. By and large, your users can get to the Internet, which by and large can't get to them. What is there left to worry about?

Well, intrusion detection would be a good idea. Don't think for a second that you've finished securing the network without it. We're going to look at monitoring and checking your network in the next chapter. We'll also come to terms with the possibility of a compromise by discussing what to do if you believe you've been hacked. Then you can go to sleep, peacefully.

## CHAPTER 11

Intrusion Detection and Response

You're sitting in your office one day, reading mail and surfing the Web, perhaps drinking tea. All of a sudden, intruders are detected on the long-range packet sniffers! Red strobe lights fill the office, the wail of klaxons fills every corridor, and the only sound that penetrates the din is the repetitive voice of the monitoring system intoning "Red Alert! Red Alert!" Calmly, you step up to the console of the firewall and bring the weapons systems online at the same moment you silence the alarms. Now, the only sounds in the Network Operations Center are your gentle (yet firm) commands to crew members: "activate packet logging devices," "fire traceroutes," "bring the tape drives online." Within minutes, the intruders are routed (no pun intended) and life in the NOC returns to normal.

Science fiction or operational fact? Sadly, for most of us, it's science fiction, and unsubtly poached science fiction at that. The fact remains, however, that a good monitoring system to look for intrusions, and a good plan for dealing with disasters—preferably one you've practiced—will stand you in good stead in a crisis. Better leave the red T-shirt at home, though.

We're not going to belabor these points, but in this chapter we'll run through some good network monitoring systems. We'll then try and talk about disaster recovery in a way which provokes ideas and makes you think about just what you would want to be able to do in such an event, and what you'd need to have ready in order to do it. But first let's get a feel for what we're up against.

Know Thine Enemies

You're not fighting Klingons or the Borg. That's the good news. The bad news is that you're probably up against a bunch of pimply teenagers that dress up as Klingons or the Borg on a regular basis. The majority of them fall into the script kiddie category. They're the most likely ones to show up at your doorstep. A few of them are good enough to be public service hackers. Unless your name is Bill Gates, or you've been in bed with Microsoft, you've got little to fear from these hackers. The pros are likely to be older and far scarier. Leave them a plate of cookies and they might decide to be nice to your network after they slide down the chimney. Let's examine each group in a bit more detail.

Script Kiddies

One word: Nuisance. Whether they're a big nuisance or a small one depends on how well you've protected yourself against them. These wanna-be hackers download pre-made hacking tools from the Internet. The vast majority of them have no idea how these tools work, but they have no problem unleashing them on random IP addresses.

The goal of the script kiddie is to gain 15 seconds of fame in the script kiddie community by hacking a well-known machine. Often this is a Web server or any exposed server on a prestigeous subnet (FBI, NASA, NSA, for example). They boast of their deed either by altering a main Web page to say something totally inane or they set up a warez FTP server or an IRC server on the compromised machine. If they're totally unsuccessful at breaking into your site, they'll probably launch some sort of denial of service attack in frustration.

Script kiddies are relatively easy to neutralize. If you built your network following the principles outlined in this book (minimize the services that go in and out of the internal network, and use a DMZ, for example) you'll keep most of the recreational script kiddies at bay. The adjustments made to the firewall in Chapter 10, "Tuning Your Firewall," will repel the vast majority of the ambitious ones. Keeping up with your patches will repel the rest of them.

Many of the tools used by script kiddies leave giant neon flags all over your network. A very simple intrusion detection system will spot most of these attacks. The relative cluelessness of script kiddies also ensures that they'll leave a very traceable trail. A few choicely worded legal documents sent to their homes will keep them and their friends off your network for quite a while.

Public Service Hackers: Friend or Fiend?

They keep finding new holes in Microsoft products. They release "exploits" which script kiddies quickly snatch up and add to their arsenal. They are "Public Service" hackers because they feel they are doing the public a great service. By making security holes public knowledge, they make it harder for professional hackers to get into a site (it's a lot easier to patch holes and watch for attempts to exploit them when you know where they are). Furthermore, their hacks force companies to acknowledge security defects. The theory is that if a company gets embarassed enough, they'll build better quality control into their development cycle to avoid future embarassments. The reality is that the company uses all the money it should have spent on quality control suing everyone that could possibly be indicted for the breach.

Public service hackers won't bother you, unless you're a software company that claims your products are secure. Even then, you'll be okay as long as your company's name isn't Microsoft. But hey, if your employer is Microsoft and you're reading this book then you've better hide it fast because your boss is standing over your shoulder with a copy of the Halloween Document and a pink slip (quick note for British readers: A pink slip is a document that turns into a UB40 in very short order indeed).

Many people debate whether this sort of hacking is a good thing. Obviously, frequently targeted companies such as Microsoft are against it. They tend to claim that the vulnerability is completely theoretical (which makes it none the less exploitable), ignore it in the hope that it will go away, or fire off lawsuits in seemingly random directions. A sort of etiquette exists for people who have discovered security holes and want to be polite about it: They should contact the maintainers of the code, who come up with a fix in a short while, then the holes and the fix are announced at the same time. Needless to say, this gets honored more in the breach than the observance: People finding holes call press conferences later the same day, vendors clam-up for weeks on end and refuse to comment on how the patches are coming along, and everyone's generally acrimonious.

Should you ever be enterprising enough to discover a hole for yourself, we strongly recommend the polite way of going about it. It's just better for everyone. Should you ever be approached by someone kind enough to be polite about the hole he or she has just found in your code, we urge you to devote your every resource to fixing it—the better to honor their public spirit and make the world a safer place.

The Pros

The pros are the Kevin Mitnicks that haven't gotten arrested yet. They're as knowledgeable as the public service hackers, but they don't share their knowledge. Instead, they keep an arsenal of unknown exploits for private and often criminal use. These guys are real criminals—they get paid to commit serious felonies. They're also really good. You might detect that they're in your system, but you'll probably have no idea how much or little they've done. You can't stop them, and there's little you can do to protect yourself from them. So don't worry about them. Unless you're doing something really secret and important, you have little to fear. If you are doing something secret and important, don't keep any of the important information on a computer that's connected to the network; otherwise you're just asking for trouble.

Monitoring Systems

Monitoring systems fall into two categories: *network monitoring*, and *host monitoring*. The former monitor the traffic on your network, and the latter monitor a machine itself. Both are useful in the context of intrusion detection. Sadly for Linux users, few of these are available in RPM format; this means you're going to have to become proficient with tar and make—the former, to unpack software distributions; the latter, to create the binaries. Unix has long been loved and reviled (often by the same people, for example, us) because all the really good software is distributed in source. That means that, in the end, you have to get good at building software. There's no way we can even begin to touch on how to build software in this book, but many packages these days come with excellent instructions, well-tuned Makefiles which automate the build, and a generally good attitude. Try it.

A passing comment on monitoring systems: They're not generally much use if they can't talk to you to let you know something's up, or down. Be prepared to have an old modem sitting on a dedicated telephone line so that whatever monitoring systems you put in place can call your beeper and let you know the bad news. If you don't have, or don't want, a beeper, then modern cellular phones can often simulate this facility. However you decide to do it, remember that these messages are short and sour, so you very rarely need more than a 9600 baud modem dedicated to this service. It's an excellent use of that old modem you've got sitting in a corner. Just make sure it doesn't answer incoming calls.

Network Monitors

These are tricky to build, but the best of breed is the Network Flight Recorder from NFR, Inc. Unfortunately, it's not free (in either sense of the word), but it is open source (in the sense that it comes with source, so you can read it). You can find out the details at www.nfr.com, but the short version is that NFR sits on your network and watches all the traffic it sees. It includes a sophisticated engine for deciding whether what it sees is something it should keep, or report, or flag as interesting, or indeed cause the NFR to start singing, and this can be configured in a whole variety of interesting ways.

Interestingly, using switches on your network makes NFR unhappy, since it wants to see everything. If you are using a switched network (good for you!), the NFR documentation addresses this issue with some joyful solutions.

Host Monitors

Host monitors themselves come in two flavors. Those that monitor a host from the network, possibly to see if it's exposing itself on the network, and those that monitor the host from inside to see if the host is internally vulnerable, and whether anyone's done anything nasty. Both types have their uses in a well-managed network.

Host Monitoring From the Network

One way hackers look for security holes is to run tools known as "port scanners" on your network. These tools attempt to connect to each IP address on your network using numerous protocols across the entire range of valid ports. The simplest ones search for open Telnet ports, mail ports, etc. One of the most famous of these is SATAN, the *System Administrator's Tool for Analyzing Networks*. It looks for classic vulnerabilities on a specified host or network. It shouldn't find anything through a well-configured firewall, so it's more useful for running on your local network to scan machines on the local network. This tool's a few years old now, but since people keep making the same old silly mistakes, it will keep finding holes in your network if you don't find them first. You can find information and the tool itself at www.fish.com/~zen/satan/satan.html. If you don't like the name, there's a patch included which turns all references to SATAN into SANTA.

There is a SATAN detector, which looks for the network traces of someone launching a SATAN probe against your network. It's called *courtney*. Along with a rather fetching picture of a small child whom we assume to be Courtney, it can be found at http://ciac.llnl.gov/ciac/ToolsUnixNetMon.html. If you have a DMZ it can be particularly worthwhile to run this on a machine in the DMZ.

A more recent, and extremely powerful, scanner is a utility called *nmap* (www.insecure.org/nmap/). Upon seeing this tool you might think it's a script kiddies delight. You'd be right. But it should be even more delightful to you. Running nmap on your own network will tell you everything the script kiddies will know. You can then use this information to plug up the holes, until there's nothing left for a script kiddie to use.

Nmap scans for most known TCP/IP weaknesses in many different ways. Simply studying its list of features can be an awareness-heightening experience:

Vanilla TCP connect() scanning (checks to see which TCP reports respond to a standard connect request)

TCP SYN (half open) scanning

TCP FIN, Xmas, or NULL (stealth) scanning

TCP ftp proxy (bounce attack) scanning

SYN/FIN scanning using IP fragments (bypasses packet filters)

UDP raw ICMP port unreachable scanning

ICMP scanning (ping-sweep)

TCP Ping scanning

Remote OS Identification by TCP/IP Fingerprinting

Reverse-ident scanning

Possibly the coolest feature of nmap is the remote OS identification system. Nothing is more useful to a hacker than the exact make and model of your OS. They can then consult tables of known security problems and take their pick of the exploit du jour. It would be a good idea to try and obscure this information as much as possible. Other features of nmap are also described on the nmap Web site:

> Nmap also supports a number of performance and reliability features such as dynamic delay time calculations, packet timeout and retransmission, parallel port scanning, detection of down hosts via parallel pings. Nmap also offers flexible target and port specification, decoy scanning, determination of TCP sequence predictability characteristics, and output to machine parseable or human readable log files.

What can we offer you besides port scanners? Often, the first sign of an intruder is the sudden unavailability of a server, or some other important service/machine. mon, the service monitoring daemon, can keep a very good eye on your important systems, and let you know if they go away. Then you can start wondering why they went away. In the words of the mon authors, "mon is a general-purpose resource monitoring system, which can be used to monitor network service availability, server problems, environmental conditions such as the temperature in a room, or any number of things." If you're interested in mon, you can find more about it at http://ftp.kernel.org/software/mon/.

The catchily-named AAFID, *Autonomous Agents For Intrusion Detection*, is a project out of COAST (Computer Operations, Audit and Security Tools) at Purdue University. It's an infrastructure of little agents that sit on individual machines, reporting on their state of wellbeing and unhackedness, and a central monitor that talks to the agents then summarises their results. If this interests you, you can read all about it at www.cs.purdue.edu/coast/projects/autonomous-agents.html.

Logging

All of the above tools are great for detecting various security holes and intrusions, but what do you do if they *don't* spot the intruder while the intrusion is happening? Your primary concern in this situation is to assess the damage done and to board up the hole they crawled through. In order to do this you'll need very accurate logs of everything that happened on your network.

One of the first things a hacker will do upon entry will be to shut down or disable any logging agents they can find. They also will try and manually edit the logs to remove any traces of their existence. An industrial strength prevention technique is to have a single system to which all other machines send their syslog information (see the sidebar on Logging in Chapter 7, "Configuring the Firewall under Linux"). This has two advantages: 1) The hacker now needs to compromise a second machine in order to hide their traces, and 2) it provides a single, central repository of data for incident evaluation.

If you choose to build a centralized logger, you need to spend some time hardening the security of the box. Such a machine should be dedicated to syslogging and run no other network services. Only trusted administrative staff should have an account on it. It should accept and process any and all syslog information that's sent to it from your internal network, breaking down the logs in some systematic way. We have provided one possible syslog.conf file on the Web site.

A busy network should not generate more than 300 Mb of logs a day, so a 10 Gb disc will allow you to hold a fair amount of logged information. For an even higher degree of security, you can devise a system where the logs are written to some write-once medium like WORM tape or CD-R in real time. Even if a hacker compromises the logging device, there's no way they can erase the logs.

Host Monitoring From the Host Itself

Tripwire is a gem of a package which allows you to automate monitoring for changes in system files. It works by obtaining a fingerprint from each critical file in your system. This fingerprint is unique, and will change if any aspect (even one little bit) of a file has been altered.

You're wondering what this does for you? It provides a simple and quick way to see if someone's changed an important file on your system. It's true that keeping copies of every important file and comparing them routinely would accomplish the same thing, but some of these files can get pretty big, and comparing them can get pretty slow. If tripwire interests you, you can find the last free version at ftp://coast.cs.purdue.edu/pub/COAST/Tripwire/. Tripwire is a *good thing* to run on a firewall, by the way.

COPS, the *Computer Oracle and Password System*, is another good old classic. One would think that nobody would release an operating system that miserably fails the basic tests in an old system such as COPS, but it happens with depressing regularity. Since the same old mistakes keep on perpetuating, running this tool can in fact be extremely useful. It's the local analogue of SATAN, in that it looks for classic security holes on a local machine. Some of these classics include: bad system directory permissions, bad device file permissions, and bad anonymous-ftp setup. COPS even tries some basic password cracking (although there are better tools for this available). This shouldn't raise any flags on your firewall system since Red Hat is careful, and OpenBSD is particularly careful, about the permissions on the default installation. Furthermore you haven't set up any network services on your firewall, and you read our section on choosing passwords earlier in the book, so you should be okay—but run it anyway. It *is* worthwhile running COPS on regular internal hosts, though. If you're interested, you can find COPS at ftp://coast.cs.purdue.edu/pub/tools/unix/cops/.

Just in case we haven't beaten the point into the ground, let us try harder. *Keep up with your host patches, particularly on your firewall.* There's no excuse for having a known security hole on your firewall. It's really embarrassing. See Chapter 12, "Loose Notes," for the locations of Red Hat and OpenBSD update pages, and for subscription details of the several good mailing lists for monitoring the state-of-the-art in hacking.

Crack in Progress, Keptin

Thank you, Mr. Chekov.

We're standing on the bridge and our excellent monitoring systems have let us know that some slimeball six timezones away has exploited a very-recently-found kernel bug and is shutting our web server down. What do we do Right Now, and what do we do after the core breach has been locked down?

Like Chapter 1, "The ABCs of Network Security," incident response breaks down well into guidelines for small, medium and larger businesses. Remember that the large company section is more a list of discussion points for good practice than a set of instructions to be used the day you hire your 101st employee. Like most things military, incident response benefits from regular planning and practice. Practice doesn't necessarily mean staging events; it can be as simple as dragging the tech team off for pizza and beer and role-playing an incident. Leave the beer until the post-incident phase, unless your training also calls for extreme situational readiness. (preparing for the inevitable massive hack-in at 6:00 P.M. on Friday, two hours into your weekly corporate beer-blast).

During an Incident

We feel organized behavior during an incident comes in four stages. Your policy for each of these stages needs to be carefully thought out ahead of time—not during the breach. The stages, in order, are notify; evaluate; disconnect or shut down; and further notification. Some of the later stages may happen in parallel, but if you cover all these bases you'll be doing well.

Notify

At some point, something will happen that alerts you to an incident in progress or an incident that went unnoticed—until now. It may happen at night, it may happen during lunch, it may be noticed by whoever's responsible for security, or it may be noticed by an operator, or a user, or an automated system. The automated system will do what it's been programmed to do: To get this right, you just need to keep it's list of conditions and responses (if A happens, page B; if C happens, page D but only if it's before midnight, otherwise page E) up to date. If an anomaly is noticed by some person not qualified to evaluate it, you will have a problem unless you have a clear policy for the situation. People need to know who to tell, and how to tell them, if they see something that's *not right*.

If you're a small company, notification is usually easy—at one of the author's sites, people are instructed to call the author's cell phone. The cell phone redirects to an answering machine at nights. This policy works well for the author. You need to work out what you can live with, tell people, and live with it.

At medium companies, you will probably already have some kind of system in place for the users to tell the computing support person (or people) what to do when something's not right. This system will already be used for messages like "no toner on printer 3," "disc's full on Gandalf again," or "the mail system's not working." If you only have one support person, and it's you, then you'll automatically get the notification of the first sign. Your problem will be separating it out from all the other noise you get during the day. To this end, just keep your mind open to the possibility that, very occasionally, it might be a security incident. Of course, usually the problem is more along the lines of someone mistaking the CD-ROM drive for a cup holder.

Large companies, with more than one support person, need to let the support people know that it's okay to escalate things to you if there's an inexplicable bug, or they see something that worries them. They need to know how to get hold of you, and they may need guidelines about what you yourself would consider worrying. You don't need to put the fear of God into them, you just need to talk about this sort of thing occasionally. You also want to write it all down and have it in hardcopy somewhere well-known.

Evaluate

Okay, notification worked. You've now been dragged out of bed at 4:30 A.M. because one of your adminstrators was logged in at 3:00 A.M. … from Latvia! (If you're at a site in Eastern Europe, please read that sentence as "from Langley, Virginia.") You are the right person to be told about this, as per your incident response plan (phase 1), which you drew up after reading the last section.

Now what? Well, you need to evaluate, based on your understanding of correct behavior on your network as a whole, whether this is a real problem. This is a judgment call, and hard to draw up tight rules for. There's no substitute for your own understanding of how your network is used normally, and what the right thing is. To continue with our example, if you know that one of your network people happens to be Latvian, and he happens to be on holiday at the moment, then evaluation might merely involve calling him at home and congratulating him on his work ethic. Boy, will he be impressed with your incident response! If, however, you can find no good reason for what caused the event that started the incident, you must conclude that you have an incident in progress.

At small companies, evaluation involves you, as network administrator, knowing what normally happens on your network.

At medium companies, you should have a policy—either in practice or in writing—that says how individual machines are laid out and how they function. This will let you quickly look at a fault and determine if it's accidental or malicious. You, as network administrator, will need to nominate a second-in-command who knows what you know and can act in your absence to evaluate an incident. If you're in bed with Martian Death Flu, life will be simpler if you can pick up the phone and croak "Make it so" to your colleague before collapsing back into bed and letting him deal with things.

At large companies, systems like tripwire will allow an automated determination of compromise to be made rapidly. A separate machine like a Network Flight Recorder or a centralized, secure logging machine will provide access to known-good data about recent network activity. You will find these logs invaluable in a disaster—at the time of writing, one of your authors had just been called to a site when a client believed that an intrusion had resulted in the deletion of a senior manager's account and email. Good logging enabled us to quickly determine that an administrator had mistyped a username when deleting a group of old users, and that there was no security incident in progress.

Disconnect or Shut Down

Once you've established that an incident is in progress, you must start responding intelligently. Some people advocate leaving things untouched while you monitor the intruder, in order to pursue him or her later. We feel this to be rather pointless. In the first place, your intruder is quite likely coming from abroad. Even if you could track him down, you can't touch him without some ludicrously complex international crime-busting warrant, which you won't get. In the second place, tracking someone down is generally nontrivial. Sure, you can see their IP address, but this is very likely some system elsewhere that they've already cracked. Only if you're extremely lucky will you find enough helpful, alert administrators at remote sites to help you trace the intruder through layer upon layer of intermediary machines. Even then, one most often ends up at a dial-in connection. Tracing a phone call involves a whole new level of legal pain. In the third place, you're not in the cracker-tracking business. You are in some other line of business which your computers exist to help you pursue. Waiting until the intruder has erased everything he or she can find just so you can prove he or she erased it may not be the single best course of action for your business. If you feel there might be some discussion regarding this point, it would be better to have it with your colleagues and management now, while you're not being cracked, rather than later, while you are.

So, you're going to shut things down. Which things? It helps a lot if you've thought about this in advance. If you have a single connection to the Internet, unplug it. If you have multiple connections in failover configuration, unplug what you need to to bring the connection down. Although Big Red Switches that cause all the humming in the machine room to stop are quite in vogue, unplugging the right cables is often the fastest way of preventing any further damage. You need to have worked out in advance which cables are the right ones.

If you don't have physical control of your own machines, if they're at a co-location facility, you will want to shut the machines down gracefully, immediately, and without warning. Your plan should have the relevant commands spelled out, in sequence.

More Notification

Now that you've managed to halt any further damage, you need to start letting people know what's happened. This is another time when a clear, pre-arranged intrusion response plan will help you immensely. It's much quicker to tell management that "An intrusion was detected at 3:05 A.M. today, and the intrusion plan of March 1999 was implemented" than try to list everything that you have disconnected.

Small companies will probably be able to get away with the grapevine, or a quick phone call to anyone relevant to let them know that things are down.

Medium companies, and anyone with external clients who rely on network access, will need to decide in advance on a method of notifying clients that the network is down. Don't assume you'll be able to do this by email! Employees, likewise, will need to be told something—notices stuck inside the lifts, or on the doors, can be surprisingly effective in spreading this kind of news. Have the notices written out in advance.

Larger companies need to have a pre-thought-out bulletin to send to employees telling them what has been shut down, why it's been done, that you're doing everything you can to restore service, and that you'll fill them in on the details later. This should form part of a comprehensive disaster-recovery plan. You might also wish to tell them what they should do in the absence of computing facilities—leaving you alone is always a good idea. You will also need to have decided on a medium for sending the bulletin—again, don't assume that you will be able to use email! If you have a voice-mail system, it may allow you to send broadcast messages. Make sure that the technique for doing this will be available to the incident response team—few incident response teams in large organisations include the voice-telecoms administrator.

After an Incident

You will have two competing priorities in the aftermath of an incident: working out what went wrong, and fixing the systems. If you spend all your time on the first, it could be days before you are able to do business again, if not longer. If you spend all your time on the second, the act of fixing things will erase all the data about the incident itself.

Fortunately, these two tasks parallelize well. The job of restoring systems from known-good backup media or re-installing systems from read-only installation media is essentially grunt work which requires technical direction, while the job of incident evaluation requires a high level of expertise but not too many people. As technical lead on the post-incident recovery, you will be able to concentrate better on the evaluation if you have planned the recovery phase. Let's take them one at a time.

Incident Recovery

The only truly safe thing to do is to reinstall all your systems from installation media, then reinstall all your programs similarly. This could take a very long time, so people are usually extremely unwilling to do it. On the other hand, sometimes a machine has been so badly compromised that there's no other safe course of action. Trying anything less can lead to a vicious cycle of restore after intrusion after restore after intrusion and general wailing and gnashing of teeth. Life will be simpler if you have some clearly defined criteria about when the bullet must be bitten. Try to make some metrics for determining when a machine must be reinstalled from scratch, when a machine must be restored from tape, and when a machine can just be patched up. Cryptographic measures such as tripwire can be a great help here, because they can very quickly tell you what has been changed on a given system.

Bear in mind that a good intrusion won't be noticed for some time; some are never noticed. Only if you can precisely pin down when an intrusion happened can you say with confidence whether any of the backups are known-good, and if so, what date they must precede to be so known. If you can't be sure about that, restores can't be safely done and reinstalls are your only recourse if a machine can't get a clean bill of health.

Your plan should lay out what tests have to be passed for a machine to get a clean bill of health. If your plan calls for restore or reinstall, it should lay out where the media are, which tape or CD drives are suitable to read them, and lay out the commands needed to perform the restore/reinstall.

Finally, you need to make arrangements for damaged systems to be backed up to tape for analysis before the damage is erased, should the recovery team get so far ahead of the analysis team that they have no other machines to check save the very ones you're analyzing. Make sure that you've got enough spare media on site, over and above your regular stocks, to allow you to keep what snapshots you need to keep in the event of an incident.

Incident Analysis

There's no roadmap to incident analysis. We can't tell you how to find system vulnerabilities; if we could, we would find them and fix them ourselves. Working out how you were compromised is much like scientific investigation. You have to be painstaking and methodical, and you have to avoid lying to yourself or accepting faulty logic.

Start with what you know—the event that triggered the incident. Summarize what you know about it. Think about how someone might have got into a position whereby they could do such a thing. Work through such a process in your mind and figure out what logging information such an activity would have generated. Check your network audit systems for evidence of such activity.

Sometimes an exploit will involve a vulnerability of which you are completely unaware. Nothing will help you in such a case; you will not be able to find a trail that makes sense. When you're confident that this has really happened to you, when you're confident that you haven't overlooked an audit trail or failed to spot the important thing in the logs, make sure you keep the tapes of the damaged systems safe for later analysis. We should stress that there are a lot of systems on the Internet these days. It's very unlikely that your site is the very first to be hit through the brand-new hole in frobnitzd 11.3(1). Search bugtraq as well as CERT and other advisories very thoroughly before you conclude that you're involved in something new.

You may also wish to notify CERT and other emergency-response teams, particularly if intrusion appears to have been caused by the exploitation of a new vulnerability in your systems rather than by an unpatched hole or a misconfiguration. Your plan should list contact numbers for all these organizations, and it should say who will decide whether or not to call them.

If you wish to pursue legal action, or think that might be a possibility, you will need to make arrangements to have your media secured. At the very least, label each tape with an exact description of the contents, and sign and date the label. Write-protect the media. If this can be done in a permanent manner, say by gluing a read-only tab in place, so much the better. Finally, make arrangements to have the media secured so that tampering would be infeasible until it's handed over to law-enforcement personnel. If you have third-party offsite storage for your backup media, making up a special box and sending it offsite may well be enough to prove that it wasn't touched. Media may become valueless as evidence if you can't prove that they could not possibly have been tampered with.

Speaking of the Old Bill (okay, "law enforcement personnel" everywhere outside of the U.K.), should you call them or not? Unless the incident involved the loss of a substantial amount of money, or real major damage, they're probably not going to be interested. Although there's no harm in telling them (they can set their own priorities quite well!), you may well not be able to lay your hands on the right policeman in the heat of the incident. When the right person does find out, much later, he or she may well regret not having been able to ask questions at the time. If you think calling in law enforcement may be an option, you should perhaps try to contact them now to find out whether they would wish to know, and whom you should talk to in the event of an incident. Put this information in your plan. In any event, your plan should say who decides whether to call them.

Laptops

This is one of these little ideas that didn't fit anywhere else. A laptop can be worth its weight in gold when portable network sniffing's in order. You don't have to shell out big bucks to get one these days; Linux and OpenBSD are much lighter OSes than some we can think of, needing less laptop to do a good job. Armed with a few tools like tcpdump, you can carry it around your building and plug it in anywhere to see what's going on. They make good portable VT100s for reconfiguring printers, switches, hubs, and routers, too.

It's worth getting a big hard drive for your laptop, since you can store more captured packets that way.

Summary

That's really all we have to say on the topic of intrusion response. A really depressingly large number of Internet sites—even companies with good security and firewalls—don't think systematically about this sort of disaster. If you do, if you spend time implementing monitoring systems and planning your response, you'll be doing better than some really big companies. Recall our comments earlier in the book about trying to make your car less stealable than your neighbors? Well, this is the equivalent of installing a Great Big car alarm on your Yugo and parking near a Ferarri. Well done.

Now, on to Chapter 12 "Loose Notes," where we run through all the resources we promised you earlier in the book—mailing lists, patch sites, discussion sites, sources of information, and system security fora. We'll wrap up the book with a few completely irrelevant remarks, so stay tuned.

## CHAPTER 12

Loose Notes

Welcome to the medley of extemporanea, which is to say, everything we needed to refer you to during the previous 11 chapters, but couldn't put in at the time without breaking the flow of the text, or getting excessively verbose, or going and looking it up ourselves.

Firstly, we'll run through the book chapter by chapter, and take the references we gave in serial order. This won't be deathless prose, by any means, but it should be edifying and it should let you find the reference you want in a hurry when you run into things like "For more information on the use of mascarpone in a really good tiramisu, see Chapter 12," elsewhere in the book.

Next, we'll touch on a few other subjects that are useful, but don't make sense to put anywhere else in the book. Ok, you caught us. We wrote half a chapter on security policies that we cut and couldn't bear to leave out entirely. So we stuck it at the back of the book and hope no one notices.

Finally, we'll wrap up with a few useful scripts and utilities that will make great strides to improving your quality of life for years to come. Trust us.

References by Chapter

In this section we've organized the references for each chapter by page number.

Chapter 1

Crack and l0phtcrack (p. 10). These are nifty utilities for determining if your password file is secure. Crack was designed to run on Unix systems, whereas l0phtcrack was designed for NT. Our crack provider of choice is CERT (www.cert.org/ftp/tools). You'll find more than just crack on this site. It'll be worth your while to experiment with some of the other things offered. To obtain l0phtcrack, point your browser at www.l0pht.com and follow the link to products. You might find some of their other tools and products interesting as well.

Sudo (p. 12). Sudo is a Unix program that allows a system administrator to provide restricted root access to certain commands for certain people on certain systems. It's available at www.courtesan.com/courtesan/products/sudo/ ; the Web page also gives an example configuration file. This file is pretty complex, and probably not suitable for simple installations, but it should demonstrate the tool's flexibility. Commands can be grouped by severity, as can machines and users by trust level, and command arguments can be limited using a fairly standard Unix glob (wildcard) syntax. The package even prevents users from wandering off and leaving their workstations empowered, since it requires the user to provide his or her own password before a command can be executed with sudo (although a short window of empowerment can be left open after one successful sudo, in order to prevent password entry from becoming laborious during extended system maintenance).

Security sites (p. 12). There are numerous sites that are one-stop security information posts. These sites try to keep abreast of all the latest security issues for one or more operating systems. Some of these sites are very good and almost always up-to-date, whereas others are commercialized junk. Here are a few of the very good ones:

- *www.cert.org* The original and best. The Computer Emergency Response Team was formed at Carnegie Mellon University in the aftermath of Morris' Internet Worm, and was just about the first formal incident response organization formed of the Internet, for the Internet. Although their mandate has changed somewhat over the last 11 years, the site is still well worth perusing, especially the CERT Advisory Archives at www.cert.org/advisories/index.html. If you are suffering from any of the holes here, you're just asking for trouble. Find them and fix them.

- *www.cs.purdue.edu/coast* The Computer Operations, Audit and Security Technology group at Purdue University hosts all sorts of interesting tools and suggestions, as well as many, many other good lnks. It has been subsumed into CERIAS, the Centre for Education and Research in Information Assurance and Security, which can be found at www.cerias.purdue.edu/ and is also well worth a long visit.

- *www.securityfocus.com* This is the new home for the Bugtraq mailing list, which is considered one of the best discussion lists for security vulnerabilities. Many security problems are discussed on bugtraq before the public ever hears of them. In addition, the securityfocus site provides a new vulnerabilities section where security holes are organized in a very friendly way. This is probably the most thorough security site on the Net.

- *www.sans.org* The System Administration, Networking and Security Institute produces excellent monthly email digests of recent major cracks and vulnerabilities which is well worth reading. Their weekly newsbites are even terser.

- *www.l0pht.com* Not only the creator of useful admin tools, the L0pht is one of the most respected hacking organizations. Their site contains information on dangerous security holes in major software applications and operating systems. They tend to have very interesting information on Microsoft-specific vulnerabilities.

- *slashdot.org* Slashdot is news for nerds, and as such you're likely to see news of a security hole here rather promptly.

- *www.openbsd.org/patches* For OpenBSD, this is the best source of information on operating system security vulnerabilities.

- *www.redhat.com/corp/support/errata/rh60-errata-general.html* For Red Hat Linux, this is the definitive source of fixes for security vulnerabilities and other brokenness.

Tripwire (p. 14). This package was originally developed by COAST (see above), but has since been licensed for development to Tripwire Security Systems. You can find the last version distributed by COAST at ftp://coast.cs.purdue.edu/pub/COAST/Tripwire/, or you can find TSS at www.tripwiresecurity.com/.

TSS seems to be making a free version of Tripwire more up-to-date than COAST's, but less so than the commercial version, available at www.tripwiresecurity.com/products/ASR1_3.html. You'll need to fill out a form to get it, but the license appears to permit anyone to run it at a single site.

Chapter 3

Firewall discussion archives (p. 63). There are numerous mailing lists which discuss firewalls exclusively. Most of these lists have been archived, and the archives are searchable via the Web. Here are some pointers to the major lists:

- *ipfilter* www.false.net/ipfilter
- *Firewalls miling list* http://lists.gnac.net/firewalls/archive.html
- *Firewall wizards' mailing list* www.nfr.net/firewall-wizards/

Many of the commercial vendors maintain discussion lists and archives that are accessible from their own Web sites. These could be useful resources for more general firewall questions.

CERT (p. 72). As we said above, CERT is a federally funded initiative based at Carnegie Mellon University. The information on the cert.org Web site is *highly* reputable, but not so thorough or timely. You can't solely rely on CERT for security information, as they do not respond to every incident, and often are the last security watchdog to respond. Nonetheless, the tools and advice offered on their site are significantly more trustworthy than quick-fixes or patches supplied elsewhere (other than those provided by the original vendor).

Kerberos (p. 99). From the MIT Kerberos site (http://web.mit.edu/kerberos/www/):

Kerberos is a network authentication protocol. It is designed to provide strong authentication for client/server applications by using secret-key cryptography.

Kerberos was created by MIT as a solution to these network security problems. The Kerberos protocol uses strong cryptography so that a client can prove its identity to a server (and vice versa) across an insecure network connection. After a client and server has used Kerberos to prove their identity, they can also encrypt all of their communications to assure privacy and data integrity as they go about their business. Numerous standard Unix applications, such as telnet, have been kerberized. There is also a Windows version of the Kerberos client suite, and Kerberos support has been properly built into the Eudora mail program.

The name Kerberos refers to the three-headed daemon of Greek lore which guards the entrance to Hades. Some readers may know of this dog by its Roman name, Cerberus (no, not the aardvark, OK?). It represents the three components of the kerberos security framework: the client, the server, and the Key Distribution Center (KDC). If you want to understand how Kerberos works, and why its very secure and very cool, check out the following amusing and low-tech document: http://web.mit.edu/kerberos/www/dialogue.html.

Chapter 10

If the thought of Pokemon sends you into a psychotic rage, then you'll be pleased to know that there's one bunny who's sick of being cute. Bun-Bun, the resident knife-wielding rabbit at www.sluggy.com may look cute, but don't tell him that.

Chapter 11

Pages with updates/patches (p. 324). Both RedHat and OpenBSD maintain pages that have information on security vulnerabilites and patches to address the issues.

- RedHat at www.redhat.com/corp/support/errata/rh60-errata-general.html
- OpenBSD at www.openbsd.org/errata.html

Good hacker sites (p. 324):
- *attrition.org* One of the better sites run by a real-hacking organization that includes lots of information and references to other sites. Some of the documents on the site can teach you volumes about common hacking techniques, especially those used by script kiddies. For example, the alt.2600/#Hack FAQ can be found at www.attrition.org/~voyager/faq014.txt. The alt.2600 is a popular USEnet news group for hacking discussion (based around the magazine of the same name), and #Hack is a hacker IRC channel. Both are almost exclusively populated by script kiddies these days. This site is definitely worth a lookover.
- *hackernews.com* This is an excellent news site for hackers with really interesting articles floating around their archives.
- *insecure.org* Fyodors Web site and the home of the excellent *nmap* security tool. On the site you'll also find ExploitWorld, a comprehensive database of many security problems and related exploits.
- *l0pht.com* (and related subsites) Mudge, Weld Pond, and Dildog, for example are denziens of the L0pht. Off of the l0pht page you can find links for Cult of the Dead Cow (creators of BackOrifice) and other hacking groups that are affiliated with the L0pht.
- *phrack.com* This is an online hackers e-zine. The contributing writers are some very smart hackers from all over the world. Their articles

describe theoretical and practical apporaches to hacking various systems and infrastructures. Some of the articles are enlightening, some are unbelievably funny, and some are so scary you'll want to cut up your credit cards and move to Montana. An offline parallel to phrack is 2600, a quarterly hackers magazine. You can subscribe from the 2600.com Web site.

Chapter 12

Recursion (p. 338). This is a powerful programming technique where a program or module makes reference to itself. It can be thought of as the practical use for circular logic. When Richard Stallman created the concept of GNU, he immediately won over hackers everywhere with the brilliant, irrefutable explanation of his idea: What is GNU? GNUs not Unix.

A Brief vi Tutorial

The first thing to note is that it's pronounced "vee eye." Not "vie," not "vee," and never, ever "six." Vi is, as we intimated earlier, possibly the most hostile editor since TECO, which is in turn the most hostile text editor ever invented. Why, then, do we suggest you use vi? Because it is canonical, it is the default editor on nearly every Unix system in the world. You can sit down at nearly any box and use vi to edit a file. If the box is primitive enough not to support full-screen editing, you can use vi's line editor mode to edit a file using a subset of vi's commands. And if you're sitting down at a box so damaged that it has no full-screen capability and no useful programs whatsoever, you can still usually find vi's hairy old grandfather, "ed," hanging around somewhere. Although ed's even more terse than vi, and speaks in a funny accent, you can usually figure out how to talk to him by talking vi commands back in the same funny accent. Don't try this unless you have to, but if you ever have to, you'll bless vi's name.

Speaking of name, you might be wondering about the name vi. It stands for visual, most likely referring to the fact that you can see what you're editing. Believe it or not, at the time of vi's creation this was quite a revolutionary idea. For some reason this feature was overlooked by the designers of earlier programs such as ed, which only lets you work on one line at a time. Don't for a second think that visual has any relationship to the Microsoft concept of visual, where pretty pictures and jumping paperclips help you drag and drop buttons and other graphical gadgets all over the screen. The most visual vi gets is a terse column of ~ marks down the left side of the screen to indicate that you've reached the end of the file and the beginning of squiggleland.

The second thing to note about vi is that it's modal, which is an unusual concept for people brought up on modern editors with drop-down menu bars and 46 function keys. In one of its two modes, it is expecting text input, and will interpret everything you type at it as text to be added to your document. In the other mode, it's expecting command input, and it will interpret everything you type at it as commands to be executed. We will call these modes INPUT mode and COMMAND mode. Just to cheer you up, vi often won't tell you which mode it's in.

Are you getting our point about user hostility yet?

Create a Test Document

Let's create something for us to work on, something that we can damage without destroying anything needed. Try:

```
cp /etc/protocols /tmp/prototest
```

and then enter vi with

```
vi /tmp/prototest
```

How Do I ESCape?

The escape key is your friend when using vi. Pressing ESC takes you back from input mode to command mode, and continuing to press it has no bad side-effects—it just keeps you in command mode (and may emit a beep or two). All vi users develop the tendency to bash on the ESC key a couple of times to make sure they're in command mode. Try it now.

How Do I Type Something?

Lets place vi into input mode. There are numerous ways of doing this. The two most common are by typing i or a in command mode. The i places vi into insert mode, whereas the a places it into append mode. Both are input modes, so what's the difference? In insert mode, the next character you type will appear before the character currently under the cursor. In append mode, it will appear after character currently under the cursor. There are other ways of getting text into the file, but these are the two commands you'll use most often. Both modes are exited by using ESC to return to command mode.

We generally use i most of the time. a is useful if you want to add something to the end of the line, because you can't move the cursor off the end of the line.

One more tip: If you just have to change a single character, you can place the cursor over the character and hit r, followed by the new character. If you want to overwrite a bunch of characters, hit R. This puts you into replace mode, which is also an input mode, but types over characters on the current line rather than inserting text. As with all input modes, you can return to command mode by hitting ESC.

How Do I Move Around?

We hope the arrow keys on your keyboard work; they're very useful. In the event that they don't, which may well be the case, or if you just want to look like a stud for not having to use the arrow keys, there are alternatives. The most useful are h, j, k, and l, which move left, down, up, and right, respectively. There's also e, which advances to the end of the next word; w, which advances to the beginning of the next word; and b, which moves back to the beginning of the previous word.

Other move-quick commands are "(," which will take you back one sentence and ")," which will take you forward a sentence. Likewise, "{" moves back a paragraph, while "}" moves forward a paragraph.

To get to the beginning of the line quickly, try "0" (zero). To get to the end of the line quickly, try "$".

To search for a word, type "/" followed by the search term. This will search forward through the document. If you want to search backwards, type "?" instead of "/".

The period (".") repeats the last command. If you want to repeat the previous search, you can use n. The advantage to using n instead of . is that you can do a few other commands between searches. n will repeat the last search, even if it isn't the most recent command.

All these commands only work in command mode (sorry if that seems a little obvious). If you want to stop entering text at the current location and enter it someplace else, you need to leave insert mode.

How Do I Delete?

To delete the letter under your cursor, hit the x key. To delete all of the text from your cursor to the end of the line, use the capital D key. For deleting larger regions of text, see the next section on cutting. Again, all these commands work only in command mode.

How Do I Undo that Last Mistake?

The u command will undo the last command. Some versions of vi, such as the one that ships with Red Hat Linux (which is really vim—vi Improved) have multiple levels of undo. With vanilla-flavor vi you only get to mess up once, and you need to catch it immediately—pressing u a second time undoes the undo and puts the mistake back!

How Do I Cut, Copy, and Paste?

In every program you've ever used, cut and paste works in almost the same way: Highlight a region of text, hit cut/copy, move to where you want to put it, and hit paste. Simple enough. The problem with vi is that there's no way to highlight text, since vi came well before the concept of highlighting. The vi system works as follows: Tell it whether you want to cut or copy, and move the cursor to the end of the region. The catch is that the movement must be the result of a single motion. This means you can't use the arrow keys to move because each tap of the arrow key is a separate motion (holding the key down doesn't help either). If you try to use the arrow keys, you'll just copy one character.

So what do we do if we want to yank a large region of text? Take a closer look at the *How Do I Move Around* section. We can use any one of these commands to get to where we want in a single motion. Let's first try cutting a single word. Go to the beginning of the word. Hit y for yank. Now hit e to move to the end of the word. You might even see something on the bottom of the screen saying you've yanked a few characters. Great! Now let's paste the word somewhere. Use the arrow keys to move somewhere special and hit the p character. Your word should be inserted under the cursor. If we had wanted to cut the word, we would have first hit the lowercase d character for delete and then hit e. Once again, p can be used to paste the cut text somewhere else.

Just as you used the e character to move to the end of a word, you could have used } to move to the end of the paragraph, or (to move back a sentence. But what if we want to copy an arbitrary region of text, for example, from the middle of one sentence to the middle of another one a few sentences later? The easiest way to accomplish this is by pulling a trick with the search command.

First, go to the *end* of the region you want to copy or cut. Hit d to cut or y to copy. Then, hit ? to perform a reverse search. Now type the first few letters of the start of the region. Hit return and voila! You've just grabbed your text. As an example, we're going to alter the following text:

```
Feel free to look. Unless you want to lose your hand DO NOT pet the
animals.
```

We're going to wreak a little havoc at the zoo. Place the cursor over the p in pet. Then type:

```
d?look
```

The resulting sentence will read:

```
Feel free to pet the animals.
```

One thing to note: The backwards search will match the first occurrence of the characters you type. For example, if we typed:

```
d?lo
```

above, the resulting sentence would be a bit confusing:

```
Feel free to look. Unless you want to pet the animals.
```

This is because the lo matches lose before it matches look (remember, were searching backwards).

Now How Do I Quit?

Most Unix applications will respond to either CTRL-C as a quit signal or CTRL-Z as a signal to suspend the program and escape to the shell. In vi, CTRL-C doesn't ever work, and CTRL-Z only works in the command mode (and then, it doesn't quit vi, it just pushes it into the background). Almost everyone who has ever used vi has the same recollection of their first encounter with vi: "I banged on a lot of keys before anything appeared on screen. Then I couldn't quit, let alone save what I had typed, and I couldn't escape to the shell or suspend the program, so I turned off the machine."

What happened here is that the initial keyboard banging shifted the vi system into the editing mode. Once it's in editing mode, control sequences are interpreted as literals, and get placed in the text file. Thus, hitting CTRL-Z or CTRL-C just puts some funny characters on the screen. Hitting the escape key has no visible effect, and typing "quit" results in the letter 't' appearing on the screen (the 'i' in "quit" puts the system in insert mode, and the 't' is inserted into the document). The lucky ones get CTRL-Z to suspend vi, and then either start reading the man page or use the kill command to terminate the suspended vi process.

The right way to quit is via the incredibly obvious command :q. Thats right—a colon before the q. Make sure you hit esc a few times first. Of course, it isn't even that straightforward. If you've accidentally made any changes or typed anything into the document, you'll need to save your file before it will let you quit. To save your file, use the command :w (stands for *write*). To save and quit, use :x or :wq. To quit without saving, use the command :q! (whenever vi starts to complain, ! can be used to force the system to comply with your wishes). By now the truth should be apparent: vi was created as a celebration of the medieval arts of pain and persuasion. The text editing features were thrown in as an afterthought. It's not supposed to be friendly, it's supposed to be light and powerful.

Look After Your Colon

In command mode, the colon precedes long-form commands—that is, commands which are more than just a single key. Try pressing : in command mode, and you'll be taken to the bottom of the screen and a colon will appear. Press <CR> and you'll be back in ordinary command mode, or type "set" and hit <CR> to see a long-form command working (it'll display a list of the current variables which have been set, and invite you to hit <CR> to return to ordinary command mode).

How Do I Get More Help?

If you want to get a list of all of the available commands on OpenBSD, type:

```
:viusage
```

The colon puts the vi system into extended command mode. There are many extended commands available, including the useful :q command we just learned about. To see the list of other : commands, type:

```
:exusage
```

You can also try:

```
:help
```

which will bring up short help screen.

On Red Hat's vim, :help in command mode will open up the full help system, which is pretty extensive.

That's the extent of our vi tutorial. Some vi implementations come with a built-in tutorial—you can learn quite a bit more from that. Additionally, there's always the vi man page—if you dare. Once you're familiar with working in vi you might begin to feel that, for all of its faults, vi is a reasonable improvement over punch cards. This feeling is only temporary and will pass with time.

The Security Policy

A well-designed security policy is your shield against the forces of evil that threaten to disrupt the very fabric of your network. Namely, your boss, your users, and hackers everywhere. Of course, it would be inaccurate to imply that every boss and user is evil, but we'll do it anyhow for simplicity's sake (and because the existence of good bosses and users has yet to be proven as anything more than a statistical possibility). Your security policy will balance the needs of your users with the realities of hackers and other threats to your network. It might even protect you from the occasional clueless command-from-above, such as: "Give my friend root access so that he can install some critical programs (read: solitaire)."

Do you, personally, need a security policy? Hard to say. If you could create one on the spot if you felt it were needed, then you probably don't, because things aren't complex enough for you to need a formal policy. If, on the other hand, you would have to get someone else's approval for such a policy, then you almost certainly do need one. In any case, you should think about the points before you reject the idea of having a policy.

We are assuming that your company is not bloated to the point where the authority to implement a major access policy requires 20 meetings with people who think security involves deleting all of their files and shredding every document on their desk every time their computer says it has performed an illegal action. If this is the case in your company and you haven't had the sanity to leave already, this book can only help you in one way: Throw it at your window to shatter the glass, making it easier for you to either get out (if you're on the first or second floor) or end the pain (if you're significantly higher). We do not recommend trying this from the third through tenth floors or if there's a large amount of shrubbery beneath your window.

What Is a Security Policy?

A security policy starts with a conceptual framework. It ultimately manifests itself as a document that describes the company policy with regards to network access, usage, support, hardware, and software. The policy discusses the methodology behind user access rights, the services that will be provided, and a procedure for requesting services or access that is not allowed under the policy. To create one, you'll need to do a lot of thinking, followed by a lot of real writing ("a lot" meaning significantly more than your average sh script, and "real" meaning sentences that don't start with grep and regular expressions that don't primarily consist of brackets, parentheses, and other punctuation characters).

Creating a Security Policy

The amount of work you'll have to do when creating your security policy grows exponentially with the size and complexity of your network and company. A full security policy for a large corporation may require months of evaluation and planning before being created. It may result in a fairly lengthy document or extensive set of documents. At the very least it involves quite a bit more than just deciding how the firewall should work. A good security policy provides the framework for controlling the flow of all digital information both into and out of your company.

It will help your effort greatly if there are other existing policies that you can reference. For example, there may already be a policy for physical access to your office space. There might be a phone access policy. If your company has a Corporate Communications or Public Affairs department, there will most likely be policies for releasing information to the public. Any of these policies would be of help here.

Before you can create your security policy, you have to make some significant decisions. These fall into three categories: *administration, risk tolerance,* and *business requirements.* You need to identify the person or people who can make executive-level decisions about security policy. Hopefully this includes you. You also need to assess the degree of risk to which your company can sustain exposure. If you are setting up a network for a top-secret military branch, you have a lot less risk tolerance than if you're setting up a home-office LAN. Finally, you'll need to determine the various ways in which people will need to use the network, both from inside the network and from the outside. Let's look at each of these areas in greater detail.

Administration

Setting any type of policy involves administration level decisions, and a security policy is no exception. There are a number of critical roles that must be defined and assigned. Even if you end up handling everything yourself today, that might not be the case tomorrow. If the roles are clearly laid out, it will be easy to re-assign them to other people as your company and network expand.

You'll also need to think about issues pertaining to compliance. How do you ensure that your users are following your security policies? Does your policy protect you and your company if a user either knowingly or unknowingly breaks the law?

There also needs to be a set of clearly defined procedures for handling a number of issues pertaining to your network security. What happens when you need to add a new user? What happens when security is compromised? What does somebody do if he or she needs greater access?

Authority

Somebody needs to have ultimate authority on the security policy. It could be you, or it could be your CEO. The answer is something you need to determine through discussion with all of the relevant parties within your organization. Once this person has been identified, they need to be made aware of the responsibility of their position. If they do not want to deal with the workload the position entails, it is their responsibility to delegate the responsibilities to others. One of the first things this person must evaluate is the importance of your network's availability. How long can you survive with a network that is down? If the answer is "not very long," then it's very important that somebody with the authority to make a decision is reachable within a short time frame in the event that something critical happens.

Roles

There are many ways in which the task of keeping a network secure can be split among individuals. We've created a set of roles that will work for the majority of organizations. You may find that some of these roles aren't necessary in your organization, and there may be other roles that are missing.

Compliance. Somebody needs to ensure that the users are complying with the security policy.

Network Monitoring. Even if you're using intrusion detection packages, someone needs to regularly monitor the network status and eye over certain log files. Talking to users helps here, since users may point out issues with the network that administrators have not noticed.

Intrusion Response. This may be a team of people, since effectively dealing with an intrusion requires a number of complex tasks to occur at nearly the same time. See also Chapter 11, "Intrusion Detection and Response."

System Maintenance. Routine maintenance of network equipment, servers, and workstations needs to be performed. The person performing these tasks should be well versed in the existing security mechanisms. This ensures that they do not inadvertently disable or bypass the security framework.

User Support. When a new user joins the group, somebody needs to give the user a machine and network access. That new user, as well as the existing user's base, needs support when something goes wrong.

Procedures

One of the most critical procedures is that of detecting and neutralizing security breaches. Refer to Chapter 11 for more information.

Maintenance. Another important procedure involves checking to make sure that all software is up to date, and upgrading any software with the latest security patches if necessary. There should be a list of all software in use. Each entry should point to a Web page or other resource for security patches.

New Technologies. New technologies appear on the Internet faster than potholes appear on I-95 between New Haven and New York (Note for UK readers: This is nearly as fast as traffic jams appear on the M25). These technologies need to be evaluated in terms of their potential utility to the organization and the security risks inherent within the protocols and implementing applications. There should be a process for identifying a new technology, evaluating the technology, and making recommendations. Often users will identify the new technology, so the procedure should include a method for users to submit new technology requests. It also should set expectations for response time frames.

Policy Changes. The United States Constitution was very well thought out, and yet it did not survive long before changes were needed. Likewise, regardless of how well you plan your security policy, you'll still need to make changes every once in a while. As it stands, every time a user has a problem with the policy, they'll come whining to you. What you need is a clearly defined procedure for requesting changes to the policy—one that allows you to discard the majority of requests with impunity. This will save you countless hours and headaches. You need to have a process for suggesting changes, evaluating the suggestions, and distributing amendments to the policy such that all employees are made aware of the relevant changes.

A Hardware Solution to Manage the Flow of Requests

Encase a paper shredder in a large metal box. Place a slit for request forms on the box such that the forms are immediately shredded upon insertion. The box should be completely sealed and unopenable or examinable by users with a padlocked door so that the shredder bag can be removed. On the front should be a sign that says, "This box contains a scanner which electronically processes the form and adds the request to the system administrator's queue. Response time could be long due to large demand. Original paper forms are compressed for efficient storage."

Compliance

There are two aspects to compliance:

1. Your users must abide by the security policy at all times, otherwise its value is greatly diminished.
2. The security policy itself should be compliant with general company compliance policies, unless the administration has specifically requested otherwise.

Enforcing security policy is hard. Unless your users are tied down with levels of security so tight they can't hit a key without an Engineering Change Order, they can probably subvert at least some of the security if they choose to. Making your policy simple, short, and easily explicable helps a lot getting your users to buy in to both the technical and the administrative sides of your policy. Getting them to sign a copy can help convince them that You Really Mean It.

Risk Tolerance

A startup company can take much greater risks than a Fortune 500 company. The close-knit nature of small companies means that nobody is expecting everything to go by the books. But once there is a larger number of employees, interpersonal problems and lack of discretion can create internal havoc. The Internet only makes the situation worse. Here we outline some of the internal and external risks presented by the Internet.

Internal Risks

Email. This is easily the greatest source of risk posed by the Internet. It should be made *very* clear to everyone in the company that sending an email is equivalent to posting your message on the big TV in Times Square. Anyone might see it, and it could stay around for a *long time*. Email messages have a habit of arriving at the wrong person's inbox with alarming regularity. Things people wrote two years ago come back to haunt them—just ask Bill Gates about his feelings on email.

The Web. The second largest risk is the Web. Someone could browse to an inappropriate Web site, and someone else could take offense. An employee might post company information onto the internet anonymously. Your company might even suffer due to someone maliciously posting inaccurate information about your company on a popular Web site. There have already been several major incidents involving inaccurate information on a Yahoo! chat forum causing excessive problems for a company.

Other Internet Services. There are plenty of other risks that come with having networked computers in your office. For example, a disgruntled employee could write programs to intercept network traffic and gain access to forbidden resources.

External Risks

Put Internet and Risk in the same sentence and you'll almost invariably find Hacker in the next sentence. Connecting a computer to the outside world means that it's only a matter of time until uninvited guests show up for dinner.

If you provide Web access to your employees, the tightest firewall in the world won't protect your internal network. By now, almost everything you can do on a computer can be done by going to a web site and possibly downloading a plug-in. This means you might *think* you're preventing employees from IRC by just allowing Web access, but a smart employee could easily gain IRC access through a Web site with an IRC plug-in or a Java applet. Furthermore, malicious Web sites *do* exist. It's not very difficult for someone to be duped into going to such a site.

Business Needs

When creating your security policy, the most important factor should be the needs of your business. To help figure out your needs, work with management to answer the following questions and you'll have a good overview of your company's networking requirements.

Internal Access. What services do your users inside the network need to get at?

Remote Access. What services do remote users need? Do they need access to data inside the network?

Public Access. What services do you need to provide to the public?

Electronic Commerce/Data Interchange. Do you need to exchange information securely with other companies?

Availability. Can your network go down? How long?

Scripts

This section contains a bunch of useful scripts that we have also placed on the companion Web site at www.wiley.com/compbooks/sonnenreich. These scripts are designed to help you configure your system.

OpenBSD Uninstall Script

```
#!/bin/sh
# detar script for OpenBSD - requires sh, awk, and tar
if [ $# -ne 2 ]; then
        echo 1>&2 Usage: $0 \<root of install\> \<tar file\>
        echo 1>&2 where root of install is usually: /
        exit 127
fi
tar ztf ${2} | awk " {a=sprintf(\" rm -rf ${1}%s\" ,\$1)} {print a} {system(a)}" -
```

This script will remove a disk set from OpenBSD. Type the above into a file called detar. Then execute the following command:

```
chmod +x detar
```

To use the script, type:

```
detar / name_of_diskset
```

Thus, to remove the comp25.tar.gz disk set, you would type:

```
detar / /mnt/cdrom/OpenBSD/2.5/i386/comp25.tar.gz
```

This particular script can be used to unistall any tar.gz file if you know the directory it was untarred into and you have the original tar file. Another use for the script is to create a tar file of programs that you want to install/uninstall often. Make sure the tar file is created with the / directory as the top level directory. Do a 'man tar' to figure out how tar works. Once you have such a file, you can run the script to uninstall the files, and run:

```
cd /
tar zxf file.tar.gz
```

whenever you want to re-install the files.

Firewall Startup under Linux

This script can be used to start your firewall up in a civilized way, and fits in with the startup/shutdown script architecture of Red Hat Linux.

```
#!/bin/sh
#

# Source function library.
```

```
. /etc/rc.d/init.d/functions

# Source networking configuration.
. /etc/sysconfig/network


[ -f /etc/rc.d/rc.firewall ] || exit 0
# See how we were called.
case " $1" in
  start)
        # Start firewall.

        echo -n " Starting firewall: "
        daemon /etc/rc.d/rc.firewall
        touch /var/lock/subsys/firewall
        ;;
  stop)
        # Stop firewall.
        echo -n " Shutting down firewall: "
        ipchains -F input
        ipchains -F output
        ipchains -P input ACCEPT
        ipchains -P output ACCEPT
        echo
        rm -f /var/lock/subsys/firewall
        ;;
  restart)
        $0 stop
        $0 start
        ;;
  status)
        status firewall
        ;;
  *)
        echo " Usage: firewall {start|stop|restart|status}"
        exit 1
esac

exit 0
```

This script should be placed in /etc/rc.d/init.d/firewall, and linked to the startup directory that corresponds to your default run level (see *Starting the Firewall* in Chapter 7 and *Now I Can Do Anything* in Chapter 10). It also requires the real firewall code, as a simple set of executable instructions, to be in /etc/rc.d/rc.firewall. Running the above script as "/etc/rc.d/init.d/firewall start" turns on the firewall; running "/etc/rc.d/init.d/firewall stop" opens up your firewall and cleans out all the chains (save the forwarding chain, because if you're doing masquerading it'll break as soon as you clean out the forwarding chain). Running this is the networking equivalent of undressing in public; this is something you may want to do for debugging, but probably not at any other time.

Some Closing Thoughts

Congratulations for bearing with us through this book. We hope it's been thought-provoking, informative, instructive, and that it helped you build a functioning firewall.